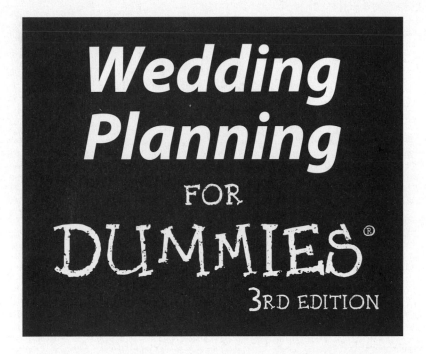

Wedding Planning FOR DUMMIES®

3RD EDITION

by Marcy Blum

WILEY

John Wiley & Sons, Inc.

Wedding Planning For Dummies®, 3rd Edition

Published by
John Wiley & Sons, Inc.
111 River St.
Hoboken, NJ 07030-5774
www.wiley.com

For general information on our other products and services, please contact our Customer Care Department within the U.S. at 877-762-2974, outside the U.S. at 317-572-3993, or fax 317-572-4002.

For technical support, please visit www.wiley.com/techsupport.

Wiley publishes in a variety of print and electronic formats and by print-on-demand. Some material included with standard print versions of this book may not be included in e-books or in print-on-demand. If this book refers to media such as a CD or DVD that is not included in the version you purchased, you may download this material at http://booksupport.wiley.com. For more information about Wiley products, visit www.wiley.com.

Library of Congress Control Number: 2012950491

ISBN 978-1-118-36035-4 (pbk); ISBN 978-1-118-43567-0 (ebk); ISBN 978-1-118-43568-7 (ebk); ISBN 978-1-118-43569-4 (ebk)

Manufactured in the United States of America

10 9 8 7 6 5 4 3 2 1

WILEY

About the Author

Marcy Blum has been creating wonderful, memorable, magical weddings for 27 years. Her sane and humorous approach to entertaining in general and weddings in particular has made her a nationally sought-out wedding and party planner. Marcy is credited with being among the first to offer couples elegant, fun, and stylish alternatives to the cookie-cutter wedding. In addition to her work as an "eventiste," Marcy is also a sought-after speaker and consultant for businesses in the wedding and special-event field. She has been a guest on *The Oprah Winfrey Show, The Today Show,* and *The Nate Berkus Show* and was a contributing editor for *Modern Bride* magazine. She has also been a guest on several wedding shows in Japan but has no idea what was said to her.

Dedication

For Destin, who keeps me remembering what really matters.

Author's Acknowledgments

Thanks a million to my agent, Sophia Seidner at IMG Literary, for picking up the ball and keeping it in play with such grace and tenacity. Gratitude to my shockingly smart agent Alexandra Machinist, at Janklow Nesbit, who will definitely harass me into finishing my novel soon.

Heartfelt thanks to Stacey Lutz, who was so helpful in using her ample brains to keep this on track while I was swamped with weddings. And to Lea Brumage, who attends to so much of our business so I can get some writing done.

Thanks also to my project editor, Alissa Schwipps, for staying several steps ahead of me and being such a sweetheart. Thanks for the expertise of my friend Terry DeRoy Gruber in helping me sort out how photography has changed since the last edition.

This is the first edition of *Wedding Planning For Dummies* that was written without my friend and co-author, Laura Fisher Kaiser, whose other writing projects are keeping her quite busy these days. It's fun to note that her own nuptials (to "the most wonderful man in the world," according to fact checkers) were planned chapter by chapter — and quite successfully — as we collaborated on the first edition. I'm sure that all her logistical wedding know-how is coming in handy for her blog, Secret Science Geek, not to mention her forthcoming book, a history of leprosy. (You read that right; even I can't make this stuff up.)

Publisher's Acknowledgments

We're proud of this book; please send us your comments at http://dummies.custhelp.com. For other comments, please contact our Customer Care Department within the U.S. at 877-762-2974, outside the U.S. at 317-572-3993, or fax 317-572-4002.

Some of the people who helped bring this book to market include the following:

Acquisitions, Editorial, and Vertical Websites

Senior Project Editor: Alissa Schwipps

Acquisitions Editor: Tracy Boggier

Copy Editor: Todd Lothery

(Previous Edition: Kristin DeMint)

Assistant Editor: David Lutton

Editorial Program Coordinator: Joe Niesen

Technical Editor: Kim King-Smith

Editorial Manager: Christine Meloy Beck

Editorial Assistant: Alexa Koschier

Art Coordinator: Alicia B. South

Cover Photos: © Peter Brutsch, © Raya Lopez, © Ettore Marzocchi, © Janice Richard © Trista Weibell, © boiling, © GrenouilleFilms, © Anna Furman, © Anthony Rosenberg /iStockphoto.com

Cartoons: Rich Tennant (www.the5th wave.com)

Composition Services

Senior Project Coordinator: Kristie Rees

Layout and Graphics: Carrie A. Cesavice, Corrie Niehaus

Proofreaders: Melissa Cossell, BIM Indexing & Proofreading Services

Indexer: Valerie Haynes Perry

Illustrator: Elizabeth Kurtzman

Publishing and Editorial for Consumer Dummies

    Kathleen Nebenhaus, Vice President and Executive Publisher

    David Palmer, Associate Publisher

    Kristin Ferguson-Wagstaffe, Product Development Director

Publishing for Technology Dummies

    Andy Cummings, Vice President and Publisher

Composition Services

    Debbie Stailey, Director of Composition Services

Contents at a Glance

Table of Contents

Introduction

. . . .

A wedding, whether it's a quiet civil ceremony in a judge's chamber or a pull-out-all-the-stops extravaganza, requires equal parts creativity, planning, diplomacy, and nerve. Often, what should be a joyously happy time in one's life is looked back on as one long stress test. Keep calm, carry on, and start reading.

The mission of *Wedding Planning For Dummies,* 3rd Edition, is to demystify and simplify myriad details that go into the Big Day, inspire you with wonderfully innovative ideas to personalize your wedding celebration, instill confidence in you to bring off a memorable ceremony and reception (no matter what your budget or wedding style), educate you on all the new tools you can use to help you, and hopefully enable you to have some fun while doing it.

About This Book

Wedding Planning For Dummies, 3rd Edition, isn't just for brides. Because a wedding (not to mention a marriage) is a joint venture, I recommend that the couple participate equally in its creation. I've also noted from the feedback on previous editions that *Wedding Planning For Dummies* has been an invaluable reference tool for mothers and fathers of brides and grooms, as well as friends helping out with a wedding, and that truly delights me. Whatever your role is, if you've done zero planning, I'll get you up and running. No matter what stage you're in, however, I won't make you go back and start over because you've done something wrong. Generally speaking, no single right way exists. Whatever makes the bride and groom happy is the right way for their particular wedding.

I've organized this book to make planning your wedding as stress-free and logical as possible. Having been a professional wedding and party planner for more than 27 years, I know just what it takes to produce a happy, hassle-free day. I've built a career of escorting couples through the exhilarating, step-by-step process of creating a joyous wedding that expresses their personal style and commitment.

Packed with wit and wedding know-how, *Wedding Planning For Dummies,* 3rd Edition, helps you figure out your own wedding style and guides you through each stage of the planning process. What size wedding is right for you and your budget? Where is the best place to have the ceremony and reception?

How can you make sure everybody will show up at the church on time? How can you save money without looking cheap or completely sacrificing style? Whatever the wedding-related issue, the answer is here in an easy-to-use reference.

Each chapter is divided into sections, and each section contains useful information, such as

- Advice on setting up a budget and sticking to it
- Tips for evaluating prospective venues for the ceremony and reception, whether for a local or destination wedding
- Thoughtful ways to make guests feel welcome
- Ideas for creating memorable menus, music playlists, and party favors
- Info on how to keep your wedding day running smoothly by creating a no-surprises schedule

Although some wedding guides love to dictate timelines about when to do what, I find that contrived deadlines produce more anxiety than efficiency. A wedding can be two years or two months in the making. Rather than lay out a strict protocol or chronology, I've organized this book according to what makes sense for real brides and grooms, for many of whom the demands of work, school, or family leave little time for wedding planning. I say: Let *your* priorities determine the timing for everything from setting the date to ducking out for the honeymoon.

The great part about this book is that you decide where to start and what to read. It's a reference you can jump into and out of at will. Just head to the table of contents or index to find the information you want.

Conventions Used in This Book

To help you navigate through this book, I've set up a few conventions:

- I use *italic* text for emphasis and to highlight new words or terms that I define.
- I use **boldfaced** text to indicate the keywords of bulleted lists and the action part of specific steps.
- I use `monofont` for website addresses.

Foolish Assumptions

Every book is written with a particular reader in mind, and this one is no different. As I wrote *Wedding Planning For Dummies,* 3rd Edition, I made a few assumptions about you:

✔ You're a newly engaged couple (or someone helping a newly engaged couple), and you've just begun really thinking about the kind of ceremony and reception you want to have.

✔ You haven't had much experience with planning weddings or even large parties, and yet you know you don't want a cookie-cutter wedding.

✔ You want basic information — tips from the pros — but you don't want to be bombarded with minutiae.

✔ No matter what size your budget, you're starting to feel panicky, wondering just how much the wedding of your dreams is going to cost — and how you're going to afford it.

I can't tell you what kind of wedding to have — that decision is completely up to you. But I can tell you how to make the most of your resources and budget. I realize that you want to know not only the traditional ways of celebrating your big day but also, in some cases, innovative ways to tweak the official rites and rituals. I can help you figure all that out. And, dare I say, make the process *fun.*

How This Book Is Organized

You have to plan so many aspects of a wedding simultaneously that picking a starting point is a difficult task — one of the reasons I'm not a fan of dogmatic timelines. I set up this book in a way that I think makes sense: big-picture visualization and budget matters upfront — plus the all-important question of where to hold the wedding — followed by party-planning strategies (invitations, weekend/destination weddings, scheduling, pre- and postwedding events, and flowers), ceremony details, reception matters, and such miscellaneous topics as registries, attire, rings, photos, and the honeymoon.

Part 1: First Things First

These initial chapters hit some of the biggest concerns upfront. Chapter 1 explains what happens from the moment someone proposes, providing a logical, step-by-step process to making your dream wedding fit your reality. In Chapter 2, I focus on the financial picture. I help you keep track of expenses with a wedding-budget spreadsheet and provide valuable tips on tipping, negotiating contracts, and surfing for deals online. Chapter 3 gets all those legal and financial technicalities out of the way, from blood tests to prenuptial agreements.

Part II: Be Our Guest

This part covers many aspects of planning the event and providing hospitality, starting with finding the perfect venue for your celebration, which I help you do in Chapter 4. Then, in Chapter 5, you start thinking about invitations, from formal to creative, do-it-yourself styles. Chapter 6 tells you how to plan the increasingly popular weekend wedding. Chapter 7 alone is worth double the price of this book, as it reveals how to design a comprehensive schedule for a snag-free wedding day. In Chapter 8, I cover other kinds of celebrations, from theme weddings to encore weddings, as well as showers, rehearsal dinners, and morning-after brunches.

Part III: Ceremony Survival Guide

The pivotal moment of all weddings is the ceremony, and in this part I detail how to make yours as special as possible.

In Chapter 9, I help you select the wedding party and explain what you can and can't expect of them. In Chapter 10, I get to the emotional center of a wedding — the ceremony — with clear explanations of various customs and rites, helping you determine the service sequence, suitable vows, and meaningful readings. I also give examples of wedding programs — a lovely guide and memento for the day. In Chapter 11, the subject is roses and whatever else your nose and eyes desire. I explain how to work with a florist to get the decorative effect you want for both the ceremony and the reception. Ceremony music is so important that I devote all of Chapter 12 to it, from choosing the songs you like to finding the right musicians to play them.

Part IV: A Rousing Reception

This part focuses on the reception, helping you decide what to serve, what to wash it down with, how to decorate, whom to hire, and what to listen to throughout.

Chapter 13 is devoted to the element that sets the tone perhaps more than anything else: the music. I include a primer on putting together a winning playlist of favorite songs for the band or DJ. Then, on to my favorite subject — food! — in Chapter 14, where I help you determine the style and scope of the nuptial feast, among other tasty topics. In Chapter 15, I order up a round of advice on what to serve in the beverage department. The wedding cake requires a chapter unto itself, hence Chapter 16. Chapter 17 focuses on making everything look stunning — décor, lighting, and tables.

Part V: Gifts, Garb, Pics, and Trips

In this part, I examine several key aspects of getting married — before, during, and after the wedding.

Chapter 18 covers gifts and registries. Then, on to Chapter 19 for choosing a bridal ensemble. You won't be fully dressed without a ring, so Chapter 20 brings you into the loop on wedding bands, diamonds, and engagement rings. In Chapter 21, I help you hire the right photo and video professionals. Finally, that hard-earned honeymoon requires planning, too, and in Chapter 22 I arrange the particulars of a blissful getaway.

Part VI: The Part of Tens

A favorite among *For Dummies* fans, this part rounds up critical information for quick reference.

In Chapter 23, I offer you some tricks to staying on budget (whatever your budget is). Chapter 24 lists some tacky trends that I implore you to avoid.

Icons Used in This Book

Icons are the nifty little pictures in the margin of this book. They each grab your attention for a different reason:

Contrary to what some fools think, even in a "traditional" heterosexual partnership, the bride *and* groom should be responsible for pulling the wedding together. Of course, a natural delineation of duties may occur, but some decisions require input from both parties. These entwined wedding rings signal a matter on which you should consult each other.

Yes, I realize that your Aunt Myrtle graduated with honors from the TJTWID (That's Just The Way It's Done) Etiquette Academy, but I'm here to tell you that times have changed, and so have certain ironclad rules of decorum. When you see this icon, expect either an alternative way for handling a sticky wedding situation or simply a heads-up on a modern approach to making everyone feel comfortable.

Although I don't advocate being a slave to calendars and endless to-do lists, every now and then a timely reminder or heads-up is in order. When you see this symbol, adjust your personal wedding timetable accordingly.

No matter the budget, anyone planning a wedding wants to get the most bang for the buck. This symbol means I'm about to impart vital information regarding a practical money matter. Although many times I tell you how to save money, I just as often explain why pinching pennies in a particular area may not be wise. I also use this icon to flag information that may save you precious time.

Weddings, like life, can be unpredictable, but you can easily avoid certain mistakes, pitfalls, and tacky traps if you know what to look for. Defuse these little bombs before they explode.

Where to Go from Here

You may find that you need to fast-forward to the reception chapters because the space you want gets booked a year in advance. No problem. This isn't a Stephen King novel — you can jump around all you want without missing any major plot twists. Check out the table of contents to find a topic that suits your fancy.

If you're just getting started, you may as well turn to Part I. Chapter 1 starts you off easy. Before you know it, you'll be planning like a pro.

Part I
First Things First

The 5th Wave   By Rich Tennant

"After all that planning and preparation it seems inappropriate
to have a sign that says 'JUST' married."

In this part . . .

Congratulations on your engagement! Now it's time to get down to business. These first three chapters help you organize a game plan that will carry you through the whole wedding-planning process. First, you need to figure out what kind of wedding you want, whom to invite, and how to pay for it. I help you create a realistic budget and stick to it. I provide valuable tips on negotiating contracts and tipping, and I give you a heads-up on new smartphone apps to assist you. I also include information on getting your marriage license, changing your name, and considering a prenuptial agreement, all aspects of your planning that are best to figure out early on.

Chapter 1

First Steps to a Wedding to Remember

In This Chapter

▶ Starting the planning for your big day

▶ Considering the help of a wedding consultant

*Y*ou came home once to find that his black cat had redecorated your white living room, and instead of pitching a fit, you thought it was hilarious. He not only wasn't embarrassed but also found it endearing the night you became violently ill on margaritas at your firm's Christmas party. This must be it then, you both realize — true love. And what comes next is the big step.

In this chapter I guide you through the beginning of the wedding-planning process. I also help you decide whether to hire a professional wedding planner or do things on your own (hint: I favor hiring a planner).

The "Ize" Have It

In spite of what you've heard, the time between your engagement and your marriage need not go down in the annals of your relationship as the Dark Ages. What follows is a series of "exercIZEs" to kick off your wedding planning and set you on the right track to pulling off the wedding of your dreams. As you familarIZE, fantasIZE, prioritIZE, and so on, the goal is to figure out what's important to both of you and to achieve your vision with as little acrimony and heartburn as possible. Okay — I admit this IZE thing is corny, but it really works.

Familiarize: Spreading the news

After you and your beloved decide to get married, I recommend that you demonstrate respect and courtesy by telling your parents first. This isn't the time, however, to ask them to foot the bill. Give them oxygen. Let them bask in the glow a bit. (If there's no glow in sight, proceed directly to Chapter 22 and start planning your honeymoon — it may be time to elope.)

This is a natural time for the first communiqué between the bride's and groom's parents if they don't already know each other. I recommend you rely on your own sense of whose parents should initiate contact. If it's a tossup, you can fall back on tradition and suggest that the groom's parents call the bride's.

If either of you has children, tell the kids before you tell other people (or other people tell them). Life isn't like *The Brady Bunch;* the merging of families can be highly charged, even if everyone seems to get along famously.

I realize that you're overjoyed with your decision to marry, but don't let your enthusiasm lead you to draft 82 people for your wedding party as you spread the news among your friends and relatives. If you've known since you were 2 who your best man or maid of honor will be, then by all means that person should be among the first few people to know. Otherwise, hold off broadcasting even tentative plans until you know how many of your 2,000 closest friends you can actually invite.

And a special caution for this age of social networking: Resist the urge to update your Facebook status or tweet about your engagement until you've told your parents (and your kids, if any) the good news. And know that after you announce your engagement online, all your friends and relatives may assume that their invitation is on the way. So if you don't plan to host every single person in your social network at your wedding, be prepared to manage expectations, and give some thought to carefully controlling your privacy settings.

Fantasize: Envisioning your dream wedding

All too often, people begin planning their wedding by setting a strict budget and then trying to shoehorn in all the things they think they *should* have in their wedding. This process doesn't work and can leave you feeling like you can't afford to have your dream wedding in any way, shape, or form.

Guest-imating your costs

You can never make a preliminary guest list *(in writing)* too early. Thinking about whom to invite and who will actually show up has a tremendous impact on the way your wedding planning evolves. The number in your head may not correspond to the reality, and seeing the names on paper helps check your natural propensity to invite anyone who's anywhere near you. Though certain costs such as space rental, officiant fees, music, and the wedding dress are usually fixed, items such as centerpieces, food, and beverages change in proportion to the number of guests attending. The difference between 100 and 125 guests is three more tables and a 25 percent increase in food and drink. Only you can decide whether those people make the day more special or simply blow your budget.

Including everyone who *really* matters while not inviting everyone you or your parents have ever met is a precarious juggling act. Before you ask your prospective in-laws to submit a list of names and/or a guest estimate, give them some parameters upfront so there's no confusion later. After you agree on a tentative number of guests, you can look for venues with a much more realistic idea of what will accommodate your group as well as your budget.

Remember that the mysterious folks who calculate wedding statistics say that you can expect 10 to 20 percent of those invited not to attend. That's the national average, but it could be irrelevant to your situation, so don't bank on this to plan the size of your venue or to determine your budget's bottom line. You may be the lucky ones blessed with 100 percent attendance.

I suggest that you work backward. Before you rein in your dreams, imagine that no budgetary or logistical constraints exist. Start thinking about all the elements that would go into your fantasy wedding. Be as specific as you can, using all your senses. How big is the wedding? Where is the wedding? What time of day is it? What color are the bridesmaids' dresses? What does the band sound like? Who's there? What does it smell like? What are you eating and drinking?

Write down these thoughts on a piece of paper and exchange them with your spouse-to-be. You may feel more comfortable brainstorming out loud together, but the point is that you should both be honest and open-minded. Take each other's fantasies seriously. Refrain from making dismissive snorting sounds. This type of open exchange is neither a mind game nor an exercise in futility, but rather a very helpful step in discovering what both of you really want.

Prioritize: Deciding what's really important

Now, take all your fantasy elements (see the preceding section) and put them in some order of importance. Are towering bouquets of white lilies more important than fine champagne? Are you flexible on the time of year? What about the time of day? Must you have a couture gown or are you willing to go with something less lavish and instead spend more money on a seven-piece orchestra? Does the wedding site have to be the country club or would Aunt Myrtle's parlor serve the same purpose?

Compare your priority list with your intended's. Maybe you both agree that having a sit-down dinner isn't so important. Perhaps you've always pictured getting married barefoot on the beach, but your better half thinks only a black-tie hotel wedding will impress everyone back home. What compromises are you both willing to make? (This is good practice for the rest of your lives.)

Visualize: Making a reality checklist

The next step is to take these priorities and paint the picture of where you're going to park your money. Start by estimating the cost of each of the most important elements. These estimates provide you with a rough budget, a way to set some parameters; you'll flesh it out later. (See Chapter 2 for more information on setting a budget.)

Remember that none of this budgeting is etched in stone, so you can afford to be flexible. Assuming you can't afford the world's most exotic flowers or rarest Champagne, assess which parts of your prioritized fantasy lineup may really work. Though you both may have in mind a caviar-and-blini bar, you may also see a band that sets you on fire. Because having both will blow your whole budget, one has to go. To help make that decision, think back on what sticks in your memory from great weddings you've been to. Was it the food? The setting? The music?

Weddings aren't planned in a vacuum, and they don't end when the cake is cut. You'll encounter both familial and interpersonal ramifications that last far longer than this one day. A good idea, therefore, is to find out at the very beginning what the highly charged issues are and, when in doubt, compromise. Doing so makes for a happier day and a happier future family life.

Dealing with kiddie complications

One of the wonderful things about weddings is that they can bring many generations together under one roof. On the other hand, you may not be delighted to have screaming infants punctuating your vows or to pay for even the most adorable Shirley Temple clone to take up a seat at your reception.

Whether to invite children to your wedding is one of the more emotional issues you may face during your premarital meanderings. As you may have noticed, people can get positively fierce when it comes to their little darlings. So what are your choices, and after you make your decisions, how do you impart them most graciously?

Don't count on guests being versed in the nuances of invitation addressing. (In other words, they probably won't realize that their children aren't invited if their names aren't on the envelope.) After you make your decision, be gracious but firm when people call and ask whether the exclusion was an oversight. The easiest way to start an all-out family war is to cave in and make an exception for some children but not others. Specifying an age cutoff is difficult. If you have young ladies and gentlemen involved in your ceremony as junior ushers and bridesmaids, they'll undoubtedly be crushed if they aren't invited to the reception. What's more, depending on your families, you may be pressured to invite other relatives of the same age if you're including these kids. And for an evening reception, trying to have any children whisked away at their witching hour without having to bid farewell to their parents is next to impossible. One solution may be to arrange a quiet area adjacent to your reception where this age group can be deposited to nap — under the supervision of a sitter — until their parents are ready to leave.

Banning children at destination weddings (see Chapters 4 and 6) is tricky. Many people won't travel without their children and consequently may refuse your invitation. One way to please everyone is to include children at surrounding events and hire a baby sitter during the wedding itself. It's up to you to pick up the tab for this sitter, as well as to arrange to have the children in one place, fed, and properly cared for.

Organize: Breaking down the details without breaking down

If the word *organize* strikes fear in your gut, then you really need to read this. And even if you're certifiably obsessive-compulsive, you may benefit from reading the following tips on getting organized and setting a budget.

Approach your wedding as any other big project in your life: Chunk it into manageable pieces. Group several little steps into segments and plot them along a timeline or calendar, setting deadlines that jibe with everything else going on in your life:

✔ **Keep track of tasks and deadlines in your calendar.** Use a flexible system like your smartphone calendar or a plain old pencil with eraser in case things change. And change they will — count on it.

✔ **Organize your time to make things easy on yourself.** If you're starting medical school, changing jobs, or moving, this is probably not the time to plan a complex wedding with a cast of thousands. Although weddings are happy occasions, they are, nonetheless, stressful. Ask yourselves, "How much are we willing to give up?"

✔ **Be ready to take notes at all times.** Those light bulbs switch on at the most unlikely moments, and even though you think you could never forget such an excellent idea, somehow it gets lost amid all that other important stuff crammed into your brain. Download a note-taking application like Evernote or Springpad for your phone if you don't already have one or do it old-school and keep a notebook (and pen) within grabbing distance. Just make sure you can capture those inspirations — "re: embroidered silk, not taffeta!" or "call baker re: apricot frosting"— as they blip across your brain waves.

✔ **Make a swatch book.** Start collecting information and inspiration in a visually inspiring way. You can use the digital pinboard at Pinterest (www.pinterest.com) to collect pictures of all those lovely flowers and cakes you see online, or try the Wedding Row application to help you create inspiration boards from images you find online or snap yourself. For all the nondigital ephemera that multiplies as you plan your big day, accordion files or clear, heavyweight, plastic sheet protectors (the kind for reports in three-ring binders) are handy. Use them to corral contracts, menus, wine labels, brochures, guest lists, fabric swatches, stationery samples, photos, receipts, magazine articles, and so on. When the wedding's over, a lot of this stuff makes great scrapbook fodder.

✔ **Start keeping track of your guests as early as possible.** Use a wedding-planning website or application, a computerized spreadsheet, or a stack of 3-x-5 index cards in a box. Each entry should contain data on everyone to whom you send an invitation — the correct name spelling, the person's address, RSVP info, gift info, the guest's spouse or significant other, and who invited the guest. Such a compilation proves invaluable when planning your seating chart (see Chapter 17).

Just as you collect ideas and pictures of things you want for your wedding, it's equally important to note things you *don't* want. That way you have a better chance of remembering, for example, to tell the caterer that Aunt Myrtle is fatally allergic to clams or to tell the band that under no circumstances are they to play "The Electric Slide."

See Chapter 6 for more on using wedding apps and blogs to help you get organized and spread the word.

All the details at a glance

As you plan your wedding, you'll make a lot of phone calls and send a lot of e-mails. It helps to have everyone's contact information pulled together in one place.

As you assemble your nuptial team, keep up-to-date contact information for all the key players. Include their phone numbers — home, office, and cell — as well as postal, e-mail, and website addresses. For vendors, include the company name and contact person. If this is a lot to keep up with, at least be sure to save all the relevant names and phone numbers in your phone contact list. At some point during your planning, the following players are sure to end up on that list.

- Attendants' attire (company or store)
- Best man
- Bride
- Bridesmaids
- Bride's parents
- Cake maker
- Calligrapher
- Caterer or banquet manager
- Ceremony musicians
- Ceremony site manager
- Florist
- Gown maker
- Groom
- Groom's parents
- Hair stylist
- Insect spraying service
- Jeweler
- Lighting designer

- Liquor services
- Maid of honor
- Makeup artist
- Officiant
- Parking services
- Photographer
- Portable toilet company
- Reception musicians
- Reception site manager
- Rental company
- Stationer
- Supplier of party favors and welcome gifts
- Tailor
- Transportation company
- Travel agent
- Tuxedo store
- Videographer
- Wedding consultant

Synchronize: Dispelling the timetable myth

With the exception of invitations, which can take up to four months to print and mail, you can accomplish almost every aspect of a wedding in less than two months. Not that I suggest waiting until the last minute, but you don't have to be a slave to someone else's timetable. Okay, now here's the big shocker: *Wedding Planning For Dummies* doesn't have the ubiquitous wedding timeline that tells you, for example, "Two days before: Polish your left toenail." I believe this etched-in-stone manifesto strikes terror in the hearts of even the most courageous couple. In devising your customized timetable, allow your priorities, budget, personal schedules, and reality constraints to come into play.

That said, I do advise that you attend to certain details sooner rather than later. In fact, even before you finalize your wedding date, you should get a jump on aspects that are hard to find, in great demand, or simply take a long time to accomplish. Generally speaking, these include

- **Band and photographer:** Good bands (and DJs) and talented photographers require that you book them several months in advance. (See Chapters 12 and 13 for info on finding ceremony and reception musicians, and see Chapter 21 for info on finding a photographer you click with.)

- **Gown:** The source of much prewedding anxiety, the hunt for the perfect wedding dress is unpredictable. Even if you score the first time you go shopping, having the gown shipped and altered can make the process interminable. Then you have to get the veil, shoes, bra . . . see Chapter 19 for the gory details.

- **Invitations:** You traditionally mail invitations six weeks before the wedding, but I suggest eight weeks. Exceptions do exist, specifically if you have international guests, who should receive invitations ten weeks ahead of time. Almost all out-of-towners need to take off extra time from work or make special arrangements to attend; either send them invitations early or send a card or e-notification alerting them to save the date six months to a year in advance, if possible. (See Chapter 5 for the skinny on invitations and other communication needs.)

- **Location:** You're not the only two people getting married in the foreseeable future, so if you want to get married in high season at a highly desirable spot, you may have to book up to a year in advance. (See Chapter 4 for info on choosing a space and Chapter 14 for info on working with a caterer.)

Picking the date

Maybe your maid of honor goes on a spa retreat at the same time every year. Or perhaps your future mother-in-law already has tickets for a three-month Arctic cruise next summer. People may put in requests, but you can't please everyone. Other factors can affect the best time to have your wedding. Perhaps you want the photographs to have a black-and-white, photojournalistic look, but the one person within 500 miles who does that is booked. Either you go with a more traditional photographer or you shift the date.

In the end, you must decide what's best for you and the majority of your guests. After you set the date, stick to it. Your guests have to deal with it, and most of them will deal very well.

Piggybacking a holiday

Having a wedding coincide with another major holiday is often tempting. (See the nearby sidebar, "Dates to bear in mind.") This can work if your family usually gets together anyway at this time or if people coming from out of town need a few extra days' cushion and the holiday provides some extra time off work.

On the other hand, sometimes people resent having their precious vacation time eaten up with a social obligation, especially if the date falls during a frequent flier blackout period. If they must sacrifice, however, they may expect the gracious host to make sure there's plenty to keep them entertained. In cases like these, you could find yourself playing social director for several days before and after the wedding. This can be both time-consuming and exhausting.

Another drawback to piggybacking your wedding with a holiday is cost. Think how much you'd charge to work on a holiday. The service staff feels the same way.

In cities with a large Jewish population, such as New York or Los Angeles, if you're willing to get married on a Friday night as opposed to Saturday after sunset, you stand a better chance of getting a good deal. Also, on many Jewish holidays a Jewish couple can't get married but a gentile couple can. However, this shouldn't be taken to the extreme — a gentile couple getting married on Yom Kippur or a Jewish couple getting married on Christmas Eve may find that many of their guests can't or won't show up.

Dates to bear in mind

Some holidays or three-day weekends seem like a perfect opportunity to have a wedding. Other times can be off-limits, depending on your religion or nationality. For example, conservative and Orthodox Jews avoid getting married during the 49 days — except on the 33rd day — between Passover and Shabbat. Still other dates may be anniversaries of painful events such as a death in the family. In any case, here are some days to take into consideration when choosing a date.

New Year's Day

Martin Luther King Jr. Day

Presidents' Day

St. Patrick's Day

Palm Sunday

Passover

Good Friday

Easter

Mother's Day

Father's Day

U.S. Independence Day

Labor Day

September 11

Rosh Hashanah

Yom Kippur

Columbus Day

Veteran's Day

Thanksgiving Day

Christmas Eve and Day

Ramadan

Choosing peak versus off-peak

Some couples are sentimental about dates — they want to get married on New Year's Eve to symbolize their new start together, or on one of their birthdays, or on the anniversary of their first kiss. Although this may seem sweet, watch out — your special spot on the calendar may fall on another holiday, an inconvenient day of the week, or at the peak (read "more costly") time of year. January, February, and March are typically slow months in most parts of the United States. The most popular time to get married is May through October.

It pays to be flexible. Booking a venue for Sunday afternoon or the newly chic Thursday evening is less expensive than a Saturday night. What's more, if you're intent on having the wedding at the most popular place in town, that spot may be booked every Saturday night for the next two years.

If your wedding guests are local and your plans simple, a weekday could make life easier — and save a few bucks.

Deputize: Choosing your team

I presume you've purchased this book because you have some vested interest in producing your own wedding. However, like it or not, in this society, money means power. If your parents or in-laws are paying for a portion of the wedding, they do get a vote. This situation may prove to be one of the trickiest you face, requiring utmost diplomacy. Other people often have specific fantasies regarding *your* wedding, and those ideas may be diametrically opposed to yours.

Measure the importance of financial contributions against your resolve for certain aspects of your wedding. This ratio is something only you can determine. If you accept a great proportion of money from others, be prepared to take a great proportion of their advice. Decide which is more important to you: more financial help or total control.

Should people become overbearing, try to turn the situation around. Listen to every word of their input, thank them with all the grace and charm for which you're undoubtedly known, and then quietly make decisions with your fiancé(e) and announce them sweetly but firmly.

Before meddlers become too meddlesome, put them to work on a simple project, such as researching places for out-of-towners to stay or tracking down Aunt Myrtle's mother's famous punch recipe. I strongly advocate the gentle exploitation of family and friends, but keep in mind that involving someone in your wedding means inviting them. Ask favors only from close friends or from people who have nothing to lose or gain from helping you. The best way to solicit help is to ask for recommendations from family or friends who've been through this. That way they feel they've done something to help you and are absolved from the responsibility of interfering further.

Think over all offers of help before accepting them. Just because your best friend says she can do calligraphy doesn't mean she's very good at it. Delegate sensibly. The idea is to save you time, not make more work, cost more money, or cause hurt feelings.

Working with a Wedding Planner

Professional wedding planners (also known as wedding producers, coordinators, or consultants) used to be considered an extravagance or relegated to the role of social secretary. In the past decade, however, more couples have begun to rely on their expertise.

You may want to consider hiring a planner if

- You can't spare at least 12 hours per week to do the job yourself — and twice that much time as the wedding date draws near
- You want to invite more than 100 guests
- You're holding your wedding in a home, garden, loft, museum, or other location that isn't a full-service venue
- You're getting married in a far-off location

If you've been to a wedding that you enjoyed and it seemed similar in taste and style to what you have in mind, ask the couple who was responsible. A tried-and-true way to find a reputable planner is to ask other suppliers such as caterers, florists, and photographers. Trade associations are another good source, but bear in mind that they provide listings, not recommendations.

The web is a possible source for finding planners, but be aware that any clever bridal entrepreneur, from photographers to caterers, may call herself a planner. To further confuse matters, people in the biz (including us) tend to use the terms *planner, coordinator, consultant,* and *producer* interchangeably. Before you make an appointment, find out whether the person plans weddings first and foremost or whether weddings are a mere sideline. Be sure to ask for references and then call them.

Considering how much help you need

The best time to hire a wedding planner is at the beginning of the process. However, you can bring in some planners at any point to handle just a few aspects or to serve as the director of events on the actual wedding day.

Most often, planners charge in three ways: a flat fee, hourly, or a percentage. Expect to pay between 15 and 25 percent of your total wedding budget for a planner to coordinate the entire wedding.

Depending on the level of assistance you require, you may choose one of the following kinds of planners:

- **Day-of planner:** This person gets involved up to a month before the wedding, touching base with suppliers and ensuring that details are in order, and coordinating and managing the wedding-day schedule (see Chapter 7). This option works well for couples who can oversee many of the details themselves but want someone around to make sure things run smoothly. Besides a fee of $1,500 to $6,000 for the wedding day, the day-of planner may charge additional fees for time before that.

✔ **Event producer/designer:** The whole enchilada — someone who both designs the décor for your entire event and does all the planning. Although a good producer takes your taste and style into consideration, be prepared to entrust the producer with complete creative control. This arrangement is best for couples with no time, a substantial budget, and the willingness to relinquish complete control. The producer charges two fees — a planning fee and a design fee — that together can run to $100,000 or more.

✔ **Full-service coordinator:** This planner can recommend vendors, accompany you on appointments, and negotiate contracts. He then schedules and supervises the entire wedding day. If you want to take an active role in the planning but want help along the way, hiring a full-service coordinator is a good way to go. The cost — usually a flat fee or a percentage of the wedding budget — ranges widely, from $5,000 to $50,000. Some full-service coordinators charge an hourly fee plus a percentage.

✔ **Hourly planner:** If you just need someone to bounce ideas off of or to help with a specific aspect of your wedding, such as finding a band or location, paying a planner by the hour can be money well spent. Most planners have a two- or three-hour minimum and charge $50 to $200 per hour.

✔ **Referral maker:** Certain professionals provide nothing more than recommendations for vendors, including caterers, musicians, and florists. Their services appear to be free, but these planners get their compensation from the vendors they recommend. Still, the help can be worth it.

Note: These fees are based on national averages and don't necessarily include any other wedding expenses.

Interviewing prospective wedding professionals

Before you talk to a planner, do a little homework. When you pick up the phone, be prepared to tell the consultant when you expect your wedding to take place, where you want it to be (or at least some possibilities), how many guests you plan to invite, and what your estimated budget is. Schedule an appointment to meet in person.

When you arrive for your meeting, the planner will probably show you a portfolio. Although the portfolio can help you get a sense of her style, it actually says more about the talent of the designer or florist whose work is represented. Be sure to ask what the planner was specifically responsible for in each photograph. Some other effective questions:

- How long have you been in this business?

- Where did you study or with whom did you apprentice?

- Do you belong to any professional organizations?

- What services are included in your contract?

- Are you comfortable working within my budget?

- Will you be able to work with vendors I choose?

- How do you charge — hourly, a flat fee, or a percentage of my total budget?

You and your intended are in this together, after all, so both of you should meet with prospective planners together. Even if your ideas haven't totally jelled, just describing them to a planner is a useful exercise. Also bring magazine clippings or digital images featuring fashion or décor elements that appeal to you. That way, the planner can get an idea of your taste and style.

Remember, you're looking for someone who has taste, style, and creativity and is organized, detail-oriented, and objective (a plus in charged situations). You also want a planner who's resourceful and an expert at getting you the most bang for your buck. Finally, as with a spouse, you want someone who is utterly dependable and who has a terrific sense of humor.

As in any great relationship, the bond you form with your wedding planner should be based on trust, honesty, and mutual respect. With that kind of foundation, you can create a day that you and your guests will remember fondly.

Chapter 2

Avoiding Those Wedding-Bill Blues

- -

- -

*B*ooks, magazines, and, perhaps worst of all, reality TV shows depict excruciatingly perfect weddings that can create a sense of false expectations. Couples may feel entitled to their own fairy-tale wedding or pressured to throw the ultimate fete. Then, as estimates from vendors start rolling in, they snap back to reality (or plunge into despair). Just figuring out how to afford this single event becomes all-consuming and, for many couples, strains their relationship.

In this chapter, I help you get a grip on the big financial picture by explaining how to set a budget and stick to it, how to negotiate contracts, and how to avoid costly surprises. I also highlight a few of my favorite cost-cutting tips, many more of which you find throughout the book.

As you look for ways to stretch your wedding dollar, remember that you have smart — and not so smart — ways to cut costs. You don't necessarily want to go with the vendor that bids the lowest, nor do you want to assume that the priciest vendor provides the best goods or services. Always get references, ask lots of questions, get everything in writing, and weigh your options carefully. If a deal seems too good to be true, it probably is. Sometimes, pennywise really is pound-foolish.

Love Is a Money-Spender Thing

First, the bad news: I can't give you a formula that tells you how much to spend on your wedding. Some experts have tried to provide such guidelines with pie chart percentages that prove utterly useless in the real world. On some websites, you can type in a dollar figure and the number of guests and — presto, change-o! — get a budget that tells you how to spend your wedding dollars. Such exercises provide a rough estimate at best. The fact is that no two weddings are alike. Who's to say what percent of your budget needs to go to food, wine, or your gown? That's a matter of your personal taste, finances, and circumstances.

Now, the good news: You *can* have an awesome wedding without breaking the bank. All it takes is the right attitude, some savvy shopping, creative planning, and diligent budgeting.

The most important idea to remember about your wedding day is that you're getting married to the person you love. Whether your budget is $3,000 or $300,000, the party's success ultimately depends on the way you conduct yourselves, the love and respect you show for each other, and the way you express your happiness. This isn't about putting on a show. It's about forging a new life as a married couple and commemorating that. The hospitality you provide should reflect your values.

In fact, I can't stress enough what a wedding should *not* be: a cause of grief and anxiety. Perhaps in the back of your mind you're worried that guests will dissect every aspect of the reception, playing that tacky guessing game, "How Much Do You Think This Cost?" Stop. Such thoughts can drive you crazy and make you skew your budget based on someone else's priorities. Besides, if you have friends who really think such things, why are you inviting them to your wedding?

Whatever you do, don't go into debt to get married. Yes, this is an important day, but it's not worth struggling to pay it off for years to come. Have the wedding you can afford and make it the best it can be. Remember, the vows say "for richer or for poorer," not "to our credit card limit."

"I Will" Make a Wedding Budget: Tracking Your Expenses

If the notion of tracking your wedding expenses and sticking to the bottom line makes you feel a little cold and clammy, don't fear. Even the most budget-phobic brides and grooms can find lots of digital support. Sites like www.weddingwire.com, www.theknot.com, and www.marthastewart weddings.com offer free tools that help you calculate your budget, track your spending, and move funds around if things change. Some even let you set up payment schedules.

Another option is a wedding budget application for your smartphone. WeddingWire offers an app for both the iPhone and Android phones that has the same features as its online budgeting tool. (Go to www.weddingwire.com and mouse over the drop-down "My Wedding" menu for links to these apps.) Other apps (for the iPhone only as of this writing) include Wedding Budget (www.weddingbudgetapp.com; it focuses on budget only), iWedding Deluxe (www.iweddingdeluxe.com), and Marrily (www.marrily.com; both of these apps include a range of other wedding planning features). The cost of these apps ranges from free to a single payment to a monthly fee. The cheaper apps have fewer features, but because you're being money-smart, shop around to find an app with features you'll really use.

Call me old-fashioned, but I think that though these new tools are great, nothing really beats a simple computerized spreadsheet for staying honest about your budget. To the uninitiated, spreadsheets may look intimidating, but they're really a breeze to use. If you're not familiar with spreadsheet software such as Excel, check out *Excel For Dummies,* by Greg Harvey (Wiley).

As shown in Figure 2-1, start at the bottom line by putting in your total budget amount, assuming you have some idea of what you're able to spend. Based on that figure, fill in guesstimates for various items. As you research vendors and bids, make adjustments in the Estimated Cost column. You may have wildly overestimated the cost of renting linens or been dreaming when you thought silk flowers were cheaper than real ones. Typically, you'll find vendors' estimates to be much higher than your guesses. Don't panic. This spreadsheet is simply to help you get some perspective. Seeing the numbers laid out helps you deal with denial — that is, from thinking that somehow all the numbers will magically work themselves out.

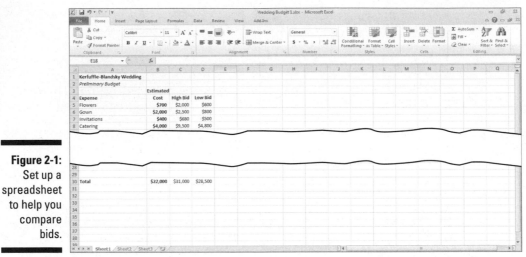

Illustration by Wiley, Composition Services Graphics

Figure 2-1:
Set up a
spreadsheet
to help you
compare
bids.

After you choose your vendors, set up another spreadsheet to help you keep track of money coming in and going out. The spreadsheet in Figure 2-2 shows you how to record expenditures, deposits paid, and outstanding balances. Creating a column that shows when payments are due is usually helpful as well. You can get as elaborate as you want, adding columns to track additional payments, record contact information, or make notes to yourself. The spreadsheet can also get quite long as you add line items. (See the "And another thing . . ." sidebar for a list of possible expenditures you may want to include on your spreadsheet.)

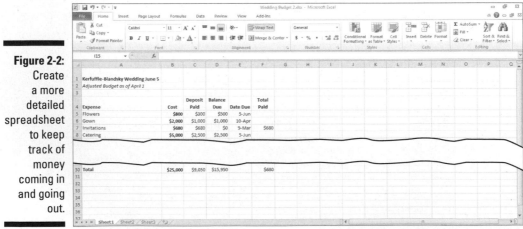

Figure 2-2:
Create
a more
detailed
spreadsheet
to keep
track of
money
coming in
and going
out.

Illustration by Wiley, Composition Services Graphics

And another thing . . .

Although I can't give you standard formulas to make budgeting a whiz (because, frankly, they don't exist), I do provide here a definitive list of the items you may need to include in your budget. If your goal is to avoid unpleasant surprises, read on:

Ceremony
Aisle runner
Church fee
Flowers
    Altar flowers
    Chuppah
    Flower baskets
    Personal
        Bouquets
        Boutonnieres
    Pew bows or flowers
    Tossing bouquet
Mass books
Officiant fee
Organist
Programs
Ring pillows
Yarmulkes

Clothing
Alterations
Attendants' attire
    Dresses
    Flower girl's
      ensemble
    Gloves
    Hats
    Ring bearers' garb
    Shoes
    Tuxedoes/suits
    Waistcoats
Bride's ensemble
    Dress or suit
    Gloves
    Hair
    Headpiece and veil
    Jewelry
    Makeup
    Nails
    Shoes
    Undergarments

Groom's garb
    Cuff links and studs
    Cummerbund
    Manicure
    Shoes
    Tie
    Tuxedo/suit
    Waistcoat

Gifts
Attendants
Bride and groom (to each other)
Parents
Party favors
Welcome baskets

Miscellaneous
Additional psychotherapy
    sessions
Baby sitter
Gratuities
Massages
Relaxation tapes
Sales tax
10 percent cushion

Music
Band(s)
Cartage fees
Ceremony musicians, choir, singers
Cocktail music
Costuming
Dance lessons
Disc jockey
Microphone for toasts
Overtime
Piano rental
Sound system

Other events
Cocktail party
Next-day brunch
Rehearsal dinner

Photography
Album fees (bound and online)
Negatives (digital or film)
Photographer's fees
    Albums
    Assistant(s)
    Film
    Labor
    Processing
Prewedding portrait
Reprints
Videography

Reception
Beverage
    Bar setups
        Fruit
        Ice
        Juices
    Bartenders
Cake
    Cutting fee
    Groom's
    Wedding (or bride's)
Centerpieces
Food
    Additional meals
        Band
        Other noncatering
          staff
        Photographer
        Videographer
Rentals
    Appropriate chairs
    Band platform
    Candles
    China

(continued)

(continued)

Coat check	**Rings**	Reply cards
Dance floor	Engagement	Save-the-date newsletter,
Glassware	Wedding	cards, or e-invitations
Linens		Wedding website fees
Portable restrooms	**Stationery and communication**	
Restroom attendants	At-home cards	**Transportation and lodging**
Restroom toiletries	Calligraphy	Bride and groom
Room treatments	Escort cards	Guests
Serving staff	Guest book	Parents
Silverware	Informals (thank-you notes)	Wedding party
Space rental	Invitations	
Special lighting	Inner and outer	**Wedding consultant**
Table numbers	envelopes	Additional staff
Tables	Reception/ceremony	Expenses
Tent	cards	Fee
Air conditioning/heat	Map and direction cards	
Floor	Place cards	
Lighting	Postage	

Whatever budgeting technique you choose, include an item in your budget for a 10 percent cushion on all expenses and for the bottom line. Unless you're a psychic, you're bound to underestimate some costs and overestimate others. This 10 percent represents the highest amount you're willing to spend. Just knowing that you're prepared with this contingency can save you from having a premature budgetary meltdown. Also, include sales tax in all your budgeting, where appropriate. Many vendors give bids that just say "plus sales tax." Or they may say "plus plus," meaning plus tax and gratuity. Take a moment to calculate the amount and add it to your costs.

Whether you use a spreadsheet or some other system for keeping track of expenses, the key to watching your bottom line is to make sure you record every single deposit you put on a credit card and every check you write. Slacking off in this department is a good way to overspend.

Controlling Costs

Because weddings tend to cost more than may seem reasonable or possible, bear in mind these ways to make the most of what you have to spend:

- ✔ **Know your limits.** If you're paying for the entire wedding or a large portion of it, schedule a session with a wedding planner (who can tell you what things cost) and an accountant or financial planner (who can help you figure out what you can really afford and how to pay for it).

- ✔ **Open a wedding account.** The simplest way to manage your wedding budget is to open a dedicated wedding account so you know exactly how much money goes in and comes out. Some people dedicate one credit card to wedding expenses.

- ✔ **Get donations upfront.** If someone else is contributing toward your wedding, try to get the money in a lump sum.

- ✔ **Earn credit card points.** When it comes to paying for big-ticket items such as the dress or the space-rental fee, charge them to a credit card that gives you something in return (like frequent flier miles). I assume that you're smart, so I don't need to remind you to pay the balance before interest accrues.

- ✔ **Enroll in awards programs.** Many hotels offer points for frequent stays. If you hold your reception at such a hotel, you may even be able to earn some free honeymoon nights.

- ✔ **Be punctual.** Stay organized and stick to your wedding-day schedule so you can avoid overtime charges (see Chapter 7).

- ✔ **Read the fine print.** Examine contracts and costs carefully and ask questions. Are tax, gratuity, and overtime included? These hidden costs can throw your budget off completely.

- ✔ **Negotiate.** Asking vendors for reasonable discounts is perfectly acceptable if you have a good reason for them to reduce the costs, such as holding your wedding on an unpopular day or cutting the amount of courses served.

- ✔ **Shop sales.** This seems obvious, but you may not realize how many wedding-related items you needn't pay retail for. Be on the lookout for sample sales for dresses (see Chapter 19), discount party-supply houses, wine sales at liquor stores, holiday department-store sales for attendants' gifts, shoe sales — you get the picture.

- ✔ **Cut the head count.** Invite fewer people or have a two-tier reception such as a cocktail party for a large group followed by a sit-down dinner elsewhere for 20 close friends and family.

✔ **Keep checking the bottom line.** Being diligent is the best way to avoid magical thinking. If you exceed your budget in one category, look for another area where you can make up the difference. Remember — something's got to give!

✔ **Elope.** This really is an option! You can plan a tiny ceremony — even just the two of you and your officiant — and add on anything else you like: a small reception with family and friends, a bouquet for the bride, a photographer, a petite cake. You don't even have to travel to do it.

Check out the blog www.elopenewyork.com; it's full of inspiring ideas, even if you don't live near New York City.

Comprehending Contracts

For every vendor you hire, get a *written* contract that specifies the deposit paid and the amount due. If you're dealing with professionals (and I hope you are), the contract should contain a list that details the specific services agreed upon. If you're dealing with a friend or relative, have at the very least a letter of agreement that spells out the service(s) to be provided. Make no exceptions! Verbal agreements are legally binding, but they're subject to amnesia and hard to prove in court. The point isn't to prepare for lawsuits but rather to make your wedding day as flawless as possible.

Contracts should be as specific as possible. Instead of "rose bouquets," say "three nosegays of yellow and orange roses, hand-tied with pale yellow satin ribbon; one bridal bouquet of pink, yellow, and ivory roses, hand-tied with ivory satin ribbon." List any possible substitutions as well. For example, "If roses are unavailable, we'll substitute a yellow flower of similar size."

Most businesses have their own formal contracts, but if a vendor fails to produce one, you may want to draft a letter or contract that lists the goods or services you ordered, the pertinent details of your wedding, and the amount you expect to pay. Ask the vendor to sign a copy; if the vendor refuses, find a new one. You don't want to do business with people who aren't willing to take responsibility for their work.

Before you sign a contract, read it carefully and don't be shy about writing in additions or changes. However, ask vendors how they want you to write them so that a legal feeding frenzy doesn't ensue. Both you and the vendor must initial all changes before signing. Never sign a partially or entirely blank contract. A vendor may try to expedite things by saying the details can be filled in later. They may genuinely be trying to speed things up, but you're nonetheless better off waiting or finding a different vendor.

If you and a vendor discuss changes by telephone or e-mail, you need to follow up with an actual letter that reiterates the changes. Keep a copy for your files. (Also keep hard copies of e-mail correspondence.) In fact, keep *all* receipts and copies of contracts in your wedding file. You'll need to refer to them several times before and after the wedding.

Depending on the type of vendor, your contract should include

✔ Business name, address, and phone number

✔ Contact person

✔ The person responsible for your event

✔ A complete description of the product or service

✔ The quantity you're ordering

✔ The number of people to be served

✔ Date and time service or product is to be available

✔ Date and time service is to end

✔ Exact prices for product

✔ Where and at what time product is to be delivered or set up

✔ Fees for delivery and setup

✔ When overtime begins and the fee per hour or half hour

✔ Policies regarding returns, postponement, or cancellation

✔ Price escalation policies and when quoted rates expire

✔ Payment plans such as layaway or three payments

✔ Acceptable payment methods (check, cash, credit card, or certified cashier's check)

✔ Whether gratuities are included or expected

✔ Business representative's signature and date

✔ Your signature and date

Forking over a little at a time

Although most contracts you've probably encountered don't require you to pay in full until all goods or services have been delivered to your satisfaction, the event world runs a little differently. Many suppliers insist on full payment before your wedding day and specify so contractually.

They also require you to put down a deposit early on. Giving a deposit is actually in your interest: Doing so tells vendors that you're serious and further commits them to your event. If you can negotiate for deposits to be refundable, more power to you. However, most vendors insist that deposits be nonrefundable as a way to protect themselves from fraud.

Remember, after you pay a deposit and sign a contract, you're legally bound to pay in full.

As you make deposits, update your wedding budget. If you pay with a check, make a note on the memo line that says exactly what the deposit is for, such as "50 percent of wedding cake." Paying deposits with credit cards is a good idea because if the vendor fails to deliver, goes out of business before your wedding date, or commits some error — and you can convince the credit card company of that — the charges may be reversed. If a check is required, use a credit check, which looks like a personal check but gets charged to your credit account.

If you cancel or postpone your wedding, don't expect a full refund of your various deposits. Some businesses charge 50 percent of their estimated fee regardless of the reason you cancel. They may have turned away other business on your wedding date; your deposit compensates them for this loss. Some vendors return deposits if you cancel because of a death in the family or if they're able to rebook the date and recoup the revenue. If you don't cancel but merely postpone, you may face a price increase.

Covering your bash

If you're the sort who always sees the glass not only half empty but also cracked in six places, you may consider taking out a wedding insurance policy. These policies generally cover postponement, photographs, dress/ attire, gifts, additional expenses, personal liability, and medical payments.

Is the one-time premium worth it? Like all insurance, it may seem like money down the drain until something goes horribly wrong. But read the fine print. A policy may cover postponement or cancellation only in cases when you incur nonrefundable expenses because of circumstances beyond your control. These circumstances may include sickness or bodily injury to the bride, groom, or anyone *essential* (whatever that means) to the wedding party, damage or inaccessibility to the wedding or reception premises, loss or damage to the bridal gown or other wedding attire, corporate or military posting, or job loss. Change of heart, not surprisingly, isn't covered.

Take a Tip: Calculating Gratuities

You want to reward the people who make your wedding day run smoothly. The rules for wedding gratuities are a lot more subjective than the 15 to 20 percent you're used to leaving on the table after a meal. The amount you tip varies according to local customs, your wedding's size (the more people, the larger the tip), and, not least of all, the quality of service.

Plan your tip distribution scheme beforehand and bring along extra cash or checks for surprise niceties. Ask your wedding planner to distribute payments and gratuities for you. If you don't have a planner, give checks for everyone who expects to be paid (bands, for example) to the banquet manager or another person in charge, and give gratuities to your best man or maid of honor. Otherwise, you'll look rather graceless sitting down at the end of your wedding, as the band is packing up and waiters are stripping the tables, scribbling a bunch of checks. Such a scenario can also be detrimental to your bottom line: Getting carried away is easy when you're on the spot, not wanting to look like a cheapskate.

Don't forget: After you tally the gratuities, enter the amounts in your budget application or spreadsheet.

Catering staff

Usually, you pay off-premise catering staff by the hour (delineated on your bill) and you pay in-house staff a percentage of the bill, about 18 to 22 percent. (For an explanation of on-premise versus off-premise facilities, see Chapter 4.) If you're unsure of local practices or percentages, check with your catering manager. Depending on the venue and the vendor, your contract may include gratuities. Even with this kind of arrangement, you may want to reward some people who go above and beyond the call of duty.

Several top catering managers I've talked to feel adamant that tipping should be based solely on merit and that a percentage standard is not only degrading for headwaiters and banquet managers but also detrimental for consumers because it can lead to subtle forms of prewedding blackmail: "If you want your wedding to go well, you better tip these five people x amount." Catering managers say that if you're really blown away by someone's performance (and only then), you may tip. If you really appreciate the job someone does for you, write a letter of praise; most vendors make their living based on referrals and recommendations.

Other vendors

For vendors such as caterers, florists, photographers, and wedding planners, a monetary tip may seem inappropriate, especially if the person you've been working with is the business owner. In such cases, you're better off giving something that's both useful and luxurious, such as a silk scarf or wine.

Officiants

In general, the lowdown on different fee/tip expectations for officiants is as follows:

- **Houses of worship** usually require a fee or donation that covers the use of the facilities. You may want to give a personal gratuity to the officiant as well. Rabbis or ministers who perform ceremonies outside a house of worship almost always charge a fee, and you should determine what this fee is (including any expenses) at your first meeting. Usually, the best man is in charge of handing over these payments so you can avoid any awkwardness.

- **Judges** are allowed to accept money for performing wedding ceremonies, although every county and municipality has its own regulations regarding how much they can accept, and it's usually dubbed a "donation." Depending on your relationship with the judge, if he's a family friend or just a judge for hire, a gratuity can be cash, a personal gift, or a charitable donation in his name.

- **Notaries public** can only perform marriages in a small handful of states (so check with the county clerk), and they generally do so for a small fee. As with judges, a charitable donation in their name may be appropriate.

- **Ordained laypeople** are recognized by most states, although some states require additional documentation, so be sure to check with the county clerk. A few organizations — the Universal Life Church (www.ulchq.org), Rose Ministries (www.roseministries.org), and Spiritual Humanism (www.spiritualhumanism.org) — offer online ordination upon request. This means you can ask your grandpa or your college sorority sister to officiate. Because you're asking a loved one to perform your ceremony, a gift is the most appropriate token of your gratitude.

Other people you may want to tip

Tip bathroom and coatroom attendants ahead of time with the understanding that they should refrain from accepting any gratuities and should politely explain that the matter has been taken care of by the hosts. You may want to post a discreet sign in appropriate places saying: "Gratuities have been paid by your host." And under no circumstances should you have a tip jar anywhere on the premises. This should go without saying, but just in case, reiterate to the manager that the sight of one will make you go bonkers.

For more detailed info about tipping, see Table 2-1 for some guidelines, which may vary depending on your area, the level of service, and the number of people served.

Table 2-1	Tipping Guidelines
Recipient	*Amount*
Banquet manager	$200 and up or a personal gift, depending on the wedding's size and complexity
Bartender (head)	$50 and up
Bartender	$25 and up
Bathroom attendants	$1 to $2 per guest or a flat fee arranged with venue management
Bride's dresser	15 to 20 percent of the fee
Catering party manager	$200 and up or a personal gift, depending on the wedding's size and complexity
Chef	$100 and up
Civil ceremony officiant	$25 to $50, if appropriate
Clergyperson	$25 and up, depending on the wedding's size
Coatroom attendants	$1 to $2 per guest or a flat fee arranged with venue management
Cooks	$25 each
Hairdresser	10 to 20 percent of the fee, depending on number of heads
Hotel chambermaid	$1 to $2 a day
Maitre d' or headwaiter	1 to 3 percent of the food and beverage fee, depending on the number of guests and the bill amount; or $150 to $300 for off-premise, depending on the number of guests

(continued)

Table 2-1 *(continued)*

Recipient	Amount
Makeup person	10 to 20 percent of the fee, depending on number of faces
Musicians (ceremony)	$25 per person or 15 percent of the fee for a large group
Musicians (reception)	$25 to $50 per member, especially if guests make numerous requests
Parking attendants	$1 to $2 per car or 15 percent of the valet parking bill (usually included in bill)
Photographer	$100 for extraordinary service if you pay a flat rate with no overtime fee
Porters	$15 each
Room captain	$50 and up
Tailor	10 percent of the fee
Transportation driver	$25 additional for a van or bus driver; 18 to 20 percent for a limo (usually on the bill), plus $25 for exceptional service
Wait staff	$20 to $50 each for off-premise (tips for on-premise wait staff are usually included in the bill's gratuity percentage)
Wedding planner	15 percent of the fee; 15 to 20 percent if charged hourly or just for the wedding day; or a personal gift

Finding Bargains Online

Thanks to the Internet, you can plan almost your entire wedding without getting up from your desk — from taking virtual tours of venues to ordering invitations to buying wedding apparel.

Depending on what you're in the market for, first try a search for exactly what you seek: *plaid cummerbund.* If that doesn't produce enough results, use general terms, such as *men's formal wear.*

 Most search engines are sophisticated enough that you can enter a string of words with no quotation marks or connecting words. However, quotation marks can help narrow the search faster: Typing *wedding gowns* brings up thousands of entries on anything having to do with Christmas or angels, but "wedding gowns" with quotation marks gives you more precise hits.

In many cases, shopping the web saves you money, but not always. To get your money's worth, remember to

- ✔ **Bare your gifts.** When shopping for attendants' gifts, be aware that gift-wrapping online orders can cost as much as $5 *per item*. Ouch. So wrap them yourself, or look for deals. For example, Tiffany sends its goodies in boxes that are so pretty they make wrapping paper superfluous, and Coach will gift-box anything for free.

- ✔ **Check out eBay.** With millions of items for sale in hundreds of categories — including one for "Wedding & Formal Occasion" — you can find almost any accouterment for your wedding on eBay (www.ebay.com). Plug in *wedding* or *bridal* on the site's search engine and you'll discover rings, dresses, veils, shoes, tiaras, jewelry, invitations, favors, flowers, candles, and just about anything else you can think of — often at prices far below retail, unless you get into a bidding war. To get the best deals, read all the instructions and policies on the site and have a good idea of retail prices.

- ✔ **Click for coupons.** Many online stores offer special promotions that you can find through coupon sites. Type in what you're looking for plus a keyword such as *coupon, discount, promotion,* or *sale* to find online coupons or special promotion codes.

- ✔ **Explore wedding blogs.** The web is an infinite source of ideas, and that includes ideas for saving money on your wedding. Loads of blogs and websites are full of money-saving wedding advice. Just do a search on the term *DIY wedding.* Particularly good is www.diywedding.org, which has gorgeous photos, money-saving tips, resources, and a community forum. Also worth a look is www.intimateweddings.com, which offers inspiration, ideas, and support for planning a smaller wedding.

- ✔ **Get your tax straight.** If you buy from a merchant that has a physical location in your state, you have to pay sales tax on your online order. When weighing tax and shipping, it may be cheaper to hunt for a smaller (as in not a chain store), out-of-state merchant or to simply buy the item in person.

- ✔ **Pit prices against each other.** Consumer sites compile databases of products sold at online stores and sort them according to price. In some cases, these sites also provide product reviews and customer-service scores and even tally the cost of tax and shipping for you.

Chapter 3

Making It All Legal

Weddings aren't all fluff and festivities. All that stuff is window dressing for an extremely serious rite of passage — a rite that you still have to make legal. Besides getting a license, you need to figure out whether to change your name and, depending on your circumstances, whether a prenuptial agreement is a good idea. In this chapter, I walk you through these tasks.

License to Thrive

First things first: A marriage *license* is the piece of paper that authorizes you to get married, and a marriage *certificate* is the document that proves you're married. Like driving, fishing, or hunting, within the United States you need a state license to get married. Same-sex couples also need a license for marriage or civil unions in the states that recognize it. Check the state or country regulations online or call the clerk of the town or city where you're getting hitched to find out about application procedures, age requirements, and familial restrictions.

Because most states have a cooling-off period (generally one to five days) between the time the license is issued and the wedding day, don't put off getting the license until the last minute. However, being super-efficient and ahead of schedule doesn't always pay. In some places, a license is good for only a certain number of days. Time your trip to the county clerk's office so your license is still valid on the day you actually wed.

Pick up the application or have it mailed to you a few weeks ahead of time, so you can fill it out at your leisure and, if necessary, have it notarized. Then you both must appear in person before the town clerk, who types up the official license, which you sign in the clerk's presence. You may need to provide one or more of the following:

✔ **Proof of identity and age:** This may be a birth certificate, passport, driver's license, state identification card, immigration record, or naturalization record. In some cases, the same document may prove both identity and age, but states may also require separate documentation. Check with the county clerk or look at the state government website to see what you need to bring. If you were born outside the United States, expect to need extra documentation.

✔ **Information regarding previous marriages or unions:** You may have to tell how many times you've been married (or had previous civil unions), the date, why the marriage(s) ended (death, divorce, annulment, and so on), whether the former spouse is living, and when, where, and against whom the divorce(s) was granted. You may also have to present a certified copy of your divorce decree or the death certificate of your former spouse.

If you need a copy of a marriage or civil union certificate, visit the website of the Centers for Disease Control (www.cdc.gov/nchs/w2w.htm), which explains where to write for vital records. Another helpful website is www.archives.com, which enables searches for vital records with membership.

✔ **Results of blood tests or premarital medical examination:** Nearly all states have eliminated blood tests as a prerequisite to getting a marriage license. At this writing, only Mississippi and Montana require them. If you do need one, ask your doctor or a local clinic for a standard prewedding blood test. What are they testing for? Mississippi requires a test of both men and women for syphilis, and Montana requires a test of women under 50 for rubella. (Neither state tests for HIV.) If one of you tests positive for the relevant disease, the state may refuse to issue a license.

Before you pay your nominal license fee, call ahead or check the state or county website to see what form of payment the clerk accepts. Some states, for example, take only money orders; others take only cash.

Whoever performs the wedding ceremony is responsible for sending a copy of the marriage or civil union certificate to the county or state agency that records them. At the wedding, your witnesses sign the certificate, which the officiant then sends back to the town clerk, who then mails it back to you after recording it.

Tying the knot abroad

In general, marriages that are legally performed and valid abroad are also legally valid in the United States. (The exception is same-sex marriages that are legal in a few foreign countries but not currently federally recognized in the United States.) However, getting married in another country can be a bit more complicated than in the States. You're subject to the residency requirements of the country where you're getting married, and the length of the waiting period varies depending on the country. Besides a valid U.S. passport, you'll probably need to present birth certificates, divorce decrees, and death certificates to the marriage registrar — and in some cases have those documents translated into the native language of that country. Some countries require that you have these documents authenticated first in the United States by a consular official of that country. This process can be time consuming and expensive. Although the United States

has largely stopped requiring blood tests before marriage, some countries still require them. And most countries also require a little item called an *affidavit of eligibility* to marry. This document — which doesn't exist in the United States — certifies that no impediment (such as still being married to another person) exists to the marriage. Unless the foreign authorities allow such a statement to be signed before one of their consular officials in the United States, you have to sign the affidavit at the American embassy or consulate in the country in which the marriage will occur. For more information, go to the U.S. State Department's website: `http://travel.state.gov/law/family_issues/marriage/marriage_589.html`. The State Department advises that the best source of information about foreign marriage requirements is the embassy or tourist information bureau of that country.

In strictly legal terms, the license shouldn't be signed until after the ceremony, but many officiants allow the couple to sign beforehand to save time after the ceremony.

When you get your marriage license, you may want to order an extra copy or two of your marriage certificate if you plan to change your name after your wedding. You must submit an original copy — not a photocopy — when applying for a new social security card and driver's license. By ordering extra copies, you don't have to worry about your only bona fide copy returning to you in several pieces or stained with coffee rings, or forever disappearing into the bureaucratic black hole.

Same-Sex Legalities

Same-sex couples wanting to wed have some special issues to consider. The legal rights they enjoy as a couple depend on the state where they get married *and* the state where they live. The majority of states in the United States don't legally recognize gay and lesbian unions (and in a few cases, explicitly ban recognizing them). But some states do recognize same-sex unions in a few different ways.

As of this writing, six states (Connecticut, Iowa, Massachusetts, New Hampshire, New York, and Vermont) as well as the District of Columbia recognize *same-sex marriage*. (And assuming recent laws aren't overturned, Washington State and Maryland will do so as of November 2012 and January 2013, respectively). In these states, gay and lesbian couples enjoy the same legal benefits granted by their state to any married couple.

A handful of other states (Delaware, Hawaii, Illinois, New Jersey, Rhode Island, and Washington) recognize *civil unions* between same-sex partners, essentially granting the same legal rights given to heterosexual married couples, even though these states don't refer to same-sex unions as "marriage."

And finally, a few other states recognize *domestic partnerships* or similar arrangements. Depending on the state, these partnerships may grant the same state-wide rights as marriage (California, Nevada, Oregon, and Washington) or just some of those rights (Colorado, Hawaii, Maine, and Wisconsin).

Couples who want to wed in states that don't recognize any rights associated with same-sex unions can of course plan a commitment ceremony. Commitment ceremonies are as beautiful as weddings and have the same personal and emotional significance; they just don't have any legal implications for the couple.

And the legal complications don't stop there. The federal Defense of Marriage Act (DOMA) denies federal recognition of same-sex marriage, which means that even same-sex couples who are legally married and receive the state benefits of marriage in their home state don't receive any of the *federal* benefits of marriage (like federal tax benefits, Social Security survivor or retiree benefits, federal employee spousal benefits, or estate planning and tax benefits).

DOMA also allows states to deny recognition to same-sex marriages performed in other states. So the rights granted by same-sex marriages, civil unions, and domestic partnerships only apply in the state where they were granted, unless another state chooses to recognize them. For instance, Connecticut and New York explicitly recognize same-sex marriage licenses granted by other states, and California recognizes same-sex marriages that were performed anywhere before November 4, 2008.

Regardless of where you live, you want to research your state's policy on same-sex unions and find out about the rights you're entitled to at the state level. State government websites are a good place to start, as is the Human Rights Campaign website (`www.hrc.org/laws-and-legislation/ state/c/marriage`), which provides an overview of marriage and other rights granted to same-sex couples by state.

Drawing Up a Pre-nup

Believe it or not, prenuptial agreements aren't just for the rock stars of the world. Also known as *pre-nups* or, more formally, as premarital contracts, these agreements are made by couples who want to circumvent the mandates of state law (concerning either marriage or civil unions) in the event of a divorce or death. You might consider drawing up a premarital contract if one of you has property that you want to keep if the marriage ends — for example, a considerable income or a family business. Perhaps most frequently, people who have children or grandchildren from prior marriages make premarital agreements. The pre-nup allows the partner to ensure that the bulk of her property passes to the children or grandchildren rather than to the current spouse. They may have a bad rap, but pre-nups need not (and should not) be a divorce rehearsal.

Even if you think you have no assets worth fighting over, peer hard into your crystal ball and think about how much things can change in a decade. Perhaps one of you will get a degree and vastly increase your earning potential. Maybe one of you will come up with an idea that takes off. This *goodwill* — an intangible asset assigned to people who have a reputation and an ability to make money on it — is worth covering in a pre-nup.

Some couples find that going through the pre-nup exercise helps them come to terms with each other's needs and desires before certain issues become irresolvable problems. Sometimes, many of the issues hashed out in pre-nup preparation simply become private pledges rather than part of a legally binding document.

That said, don't underestimate the possible psychological repercussions of a pre-nup. Before you broach the subject, ask yourself whether such an agreement is worth the effect it may have on your relationship. You can explore the potential benefits of a pre-nup at the legal website Nolo (`www.nolo.com/ legal-encyclopedia/prenuptial-agreement`). And the site `www. prenuptialagreements.org/` includes lots of tips for talking to your partner and negotiating a pre-nup.

If you decide to negotiate a premarital contract, you and your partner should each get your own lawyer. Instruct the lawyers to write the agreement in plain English as opposed to legalese and to follow the Uniform Premarital Agreement Act or similar state laws. Include an amendment clause. Negotiate the specifics and sign it as early as possible in the wedding-planning process. Getting a head start makes sense for two reasons: first, because an agreement signed under duress may not hold up in court, and second, because you don't want financial negotiations to be foremost in your mind as you walk down the aisle. Be flexible and certain that every negotiation reflects your love for each other. You may find that trusting each other and talking things through brings you even closer.

Playing the Name Game

Deciding what to call yourselves after your marriage isn't the simple wife-takes-her-husband's-name scenario it once was. Although many newspapers still feel compelled to note when the bride is keeping her name, upon marriage, a woman's *surname* (her family or last name) doesn't automatically change to her husband's, nor is she legally *required* to change it. A woman must choose to change it and then take certain measures to make the change official (that is, legal). Sites such as www.missnowmrs.com can help you change all your legal documents easily and efficiently. Note that if you're not among the 90 percent of women who choose to take their husband's name, you're still entitled to a portion of your husband's pension, Social Security, or other rights associated with the marriage contract.

Deciding whether to change your name

These days, a variety of name options are both possible and socially acceptable:

- The bride takes the groom's name.
- The bride keeps her birth name.
- The bride keeps her birth name for professional circumstances but takes her husband's name in all other cases.
- The bride and groom use both their last names, with or without a hyphen.
- The bride uses both her birth and married surnames, with or without a hyphen.
- The groom drops his name and takes the bride's.
- The bride and groom meld their names into a new one altogether.
- The bride and groom pick out an entirely new name.

If you're a same-sex couple, you may feel less bound by tradition, but basically the same name-change options are open to you. You may keep your own names, take or add the other's name, combine your names with or without a hyphen, meld your names into a new one, or choose an entirely new name. Note that in states that allow same-sex couples to marry or enter into civil unions, you're permitted to change your name in light of your marriage. This is recognized at the state level (so you can change your driver's license or state ID card). Though current federal convention generally recognizes the state name change, DOMA doesn't permit federal recognition of same-sex unions, so the ability to change your name on your passport or Social Security card isn't a guarantee, which may create some confusion in your life.

For a woman, adopting her husband's name can have some drawbacks. If a man has been previously married or comes to the marriage laden with some unfortunate financial or legal baggage, a new bride could find herself being harassed by credit-collection agencies as a result of mismerged data — that is, when an ex-spouse's financial information winds up in a new spouse's credit report. If your hubby-to-be owes back taxes, has tax liens on his property, has been the victim of identity theft, or has some other complicated financial history, you may want to hold off changing your name until those issues are resolved so you can protect your own assets.

Another issue to consider is whether your career will suffer by changing your name. As people are marrying later in life — the average American woman marries at age 25 today, up from age 20 in the 1950s — many women find that they've established themselves enough that changing their name would confuse colleagues. This is particularly true in industries where referrals and networking are integral to the job. On the other hand, announcing your new name could be a wonderful opportunity to touch base with clients and colleagues.

Updating your records

You should decide by the time of your wedding what names you'll use legally, professionally, and socially. If you change one or both of your names, start using the new ones as soon as you're married, and then be sure to change your name on all your identification, accounts, and important documents.

Start with Social Security — it's hard to get any other institution to acknowledge your new identity until Big Brother does. To apply for a name change, go to the Social Security home page (www.socialsecurity.gov) and click Name Changes under the Useful Links heading. You'll get information about relevant documents and an application you can print and mail. Next you want to change your driver's license. In both cases, you need a certified copy of your marriage certificate, which should arrive by mail a few weeks after your marriage ceremony.

When you have your new Social Security card and driver's license, you're ready to update all your other legal and financial records. Just when you think you've changed every last one, you're sure to discover another. After you start, you must change everything; otherwise, you leave yourself vulnerable to such annoyances as nasty notices from the IRS and canceled plane tickets because the name on your passport doesn't match. Here are a few things you need to change:

- Bank accounts (if you're still using them, order new checks, too)
- Business cards
- Credit cards
- Frequent flier programs
- Income tax forms
- Insurance policies (change your beneficiaries as well)
- Passport
- Retirement accounts (again, change your beneficiaries)
- Stationery
- Voter registration card

Also be sure to notify your employer's accounting office and office manager of your name change. If your marriage coincides with a move to a new address, update your address where necessary.

Many companies allow you to update your information by phone or e-mail. However, others, such as banks and credit card companies, require a written request and, in some cases, a copy of your marriage certificate. Be sure to sign each letter and, if circumstances require it, have your spouse sign as well.

Take a copy of your marriage certificate with you when you travel or have to sign anything official, such as the papers when you close a home sale. After you have new forms of ID, you can leave the certificate at home.

Alerting the Media

In this age of reality TV and confessional talk shows, going public with details of your engagement or wedding in the local newspaper seems positively low-profile. Nonetheless, you need to undertake these formalities with care to present yourselves as a couple in the best possible light for the public record.

Announcing the engagement

Sending out engagement announcements is frowned upon because it looks like a ploy to get gifts. (However, don't confuse engagement announcements with save-the-date cards, which I discuss in Chapters 4 and 5.) You may decide to announce your engagement to the multitudes through your current local newspaper, your hometown newspaper, or the paper in the city where your parents currently reside.

Many papers, however, have abandoned these listings because they discovered that vendors deluged couples with solicitations and also that engagements don't *always* end in marriage. The papers figure that it's better to run an announcement after the couple crosses the finish line. Call the newspaper you want to place your announcement in and see whether you have to fill out a form. In some cases, a simple letter from the bride's parents suffices.

Engagement parties are another popular way to share your news. If you're lucky enough to have friends or family who will host a party to celebrate your engagement, the party invitation serves as an announcement in itself.

News of the wed

Some newspapers publish wedding announcements as a free service to readers; others treat them like classified ads and charge a fee. You usually have to fill out a form (see the example in Figure 3-1). You can often find the form along with procedures, deadlines, and photo specifications on the paper's website. The wedding pages have traditionally been a notoriously snooty section of most newspapers, but some show signs of loosening up. Although the *New York Times, Boston Globe, Washington Post,* and other leading newspapers now run announcements for same-sex commitment ceremonies and weddings, it remains to be seen whether many more papers will follow suit.

Papers like to publish wedding announcements the day of the wedding or shortly afterward. To get your wedding announcement in the newspaper, send in your vital statistics at least six weeks in advance.

For newspapers that run the announcements late, you should be able to choose a digital image the night of the wedding with your photographer to submit electronically.

If you want a formal portrait to appear with your announcement the day after your wedding, schedule a session with your photographer several weeks ahead of time. Check with the newspaper first for its photo requirements — many have composition rules that stipulate things like the couple's heads must be at the same level or their eyebrows must be in the same plane.

Sample Newspaper Wedding Announcement Form

Indicate when a middle name is used as a first name, such as Mary Margaret Jones (known as Margaret) or Thomas Edward Smith (known as Edward). For names like Maryanne and Mary Anne, make clear whether the name is one word or two and which letters are capitalized.

Bride's Full Name:_____
Address: _____
Community/Town: _____
Phone:
(Home)_____(Business)_____

Bride's Parents' Full Names: _____
Address:_____
Community/Town:_____
Phone:_____

Bridegroom's Full Name:_____
Address:_____
Community/Town:_____
Phone:
(Home)_____(Business)_____

Specify if parents are deceased, stepparents, divorced, or separated, and where each lives.

Bridegroom's Parents' Full Names:_____
Address:_____
Community/Town:_____
Phone:_____

CEREMONY

Phone numbers are critical for clarifications under deadline. Numbers should be "good" 9 a.m. to 5 p.m. so that responses are not delayed by answering machines or voice mail.

Place of Ceremony: _____
City:_____ State: _____
Date, Hour: _____
Mass?_____
Ceremony performed by:_____
Of: (church, affiliation, location)_____
Place of Reception: _____
City:_____ State:_____
Honeymoon: _____
Future Address: (will publish community only)

_____

WEDDING PARTY

Even though they might be your oldest friends, use formal first names such as Antoinette (not Toni), Suzanne (not Sue or Susie), Robert (not Bob or Rob), Anthony (not Tony), and so on. Include last names.

Escorted to the altar by (full first name):
_____ Relationship:_____
( )Maid ( ) Matron of Honor:_____
Relationship:_____
Best Man: _____ Relationship: _____
Bridesmaids:_____
_____
Ushers: _____
Flower Girl:_____
Ring Bearer:_____

Figure 3-1: Make clear the pertinent details of your wedding.

Illustration by Wiley, Composition Services Graphics

Recognizing that most couples are out of town on their honeymoon by the time their wedding announcement runs, some newspapers have developed a sideline of selling newly minted couples a "professionally" mounted copy of their announcement. In fact, the first call you get upon your return is likely to be a salesperson trying to take your order before the newlywed glow wears off. Save a few bucks and ask someone to save extra copies of the paper for you. Then you can decide at your leisure how to preserve this keepsake.

Unplanning a Wedding

If you're in the throes of planning your wedding and you need to cancel or postpone it, I realize that what you're going through is traumatic. Whatever the culprit, you're faced with an awful task, made all the more unpleasant by unnecessary financial losses in addition to the psychological stress.

For details on the social aspects such as alerting guests that the wedding is off, see Chapter 5. To figure out what to do with gifts you've already received, see Chapter 18. Continue on, dear reader, for tips on dealing with contracts and money matters and deciding what to do with the engagement ring.

Settling up

Depending on how far along you are in your planning, you must call your venue, caterer, and other vendors and attempt to get all or some of your deposits back. If you specified a refundable deposit clause in your contract, that makes things easier and less of a financial hardship. If a vendor refuses to refund any money you're due, you can dispute the charge on your credit card statement (if you read Chapter 2 and paid by credit card, that is) or take up the dispute with a third party mediator such as the Better Business Bureau or your local consumer affairs department. In general, vendors assess the cause of the cancellation, the possibilities of their rebooking the date, and the amount of time they've already invested in your wedding to calculate a possible refund.

Even if your attendants were going to pay for their own dresses or other attire, you now need to reimburse them for the money they've spent or the deposits they may have lost. If they ask you to pay them back for the shower they threw in your honor, you're not obligated to do so. But do return their gifts (or, if used, an identical gift) with a note of "Thanks, but . . ." as described in Chapter 18.

If you need to iron out some financial details of your split with your ex (such as reception payments spent), retaining legal counsel is probably a good idea so that discussions are kept businesslike.

Who keeps the ring?

Whether she's the jilter or the jiltee, every bride wants to know: "Do I have to give the ring back?" The answer is usually yes, although more than 100 cases on the books — some going all the way to state supreme courts — have grappled with this question and reached different conclusions. The main point of contention is whether an engagement ring is just a gift or contains an implied condition of marriage. And though some judges think the ring should go back to the purchaser, regardless of who broke up with whom, others think that if the man (the "donor," in legal parlance) broke off the engagement, he can't recover the ring.

I happen to feel that, no matter who or what's to blame, the ring should go back to the person who gave it.

Part II
Be Our Guest

The 5th Wave   By Rich Tennant

"It's an electronic wedding planner. It'll create
all your checklists and timetables, and after
the ceremony it turns all the documents into
confetti and throws it in your face."

In this part . . .

I show you how to be an incredible host, because a wedding isn't just about two people getting married — it's a full-fledged display of hospitality. That doesn't necessarily mean spending a fortune to wow your guests. Even if you turn your ballroom into Versailles, top every table with life-size ice sculptures, and shoot yourselves from a cannon, the most meaningful (and memorable) wedding touches are those that show how much you care for each other and for those around you. That message is conveyed in every detail — from your choice of venue to the wording of the invitation, from the wedding-day schedule to the extracurricular activities — and the thoughtfulness with which you approach them.

Chapter 4

Venue Victories: Finding the Ideal Location

*W*hether you choose a religious ceremony in a local house of worship followed by an old-fashioned reception at home or you invent new traditions somewhere faraway, finding a tie-the-knot spot is one of the first tasks to cross off your list. Hot venues are often booked a year in advance, and in popular resort areas, hotels and other lodgings fill up quickly as peak season approaches. And, of course, until you know where you're getting married, moving on to other decisions, such as ordering invitations and finalizing the menu, is impossible.

Looking for Love in All the Right Places

Start with the big picture: Narrow down the location by region, state, city, and venue. Money is power, so you need to take into account who's covering the cost and where *they* want to have the wedding. Consider also who may actually come (which isn't always the same as whom you *want* to come) and how far they have to travel. Where do most of your friends and relatives live?

Tradition favors having the wedding in the bride's hometown, but that's not always feasible or desirable. If neither of you has roots in your present community, you may opt for neutral territory or a favorite vacation spot. However, are you prepared to pay guests' travel costs or are your guests well-heeled enough to cover the expense? How often are the local airports shut down because of weather? And if you're looking at a resort town, are peak-season costs sky-high? Often, two cities that appear equal in every other way vary greatly in cost of living.

If you're planning a religious ceremony, hold off on booking anything until you clear the dates, location, and timing with the priest, rabbi, or minister you want to officiate. Even though you may be of a particular religion, some local clergy have autonomy over their physical plants and the order of service. A clergyperson may deem your ceremony plans inappropriate for reasons you never dreamed of, such as secular music, contemporary readings, or your edited version of traditional vows.

Should you come upon a church or synagogue within reasonable proximity of your reception, don't expect to be able to just walk in and book it as if it were a catering hall. Many sensitive issues are involved, and the church may charge fees for nonparishioners. If you have a relationship with a clergyperson or some other official religious authority through your family or as a couple, enlist his help in communicating with the powers that be at the house of worship you're interested in.

Finding great spaces

Before you set out on a wild goose chase, spend some time amassing as much material on various locations as possible. You can find information about wedding sites in a variety of places, including

- ✔ **Bridal and event shows:** Location vendors display at these exhibitions, which range from huge bridal fairs to invitation-only events at department stores. See the Bridal Show Producers International website to find a show near you (www.bspibridalshows.com).

- ✔ **Caterers, florists, and photographers:** Because off-premise locations are their stock in trade, caterers are tuned into what's available. Florists and wedding photographers also tend to know the good spots in their area. To find a unique space, interview these professionals for suggestions. Because many wedding professionals now maintain blogs, you can also explore the photos on their sites for places that appeal to you. If a photo of a place you like is uncredited, send an e-mail to ask where it was taken.

- ✔ **Consumer magazines:** Besides the requisite *Brides, Bridal Guide,* and *Martha Stewart Weddings,* other consumer magazines (*Town & Country* and *New York,* for example) put out special wedding issues. Look for regional magazines such as *Hawaii Bride & Groom* and *Inside Weddings* (for the West Coast). The lesser-known magazine *Grace Ormonde Wedding Style* and the Canadian magazine *WedLuxe* are also worth checking out.

✔ **The Innkeepers' Register:** The Independent Innkeepers Association publishes *The Innkeepers' Register,* a printed guide to more than 300 country inns in North America. The guide evaluates member inns for quality and includes photographs and information for each inn. See www.travelassist.com for ordering information.

✔ **Internet:** Type the word "wedding" into a search engine, along with "planning," "vendor," or the name of a town or state to access numerous sites. At this writing, some of the top wedding websites include www.theknot.com, www.weddingchannel.com, and www.weddingdetails.com.

  • **Venue databases online:** These sites let you search for venues by your preferred location. Unique Venues (www.uniquevenues.com) offers a vast database of conference centers, colleges, universities, movie theaters, entertainment venues, and other special places you may not have thought of. Or try www.venuesonline.com, which features both venues and vendor information. The My Wedding site (www.mywedding.com) lets you click a map to explore local venues and vendors, and Romantic Places (www.romanticplaces.com) lists romantic hotels and inns all over the world. Another site, www.eventlocations.us, lets you explore a wide variety of venues in New York and New Jersey. Finally, BizBash (www.bizbash.com), a media company for the events industry, publishes area-specific print magazines and maintains a website with great event coverage articles as well as venue guides by city. Although its output is geared toward the trade, browsing the website or magazine for your area can still give you some great ideas for your event.

  • **Wedding blogs:** Try searching the web for "wedding blog" plus your desired location (like "wedding blog San Francisco" or "wedding blog Charleston") and explore the results for venue ideas. If you're undecided on city or country, just find some blogs you like and go from there. The site www.weddingblogs100.com lists the top 100 wedding blogs of the year with descriptions, so you're sure to find blogs with a style that appeals to you. I particularly like the www.stylemepretty.com blog for national and international recommendations and the charming www.junebugweddings.com for resources and vendors in Seattle and Southern California.

  • **Your social network:** Both in person and online, your family, friends, and colleagues can be a great source of recommendations. Put the word out and ask via Facebook or Twitter whether anyone has been to a good venue lately.

✔ **Newspapers:** Peruse the wedding announcements in your local newspaper or the paper in the city where you want to be married. Besides telling where the ceremony is held, they also sometimes mention the reception site.

Remember, your own attitude plays a key role in your search for an original, magical place to get married. Think of yourself as a daring investigative journalist of wedding venues, meaning you should

✔ **Be gutsy:** Get personal suggestions from people whom you consider arbiters of taste and style, including bridal magazine editors.

✔ **Be curious:** Perhaps you or someone you know attended a wedding that was stunning, but for some reason — cost, location, or size — the venue isn't quite right for you. Find out what other spots the couple passed up. Their reject list may contain your dream site.

✔ **Be creative:** Inquire about unconventional spaces to rent, such as private homes, lofts, museums, galleries, boats, and private gardens. Owners who've never thought of renting out their property may consider it for a wedding.

If you have your eye on a private club, you need to be sponsored by a member or be a member of a club that has a reciprocal agreement. This can be a Catch-22 because often the club won't even let you check out the site if you don't have a sponsor — and how do you find a sponsor without finding out who the members are? In addition to having an in-house caterer, clubs may have stringent or seemingly peculiar rules.

Although I encourage you to doggedly pursue all leads, this is no time to launch into your entitled heiress impersonation, especially when you start barraging vendors with questions. Food and beverage personnel are people, too, and wherever you wind up holding your wedding, they'll remember you, for better or for worse.

Getting more info by phone

You may narrow down your choices online, but if you're really interested in a space, you need to make a phone call. The phone interview lets you preview the kind of service you can expect. Does someone at the venue return calls promptly? Does the person seem flexible or does she have a more take-it-or-leave-it attitude? Do you get the sense that she'd be happy (not desperate, just pleased) to host your wedding? Is she too busy to talk to you? Is she condescending, rude, or evasive? Your first impressions are a huge tip-off to the quality of service you'll find during your planning.

During the initial phone call

✔ Get the name and title of the person on the other end of the phone. You'd be amazed at how often busboys quote prices and availability.

✔ Ask what room(s) is available for your wedding date and time. If another event is booked in the space earlier in the day, how much setup time is allotted between events?

✔ Ask for photos of the room and a layout that shows a similar number of guests to your total.

✔ Confirm whether the prospective reception venue is an on-premise or off-premise site:

- In general, *on-premise* refers to hotels, restaurants, banquet facilities, private clubs, and any other place that has a full-service, in-house food and beverage operation on the premises. If you're interested in an on-premise site, ask for food and beverage price estimates. (For a breakdown of what those estimates may be, see Chapters 14 and 15.)

- When a venue is *off-premise,* you have to contract separately to rent the site and the outside caterer. Examples of off-premise venues range from a tent in your backyard to a museum to a private mansion. Some of these spaces have lists of off-premise caterers they allow or recommend. Whether you've fallen in love with a particular off-premise space or have designs on a brilliant caterer, be certain that the venue and caterer can work together. If you feel the food is more important than the space, start by finding a caterer, who in turn may lead you to the space. (See Chapter 14 for tips on finding a great caterer.)

Do You Need More than One Space?

If you're not going to be married in a house of worship, you need a place to have a ceremony, a cocktail hour (if you have one), and a reception. Your first choice should be a site that can handle all three in separate spaces.

The turning of the room

Finding versatile, multiroomed spaces isn't easy. Consequently, you may need to *turn* a room. This banquet term refers to resetting a room for another function. A space that must double as both a ceremony location and a cocktail area requires that chairs be moved and bars unveiled while guests are still in the room. If the ceremony and reception are in the same room, guests are ushered to a separate cocktail area while the ceremony room is turned.

An elaborate decor may involve extra labor costs or may be impossible to carry off in the time between ceremony and reception. Your decor concept shouldn't dictate the length of the cocktail hour. Sculpting miniature English gardens on each table, for example, may take an inordinately long time. By the time they're seated, some guests may be too sloshed to notice or care whether they have a rose tree or a redwood towering above them.

Does the price include tax and tip?

Catering halls, restaurants, hotels, and banquet facilities often offer space-food-liquor packages, so asking about one without considering the others is almost impossible. The terms to know are

✔ **All-inclusive:** Covers food, beverage, tax, and tip, but may not include such extras as bartenders, bathroom attendants, cake, carvers, coat room, and valet parking.

✔ **Plus-plus:** Tax and gratuity are added to your food and beverage price. This figure may skew your whole budget, so don't ignore it. For example, if your meal and bar price is $75 per person plus-plus, with a sales tax of 8.25 percent and a gratuity of 20 percent, that comes to an additional $21.19 per person, making your actual cost $96.19 per person. To make matters worse, in some states, the gratuity is also taxable. Oh well, you didn't need to have any flowers, right?

Ceremony here, reception there

Even if getting married in a house of worship isn't a priority, you may opt to have the ceremony and reception at different locations to avoid any room-turn awkwardness. Doing so, however, may incur additional expenses, such as fees for the ceremony site, dual sets of flowers and other decor for both sites, and transportation for your guests. In fact, don't assume that shuttling guests from the ceremony to the reception isn't your responsibility. Unless your guests are all driving, think what happens when 200 people pour out of a church in a rainstorm with not a cab in sight. Not pretty.

What's more, the timing between the two sites must jibe. If the ceremony ends at 5:30 and the reception space, which is 35 minutes away, won't be ready until 6:45 (need a calculator?), don't think you can fudge it. Invariably, your guests will arrive 20 minutes before the space is set — in time to see the band lugging their amplifiers across the dining room floor. Horrors! For a sample wedding-day schedule, see Chapter 7.

Taking a Space Walk

After you do your preliminary nosing around, investigate spaces in person with your fiancé(e) or a close friend whose opinion you trust. Don't take your parents or future in-laws on this qualifying round. You want to have intelligent, researched responses to the possible downsides before they spot them and panic.

Whom should you ask to see? If you're looking at an on-premise catering location, you deal with someone from the banquet department or the food and beverage department. For off-premise locales, you talk to a site coordinator, although this person may not be able to answer your food and beverage queries. Save those questions (which I provide later in this chapter) for the caterer.

As you check out a space, take copious notes. Ask for brochures and photos of other events that have taken place there. If none are available, snap a few photos — but ask permission first, because some places consider their layout and decor proprietary information. Notes and photos help because by the time you've seen the 12th place, you won't remember which hotel had the striped mauve walls you hated or the fluorescent lights reminiscent of a New York subway.

Remember, you're still in the preliminary stages. Go with your gut reaction. This isn't the time to start thinking about how you can transform a space you basically don't like. If the place depresses you or offends any one of your five senses, move on.

Asking the right questions

As you scout various options, you need to ask different questions, depending on whether the space is on-premise or off-premise and whether you intend to use the site for both the ceremony and reception or just the reception.

For starters, ask specifically what parts of the space are available. You may envision the inn's exquisite rose garden as the perfect backdrop for photos, only to find out on the day of the rehearsal that it's off-limits.

Also, if another event will be taking place at the same time, ask the manager how the staff keeps attendees from running into one another. A "bridal crossing" experience can put a real damper on your day.

The list of questions in Figure 4-1 helps you zero in on the specifics.

Many places refuse to hold tastings of their menus for shoppers, and I do empathize. Producing a meal for two (or four) is both costly and labor-intensive, especially for off-premise caterers. I feel, however, that after you book the facility or caterer, you're entitled to a tasting, and you should negotiate this upfront before signing the contract. If the food isn't up to par, you're entitled to repeat tastings until it is (but definitely take this as a warning sign).

As you question a prospective caterer or banquet manager, get a clear idea of the rules regarding bar service, as that affects overall cost and logistics. (For a complete rundown of your bar needs, see Chapter 15.)

Reception Sites Checklist

Dates and Times

❑ Might the establishment book other weddings or events on the same day as your reception? (Besides privacy issues, another event before your reception might make your floral set-up tight for time and an event after your reception means you would not be able to request to stay later.)

❑ How far in advance can or must a reservation be confirmed?

❑ What time would your vendors (florist, caterer, and so on) be able to set up?

❑ Do you have to pick up everything that evening, or can you arrange for next-day pickups? (Vendors may charge more for late-night pickups.)

Capacity, Logistics, and Floor-Plan Dimensions

❑ What is the square footage?

❑ What rooms are available?

❑ How many people can you seat (with dancing) for either buffet stations or a sit-down dinner? Ask to see floor plans, diagrams, and photos including pictures of events they've held other than weddings, to give you decorating ideas.

❑ What do they consider to be the optimum number of guests for the site?

❑ How does the space work? (Where do guests enter? If the venue is on the 90th story of a building and you must get to it via an elevator, will a doorman or an elevator operator be downstairs to direct your guests? How are guests directed after they arrive on the floor?)

❑ What are the parking facilities? Is valet parking available?

❑ Is the site handicapped accessible?

❑ Where is the coat room?

❑ Where should the escort card table go?

❑ Where would you serve cocktails?

❑ How long does it take to turn the room?

❑ Where can the bride get dressed? The groom?

❑ Where can you take photographs? What do they recommend in terms of lighting, glare, and weather conditions?

❑ What is the rain plan if part of the event is to take place outside?

Fees

❑ What is the space rental fee?

❑ Do you get the space for a maximum number of hours? When does overtime kick in, and what's the rate?

Figure 4-1:
Asking the right questions helps determine whether a site is viable for a ceremony, reception, or both.

Illustration by Wiley, Composition Services Graphics

❑ Do you have to pay fees for additional rooms?

❑ Does the establishment offer discounts for certain days or months?

❑ What are the hidden labor costs — security guards, bathroom attendants, coat check attendants, porters, or union electricians?

❑ What kind of security deposit is required? By when? What's the schedule for other payments?

❑ What's the refund policy?

❑ How long will they hold the space for you without a deposit? Will they give you a right of first refusal?

❑ What does the price include (china, glass, linens, silverware, tables, and so on)? How much are rentals?

❑ Is any part of the fee tax-deductible?

Dancing and Music

❑ Is dancing allowed? Does the facility have a dance floor? Is it built in, a roll-out, or in parquet squares? What is the maximum number of dancers the floor will hold?

❑ Do you have access to a piano on the premises? Upright or baby grand?

❑ Is a sound system available? Do you have to pay a rental fee for it or for additional microphones?

❑ What are the acoustics like? Does sound *bleed* (meaning music and laughter travel from one room to another)?

❑ Do you have to abide by a music curfew?

Food and Drink

❑ How many alternate entrees do they usually prepare?

❑ What do they offer for diabetic, kosher, or vegetarian guests upon request?

❑ If the space is *off-premise* (meaning you have to hire an outside caterer), does the caterer feel that the kitchen space is adequate? Must a kitchen be "built" (which requires extra rentals)?

❑ Has the caterer worked in the space before?

❑ Is the wedding cake included in the overall package? (See Chapter 16 for more cake questions.)

❑ Does the site hold a liquor license?

❑ May you provide your own liquor?

Decor

❑ Are tables and chairs included, or do you have to rent them separately?

❏ If the facility has glaring problems such as chipped paint, scaffolding, or broken mirrors, will they assure you in writing that they'll fix the problems by your wedding date?

❏ Can you choose the china? If so, do you have to pay a surcharge?

Lighting

❏ Are the chandeliers clean and all the bulbs working?

❏ How does the lighting look best? Do the lights have dimmers?

❏ Are candles allowed? Do they supply them?

Heating, Cooling, and Plumbing

❏ Does the site have central air conditioning? Does it work well?

❏ Is the venue heated? Do they provide portable heaters for outside terraces and patios?

❏ How well is the site ventilated? Can you open windows?

❏ What are the smoking rules?

❏ How many bathrooms does the facility have, and what do they look like? (*Very important.*)

Services and Staff

❏ Must you use the facility's vendors? (For example, a hotel's approved florist or band.)

❏ Will the person showing you the space work with you throughout the entire process? If not, who will?

❏ What uniforms does the wait staff wear? Are both males and females on staff?

❏ What's the method of service — French, Russian, or á la carte? (See Chapter 14 for the scoop on service styles.)

❏ Can the caterer provide references?

❏ How many room captains will be on board? How many servers per table?

❏ Will they feed your staff (photographer, band, and so on), and at what cost?

Fine Print

❏ How much and what kind of insurance is required? Does the caterer have insurance, and will it cover you?

❏ Are permits, such as a certificate of occupancy or parking, necessary?

To compare the total *real* costs for your food and beverage service at an off-premise site with those at an on-premise site, you must get estimates from outside caterers for the off-premise site. Comparing sites based on rental fees alone doesn't give you enough financial information to make a decision. For this reason, I include the questions to ask in preliminary interviews with caterers in Chapter 14.

Understanding square footage without spacing out

In determining whether a space is large enough for various parts of your wedding, take the venue's square footage estimates with a grain of salt. Not that banquet managers would lie, but their job is, after all, to fill spaces with warm bodies. Most venues now have CAD ("computer-aided design") plans of their spaces, which provide precise information about dimensions and configuration. If the CAD plan isn't available online, ask the venue to e-mail the file to you. Whipping out a tape measure doesn't hurt either. When in doubt, refer to Table 4-1.

Note: The list in Table 4-1 is a guideline; you also must take into account the room shape, sightline obstructions such as columns, and the amount of unusable space.

Table 4-1	Square Footage Recommendations
Space	*Square Feet per Person*
Ceremony	8
Cocktails without seating (pre-meal)	6–8
Cocktails with dance floor and partial seating	8
Cocktails with hors d'oeuvre stations and partial seating	12–13
Seated and served meal with dancing	13–15
Band	20–25 per instrument
Dance floor	3

For places such as hotels or catering halls whose main purpose is hosting banquets, mapping out the room is easy because these spaces lend themselves to parties. Banquet managers are usually well versed in the possible scenarios of a particular room. Other locations, such as schools and museums, however, may require ingenuity in creating a room arrangement conducive to a wedding reception. Consider innovative ways to arrange tables — such as varying sizes — to utilize the space rather than sticking to a traditional banquet setup.

Measurement converter website Convertalot features a room-size calculator that can estimate the square footage needed for a certain number of guests sitting at 60-inch or 72-inch round tables. You'll find the site at `www.converta-lot.com/room_size_calculator.html`.

When There's No Place Like Home

Although your sunny little hamlet may seem perfect for a wedding, the only time to really assess its appropriateness is during a monsoon. That said, consider these questions:

- ✔ Should a weather disaster strike and you're having the wedding outside, is the house big enough to use as a backup?

- ✔ What's the capacity of the bathroom(s) and, if applicable, septic system?

- ✔ Where will guests park?

- ✔ Do you need to make any major home or landscape improvements to make the property suitable for a wedding? This can be a significant hidden cost.

- ✔ Assuming that you're lucky enough to have a beautiful day and you'll be outdoors, what's the fly and/or mosquito population? Do you need to fog the property with pesticide?

- ✔ How up to date and powerful is the electricity? Plugging in a single 100-cup coffee urn can cause an entire house to go dark. Do you have a generator?

- ✔ Does your kitchen have sufficient space for a caterer?

- ✔ Who's available to receive deliveries of rentals, flowers, food, and so on?

- ✔ How much time for *setup* and *breakdown* (assembling and dismantling the tent and so on) is required, and can you live in your house during it? Who's responsible for putting your house back in order? If you are, do you have time to work miracles before you leave for the honeymoon?

Tents and pretense

Although at-home and estate weddings can be utterly picturesque, they're neither simple nor inexpensive. The reason: You usually have to erect a tent. Because most houses lack a ballroom or an indoor tennis court that can accommodate row upon row of chairs — unless you limit the guest list to a handful of deserving souls — at least part of the wedding must take place outdoors. Putting up a canopy is neither costly nor complicated, but a flimsy awning does absolutely no good if it's raining, freezing cold, or stifling hot. The only way to be absolutely secure is to have a full-fledged tent.

Tents generally come in one of four designs, as shown in Figure 4-2, and the style you choose depends on the number of guests, the location of the dance floor and food stations, and the property setting. The basic styles are

- **Frame:** This tent, also called a *clear-span frame tent,* is supported by a frame with no poles down the center.
- **Pole:** This tent has quarter poles around the perimeter and center poles down the middle. Pole tents must be staked to the ground, which means that they don't work very well in rock gardens or on asphalt.
- **Century:** This tent is defined by its shape rather than its structure. It has one or several peaks and can be either a frame tent or a pole tent.
- **Aluminum structure tent:** Sometimes called a *European-style structure* tent, this is similar to a frame tent but with no central poles and a more elaborated, grid-like frame. Because it's usable on any surface and able to span a much wider area than other kinds of tents, it's often used for very large events and weddings.

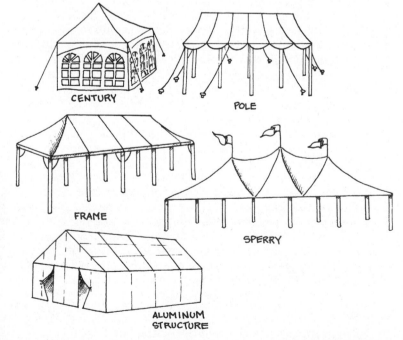

Figure 4-2: In these cases, the century tent has windowed sides, while the pole and frame tents have their sides up.

CENTURY

POLE

FRAME

SPERRY

ALUMINUM STRUCTURE

Illustration by Elizabeth Kurtzman

A popular tent choice is Sperry (www.sperrytents.com), which is a brand rather than a structure type. Sperry tents come in many shapes, have a distinctive look, and provide the option of lovely wood flooring.

After you've decided to have a tented wedding, you need to consider several issues:

✔ **Comfort zone:** Heating, albeit primitive, is affordable, but air conditioning is very expensive and energy-scarfing. Anybody who has been to a tent party where the power conked out will urge you to spring for a backup generator. Just be sure to place it far enough away so guests don't have to shout over the incessant hum. If you're imagining the drama of a starlit sky through a clear tent ceiling, keep in mind that without air conditioning, tents tend to fog up, and under a sunny sky, they can turn into hot, miserable terrariums.

✔ **Décor dilemmas:** Consider how you'll light and decorate the tent. Even if you plan something simple, you're looking at a great white expanse punctuated by glaring industrial tent poles. Disguising all of this can be heart-stoppingly expensive. (See Chapter 17 for tent-decorating ideas.)

✔ **Multiple tents:** In addition to the main tent, you may need a tent for the caterer and a separate lighted tent for portable toilets (especially for evening weddings) or to obscure a mobile bathroom vehicle. To connect these areas you'll need walkways with canopies.

✔ **Proper placement:** Make sure your property has an appropriate spot to put the tent. If your backyard resembles the Badlands, erecting a tent without flooring is risky. Floors can be prohibitively expensive because of the labor, but not having a floor leaves you vulnerable to potential fiascoes such as off-balance tables and chairs, an uneven dance floor, and, most ruinous, water seepage. A downpour on your wedding day isn't the only weather report you have to worry about. If it has rained recently, water seeps up from the ground, even if the tent is on a hill. Add a hundred pairs of high heels poking divots in the lawn and so much for the verdant expanse that made you decide your home was the perfect spot for the most important day of your life. (Anyone for a little white-water rafting?)

Tent contracts are particularly tricky. Suppliers usually erect tents several days before a wedding, so even if you (bravely) believe the weather forecast is so unfailingly positive that you don't want to erect the tents at all, you must still pay 50 percent or more of the estimated bill to cover labor, on the assumption that the tent supplier turned away other jobs for your wedding. You usually have a 48- to 72-hour window for a final decision (as specified in your contract) regarding whether to connect tents and canopies. For these you usually pay only 25 percent of the deposit if you decide not to have them erected.

Have venue, will travel

Taking the tent concept a step further, a British company called Innovations Extreme (www. inflatablechurch.com) has come up with an inflatable church. The air-filled building is 47 feet long, 25 feet wide, and 47 feet high, and it holds about 60 people. Made of polyester and PVC, the blow-up building resembles a quaint (albeit pneumatic) Gothic church, complete with steeple, plastic "stained glass" windows, and airbrushed religious artwork. Inside it has an inflatable organ, altar, pulpit, pews, candles, and gold cross. Even the doors are flanked by air-filled angels. The makers say the church can be built in three hours and disassembled in less than two. At this writing, the mobile space costs about $4,000 a day to rent. If the idea of getting hitched in a moonwalk pumps you up, the inflatable church is one way to blow.

An equally quirky but more modest choice is Reverend Darrell Best's mobile wedding chapel, a converted 1942 firetruck complete with stained glass, organ, altar, and two pews. The Reverend (www.bestwedding chapel.com) is located in Shelbyville, Illinois, but in season he charges $200 plus $2 per mile round trip to drive to where you want to get married. He officiates the ceremony too, of course.

The flushing bride

In the category of "little facts you never dreamed you'd need to know but aren't you glad I'm printing them here," the toilet situation requires utmost attention. Just like parking, coat room organization, and guest transportation, bathrooms shouldn't be an afterthought. People are often reluctant to spend money on such an unglamorous detail of their wedding, but adequate and "commodious" toilet facilities are a crucial aspect of hospitality.

When renting portable toilets, keep in mind that each one is good for a maximum of 125 uses. As a general rule, an average person uses the toilet once in three hours. If you have 500 guests for three hours, you need four toilets (500 ÷ 125 = 4). If they're staying for six hours, you need eight toilets.

Designate one set of toilets for men and another for women. Even if the guest ratio of men to women is one to one, have more toilets for women because, as everybody knows, they take longer. At all costs, you want to spare your guests mistaking a long snaking bathroom line for the conga line.

Portable toilets range from rustic construction-site designs to trailers fully outfitted with toilet stalls, mirrors, sinks, and faux marble vanities. Whichever you choose, having tented walkways and a separate lighted tent for the toilets (especially for evening weddings) makes sense. Portable toilets with lighting need electricity. Even with trash receptacles, you may need an attendant to keep the facilities pristine.

Anticipating special needs

If you have guests who are elderly, handicapped, or ill, make them as comfortable as possible by providing transportation and making sure the ceremony and reception — including portable toilets — are wheelchair-accessible when necessary. Because people who can't see or move well can often get left out of the fun, be especially gracious by seating them in places of honor, devoting quality visiting time with them, and appointing someone to keep on top of special hospitality needs.

Even if you have enough toilets in your house, be sure to double-check the septic capacity. You often have to drain septic tanks beforehand so that your restrooms can accommodate the number of guests.

Planning a Destination Wedding

More and more couples are now opting for a *destination wedding* — a wedding whose location requires some traveling on the part of you and the majority of your guests in order to spend a few memorable days with the group. Typically, these events take place over a long weekend (see more about weekend weddings in Chapter 6) and entail a special level of research, logistics, and hospitality. But having your wedding in an exotic location or someplace that's especially meaningful for you makes it all the more distinctive. In spite of the complicated logistics, destination weddings provide ample opportunity for originality, freedom, and intimacy. You also have the advantage of neutral territory if you're worried about family feuds or power issues.

Another reason to go the distance: cost. Destination weddings usually attract fewer guests, and you can often get more bang for the buck in an all-inclusive resort than in a major metropolitan area. Be aware, however, that some places are so inaccessible that saving money is impossible, especially if you have to "import" what you need. But you have ways around this. For starters, take advantage of a location's natural beauty instead of duding it up to look like someplace else. Trying to turn a beach setting into a chandeliered hotel lobby or a quaint town into downtown Manhattan makes no sense.

Also, you may have fee leverage with some vendors if you get married in a wonderful, exotic location. For example, finding a first-rate photographer in an out-of-the-way spot is often impossible, but you may be able to barter a photographer's services in exchange for a few free days at the location plus airfare.

Finding a faraway venue

The destination you choose may be one you're intimately familiar with, such as your hometown or a childhood vacation spot, or it can be an entirely new, different, and fascinating location. Figure 4-3 is a destination location checklist that helps you sort out all the factors so you can decide on a destination venue that works for you and your guests.

Destination Location Checklist

❏ What are the legal and religious requirements for getting married there?

❏ What are the residency requirements?

❏ How difficult is it for your guests to get to? Is a change of planes necessary?

❏ Are airfare and lodging affordable for guests?

❏ Are blood tests or immunizations required for marriage licenses?

❏ Will guests require vaccinations? Can the certifying doctor be in the U.S.?

❏ What are the necessary documents to get married in this destination?

❏ Must proof of divorce or proof of being a widow(er) be certified?

❏ Do documents need to be translated into the native language? Are the original documents necessary?

❏ Do these documents need to be sent in advance?

❏ How long do you have to wait after your arrival to obtain a marriage license?

❏ After getting the license, how long is the waiting period?

❏ Are witnesses necessary? Must they be citizens of that country?

❏ Are civil ceremonies allowed? Which religious ceremonies are permitted?

❏ What is the name of a reputable wedding coordinator and/or a travel agent specializing in destination weddings who can help with bookings for your guests and with hiring vendors?

❏ Can you make at least one site-inspection trip?

❏ Would you like to spend your honeymoon there?

❏ What's the weather like in the season you're planning to get married?

❏ How long before your wedding is it suggested you arrive?

Figure 4-3:
Research
the perfect
destination
for your
wedding.

Illustration by Wiley, Composition Services Graphics

Honeymoon-weddings

Another option is to get married with just each other (and two witnesses) in the same locale as your honeymoon. Some resorts (Walt Disney World and Sandals, for example) specialize in intimate honeymoon-weddings, which are smaller and less complicated than full-blown destination weddings. These add-on weddings are inexpensive — even free in some cases. Unsurprisingly, the weddings are pretty formulaic, held in only certain areas of the properties with a set style and ceremony length and topped off with some fizzy stuff and a cake product.

Ask the wedding department at your destination to send you a full description of how it conducts these ceremonies and mini-receptions. If details are important to you, make a trip to the destination to meet with the person who'll be overseeing your wedding. If you want something different from what the resort ordinarily provides (and are willing to pay for special plans), notify the people at your destination far in advance — in writing — and ask them to send back a letter of agreement.

Arrive a few days early to arrange things the way you want them. An on-site wedding coordinator should be able to assist you in whipping your wedding into shape.

Honeymoon-weddings can be the simplest to carry off, especially if the emphasis is on the honeymoon and you don't invite any guests. In such cases, the resort provides all the accoutrements, including the witnesses. You might send out announcements or even have a celebratory bash when you return. These postwedding parties tend to be less expensive and less stressful than the typical wedding ceremony followed by a same-day reception.

To search for a destination wedding location, a good place to start is www.destinationweddingmag.com. The site features articles, photos of real weddings, and a destination list. You can even click on the international destination that interests you to explore legal requirements, locations, and hotels. (*Destination Weddings & Honeymoons* magazine also offers an application for the iPad that lets you explore photographs, details, and contact information for a host of beautiful destination venues. Search for "Destination Weddings & Honeymoons" in the iTunes store.) And if you're interested in a particular country, check the web for its travel and tourism board, which often lists wedding and venue information.

The number of guests you invite (perhaps only close friends and relatives) and the portion of their tab you pick up depends on what you decide is reasonable to spend.

Inquire with hotels, resorts, and airlines about group rates and package deals. Find a good travel agent and have all your guests book through that person so you don't have to be a travel clearinghouse.

Taking care of foreign affairs and red tape

Before deciding to get married in another country — or even spending time looking for a venue there — take a good look at the logistics involved, particularly the length of the cooling-off period and the residency requirements. In some countries, you need to have lived there six months or more, while others allow only citizens to marry! Other factors to consider are whether you need a blood test and if one from your doctor back home will suffice, and whether you need both a civil ceremony and a religious one for the marriage to be legally binding. (While you're at it, find out the business hours of the office where you apply for the license; you may need to arrive a few days early to process this paperwork.) Before you decide on a country, consult its consular office in New York or its embassy in Washington, D.C. The U.S. State Department can provide marriage requirements and lists of U.S. consular offices abroad where you can have your marriage certificate authenticated (see Chapter 3).

Getting married on a cruise ship isn't automatically a matter of having the captain perform the nuptials. As a matter of fact, with just a couple of exceptions, marriages performed at sea aren't legal. At this writing, Princess and Celebrity are the only cruise lines where the captain is able to perform a legally binding wedding ceremony at sea. Keep in mind that your marriage license will be from Bermuda (where Princess is registered) or Malta (where Celebrity is registered), and make sure that it'll be legal in the state you live in. But if you'd just like to get married aboard a ship and aren't picky about actually being *at sea* at the time, you have lots of options. Most other cruise lines offer special wedding packages, which include a civil ceremony either on embarkation day while the ship is docked (so that you can have guests at your ceremony), on board, or in a port of call.

Essentials for getting married abroad

In addition to my list of honeymoon goodies in Chapter 22, you may need the following for a long-distance or destination wedding:

✓ Birth certificate (authenticated)

✓ Confirmation, baptism, and pre-Cana records (for Catholic weddings)

✓ Immunization and other health records

✓ Passports

✓ Proof of economic solvency

✓ Proof that you're free to marry, such as a divorce decree or death certificate (authenticated and perhaps translated)

Chapter 5

By Invitation Only

. . . .

In This Chapter

▶ Wording both formal and less traditional invitations

▶ Getting familiar with printing methods, paper, and more

▶ Seeing how to address outer and inner envelopes

▶ Creating your own invitations

▶ Mailing your invitations — through the post office or electronically

. . . .

The invitation is meant to convey the necessary facts about your upcoming ceremony and the celebration following. If things were as simple as who, what, when, and where, I could do away with this chapter and you could save a bundle by relaying the salient information by telephone, Facebook, or paper airplanes.

As you're well aware, that isn't the case. The wedding invitation — from its wording, form, and addressing to its printing style and ink color — is the subject of etiquette controversies; long, long chapters in wedding books; and dictatorial outlines. To flout the rules, these sources imply, is to risk massive embarrassment, if not complete social disgrace.

Such scare tactics aren't my m.o., but I do believe you should be familiar with what the social wags consider proper before you get creative. Therefore, I first cover all the rules for writing traditional, formal invitations. Then I move on to tips and ideas for giving your invitations a personal twist. No matter what kind of stationery you choose, you should know about card stock, print fonts, and other technical details, so I provide a primer on that, too. And yes, I address your burning curiosity (or shudder of horror) about e-invitations.

Preliminary Planning

Play it safe. Order your invitations three to four months — and send them no later than six to eight weeks — before the wedding. Send invitations to guests coming from abroad ten weeks in advance. If you plan on getting married over a holiday weekend, send invitations eight to ten weeks ahead of time, unless you've already sent a save-the-date card.

In figuring the number of invitations you need, a classic mistake is to think that if you're inviting 200 people, you need 200 invitations. Guess again. Look at your list. Chances are that a good number of those people are couples, which means you need send only one invitation, not two. However, you do want to order 25 extras; reordering afterward is more expensive.

A way of branding your celebration is to select a motif, theme, or typeface that appears on all your wedding-related stationery — from save-the-date cards to thank-you notes — and on such incidentals as cocktail napkins, menus, and seating cards. Similarly, a consistent color palette gives your event cohesiveness and conveys the amount of thought that went into your wedding.

Ordering your entire stationery wardrobe, from invitations to thank-you notes, at the same time may save you money and also helps ensure consistency in color, paper weight, and art. But this requires an enormous amount of forethought, particularly if you want to have a monogram or other emblem designed for use throughout.

If you're not up to placing your stationery order so far in advance, you can send a picture postcard of the area where you plan to marry with something like

Larkin and Gilbert are getting married!
August 10, 2013
Bar Harbor, Maine
Please save the date
Invitation and details to follow

If you don't like the idea of sending postcards, you can find lots of clever alternatives, from refrigerator magnets (found on many wedding websites) to wall calendars, with the day and month of your wedding circled. And although I'm old-fashioned enough to prefer paper for your invitations, I think e-cards are a great option for asking your guests to save the date.

The year is considered mandatory on announcements and optional on invitations. You may want to include it on the invite, though, particularly if you're the sentimental type and you plan to frame your invitation as a keepsake. Including the year is also helpful as a reference in years to come for those who are anniversary-challenged.

For a wedding held in a tourist area during peak season, when accommodations are at a premium, a longer letter may be in order, detailing travel and lodging options.

Guest who?

Before you can figure out how many invitations to order, you need to get a grip on your guest list. The complete guest list can represent the merger of a minimum of four lists — the bride's, the groom's, and that of both sets of parents. The recipe for the final number should comprise one part realism (budget and logistics) and two parts graciousness and hospitality. Consider this a casting call for all the supporting players in not only your two individual lives but also the lives of your two families together. Being stubborn now about someone who's important to your future mother-in-law may strain relations for eternity.

Be as tolerant as possible of your parents' requests. Nostalgia is a major draw for weddings, and later you may be very touched that your parents' oldest friends and long-lost relatives care enough to reconnect as you realize that they do in fact make your circle complete.

If you're looking for where to draw the line, remember that weddings aren't an opportunity to pay back social obligations or recoup your investment on wedding gifts to others in the past. And never make the mistake of sending invitations to people you really don't want to come on the assumption they won't. They're often the very first souls to accept.

Some people may never speak to you again if you don't invite them. If you can live with that, leave them off the list. Otherwise, add them and don't look back.

Formalities First

What constitutes a traditional, *formal* wedding invitation? It is written in the third person, engraved on folded paper or heavy card stock in black ink, and mailed inside two envelopes. The inner envelope has no glue. The invitations are usually ecru, although some couples prefer the look of pure white. For invitations engraved on card stock, the edge may be beveled with gold or silver.

Getting the wording just right

The rules of composition for formal invitations are quite specific:

- **Abbreviate and punctuate (almost) nothing.** That means you spell out words like *Doctor, Street, Road,* and *Apartment,* as well as state names (including the District of Columbia). The exceptions are Mr., Ms., Mrs., and Jr., which are abbreviated and take periods.

- **Use commas in only two spots.** They go between days and dates (Saturday, the nineteenth of July) and between cities and states (Spur, Texas).

Attention!

On invitations, you may list enlisted personnel and noncommissioned officers with their military branch beneath their names:

Frederick Homer Cooley
United States Army

Senior officers (above captain in the army and lieutenant senior grade in the navy) appear with their rank before their name and their branch underneath:

Commander Troy William Sloane
United States Navy

The titles of junior officers go on the second line with the branch:

Melinda Anne Turner
Second Lieutenant, United States Air Force

✔ **You may omit the state if the city is well-known,** such as New York City, Dallas, or Seattle.

✔ **Employ British spellings of *favour* and *honour*.**

✔ **Use *the honour of your presence* for ceremonies in a house of worship.**

✔ **Use *the pleasure of your company* for ceremonies in secular locations,** such as a home, hotel, club, or other nonreligious venue, or solely for the reception.

✔ **Write out the numerals for long numbers in street addresses,** unless the numbers are particularly unwieldy.

✔ **Write out times, including the word *o'clock*.** For example, *two o'clock*.

✔ **Use *half after* or *half past* in lieu of *-thirty* for half hours.** For example, *half after five o'clock* or *half past five o'clock,* not *five-thirty o'clock*.

✔ **Write out years.** Whichever way you want to write this is fine: *Two thousand and thirteen* or *Twenty hundred and thirteen*. In the tradition of needless nuptial debates, whether to capitalize the year ranks as a biggie. I like the look of capitalizing it, but whatever you choose is correct.

✔ **Always put the bride's name before the groom's.**

✔ **Note that while *Mr.* is always used with the groom's name, the bride's name doesn't take *Miss* or *Ms*.** In the case where the groom's parents are hosting the wedding, the rule is reversed.

- ✔ **Use military titles for brides and grooms on active duty.** Fathers may use their military titles whether on active duty or retired.

- ✔ **Use professional titles *(Doctor, Judge)* for grooms.** Ditto for fathers.

- ✔ **Do not, however, use professional titles for brides or mothers.** The one exception for brides is if both mother and daughter are issuing the invitations.

Who's throwing this shindig?

The crux of traditional formal invitations lies in meticulous placement of names to convey who's related to whom and who's hosting the wedding. If the **bride's parents** are hosting the wedding:

Mr. and Mrs. Garthwaite Stubbs Kerfuffle
request the honour of your presence
at the marriage of their daughter
Ida Hortense
to
Mr. Wylie Beauregard Blandsky
Saturday, the tenth of August
Two thousand and thirteen
at half after four o'clock
Saint Agnes Church
Wigglebury, Vermont
and afterwards at the reception
The Neptunian Society Pavilion
Forty-two Sweetbirch Drive

RSVP

You ask for a reply by printing one of five things under the text or in the bottom left corner: *Kindly respond, The favor of a reply is requested, RSVP, Rsvp,* or *r.s.v.p.* The abbreviation RSVP is short for *Repondez, s'il vous plait,* which is French for "respond (if you please)." Include the address where the response is to be sent because the return address on the envelope is often blind embossed, which is hard to read, and recipients often discard the envelope.

If the wedding is **not in a church,** you can word it this way:

> *Mr. and Mrs. Garthwaite Stubbs Kerfuffle*
> *request the pleasure of your company*
> *at the marriage of their daughter*
> *Ida Hortense*
> *to*
> *Mr. Wylie Beauregard Blandsky*
> *Saturday, the tenth of August*
> *Two thousand and thirteen*
> *at half after four o'clock*
> *Town Green Gazebo*
> *Wigglebury, Vermont*
> *RSVP*

The **most formal** invitations contain the name of the recipient, written by hand:

> *Mr. and Mrs. Garthwaite Stubbs Kerfuffle*
> *request the honour of*
> *Mr. and Mrs. Franklin B. Langley's*
> *presence*
> *at the marriage of their daughter . . .*

If the **bride's mother is a widow or divorced** and goes by her ex-husband's surname:

> *Mrs. Cassandra Kerfuffle*
> *requests the honour of your presence*
> *at the marriage of her daughter . . .*

If the **bride's mother is divorced,** she may combine her maiden name and married surname:

> *Mrs. Bloomberg Kerfuffle*
> *requests the honour of your presence*
> *at the marriage of her daughter . . .*

Although etiquette mavens have always maintained that no such person as *Mrs. Annabelle Kerfuffle* — in other words, Mrs. with a woman's birth name — can exist, as more women are combining their first name with Mrs., the rules seem to have relaxed of late. I can simply shrug my shoulders. It's your call.

If the **bride's father is a widower or divorced** and he's hosting the wedding:

> *Mr. Garthwaite Stubbs Kerfuffle*
> *requests the honour of your presence*
> *at the marriage of his daughter . . .*

If the **bride's mother is remarried** and she and her new husband are hosting the wedding:

> *Mr. and Mrs. Malcolm Holliday Harglow*
> *request the honour of your presence*
> *at the marriage of her daughter*
> *Ida Hortense Kerfuffle . . .*

Note: You can substitute the words *Mrs. Harglow's daughter* for *her daughter*.

If the **bride's widowed father is remarried** and he and his wife are hosting:

> *Mr. and Mrs. Garthwaite Stubbs Kerfuffle*
> *request the honour of your presence*
> *at the marriage of his daughter . . .*

Note: You can substitute the words *Mr. Kerfuffle's daughter* for *his daughter*.

If the **bride's father is deceased** and her stepmother gives the wedding:

> *Mrs. Garthwaite Stubbs Kerfuffle*
> *requests the honour of your presence*
> *at the marriage of her stepdaughter*
> *Ida Hortense Kerfuffle . . .*

If the **bride's parents are divorced, both are remarried,** and all are sponsoring the wedding:

> *Mr. and Mrs. Malcolm Holliday Harglow*
> *Mr. and Mrs. Garthwaite Stubbs Kerfuffle*
> *request the honour of your presence*
> *at the marriage of*
> *Mrs. Harglow and Mr. Kerfuffle's daughter*
> *Ida Hortense Kerfuffle . . .*

The names of the bride's mother and her new husband go first. If you think your guests can assume whose daughter she is, you may omit the line before the bride's name (*Mrs. Harglow and Mr. Kerfuffle's daughter,* in this case.)

If the **bride's parents are divorced** and her mother goes by her ex-husband's name:

> *Mrs. Garthwaite Stubbs Kerfuffle*
> *and*
> *Mr. Garthwaite Stubbs Kerfuffle*
> *request the honour of your presence*
> *at the marriage of their daughter*
> *Ida Hortense Kerfuffle . . .*

Listing the parents on separate lines indicates that they're divorced or separated.

If the **groom's parents** are giving the wedding:

> *Mr. and Mrs. Edgar Montague Blandsky*
> *request the honour of your presence*
> *at the marriage of*
> *Miss Ida Hortense Kerfuffle*
> *to their son*
> *Wylie Beauregard . . .*

Note: In the preceding case, use *Miss* for the bride and omit *Mr.* for the groom.

If the **groom's father is deceased** and the groom's mother is hosting the wedding:

> *Mrs. Edgar Montague Blandsky*
> *requests the honour of your presence*
> *at the marriage of*
> *Miss Ida Hortense Kerfuffle*
> *to*
> *Wylie Beauregard . . .*

If **you're hosting your own** wedding:

> *The honour of your presence*
> *is requested at the marriage of*
> *Miss Ida Hortense Kerfuffle*
> *to*
> *Mr. Wylie Beauregard Blandsky . . .*

or

> *Miss Ida Hortense Kerfuffle*
> *and*
> *Mr. Wylie Beauregard Blandsky*
> *request the honour of your presence*
> *at their marriage . . .*

If the ceremony is **very small,** you can invite people by phone or include a ceremony card with the reception invitation for the few invited to both:

> *The honour of your presence*
> *is requested at the marriage of*
> *Miss Ida Hortense Kerfuffle*
> *to*
> *Mr. Wylie Beauregard Blandsky*
> *Saturday, the tenth of August*
> *Two thousand and thirteen*
> *at half after four o'clock*
> *Saint Agnes Church*
> *Wigglebury, Vermont*

You don't need to put *RSVP* on invitations that are for ceremonies only. Most likely, the church or synagogue can accommodate all guests.

If the recipient is **invited only to the reception:**

> *Mr. and Mrs. Garthwaite Stubbs Kerfuffle*
> *request the pleasure of your company*
> *at the wedding reception of their daughter . . .*

This type of invitation is useful for belated receptions held, for example, after the couple has returned from their honeymoon or if the ceremony was held in another town (see Chapter 4 for information on faraway weddings). This invitation also works for extremely small ceremonies consisting of just family or just you and witnesses. Bear in mind, however, that anyone you care enough to invite to the reception would probably love to see you walk down the aisle. Think twice before depriving them of this pleasure.

If the **reception and ceremony are in different locations** or you can't fit all the information on the invitation, you may have a separate reception card:

> *Reception immediately following the ceremony*
> *Neptunian Society Pavilion*
> *Forty-two Sweetbirch Drive*
> *Wigglebury, Vermont*
>
> *RSVP*

If the reception isn't immediately following the ceremony, add a line indicating the time it will begin.

In countries where **double invitations** are customary, two complete sets of text are printed side by side, with the bride's on the left and the groom's on the right. This solution is perfect for invitations printed in two languages. A similar concept known as a *French-fold invitation* — folded in half twice, once horizontally and then vertically — is also back in vogue and useful for weddings hosted by both the bride's and groom's parents. The bride's information appears on the left, the groom's on the right, and the where and when is centered beneath:

Mr. and Mrs. Jaime Puente
request the honour of your presence
at the marriage of their daughter
Juanita
to
Mr. Antonio Jicama
Mr. and Mrs. Geraldo Jicama
request the honour of your presence
at the marriage of their son
Antonio
to
Miss Juanita Puente
Saturday, the sixteenth of November
at two o'clock in the afternoon
Our Lady of Angels Church
New York

Following up with announcements

Announcements go to anyone you didn't invite to the wedding but want to inform of your nuptials. Address and stamp announcements before the wedding so that they're ready for a friend to mail the day after the wedding. In response, you should expect nothing more than a note of congratulations.

Wedding announcements can be from the bride's parents or both sets of parents:

Mr. and Mrs. Garthwaite Stubbs Kerfuffle
and
Mr. and Mrs. Edgar Montague Blandsky
have the pleasure of announcing
the marriage of
their children
Ida Hortense Kerfuffle
and
Wylie Beauregard Blandsky . . .

Extra, extra

If you get really stationery-happy, you may end up with more enclosures than the Publishers Clearing House Sweepstakes. Use them only if they serve your purposes, not because you think the bulkier the invitation, the more important it appears.

✔ **At-home cards:** These are traditionally used to tell guests of the couple's new address after they move in together following the wedding. As many couples today live together before marriage, these cards have a new purpose: to tell people how the bride and groom want to be known after the wedding.

✔ **Maps:** Maps may be hand-drawn and offset printed but should be in keeping with the style and ink color of the invitation. Top them with a heading that says *Directions to [your first names'] Wedding.* If you don't want to overwhelm your pristine invitation, send maps separately or include them in the rehearsal invitation or other invitation. If you have maps from the ceremony to the reception, have extras to give out after the

ceremony. (See Chapter 6 for help finding maps on the Internet.)

✔ **Pew cards:** These are small cards that say *Pew Number___* to tell close friends and family in which pew they're to sit. Cards may say *Within the ribbon,* meaning that several pews (designated by a ribbon along the aisle) are reserved for special guests but no specific pew is assigned. You may include pew cards with invitations or send them later, after receiving replies. In the latter case, cards must be large enough to meet postal regulations — at least 3½ x 5 inches in the United States.

✔ **Rain cards:** If you're having an outdoor ceremony, you need to have a backup site in case of inclement weather. If that location isn't near the original site, a rain card informs guests where to show up. Because people have differing definitions of a monsoon, you may post someone at your original site to send weather-oblivious guests to the alternate site.

The happy couple may announce their marriage themselves:

Ida Hortense Kerfuffle
and
Wylie Beauregard Blandsky
have the pleasure of announcing
their marriage . . .

When things don't go as planned

If the wedding is canceled after you mail invitations, you (or your maid of honor, close friends, or relatives) must call each guest personally if time doesn't permit you to send written word. If you do send a formal announcement, you're under no obligation to explain your decision.

A cancellation announcement may read

Mr. and Mrs. Garthwaite Stubbs Kerfuffle
announce that the marriage of
their daughter
Ida Hortense
to
Mr. Wylie Beauregard Blandsky
will not take place

If a wedding is postponed because of death or other unforeseen circumstances after you mail the invitations, you may call with the information or print a formal announcement of the change:

Mr. and Mrs. Garthwaite Stubbs Kerfuffle
regret that
owing to a death in the family
the marriage of their daughter
Ida Hortense
to
Mr. Wylie Beauregard Blandsky
has been postponed
to Saturday, the twenty-eighth of September

If the invitations have been printed but not mailed, you may enclose a card (rush printed) saying:

Kindly note that
the date of the wedding has been changed
to
Saturday, the twenty-eighth of September

How Else Can We Put This?

You may feel that the traditional style of invitations is a little too formal or a little too flat. And if you're a same-sex couple, you may find that formal styles that differentiate between bride and groom just don't feel right. Either way, you're up for something more creative, more ambitious, more *you*. In that case, you may adapt traditional wordings to your own means. Feel free to break the rules as long as you don't leave your guests scratching their heads or guffawing.

For starters, consider these alternatives to the tried-and-true wedding-invitation formulas:

- **Use American spellings.** *Honor* and *favor,* not *honour* and *favour.*
- **Better yet, drop the pretense.** Consider not using *honor of your presence* or *pleasure of your company* at all. (See examples later in this section.)
- **Use first person** *(We cordially invite . . .)* as opposed to third person *(Mr. and Mrs. William Dinkel request the pleasure . . .)* and close with your names at the bottom of the invite, similar to a signature.
- **Use *Ms.* instead of *Miss.*** Or omit social titles altogether.
- **Skip *Mr. and Mrs.*** Use the first names of both parents and stepparents instead.
- **Use professional titles for brides and their mothers, just as you would for the guys.** The fact that they're doctors, dentists, judges, or active military isn't a state secret.
- **Include a stamped, addressed envelope with an RSVP card.** In addition, put *Kindly respond* in the lower left corner of the invitation.
- **Put *Respond by [date]* on RSVP cards.** If you're planning on issuing more invitations after you receive regrets, have some response cards printed without a date. Remember, however, that yes responses generally come in early, while no's delay their responses as long as possible.

Striking a less-formal tone

As long as you're loosening up a bit, feel free to use more informal wording. Here are some variations, starting with if **your parents are hosting:**

Mr. and Mrs. Garthwaite Stubbs Kerfuffle
and
Mr. and Mrs. Archibald Hasabebe
invite you to join them at the marriage of
their children . . .

or

Jane and Kermit Winkler
would be delighted to have you
join them
as their daughter
Melissa Hope
and
Harry Crichna
pledge their love to each other . . .

If you **host your own wedding,** the invitation may read

Ida Hortense Kerfuffle
and
Wylie Beauregard Blandsky
would be delighted
to have you share
in the joy of their marriage
Saturday, the tenth of August
at half after one o'clock
Temple Beth Israel
Tel Aviv, Texas
and afterward at the reception
K-Brand Ranch
Cricket, Texas

Another variation:

Ida Hortense Kerfuffle
and
Wylie Beauregard Blandsky
invite you to celebrate with us
at our wedding . . .

Invitation turn-offs

The social haiku of invitations is intended to prevent you from oversharing. Some things to avoid in your creative frenzy include

- Cloying poetry and trite, drippy sentiments
- Bad art
- Tiny, messy things such as Day-Glo confetti, glitter, and adorable metallic musical notes that spill forth as you remove the invitation from the envelope and surface in carpets, chair cushions, underwear drawers, and even more exotic places for years to come, despite the use of industrial-strength cleaning contraptions

- Telling guests where you're registered and what particularly you're hoping to receive (see Chapter 18 for the scoop on registry etiquette)
- Noting that children aren't welcome (pointedly excluding anyone on an invitation is hostile); see Chapter 1 for tips on handling this doozy
- So many names as hosts that guests know without a doubt who's on the committee that's paying for the wedding

When the **ceremony and reception take place in the same venue,** you may think that mentioning both events is unnecessary. After all, you assume, guests know you wouldn't drag them all this way without feeding them. But you know what happens when you assume, don't you? To be absolutely certain that guests won't make a fast break for the nearest restaurant after the ceremony, try

Ida Hortense Kerfuffle
and
Wylie Beauregard Blandsky
invite you to witness our vows
and join us afterward for dining and dancing
under the stars
Saturday, the tenth of August
six o'clock in the evening
K-Brand Ranch
Cricket, Texas

If **the couple and both sets of parents host** the wedding:

Ida Hortense Kerfuffle
and
Wylie Beauregard Blandsky
together with their parents
Mr. and Mrs. Garthwaite Stubbs Kerfuffle
Mr. and Mrs. Edgar Montague Blandsky . . .

Many couples of all religions are adopting the Jewish custom of listing both sets of parents on the invitation, not necessarily because the groom's parents are helping foot the bill but simply out of respect:

Mr. and Mrs. Garthwaite Stubbs Kerfuffle
request the honor of your presence
at the marriage of their daughter
Ida Hortense

to

Mr. Wylie Beauregard
son of Mr. and Mrs. Edgar Montague Blandsky . . .

If, out of respect, you want to **include the name of a deceased parent,** make sure that it doesn't read like a dead person is giving the wedding.

Mrs. Garthwaite Stubbs Kerfuffle
requests the honor of your presence
at the marriage of
Ida Hortense
daughter of Mrs. Kerfuffle
and the late Mr. Garthwaite Stubbs Kerfuffle
to
Mr. Wylie Beauregard Blandsky . . .

All the options I list here work for same-sex couples, too. The order in which you list your (and your parents') names is up to you. Doing it alphabetically by either first or last name is a nice, egalitarian choice.

RSVP remedies

Even if you don't have other events to worry about, a fill-in-the-blank reply card is the most expedient method for guests to reply to the wedding invitation:

*M*_____

_____*accepts*

_____*regrets*

For Saturday, the tenth of August

Another variation:

Kindly reply by the eleventh of July

*M*_____

will _____*attend the wedding*

Response cards never ask the number of guests coming. Guests should assume that only the people listed on the envelope are invited. They then write in only the names of the invitees who can make it.

A compromise between the traditional lack of a reply card and a fill-in-the-blank reply card is a card that says, simply, *Kindly respond by [the date]* or *The favor of a reply is requested.* Guests then write a gracious note in the blank space. If the thought of leaving your friends and relatives to figure things out scares you, consider adding *for [your wedding date]* at the bottom.

The date on the response card should be three to four weeks before your wedding, depending on how early you mail your invitations. If you're really pressed for time and your wedding is informal, consider asking guests to RSVP by phone or e-mail rather than by mail.

In light pencil, number the back of each RSVP card to coordinate with your numbered guest list. Doing so enables you to cross-reference cards of guests whose handwriting requires a Scotland Yard decryption unit.

Dress codes: Now wear this

One of the most difficult decisions for many couples is whether to dictate guests' attire. An engraved invitation or one for a wedding after 6 p.m. doesn't automatically direct people to dress in black tie. If seeing every male guest in a tuxedo and all the women in their fanciest dresses is important to you, print *Black tie* on the invitation. If you're determined that the aesthetics of your wedding will be marred if the guests are underdressed, consider these rarely used but *very* specific directions: *Black tie, Evening gowns, Very formal,* or *Very black tie.*

The rather trendy *Black tie optional* seems to encourage guests *not* to wear black tie, while *Black tie invited* is even more confusing.

Other dress codes you may specify include *Dress for an evening in the country* (hopefully a hint for women to leave their spike heels at home), *Garden party attire,* or *Festive dress.* There's a trend for even more specific dress codes intended to create a distinctive, hopefully celebratory, atmosphere. Some examples include *Creative Black Tie, Beach Formal,* or *Glamorous.* Just remember that the less traditional your dress code, the more license your guests have for interpretation.

The nonprinted invitation

If you're having an extremely small wedding, you may invite guests with a handwritten note:

> *Dear Prudence,*
>
> *Wylie and I are getting married Saturday, August 10th. We would be delighted to have you join us for the ceremony at 3 p.m. on the town green in his hometown, Wigglebury, Vermont, and afterward for tea at the home of his aunt, Hazel Twig, 42 East Bean Street.*
>
> *Affectionately,*
> *Ida*

Illustration by Wiley, Composition Services Graphics

Rehearsal Dinner Invitations

Traditionally, the groom's parents host the rehearsal dinner. If the rehearsal dinner is small, you can simply let invitees know when and where by word of mouth. These invitations may have a touch of whimsy (see Chapter 8) or rely on a classic format:

Sally and Edgar Blandsky
invite you to a rehearsal dinner
in honor of
Ida and Wylie
Friday, August 9th
7 p.m.
Wick's Steak Palace
777 South Beaumont Avenue
Spur, Texas

RSVP
516-555-1234 (Sally Blandsky)

For a different twist, use the words *prenuptial dinner* instead of *rehearsal dinner.*

Extracurricular Events

Often, the bride's parents, grandparents, or close friends host a brunch the morning after the wedding, particularly if several of the guests are from out of town (see Chapter 8 for details on other kinds of parties). If the same guests are invited to the rehearsal (or other prewedding event), wedding, and brunch, for efficiency and economy, you may combine the before-and-after events in one invitation and enclose them with the wedding invitation:

Please join us for a
prenuptial cruise and jam session
Friday, August 9th
The Sabine Queen
boarding at 6:30 p.m.
setting sail at 7 p.m. sharp
Pier 20, Port Gusher
Bring instruments

— Ida and Wylie

~

Gladys Melarkey
invites you to join her for a
postwedding brunch
Sunday, August 11th
at her home
45 Pansy Way
Spark, Texas

To make things easier, you can use one RSVP card for several events. Guests send the card back — in a stamped, preaddressed envelope — to whoever has the most time to keep running tabs on the various head counts.

Please respond by July 11th
M _____will attend the wedding
M _____will attend the cruise
M _____will attend the brunch

Typefaces and Other Technicalities

To help you design the invitation you have in mind and ensure that your order gets placed correctly, understanding a few points about the stationery trade helps. What follows is a primer on paper and printing.

Printing methods

The way your invitation is printed conveys as much about your wedding style as the words themselves. You can choose from among several printing methods to suit your invitation, including

- ✔ **Blind embossing:** Letters are etched into metal plates, which are pressed against paper without ink so that you just see the imprint, no color. Usually used for monograms, borders, and return addresses.

- ✔ **Calligraphy:** Handwritten with special pens and inks, usually for addressing. Can be done in a print style to match the invitation, use a calligraphed original to make a plate for an engraved invitation, or be the prototype for an offset invitation.

- ✔ **Computerized calligraphy:** Done by a special machine with mechanized pen and laser printer. Meant to look hand-calligraphed; some fonts are more successful than others. Used for both invitations and addressing.

- ✔ **Digital printing:** A digital file of your invitation image is sent to a professional digital printer, which gives you a high-quality image similar to offset printing. This is a relatively casual option best for light, smooth paper, but it lets you use the full color spectrum, and it's the most economical option short of printing invitations yourself.

- ✔ **Engraved:** Letters are etched into a metal plate, which is then rolled with ink and wiped off. Ink remains in each etched letter. The paper is pressed onto the plate, leaving a raised image and a "bruise" on the reverse side, which means you need soft but heavy paper. Engraving in black ink is considered the appropriate mode for formal invitations. You may need to include a sheet of tissue paper over the type when mailing to prevent it from smudging.

- ✔ **Foil stamped:** As with engraving, letters and design are etched onto a metal plate, but then the plate is heated to press a thin, film-backed material in gold, silver, or flat colors (the foil) onto paper, imprinting the design. Foil stamping is good for complex designs and heavy, textured paper. It gives a look similar to that of letterpress (see the next bullet) but allows for a wider range of designs.

- ✔ **Letterpress:** Created on an old-fashioned movable type machine. Raised type is inked and stamped on the paper. Very popular for the handmade effect it gives to invitations. Borders and other letterpress designs are quite beautiful. Unlike other processes, letterpress works well on handmade paper.

- ✔ **Lithography, offset, or flat printed:** An inked impression is made on a rubber-blanketed cylinder and then transferred to paper. Produces a crisp, flat image.

> ✔ **Thermography:** Heat-sensitive powder is sprinkled onto ink, which is heat-treated to form letters that are raised but not indented. A popular, less-expensive alternative meant to mimic engraving. Can be shiny and isn't good for dark paper.

Paper

Paper is measured in *bond weight.* Cards are three-ply stock; sheets are 32- to 42-pound bond. The most desirable paper is acid-free, 100 percent cotton rag as opposed to paper that contains a high percentage of wood pulp.

Most invitations come in one of two standard sizes: *embassy,* which is 5½ x 7½ inches; and *classic,* which is 4½ x 6¾ inches. An invitation may be a single, heavy card; a single-folded sheet with printing on the outside; or a double-folded sheet with the printing on the inside. In either case, the words can run horizontally or vertically.

If you depart from these standard sizes, you may have to buy handmade envelopes, which can be pricey.

If you opt for a nontraditional style, you can use special papers for creative effect. *Vellum* is a strong, translucent paper resembling parchment and is used either as an overlay or as the actual invitation. *Gilt-edged vellum,* which is rimmed in gold ink, is expensive yet beautiful. Sold by the sheet, special handmade papers may have nubby textures and be embedded with leaves, dried wildflowers, or metallic threads. Often impossible to print on, they make beautiful backgrounds for mounting invitations printed on plain card stock. If these options prove too expensive, consider using them for a smaller event such as the rehearsal dinner or brunch.

Fonts

Although some printing companies invent their own names for specific type styles, or *fonts,* they're all variations of the same styles. You can choose from several printing styles, ranging from what's usually called Antique Roman, a fairly staid but respectable-looking block print, to Copper Plate, a swirly script. Many typefaces come in shaded versions that add a three-dimensional look to the font. Discuss the merits of various *point,* or letter, sizes with your printer. Using a specific font on all your wedding stationery is one way of creating a unified look.

To do a little preliminary research on the style of font that appeals to you, browse websites like www.dafont.com or www.1001freefonts.com and print some sample fonts that you like to show to your printer.

Professional calligraphy is a really nice touch (although it isn't cheap). If you use a calligrapher to address your envelopes, you must provide an accurate, alphabetized guest list. If you don't know all the zip codes, don't expect the calligrapher to. Look up zip codes in a directory (www.usps.com) or call the post office.

Some calligraphers are conscientious enough to catch mistakes and correct them free of charge. Mistakes that are your fault, however, will cost you in both labor fees and extra envelopes.

Ink color

Aside from the traditional dark black, many ink colors are available, from deep gray to violet. If you want the type on your invitations to be the same shade of cornflower blue as your beloved's eyes, you can find a matching PMS (Pantone Match System) color at your printer.

Envelopes

If you use double envelopes and you choose to spiff up your invitation with a lining, the lining goes in the inside envelope but not the outer. Linings can be anything from black satin moiré to tie-dyed papers.

Tradition has dictated that the return addresses on outer envelopes are blind embossed at most, but you won't win any friends at the post office this way. Calligraph or print the return address — with no name for a private home or no apartment number for an apartment house — on the back flap. The address should be that of whoever is hosting the wedding. Traditionally, even if the bride's parents are hosting the wedding in name only, the reply cards go to them. If you're keeping track of regrets and acceptances, the parents then pass on that information or merely drop off the weekly returns in a pillowcase for you to tabulate.

If you have oversized invitations, you may mail them in oversized boxes (similar to a scarf box) with the invitation wrapped in tissue. Many companies sell transparent mailing tubes perfect for scroll-like invitations.

Besides taking into account special postal costs (not just for weight but for nonstandard sizes as well), consider where you're mailing the invitations. Your exquisite packaging may get karate-chopped and crumpled as it's crammed into a tiny apartment mailbox.

When recipients open the envelope, they should be able to read the invitation without turning it around. Folded invitations go in the envelope fold first. You may put the enclosures either on top of the invitation or in the fold. Tuck reception response cards under the envelope flap, not inside the response envelope. Don't put the response card behind the invitation, because some guests may not see it.

Proof it all night

After ordering invitations, you receive a reader's proof of the text. Read this proof over very carefully; any mistakes you overlook aren't considered the printer's fault. Then have someone else — preferably someone who knows nothing about your wedding and thus doesn't have the same blind spots you do — proofread everything. Obvious typos are often the easiest to miss.

With some engraved invitations, the proof is made from the actual printing die, on which all the text appears backward and requires a mirror to decipher. After the invitations are printed, if you can get the die from the printer, you may want to turn it into a small tray or have it mounted, a custom popular in Victorian times.

Addressing Traditions

As with other aspects of traditional formal invitations, outer and inner envelopes subscribe to precise rules of decorum. For starters, address envelopes by hand or have them calligraphed. Never use laser printers or labels. The following sections cover other rules.

Outies

Follow these guidelines for addressing outer envelopes:

- ✓ **Use formal names.** If you use middle names, you must use them in full. Middle initials don't suffice; if you don't know the middle name, skip it.

- **Spell out words such as *Apartment, Avenue,* and *Street,* as well as state names.** Although the U.S. Postal Service prefers that you use two-letter state abbreviations and no comma between cities and states so letters can be scanned by machine, your invitations won't be sent back to you if you do otherwise.

- **Abbreviate only Mr., Mrs., Ms., Jr., Messrs., and Esq.** Write out professional titles, including Doctor.

- **Address envelopes to both members of married couples, even if you know only one:** *Mr. and Mrs. Travis Twig.*

- **Address envelopes to unmarried couples as *Mr. Huck Porter and Ms. Wanda Guernsey,* with the names on separate lines.**

- **Send separate invitations to children over 13.** (*Note:* Some experts say children over 18; use your discretion.)

- **You may send joint invitations to siblings of the same sex younger than 13.** Address them as *The Misses Twig* or *The Messrs. Twig.* If you're sending to both boys and girls, write the names on the same envelope, like this:

  The Messrs. Twig
  The Misses Twig

- **You may write *Miss Daisy Twig* or *The Misses Twig* under *Mr. and Mrs. John Twig,* but *The Messrs. Twig* receive a separate invitation.**

- **Because adults should receive their own invitation no matter what, only use the phrase *and Family* when everyone under the same roof is invited.** Such open-ended generalizations can, however, get you in trouble; some people have very large families, and you may not want to meet all of them on your wedding day.

Innies

If you also use inner envelopes, address them as follows:

- Address married couples as *Mr. and Mrs. Twig,* with neither the first names nor address.

- Use only first names for children: *Pearl, Pablo, and Gus.*

- Put a young daughter's name below her parents' if the outer envelope is addressed to both the parents and her: *Miss Felicity Twig.*

- You may address intimate relatives as, say, *Aunt Hazel and Uncle Woody* or *Grandfather.*

- If you ask a friend to bring a guest, write *and Guest* on the inner, but not the outer, envelope. Better yet, find out the guest's name.

In a perfect world, all your guests would realize that only those people whose names appear on the inner envelopes are actually invited. That's not always the case, however. This is especially true when it comes to children, and you may need to employ some proactive diplomacy where precious darlings are involved. For more information on negotiating this sticky wicket, see Chapter 1.

Fit to be titled

As if you don't have enough rules to remember in writing a simple address, professional titles can put you out of your tree. Traditionally, the rule has been very simple: No matter what, you never list women with professional titles or, if they're married, their own first names. That's simple enough, yes, but these days, ignoring a woman's professional and personal identity strikes many people (including us) as sexist, to say the least. The fact that many women are keeping their names after marriage complicates things even more.

I believe that you should use professional titles for either everyone or no one. If you're stumped about how to list the names, go with this simple rule: alphabetical order unless superseded by title. For example:

Judge Jane Silk and Mr. Ty Bickle

In the preceding example, although *Bickle* would normally go before *Silk,* because Jane Silk has a title — judge — she goes first.

However, if the partners have different names and each has a title, list them alphabetically by last name:

Judge Felix Bipp and Doctor June Pickle

If the couple has the same last name, put the titled person first:

Doctor Whit Fink and Ms. Camela Fink
Doctor Mathilda Burr and Mr. Rip Burr

Unless you hobnob in diplomatic circles or work as an executive assistant to some corporate titan or socialite, you probably don't have to worry very often about addressing personages with fancy professional, political, or religious titles. But now that you're getting married, here's your chance. You can go with just first names on place cards, but if you want to use professional titles, Table 5-1 explains how.

Although people in the South sometimes refer to a person with a PhD as "Doctor," usually the title is reserved for a medical doctor.

Table 5-1 Titles of Address

Official	Envelopes	Introduction	Place Card
Protestant clergy with degree (male)	The Reverend Doctor Peter Pickle and Mrs. Pickle	Dr. Peter Pickle	Dr. Pickle or Dr. Peter Pickle
Protestant clergy with degree (female)	The Reverend Doctor Jane Cash and Mr. Cash	Dr. Jane Cash	Dr. Jane Cash
Protestant clergy without degree (male)	The Reverend Peter Pickle and Mrs. Pickle	Mr. Pickle	Mr. Pickle or Mr. Peter Pickle
Protestant clergy without degree (female)	The Reverend and Mr. Cash	Ms. Cash or Mrs. Cash	Ms. Cash, Mrs. Cash, Mrs. Buck Cash, or Ms. Jane Cash
Bishop of the Episcopal Church (male)	The Right Reverend Peter Pickle and Mrs. Pickle	Bishop Pickle	Bishop Pickle or Bishop Peter Pickle
Bishop of the Episcopal Church (female)	The Right Reverend Jane Cash and Mr. Cash	Bishop Cash	Bishop Cash or Bishop Jane Cash
Bishop of the Methodist Church (male)	The Reverend Peter Pickle and Mrs. Pickle	Bishop Pickle	Bishop Pickle or Bishop Peter Pickle
Bishop of the Methodist Church (female)	The Reverend Jane Cash and Mr. Cash	Bishop Cash	Bishop Cash or Bishop Jane Cash
Mormon Bishop	Bishop and Mrs. Peter Pickle	Mr. Pickle	Mr. Pickle or Mr. Peter Pickle
Roman Catholic Bishop and Archbishop	The Most Reverend Peter Pickle	His Excellency	His Excellency Bishop Pickle
Monsignor	The Right Reverend Monsignor Peter Pickle	Monsignor Pickle	Monsignor Pickle or Monsignor Peter Pickle
Priest	The Reverend Father Peter Pickle	Father Pickle	Father Pickle or Father Peter Pickle
Nun	Sister Mary Margaret	Sister Mary Margaret	Sister Mary Margaret or Sister Cash
Eastern Orthodox Communion Bishop	The Right Reverend Peter Pickle	His Excellency	His Excellency Bishop Pickle
Eastern Orthodox Communion Priest	The Reverend Father Peter Pickle	Father Pickle	Father Pickle or Father Peter Pickle

(continued)

Official	Envelopes	Introduction	Place Card
Rabbi (male)	Rabbi and Mrs. Isaac Pickle	Rabbi Pickle	Rabbi Pickle or Rabbi Isaac Pickle
Rabbi (female)	Rabbi Rachel Cash	Rabbi Cash	Rabbi Rachel Cash and Mr. Cash
U.S. Senator (male)	Senator and Mrs. Peter Pickle	Senator or Senator Pickle	Senator Pickle or Senator Peter Pickle
U.S. Senator (female)	Senator Jane Cash and Mr. Cash	Senator Cash	Senator Cash or Senator Jane Cash
U.S. Representative (male)	The Honorable and Mrs. Peter Pickle	Mr. Pickle	The Honorable Peter Pickle, Mr. Pickle, or Mr. Peter Pickle
U.S. Representative (female)	The Honorable Jane Cash and Mr. Cash	Ms. Cash or Mrs. Cash	Ms. Cash, Mrs. Cash, or Ms. Jane Cash
Mayor (male)	Mayor and Mrs. Peter Pickle	Mayor Pickle	The Mayor of Wigglebury
Mayor (female)	Mayor Jane and Mr. Buck Cash or The Honorable Jane Cash and Mr. Buck Limestone (if his name is different from hers)	Mayor Cash	The Mayor of Wigglebury
Judge (male)	Judge and Mrs. Peter Pickle	Judge Pickle	Judge Pickle or Judge Peter Pickle
Judge (female)	The Honorable Jane Cash and Mr. Cash	Judge Cash	Judge Cash or Judge Jane Cash
Ambassador (male)	The Honorable Peter Pickle, Ambassador of the United States	Mr. Ambassador	Ambassador Pickle or Ambassador Peter Pickle
Ambassador (female)	The Honorable Jane Cash, Ambassador of the United States	Madam Ambassador	Ambassador Cash or Ambassador Jane Cash
Doctor (male)	Dr. and Mrs. Peter Pickle	Dr. Pickle	Dr. Pickle or Dr. Peter Pickle
Doctor (female)	Mr. Buck and Dr. Jane Cash	Dr. Cash	Dr. Cash or Dr. Jane Cash
Doctors	The Drs. Billy and Betty Bopper	Dr. Bopper	Dr. Bopper or Dr. Billy Bopper, Dr. Betty Bopper

A word from some distinguished guests

In the your-tax-dollars-hard-at-work department, if you send an invitation to the U.S. President and First Lady, you'll get a lovely note congratulating you on your marriage. (You must be United States citizens.) The address is

The White House
Greetings Office, Room 39

1600 Pennsylvania Ave. NW
Washington, D.C. 20502-0039

Include the name of the president (addressed as *The Honorable*) and his wife (addressed as *Mrs.*) Send your invitation at least six weeks in advance if you'd like your reply in time for the wedding. Be sure to include your married names and both your old and new mailing addresses. You can also send an invitation to the Pope and receive a papal blessing for your marriage. Ask your parish priest to provide you with information on precisely where and to whom to send an invite.

Printing Your Own Invitations

Many couples choose to design their own invitations or hire a graphic artist to assist them in creating something one-of-a-kind. But if you're ambitious, creative, and eager to save money, you can try *literally* making your own invitations. For something really down-home and whimsical, invent your own style.

With the advances in computer software and online services, you can create or purchase a design for your invitation that's nearly professional quality. However, unless you invest in your own printing press, you can't approximate an engraved product or even a thermographed one. But if you seek a casual style, then the do-it-yourself route works fine.

Printing your own wedding invitations doesn't always save you money. Although you eliminate the middleman — the printer — you may still have to buy the paper, the design, and the ink. And you should also take into account your own time, experience, and anxiety level. How many sheets of gilt-edged vellum will you mess up before you get the process down pat?

One way to go is to have the invitation card printed professionally and then assemble your own multifaceted creation. Many Internet companies offer such services and supplies.

If you do decide to DIY, you'll need an electronic file of your invitation design. If you're great at using graphic design programs, you can try creating the design yourself. But if you're like most people, you'll want to purchase a design instead. A number of online companies offer a range of lovely designs and even allow some customization for an additional fee. Two good sites are www.printablepress.com and www.empapers.com. Another great source is Etsy (www.etsy.com). Just enter *printable wedding invitations* into the search box for thousands of results. You can narrow your results by style by adding a term like *art deco, modern,* or *Victorian* to your search. When printing your own invitations with the goal of saving money, be sure to choose a design that's not too ink-heavy or you'll end up blowing your budget on cartridges. And as with printed invitations, you'll get an e-mailed proof of your design. Read it carefully and do a test print. The number of changes you can make to the design without additional charges is limited.

After you choose your design, you'll need paper. If you search for *imprintable papers* online, you'll find many places that sell interesting papers for laser printing your own invitations, place cards, wedding programs, and so on. A couple of good sites are www.paper-source.com and www.myexpression.com. Be sure to order some extra cards and envelopes because you'll need some test copies.

If you're printing your own invitations, you may want to supplement them with a wedding website for RSVPs, itineraries, maps, and other details so you don't have to fuss with printing lots of inserts. (See Chapter 6 for more on wedding websites.)

After choosing and printing your design, you still have more ways to make your invitations special. These days, crafts and stationery stores stock an impressive array of do-it-yourself supplies and embellishments. Among the items you may need are

- ✓ **Deckling ruler:** A special tool with a wavy, sharp edge. You lay it on the paper and tear-cut along the sharp edge to create the hand-torn effect.

- ✓ **Embossing stamp:** Emboss a simple image or monogram on your card stock or envelope.

- ✓ **Glue sticks or a glue gun:** For mounting papers and attaching doodads.

- ✓ **Hole punch:** For threading ribbons.

- ✓ **Ribbon:** A simple bow or wisp of organza is perhaps the least expensive way to transform a plain card into an elegant invite. Buy several rolls — you can extend the theme by using it to tie napkins, accessorize place cards, and tie bows on guest baskets.

- ✓ **Sealing wax:** Create an embossed seal on the outer envelope by using a decorative press and wax in a color that matches your overall theme. Because true sealing wax doesn't fare well in the U.S. mail, use one of the many faux versions out there (you can find them advertised as such). They seal like wax but don't crack when put through a stamping machine.

- ✓ **Special papers:** Combine different textures — vellum, crepe, handmade flower paper, and so on — to mat your invitation for a sophisticated layered look.

- ✓ **Trinkets:** A small brass charm glued onto the invitation is another quick way to add interest.

It's a Mail Thing

In calculating the cost of your invitations, be sure to include postage. When you have a sample — including response card, direction card, map, and all other inserts — take it to the post office to have it weighed (twice). If you're using special handmade papers or envelopes, bring several; some may weigh more than others, and you don't want any invitations to wind up back in your mailbox marked with the heart-stopping words *insufficient postage.* Be prepared to put up to three stamps on each envelope. Don't pinch pennies here: Go for all matching stamps, which look more finished, even if you have to pay a few more cents to mail the invitation.

Don't forget to send invitations to your officiant and parents. You'd be amazed at how often these very important people get overlooked. Also send an invitation to yourselves before the others go out so that you can see how long it takes to arrive and in what condition.

The cherry on the sundae of your printed invitation may be a beautiful stamp. The U.S. Postal Service offers floral-, romance-, or wedding-themed stamps at a premium price, and Perfect Postage (www.perfectpostage.com) stocks an even wider variety of wedding, monogram, save-the-date, and other specialty postage. Perfect Postage, Zazzle (www.zazzle.com), and other sites also let you upload a favorite photo, which they can transform into customized, valid stamps. They also offer monogrammed stamps and stamps with your own custom designs. Note that these services are pricey — meaningfully more than the face value of the stamps.

Putting stamps on the response envelopes encourages your lazier guests to mail them in. However, stamping reply envelopes for guests abroad is useless — they must use their own postage.

After you've gone to all the trouble of painstakingly inscribing each envelope and choosing special stamps, you don't want the effect ruined by having your invitation run over by the post office's vicious canceling machines. A hand-canceled envelope looks more elegant and keeps calligraphy and sealing wax intact. In many areas, unfortunately, you must promise your firstborn to get the post office to hand stamp anything. However, the look of a hand cancel is worth your most charming powers of persuasion.

One for the record

The simplest way to preserve your invitation is to mat and frame it or include it in your photo album. If you have a lot of time on your hands, you may decoupage it on a plate, serving tray, or hope chest in which you keep other wedding mementos. Or save time by sending it to a company that backs invitations with velvet and mounts them in shadow boxes.

Or Maybe It's an E-Mail Thing

According to the *New York Times,* one in five couples now issue wedding invitations by electronic means. Though I do think there's nothing quite like a beautifully designed paper invitation, if your budget or your ecological consciousness just can't tolerate paper, you can find some online services that elevate electronic invitations far above a standard e-mail.

Paperless Post (www.paperlesspost.com) and Greenvelope (www.greenvelope.com) both mimic the experience of opening a paper invitation through Flash animation, and both sites keep track of guest RSVPs. Paperless Post offers a number of free and low-cost designs, while the somewhat pricier Greenvelope allows you to personalize one of its designs, work with a staff designer, or upload your own design. Greenvelope also makes a donation to an ecological nonprofit with every purchase.

If you do decide to go electronic for your invitations, any service that grants some formality to the invitation and reply process is a good choice. Those plain old e-vites that you'd use for your Super Bowl Sunday party, though, are *not.*

If you're committed to a formal paper invitation but still concerned about trees (or just want to make things easier on yourself and your guests), you can sign up with an e-RSVP service instead of requesting written responses or including response cards. These services provide an event code or custom URL that's included in the invitation. Guests simply go the website (some also allow guests to call a toll-free number) and record their reply. The site keeps track of all responses and provides an instant guest count at any time. If this interests you, check out www.rsvpmenow.com, www.myrsvplive.com, or www.rsvphq.com.

Even if you're a traditionalist who wouldn't dream of sending e-invitations for a wedding, I think these e-invitation sites are a great option for save-the-date communications and invitations to the welcome dinner or post-wedding brunch, where the same level of formality isn't expected.

Chapter 6

The Weekend Wedding

The term *weekend wedding* encompasses a variety of celebrations that include several events over several days. Perhaps you and your guests are flying to a Caribbean resort (a *destination wedding* — see Chapter 4 for more information) or your parents are playing hometown hosts to a slew of out-of-towners. In any case, be prepared to take on multiple roles for this temporary community. It's a big project, but the lasting memories are well worth it.

As early as possible — eight months to a year ahead in popular destinations — reserve a block of rooms at a hotel (or two or three hotels in the same neighborhood at different rates, if possible). Settling all your guests in the same area not only eases your (and their) logistical problems but also helps create a sense of community, even among those who haven't met before. And community is one of the key elements that make for a truly memorable weekend.

A Typical Timeline

To give you an idea of how the festivities might unfold, here I show you a sample day-by-day breakdown of events for a Thursday-through-Sunday wedding weekend, in which the ceremony and reception take place on Saturday night:

✔ **Thursday evening:** Bride, groom, parents, and perhaps siblings have dinner, which can be anything from a casual, at-home meal to elegant dining in a restaurant. This gives the families a chance to spend some private, calm-before-the-storm time. Other early arrivals are on their own, but try to have their welcome packages in their rooms when they arrive (see "Winning Welcomes for Weekend Weddings," later in this chapter).

✔ **Friday:** The majority of guests start arriving and checking in. Although picking them up at the airport isn't necessary, make sure they know the easiest and least expensive ways to get to the hotel. If you can swing it, a simple hospitality suite or gathering area designated as Wedding Central is a fun part of a weekend wedding. Stocked with sodas and snacks, it becomes a great place for friends and families to congregate and get to know one another.

✔ **Friday, late afternoon:** Rehearsal takes place for the wedding party and others involved in the ceremony (readers, singers, and so on). Usually (but not always), you rehearse where the ceremony will actually be performed.

Although you may be tempted to skip a formal rehearsal and just do a run-through the day of your wedding, I strongly advise against that — the run-through will either be nerve-wracking or won't take place at all.

✔ **Friday evening:** After the rehearsal, the wedding party goes to the rehearsal dinner. Who else gets invited to this prenuptial event is a source of great debate in bridal circles. I believe that if you ask people to travel to your wedding, you should entertain them in some way. You don't need to invite people who live in the area to the rehearsal dinner, unless they're in the wedding party, of course. (See the sidebar "Rehearsal-dinner options," later in this chapter, for ways to finesse the situation.) Do provide transportation to and from the event.

The rehearsal dinner (or luncheon) works well with a casual feel (see Chapter 8 for more information). A postrehearsal hoedown or beachside clambake works well as the opening fete of the weekend, particularly if the reception is a formal, seated affair. The main purpose is to welcome friends and family and let them get to know one another. Mixing up the seating also makes the wedding itself more fun as people have made new friends.

✔ **Saturday:** Wedding day! Schedule some group activities during the day — a softball game, antiquing, or diving, for example — but make sure they're optional; some of your guests may want to sleep in. In an urban setting, recommend museums or landmarks to see. You might also schedule spa or salon appointments or provide gym passes for guests.

✔ **Saturday evening:** If getting to and from the ceremony and reception sites from where guests are staying is tricky, provide transportation if possible. If your wedding doesn't go until the wee hours, possibly offer a late-night bar or a coffee-and-dessert option after the reception at the hotel where the guests are staying for those who want to party on.

✔ **Sunday:** Have brunch, usually hosted by a relative or friend. Keep it very casual, more of a drop-in affair than a seated lunch. Although you aren't obligated to attend the brunch (people understand if you've already left for your honeymoon), if you're still around, stop in and say your goodbyes.

Rehearsal-dinner options

Okay, you want to be hospitable to out-of-town guests, but you really want an intimate rehearsal dinner. One solution is to hold two parties that night: a private dinner for the wedding party and immediate families followed by a dessert or cocktail reception that includes all your guests. Or ask a friend or relative to act as host for a separate event that the majority of your guests can enjoy. This get-together might consist of a barbecue, a boat ride with refreshments, or a cross-country ski outing followed by a fireside supper.

A religious Jewish ceremony can't take place between sundown on Friday and sundown on Saturday (the Sabbath). Consequently, these weddings often don't have rehearsals at all. A Conservative or Orthodox Jewish weekend wedding in the spring or summer — when sundown is obviously quite late — often consists of a dessert party for guests arriving on Saturday night after sundown, a Sunday wedding, and a Monday-morning farewell brunch.

Resist the urge to overplan your wedding weekend. Leaving guests to their own devices is fine — some may prefer to come up with their own impromptu activities and excursions.

Asking Guests to Save the Weekend

With everybody's crazy schedules, pinning down one day for a wedding is tough enough, much less a whole weekend. To ensure that your favorite people aren't off skiing in St. Moritz, hosting their own nuptials (with the same guest list), or scheduling elective surgery for the week of your wedding, the earlier you inform your guests, the better. Here are some target dates for sending out bulletins:

- **Save-the-date cards, letters, or e-cards:** Four to six months' advance warning is adequate; eight months isn't unreasonable. If you know where you're having the wedding, you might include the city and state or country.

- **Follow-up details:** Four months later, if you didn't include all the particulars with the first heads-up, send a more-detailed missive or a link to your wedding website. For particulars on this prewedding info, see the section "Telling Guests What They Need to Know," later in this chapter.

- **Invitations:** If you've sent save-the-date cards and followed up with more details, six to eight weeks before the wedding is enough time to send the official invitations. If you haven't sent any previous notice of your weekend wedding (particularly if guests need to travel or it's on a holiday weekend), send the invitations at least two to three months before.

A save-the-date card can be a short-and-sweet postcard or a chatty letter. If you just want to get the word out and then give more details when you have the time, an e-mail will suffice. Figures 6-1 and 6-2 show two different styles for asking guests to save the date.

Please Save the Date
for the wedding of

Molly Fox
and
Joseph Hall

To be held on Saturday, April 6, 2013
On the Island of Jamaica

Please plan on joining us for a wondrous weekend
of Red Stripe, Reggae, and Rejoicing!

Details and Invitations to follow

Figure 6-1: A short-and-sweet save-the-date card.

Illustration by Wiley, Composition Services Graphics

The easiest and least expensive way to create a save-the-date letter is to use an e-invitation service, such as Paperless Post (www.paperlesspost.com). These services have a wide variety of elegant designs to choose from and provide you with constantly updated info on who has received and/or opened your letter. If you want something a bit more substantive, you can type and print save-the-date cards or letters yourself. Many attractive decorative papers are now made for specific printers. For postcards, you can hand-write your note and photocopy it onto card stock on a high-performance machine. If you want something more formal, perhaps with a logo that you use on all the items you send out, see Chapter 5.

Whom you invite to which parties can get tricky with a large group. If you invite everyone to all events, you don't need to send everyone four different invitations. One card included with the wedding invitation can have all the particulars for various events: *Grandma Rose is hosting a prenuptial pig roast on Friday; Join the Smiths for a brunch on Sunday;* and so on. In this case, the least complicated response system is one card that covers all bases:

M_____

Will___attend the Friday night pig roast

Will___attend the wedding

Will___attend Sunday brunch

Dearest friends and family,

Well, it's really happening. We're actually going to make it legal. Of course, you wouldn't expect us, with our odd predilections, to get married here in Chicago, would you? That would be too easy! Sooo:

Please Save The Dates

The weekend of Friday, April 5–Sunday, April 7
to join us as we formalize our bond, on the island of Jamaica.

We would be truly delighted to have you there!

Further details to follow shortly . . .

With love,

Molly and Joe

Figure 6-2:
A chattier
save-the-
date letter.

Illustration by Wiley, Composition Services Graphics

Telling Guests What They Need to Know

In order for your guests to plan accordingly, give them a detailed idea of what to expect, including background on the destination and the weekend's itinerary. You can do this in a printed letter (Figure 6-3 shows a sample wedding preview letter that tells guests everything they need to know), on a wedding website, or using a smartphone application.

Molly and Joe are getting married!!!

By now you've heard the fantastic news that we are getting married on April 5, 2013, in Jamaica. We are tickled pink that you are planning to join us for our wedding and a weekend of festivities to celebrate.

Why Jamaica?

There were many trips to Jamaica as single souls, where we both fell head over heels in love with this magical island, never knowing that each other existed. And then — one trip together that cemented our relationship and sealed our futures together. It seemed like the only place for us to commit to each other surrounded by our dear friends and family.

Air reservations

Due to the popularity of trips to the islands at this time, we urge you to call early to make your airline reservations. We have contracted with "Fly By Night" travel agents, at 1-800-233-4272 or www.flybynight.com, for a discounted rate for our guests on both Delta and Air Jamaica. If you wish to ask specific questions, please contact Celeste at extension 23 and tell her you are with the Fox-Hall wedding.

Accommodations

We have blocked rooms at a discounted rate at the Island Heaven resort and spa. The rates vary from rooms in the Lodge ($) and the Poolside Cottages ($$) to the Fantasy Suites ($$$$). The rest of your stay is included in your room rate, or as our guests.

Please be certain to say you are a member of the Fox-Hall wedding party when booking. The rooms are reserved for us until February 15, after which they will be released. Please call early so as not to be disappointed (and disappoint us, of course).

Transportation

A shuttle bus from Island Heaven will meet every flight that has our guests arriving on it. There will be representatives from the resort directly outside the customs area, with signage. If you prefer to rent a car (which we don't recommend as driving is on the "other side" of the road, and the roads aren't exactly state of the art), there is a rental agency at the airport, and our travel agent will reserve one for you in advance. Just ask her when you make your other reservations.

Figure 6-3:
Give your guests the pertinent information.

Activities

There will be a beach barbecue on Friday evening, the Main Event on Saturday at 5 p.m., followed by dinner and dancing under the stars, and a farewell brunch on Sunday at 10 a.m. (for those of you who can tear yourselves away from paradise). We will be going into honeymoon seclusion after that, so be sure to get your fill of us beforehand as we will be definitely incommunicado!

Golfing, tennis, scuba, snorkeling, coladas, daiquiris, rum punch, naps, sun, naps, sun. . . . If you wish to book any spa services, such as a massage or hair styling, it is best to book these early as well. Call the spa directly at 1-800-234-5678.

Weather

The average temperature is a perfect 85 degrees — balmy, not humid. A light sweater or jacket may be necessary at night. The rest of the time, wear plenty of sun block and something to keep it in place.

Dress

With the exception of our wedding ceremony and the celebration that follows on Saturday — which is island-dress-up (you interpret) — all other activities are strictly casual. Penalties for overdressing will be administered.

Babysitting

We are aware that many of you may be bringing your kids and making this a family vacation. They are welcome to all events — WITH THE EXCEPTION of the ceremony and the party following. We have contracted with a bonded child care service that was recommended by our wedding consultant. They can be reached at We Be Kid-Care, 1-800-231-6789.

Questions

If there is anything we haven't covered here please call or e-mail either of us:

Molly: 212-555-9878 or Mfox@baddabing.com
Joe: 212-555-7865 or Jhall@baddabing.com

Watch for more mailings and information as April approaches. (You know we can't help ourselves!)

We are really looking forward to seeing you in Jamaica, mon.

Love,
Molly and Joe

Personalized wedding websites have become a very popular way of communicating with guests and can be created in addition to the printed preview letter or in place of it. Your site can inform guests about all the usual details and include interactive maps, links to online hotel bookings and vendor information, and other useful information. Because guests can always access your website, it can be a real help to those less-organized loved ones who've somehow misplaced their invitation. Guests can also use the site to RSVP, view the guest list, and even book local attractions. But make sure that the only events posted on your site are those that include all your guests. Don't post events with a restricted guest list, like showers or the rehearsal dinner, for everyone to see. (The same goes for Facebook — use those privacy controls!)

With the explosion of popularity in wedding websites, there are now legions of providers out there hoping to host your site. They can vary in their cost, in the templates and designs available, and in the additional services they offer (such as blog-hosting, registry management, or help with budgeting), so be sure to do some comparison shopping before you choose. There is usually a strong relationship between the cost of the service and factors like how long the site will remain active, the number of pages and types of media available, and whether advertising appears on your website pages.

Another option for getting wedding information to your guests is a smartphone application. The miWedding app for iPhone (coming soon for Android as of this writing; see `www.bottegasol.com/miwedding`) lets you and your guests communicate with one another. You can use it to provide your weekend itinerary and directions to your wedding venues and local attractions. You can also create a shared photo album so guests can share their weekend photographs with you. Of course, a smartphone app only works for wedding guests who actually have smartphones, so you may need a backup plan for Aunt Myrtle, who's perfectly happy with her landline phone, thank you.

Regardless of the medium you choose for communicating with your guests, the prewedding info they need includes any or all of the following vital data:

- Reservations phone number for hotel(s), web addresses, general price variables, and how your group is listed ("The Rawly-Pawly Wedding," for example).

- The name of a contact person at the hotel.

- Travel agent information or recommendations on booking air travel.

- Information on transportation to and from the venue (see Chapter 7).

- Travel requirements such as vaccinations, passports, and visas.

- An overview of the destination, including a map (see the sidebar "Mapping the way" for more information).

- Typical weather for that time of year.

- ✔ A rundown of the festivities, a preliminary schedule of events, general dress codes, and suggestions of what to bring, such as golf clubs or tennis racquets.

- ✔ Child-care information.

- ✔ Phone numbers and the names of contacts for services that need to be booked in advance, such as spa treatments, scuba diving, or skiing lessons.

- ✔ A questionnaire that asks whether guests are interested in spa services or sports such as sailing, tennis, or diving. Although this may seem a bit much, at small resorts, these services book up fast. Based on this questionnaire, you can give the management a heads-up so they aren't caught short-staffed.

- ✔ A festive touch such as a sun hat with your combination monogram and wedding date on it (it's considered bad taste to use your married monogram before you're actually married) and instructions to wear upon arrival (very cool for group shots).

- ✔ Preprinted room reservation cards to be mailed back by your invitees. Some resorts and hotels provide these free of charge.

Generally speaking, guests pay for their own travel and accommodations, and you're responsible for the events that take place over the weekend.

Negotiate a group rate based on the maximum number of guest rooms you feel comfortable guaranteeing. These contracts can be complicated and often require you to furnish a credit card to hold the rooms until your guests furnish theirs. *Note:* Be certain you understand what you're financially responsible for if the rooms you blocked aren't taken. Negotiate other variables at the same time such as a hospitality suite, farewell brunch, and delivery fees for welcome baskets (which can run over $5 per basket at some locations).

Mapping the way

An accurate and attractive map is a key part of any destination preview package for an exotic or out-of-the-way locale (and often a good idea as an insert with the invitation).

If the directions are simple and you have some artistic ability, you may want to draw a map, complete with cute landmarks and street signs. Or you can take a ready-made map and star favorite sites — "The world's best hot dogs!" — and write a legend.

The web also offers resources for creating maps. Try www.mapfling.com (a free site that adds custom markers to Google maps and gives you a link to share with guests) or www.weddingmapper.com (which can customize a map with your markers and offers professional and custom designs).

For do-it-yourselfers, you can print out maps complete with driving directions as well as shopping, lodging, and other businesses near your target destination.

Winning Welcomes for Weekend Weddings

A great way to show appreciation for those who've decided they can't miss your wedding, even if it's on the other side of the equator, is a welcome package that says, "We're glad you're here." One of the loveliest expressions of thanks is a little something in their room upon their arrival. The gift can come in the form of a basket, a box, or a door hanger. Something thematically appropriate is nice, such as a tote bag for an urban wedding (maybe personalized with your names and wedding date) or a beach bag for tropical nuptials. The contents don't need to be elaborate or expensive; just try to make them as thoughtful as you can. Choose items that reflect when and where you're celebrating and adjust the contents a bit for each recipient. (For example, guests arriving late at night may need extra snacks, and your cousin who's on the wagon shouldn't get that charming mini-bottle of champagne.)

A creative welcome package may include some combination of the following:

- **Welcome/thank-you letter:** All welcome packages should include a brief but heartfelt message that welcomes and thanks guests for making the journey.

- **Wedding information:** Either as part of your letter or separately, provide a day-by-day synopsis of the weekend, remind guests exactly when the wedding and reception will take place, supply a map to wedding locations, and give directions to the hospitality suite, if you're having one. Another nice idea is to include contact information for someone guests can call with questions. This shouldn't be you — you're going to be very busy! — but can be your wedding consultant or a kindly local relative who knows the area and your wedding details.

- **Wedding-party particulars:** Include a separate insert just for bridesmaids, groomsmen, and other wedding-party members that details where and when the rehearsal is and any other events that pertain to them. (See Chapter 7 for info on the wedding-day schedule.)

- **The inside scoop:** You want to help your guests have a good time even when they're not attending wedding events. Provide a good local guidebook and mark the spots you recommend or you customize a map to show the area and pinpoint your personal favorite places. In a city, you might feature art galleries, flea markets, shops, and restaurants. At a resort, you might highlight snorkeling spots or the best bartender. (See the sidebar "Mapping the way," earlier in this chapter, for tips on creating maps.) In addition to your recommendations, vouchers for a local tour are a particularly generous touch. Also include directions and transportation details, as well as phone numbers of baby sitters, doctors, and other local troubleshooters.

✔ **Snacks and drinks:** These are particularly thoughtful for guests who arrive before or after usual meal times, but everyone appreciates provisions when travelling. You can supply bottled water, gourmet coffee or tea, fruit, cheese and crackers, and/or chocolates. Just about any packaged good can be personalized nowadays, and water bottles or candy bars emblazoned with your wedding logo can be charming. When choosing snacks, local taste treats make your gift more special. For example, in New York City, you could include Zabar's bagel chips and New York State apple cider. In the Caribbean, include the brand of rum the island is noted for (Cocksbur in Barbados, for example) and tropical fruits.

✔ **A bit of bubbly:** To enhance the celebratory mood, you can greet your guests with standard or favor-sized bottles of sparkling or still wine. A number of companies offer personalized labels; just enter "wedding wine labels" into your search engine. And Francis Coppola Winery offers Sofia Minis, small pink cans of their popular sparkling wine.

✔ **Personal pampering:** Your wedding weekend may be your guests' mini-vacation, so help them relax by including items like bath salts, lotion, a mud mask, or a sleep mask.

✔ **In case of emergency:** Supply the items people have in the medicine cabinet but often miss when travelling: tissues, pain reliever, or mints, for example. Your patented hangover cure may be particularly appreciated. I also love the idea of "before and after" items, such as hair styling products for before the reception and Alka-Seltzer for afterward.

✔ **Preparation, preparation:** If she's anything like ours, your mom reminds you to prepare before going outside, and you can help your guests do the same. Sunscreen, insect repellent, or a fan is thoughtful for a tropical destination, while a wooly scarf or mittens are a gracious gift for a fall or winter urban wedding.

✔ **Treats for the kids:** Children should get a welcome gift too — something different, and less expensive, than the adults'. Depending on the age, candy, coloring books and crayons, inexpensive games or toys, or a scrapbook for them to fill with details of the trip will delight them and convey that you're especially glad they came.

Chapter 7

Creating a Foolproof Wedding-Day Schedule

In This Chapter

▶ Figuring out the flow of events

▶ Transporting the players

▶ Coordinating the receiving line

*W*hether you have hired a wedding consultant, are arranging things yourselves, or have placed yourselves totally in the hands of a banquet manager or caterer, you'll find that composing a wedding-day schedule is very helpful.

The schedule tells all the players — members of the wedding party, vendors, and staff — what to do and when to do it. More important, the schedule serves as your personal prompter and helps you envision exactly how you want the day to flow. Granted, you're not masterminding D-Day, but a little organizational wizardry in advance never hurt any wedding.

Realize that scheduling your wedding on paper is primarily a tool that helps get everyone — namely your wedding party and your vendors — on the same page. You don't have to treat the schedule as gospel or follow it to the letter with blind obedience. In other words, leave room for the day to evolve naturally.

Putting Everyone on the Same Page with a Wedding-Day Schedule

Every wedding is unique, which makes creating a one-size-fits-all wedding-day schedule impossible. However, here's a generic prototype to give you an idea of how to create your own version. The best approach is to create two versions of your wedding-day schedule:

✔ **Master:** This comprehensive version delineates *every* detail of the day with minute-by-minute precision, from a few hours before the ceremony to after the last song. Give this list to everyone on the team involved in making your day happen — caterer, band, florist, photographer, cake maker, banquet manager, and anyone else who needs to know all the players and how they interconnect.

✔ **Ceremony only:** The abridged version of the master schedule focuses exclusively on the ceremony. Give this information to the attendants, your officiant, parents, and other ceremony participants. Distribute this schedule at the rehearsal and go over it carefully. Also ask someone to bring copies to the actual ceremony — unless, that is, your attendants are all soap opera stars, able to memorize a script in one reading.

The rehearsal shouldn't be the first time you tell everyone the way you want your wedding day to flow. Create a preliminary order of events and have key people give it a once-over to offer suggestions for improving the flow and timing. You may revise it up to the last minute, but make sure that everyone keeps up with the latest version to prevent your parents from waiting at the ceremony site for a receiving line that you nixed long ago.

The master schedule includes

✔ A roster of all the players, including postal addresses, e-mail addresses, and all relevant phone numbers. (See Chapter 1 for information on assembling everyone's pertinent stats.)

✔ Transportation logistics, including names and times of arrival for everyone involved.

✔ Directions to sites.

✔ Delineation of steps before, during, and after the ceremony.

✔ Specifics for the ceremony.

✔ Estimated timing for each activity, including toasts.

✔ Specific notes or addenda for each vendor, as applicable.

✔ A highlighted list of important details.

Develop the master schedule in tandem with your vendors and your wedding consultant, if you have one. The banquet manager can tell you how long it takes to serve and clear each course; the bandleader can give you the timing for a dance set; and so on. Send the first draft of your schedule to all your vendors to get their input. Let them make notes on it and return it to you so you can incorporate any changes in the finished schedule.

Addressing Transportation Plans

Ask professional wedding planners what causes the most problems for them and they'll inevitably answer, "the transportation." This section helps you iron out any kinks in advance by showing you how to approach this facet of your wedding carefully and efficiently.

Transporting the wedding party

On the wedding day, you may want to arrange separate transportation to the ceremony for just your wedding party and your parents to have them all in one place at the same time.

For limousines or town cars, negotiate rates with the booking agent and ask about cheaper rates on less-luxurious models. (Some companies actually charge less for untinted windows.) Be specific about the number of guests that cars hold and whether the cars have *jump seats* (extra fold-down seats). Keep in mind that having a limo wait for you for several hours usually costs the same as having it return to pick you up (because the driver likely doesn't have time to handle a job in between).

Of course, a limousine isn't a necessity. Consider less-pricey vehicles such as a town car or larger vehicles such as a minivan or an SUV, which hold more people and, consequently, can be less costly.

After the section that lists contact information, the next page of the master wedding-day schedule looks like Figure 7-1, which indicates where members of the wedding party are during the day and how they're getting there. Give this sheet to anyone whose name appears on it, as well as to the drivers.

Wedding Transportation Schedule

Pick-Up Time and Location	Drop-Off Time and Location	Driver Wait?	Passenger(s)	Car Number and Type
10 a.m. Groom's parents' house	10:20 a.m. Hotel Fabulosity	No	Mrs. Harry Badger (Madge, groom's mother) and Buffy Badger (groom's sister)	#1, Lincoln Town Car
3 p.m. Hotel Fabulosity	3:20 p.m. Pelican Memorial Church	Yes	(Bridesmaids) Mimi Marmot, Kitty Lidder, and Poppy Porpoise	#2, Limo
4:30 p.m. Pelican Memorial Church	4:50 p.m. Hotel Fabulosity	No	(Bridesmaids and ushers) Marmot, Lidder, Porpoise, Rod Weiler, Bob Boar, and Jay Seegawl	#2, Limo

Figure 7-1: Coordinate pick-ups and drop-offs for the wedding party and their drivers.

Illustration by Wiley, Composition Services Graphics

Arranging transportation for guests

Unless you're holding all your events in the hotel where your guests are staying (or within walking distance), if your budget permits, you may want to arrange to get everyone from one place to another, comfortably and safely. Although this may seem an unnecessary expense, it'll be worth every penny in case of rain not to have 300 guests trying to hail taxis from the church at the same time.

Plan for the vehicles to leave from a central location, and stagger the departure times to allow for stragglers. If you have elderly or handicapped guests, consider providing them with special transportation. Assign friends who want to be helpful to transportation patrol — corralling strays and checking that everyone is accounted for. If the hotel allows it, a poster in the lobby with the transportation details and itinerary is very helpful.

Directing traffic

You also need to provide an addendum in case someone isn't familiar with the town or venues. Include the address of the ceremony and reception sites, directions, and information for such intermediate stops as the location where the bridal party is dressing. Cover all bases by giving directions from several key locations such as the airport, downtown, or the hotel where you've reserved rooms. To save yourself time, print out maps and routes by using an Internet map site (see Chapter 6).

Creating the Master Schedule

Your master schedule (even if it's for your eyes only) begins with the pre-ceremony rituals of getting dressed and — if you're not waiting until after the ceremony — taking photographs. The timing of what has to happen before the ceremony is crucial. Make sure you take into account even seemingly little things, such as when you'll have time to eat before the ceremony. Putting these items on your master schedule acts as a reminder on a day when time can be on warp speed.

In many hotels, check-in time is 2 or 3 p.m., so the bride should either stay in this room (perhaps with her maid of honor) the night before the wedding or try to negotiate with the hotel for an early check in. Even couples who live together often spend the night before the wedding in separate places.

Whether the attendants get dressed in a hotel or at someone's home, always arrange for lunch or tea. They won't be eating for hours, and the combination of starvation and the first glass of champagne can be explosive. Also, the bride should usually be last to have her hair and makeup done so that she waits the least amount of time "done up" before the ceremony.

Then you have the ceremony itself. In Chapter 10, I cover the elements of major religious ceremonies, chapter and verse, so to speak. That's where I help you create a specific schedule and script, complete with music cues, readings, and other details. For the master schedule, you're just interested in the broad strokes.

Finally, the master schedule segues into the reception. Your caterer, band, bartender, and other vendors should know exactly when (at least in theory) you want to eat, dance, and toast. Again, it's a good idea to send the vendors the details of their duties a week before in the succinct format I supply throughout the book.

I base the sample master schedule in Figures 7-2, 7-3, and 7-4 on the increasingly popular choice of taking photos *before the ceremony.* (See Chapter 21 for photo-scheduling details.) Many couples still prefer not to see each other before the ceremony, though. If you prefer to slip away and have formal portraits taken while the guests are having cocktails, configure your schedule that way.

Sample Wedding-Day Schedule

Pre-ceremony Schedule		
Time	*Events*	*Notes*
1:00–2:30	Hair and makeup.	Makeup artist and hair stylist to arrive at bride's hotel suite at 1.
2:30–3:30	Bride and attendants dress.	
2:30	Have snack.	Order from room service day before.
3:30	Dressing room photos.	Photographer to arrive at suite at 2:45.
4:00	Ushers arrive for pre-ceremony photos.	Location: Hotel Fabulosity garden.
4:00	Florist distributes boutonnières, corsages, and bouquets.	
4:10	Tête-à-tête between bride and groom before photo session.	
4:30	Family and other members of wedding party arrive for photos.	Attach shot list to this schedule. Designate someone to help pose subjects.
5:20	After photos, leave for ceremony.	

Figure 7-2:
A pre-ceremony schedule helps everyone get to the wedding site on time.

Illustration by Wiley, Composition Services Graphics

The do-si-do of the first dance and cut-ins becomes infinitely more complicated if you have myriad sets of parents who don't speak to each other, widowed parents, or hypersensitive mothers. If the groom's mother feels that she should be first to dance with him — after the bride, hopefully — then comply with her wishes. If a parent is partnerless, be sure to pair the person with someone and give them top billing in the dance order. If the entire situation seems too complicated, give up and invite everyone onto the dance floor simultaneously, after your first dance.

Ceremony Schedule		
Time	*Events*	*Notes*
5:45	Church doors open. Prelude begins.	Invitation is for 6.
6:00	Ushers hand out programs and seat guests. Bride and bridesmaids wait in side room at church.	Aunt Ella Fant bringing programs from printer.
6:15	Processional music begins.	
Till 6:25	Processional.	See attached sheet of who walks with whom.
6:25–7:00	Ceremony.	Approx. 35 minutes. Cue recessional music after officiant says, "I now pronounce you . . ."
7:00	Recessional music begins.	
7:00–7:05	Recessional.	See attached sheet of who walks with whom.
7:05	Bride and groom, wedding party, family, and so on leave for reception in assigned cars.	See attached transportation sheet.
7:15–7:30	Postlude music plays until all the guests have left the church.	

Figure 7-3: Creating a ceremony schedule helps everyone be in the right place at the right time.

Illustration by Wiley, Composition Services Graphics

If you're having ethnic dancing, such as a hora or tarantella, schedule it after the main course to get guests moving again after eating and drinking.

When the guests are seated for the main course, some of the band (those members not required to play subtle background music during the meal), the photographer, and the videographer should eat as well. Assistants should eat when the others are finished so someone is watching the room for any spontaneous toasts. Arrange with your caterer ahead of time to serve them something appetizing, even if it's not exactly what you serve your guests.

Reception Schedule		
Time	*Events*	*Notes*
7:15–8:30	Cocktail hour begins on Turtle Terrace at Hotel Fabulosity. Guests start arriving.	Waiters ready with trays of wine; bars open. Background music: Barry Badger Trio CD.
7:15	Weather permitting, bride and groom take outdoor portraits.	
8:15	Banquet manager adjusts lighting in dining room. Final sound check.	
8:20	Bride, groom, and parents look at room before guests are escorted in.	Banquet manager or wedding consultant to arrange.
8:25	Band starts.	
8:30	Guests escorted in and take seats.	
8:45	Wine poured. First toast by best man Barry Cuda.	
8:50–9:15	Appetizer served and cleared.	
9:15	First dance. Cut-ins. Dance set (20 minutes).	See attached choreography list for cut-ins.
9:35–10:20	Main course served. Three toasts during main course by Bunny Hopper, Mara Supial, and Sally Mander. Places cleared.	
10:20–10:45	Dance set.	
10:45	Champagne poured, cake cutting, bride and groom toast, cake served.	
11:10	Coffee and sweets served.	
11:10–12:30	Band plays. Bandleader announces last dance at 12:25.	

Figure 7-4: Determining the sequence of events makes for a happy party.

Illustration by Wiley, Composition Services Graphics

Tossing the bouquet

The bouquet toss is increasingly going the way of the pay phone — many brides find it sexist or archaic. If you do want to include this tradition but don't have a critical mass of single friends at the wedding, you may want to simply present the bouquet as a memento to a favorite aunt or other person you want to honor. If you're planning on tossing it or giving it away and want to keep your real bouquet for yourself, make one specifically for the toss, as I describe in Chapter 11.

Schedule the bouquet toss late in the evening, after the cake cutting, so it isn't disruptive to the party. A headwaiter should be prepared to choreograph the toss. Participants should be several yards behind the bride, arranged into a semicircle. If possible, gather participants on a softer surface than a dance floor; competition can be ruthless, and people have been known to go down.

The bride should stand with her back to the crowd, in a place with no chandeliers or other possible impediments to a high, vigorous fling. To the sounds of a drum roll, if possible, the bride bends ever so slightly at the knees and tosses the bouquet over her head, aiming high. If the bouquet collides with the ceiling or some other stationary object, the toss results in a foul and she must attempt it again.

Taking a Closer Look at Receiving-Line Logistics

If you have 125 guests and allot each one 30 seconds, you're looking at an hour-long receiving line. In spite of this fact, many wedding manuals still consider receiving lines a must. A receiving line does ensure that the couple greets all the guests, but you can greet them by making your rounds at the reception, which is more hospitable, anyway. If you feel you must have a receiving line, keep it short. You don't need to have all 24 of your attendants glad-handing the guests. The fastest way, if possible, is to hold the receiving line at the door of the ceremony site as guests are leaving. Even that, however, doesn't prevent traffic jams. And having the line at your reception shouldn't mean torture for your guests. Make sure someone offers them drinks and hors d'oeuvres while they're waiting.

An ample receiving line includes, from left: the bride's mother, the groom's mother, and the bride and groom. A longer one has, from left: the bride's mother, the bride's (or groom's) father, the groom's mother, and the groom's (or bride's) father. If time isn't an issue, you may include the maid of honor and, even though he's not considered part of the standard lineup, the best man. Anything longer is for the Rockettes. If issues exist with divorced parents, be kind. Don't force people who can't bear each other to stand side by side, smiling through clenched teeth.

The receiving line is like a good game of telephone. Guests introduce themselves to the bride's mother, who then introduces them to the groom's mother, who introduces them to the bride, and so on. Of course, by the time Harriet Luce gets to the end, she has become Harry Caboose.

Although I discuss in Chapter 21 whether to take formal photos before or after the ceremony, one thing is certain: If you have a receiving line and your guest list is anything but teeny, you need to take your formal photos, including those of the bride and groom together, *before* the ceremony — unless you want to make your guests wait three days to eat.

Weather art thou?

Obsessing about the weather is a big part of wedding planning. Several websites are tailored to this compulsion at no charge, including

✔ The Weather Channel (www.weather.com)

✔ The National Weather Service (www.weather.gov)

✔ AccuWeather.com

And the Weather Channel offers a special wedding planner feature that helps you select the best dates for your wedding or track weather for a date you've chosen. See www.weather.com/activities/events/weddings/.

Chapter 8

Other Creative Celebrations

Although no two weddings are identical, some are clearly traditional, while others are quirkier. In this chapter, I cover the spectrum, from the playfulness of theme nuptials to the precision of military weddings. I include the increasingly popular vow-renewal ceremonies as well as my thoughts on second (or third or fourth) weddings. These ideas won't appeal to every couple, but this chapter does reconfirm that wedding-style possibilities abound.

Also in this chapter, I help you plan a rehearsal dinner that's the perfect prelude to the main event. And I cover your role in the various kinds of fetes that may be thrown in your honor — showers, engagement parties, bachelor bashes, and the like.

Dream Themes

Even couples who love the idea of a theme wedding often don't go for a full-scale production. A circus theme, for example, where you're seated by a ringmaster, eat in different rings, and devour a dessert garnished with animal crackers seems more suited to a sweet-sixteen party than a wedding. Theme weddings can be complicated, costly, and a little confusing for guests, but if your heart is set on a *Hunger Games* wedding, for example, go for it — hey, it's your wedding. Just remember that a little theatrics go a long way: Having bow and arrow props in your photo booth may be charming and fun, but making your attendants carry them down the aisle is asking a lot and will definitely detract from the wedding itself.

You can build a theme around almost anything that reflects your personalities, hobbies, lifestyles, or your own style. Even extremely elegant weddings may incorporate thematic elements. If you're considering having a full-blown theme wedding, the most important aspect is the location. Choose a site that goes along with your theme *or* create a theme because you've chosen a location that lends itself to one. For example, a tent is a perfect venue for a Moroccan-style wedding, whereas a city loft might evoke a theme based on art or artists. With rare exceptions, however, the most successful wedding themes are the most subtle.

In the following list, I offer a few ideas for décor, props, foods, and entertainment to get your creative juices flowing:

- **Black and white:** The black-and-white wedding is a classic that can be adapted to suit just about any couple's personal style. Start with a crisp black-and white-invitation. You'll want chic, black-and-white raiment for the bridal party. In their recent bridal collections, many designers, such as Isaac Mizrahi and Vera Wang, have shown elegant white gowns with black ornamentation for brides and black gowns for attendants. (You can even ask guests to wear black and white.) For flowers that reflect your theme without going gothic, consider anemones, black-centered gerbera daisies, almost-black callas or hellebores, or pure white roses interwoven with black ribbon. You have lots of choices of table linens and china, and you can extend your theme to a graphically decorated cake, black-and-white cookie or candy favors, and beyond. For decorative accents, any stereotypically black-and-white objects, from chess pieces to cameos to sheet music, can personalize your theme. And for fun, consider a photo booth that produces black-and-white pictures.

- **Holiday:** Valentine's Day, Independence Day, Halloween, Christmas, and New Year's Eve all make for spectacular theme weddings. The possibilities for creative décor are numerous, and because these days are already imbued with a festive atmosphere, getting your guests into a partying mood is easy. Two caveats, however: As I mention in Chapter 1, many people reserve certain holidays for close family gatherings, so they may not be able to attend your holiday wedding; and second, paying holiday rates (usually time-and-a-half or double-time) for staff wages may be excessive. On the bright side, some spaces may already be decorated for the holiday, so you'll need only minor additions.

- **Seasonal:** Weddings that reflect the season always feel right, and they take advantage of flowers and foliage at the peak of their beauty (and lowest cost). An autumn theme, for example, may have centerpieces composed of colorful fall leaves, miniature pumpkins, gourds, and apples to evoke a feeling of harvest. With the table linens in rusts and burgundies and a menu that showcases seasonal items, the wedding reception would be stylized without seeming bizarre. You could even host a hayride the night before the wedding and give small jars of preserves or marzipan fruits as favors. That theme, however, would cease to be charming if you stuck bales of hay and a pitchfork in the middle of a hotel ballroom.

Trendy touches

The most delightful aspects of a wedding celebration are sometimes the least traditional. My favorite newfangled extras for a wedding involve photographs, whether it's the self-service photo booth (complete with props and chalk message board; see Chapter 21) or a photographer hired to videotape guests and transform the shots into virtually instant flip books, which are great fun at the reception and a lovely memento for guests to take home. Some couples may want to add more interactive entertainment possibilities such as tango dancers to coach guests on the dance floor or DJs who interact with live musicians to get the party started.

✔ **Vintage:** Inspired by the look of your favorite show (*Mad Men* and *Downton Abbey* come to mind), music you love (always had a fondness for "In the Mood"?), or the date your reception venue was constructed, weddings styled after a particular era — from Victorian to Roaring Twenties to swinging sixties — can be beautiful, unique, and lots of fun. The era you choose can influence your invitations, your attire, your décor, and your flowers. Just do a little web browsing of images from the era to inspire your ideas. Extend the theme beyond the visual to include reception activities (garden croquet for an Edwardian wedding or swing dance lessons for a 1940s do), guestbook ideas (pressed flower stationery or a vintage typewriter for guest messages to the happy couple), and favors (which can include inexpensive items from the period, such as vintage postcards or souvenir spoons).

The websites www.vintagetextile.com, www.antiquedress.com, and www.thefrock.com are sources of exquisite period gowns.

Strategizing a Military Wedding

Military weddings are extremely traditional affairs, usually held in a base chapel or house of worship. If a military chaplain performs the service, you never have to pay a fee. Consult the chaplain before hiring musicians or a photographer, though. As for the reception, military custom dictates that you extend a formal invitation to the chaplain and his or her spouse.

Dressing to code

Figuring out what to wear to a military wedding is easy if you're in the service:

✔ **Officers:** Evening dress uniform conforms to civilian white tie and tails. Dinner or mess dress uniform is in accordance with black tie. A female officer may marry in uniform or in a traditional bridal gown. White gloves are a necessity for all saber (sword) bearers.

> ✔ **Noncommissioned officers:** Dress blues or Army green uniforms are appropriate at both formal and informal weddings.
>
> ✔ **Military guests:** They may attend the wedding in uniform if they want.

No matter what the person's rank, a man should never wear a boutonniere with his uniform.

Passing under the arch of sabers

A military wedding is no different from a civilian wedding except at the end, when the bride and groom make a dramatic exit under an arch of sabers (Army and Air Force) or swords (Navy and Marines). As soon as the ceremony is over, the attendants line up on either side of the aisle. For Army and Air Force weddings, the senior saber bearer issues a quiet cue, and all saber bearers turn, proceed to the center aisle in pairs, face the guests, and stop at a point just forward from the first pew line. With the command "Center face!" they pivot so that the officers are in two lines facing one another. At the "Arch sabers!" command, they raise their sabers (in their right hands, blade up) until the tip touches that of the saber directly opposite. As the guests stand, the bride and groom start the recessional, passing beneath the arch. After the newlyweds walk through, the commands "Carry sabers!" "Rear face!" and "Forward march!" move the saber bearers to the outside of the chapel to prepare for the second arch.

(The Navy/Marines version is virtually the same except for the command "Officers, draw swords!" when the attendants draw their swords from their scabbards in one continuous motion and lift them gracefully to touch the tip of the opposite sword. Then, at "Invert swords," they quickly turn their wrists so that the sharp edge is up.)

After the couple passes through the second arch, the head usher commands, "Return sabers!" and the attendants return them to their sheaths. Only the bridal couple may pass under the arch. The recessional continues after the saber bearers have exited the chapel.

If the bride is a civilian, there's one more step: As the couple passes under the arch, two officers at the end lower their sabers/swords in front of the couple, detaining them momentarily. The one on the right gently swats the bride on the rump with his or her saber or sword and says, "Welcome to the Army!" (or the appropriate branch of service).

At the reception, the couple cuts the cake with a sword or saber. Besides flowers, the decorations often include the American flag and the standard of the military unit. See Chapter 5 for use of military titles on invitations.

Surprising Your Spouse-to-Be

Virtually unheard of until recently, surprise weddings are gaining popularity among couples who've been married before and/or can handle planning a party but not a full-scale wedding. In this situation, the couple sends out invitations for some sort of celebratory occasion, perhaps a graduation or birthday. After their lucky guests are assembled, the couple announces that the guests are about to watch them get married. I know of one couple who threw a Halloween party and dressed as a bride and groom. Halfway through the evening, the couple asked for everyone's attention and announced that earlier in the day they had gotten hitched at city hall and wanted to thank everyone for coming to their wedding reception.

The other kind of surprise wedding is risky to say the least, and you better be absolutely sure of yourself before attempting it. In this scenario, multitudes of friends witness the bride or groom spring a proposal on the other and then (hopefully) the wedding that follows.

Private Ceremony, Public Party

If you have a destination or honeymoon-wedding (see Chapter 6) or for other reasons have only a few guests at your ceremony, you may want to throw a bash sometime after the fact. Whether you host or your parents host, this party should be an all-out celebration. Display large photos of yourselves getting married; guests love to see them. Mount a montage of photos and prop it on an easel or on the escort card table. In a pithy toast to your parents and/or the guests, diplomatically explain why you chose to have your wedding this way. ("We felt we wanted our vows to be private, and they were exactly as we hoped they would be. And now, to have the best of both worlds and be able to celebrate with our loved ones makes everything perfect.") The goal is to tie the two events together so everyone can share your happiness.

Giving Marriage Another Try

When it comes to "encore" weddings, the rules are no longer different from the first time around. If you're one of those people who speak of your first wedding as if it were a dream directed by your parents, now's your chance to create a ceremony and reception that are truly yours. (Think of Samuel Johnson's definition of remarriage: "the triumph of hope over experience.") That may mean you approach the altar in full wedding regalia — lace, tulle, white tie, tails — or skip the traditional wedding hoopla in favor of an understated luncheon with you both in elegant suits. Do what's meaningful to you.

One of the most sensitive issues in remarriage is dealing with children from a previous relationship. As with every aspect of child-raising, don't assume anything. To appoint a child best person, which you see as a great honor, may in fact leave the child feeling enormously guilty about the other parent. But to leave children out of the ceremony altogether without giving them a choice as to their level of participation may alienate them from the new family unit you're forming. Their role in the ceremony should depend on their age, attitude, and relationship with each of you (old and new spouses alike). If any of the children are teenagers, let them invite some friends to the wedding, too. And if the children are younger, plan some special activities just for kids over the wedding weekend. Such overtures can go a long way toward developing peaceful relations for the future.

Say It Again: Renewing Your Vows

Some couples choose to reaffirm their vows because they didn't (or couldn't) have a religious ceremony the first time and want to be wed in holy matrimony. Other reasons for reaffirmations include wanting an elaborate party if the original reception was very simple, celebrating a spiritual or emotional renewal, or marking a significant family event, such as the birth of a grandchild. Because reaffirmation isn't a legally binding ceremony, the couple may have anyone they want officiate (or just exchange their vows with no officiant). Having the same officiant and attendants as at the original ceremony can be touching. Religious vow renewals often take place during the regular services in the couple's house of worship. Otherwise, both the ceremony and reception may be at home or, for a blowout party, in an event space (see Chapter 4).

If you're planning on inviting guests to a vow renewal, make it clear that gifts are out of the question. People may get the no-gift idea if you have a private ceremony and a big bash, but you may have to convey your wishes by word of mouth. This is especially important if you renew your vows fewer than 15 years after your original ones. Unless you've experienced an extraordinary situation, people may feel strange attending a renewal of vows so soon.

Usually, the couple issues the invitations, but sometimes their children or, more rarely, other family or friends host the event. Chapter 5 provides a comprehensive look at invitation wording, but here's how a typical renewal invitation may read:

The pleasure of your company
is requested at the reaffirmation
of the wedding vows of
Mr. and Mrs. Wylie Beauregard Blandsky
[Wylie Beauregard and Ida Kerfuffle Blandsky] . . .

Or, if you want something less formal,

Join us as we celebrate
our twenty-five years
of joy together
and renew our promises
for eternity . . .

Partying Before and After the Wedding

You may find yourselves being honored at several events, including engagement parties, showers, and bachelor/bachelorette parties. The following sections help you figure out the rules for these occasions and invite you to invent traditions of your own.

Remember! Send a note and a gift thanking anyone who hosts a party for you.

Opening rounds: Engagement parties

Engagement parties may be as simple as an at-home dinner with your families followed by a round of toasts. Or they may be a major bash, complete with themed entertainment and foods. The most common scenario is a party at someone's home.

Traditionally, the bride's parents held the first engagement party. If that wasn't feasible, the duty fell to the groom's parents. Nowadays, friends of the couple often honor the couple with a shindig, particularly if the couple lives far away from their parents or if complicated family relationships make it awkward for the parents to throw a party.

Although you (or your parents) may announce your engagement in a newspaper (see Chapter 3), mailing printed engagement announcements may be seen as a "send gifts" alert, and neither engagements nor engagement parties are occasions for gifts. Writing personal notes to or calling friends and relatives you want to inform personally, however, qualifies as a sign of affection. Of course, under no circumstances should you place a newspaper announcement of your engagement if either of you is still legally married.

You should invite everyone from the engagement party to the wedding, if the same people are hosting both. (Otherwise, guests may wonder what they did at the first party to keep them from being invited to the wedding.) You can make exceptions in two circumstances: when the engagement party is significantly larger than the wedding and when friends or relatives who have no control over the wedding guest list host the engagement party.

Getting showered

The bridal shower is said to have started a few centuries ago with a poor yet beautiful girl in Holland whose father betrothed her to a prosperous pig farmer. Her father, miser that he was, refused to give her a dowry if she married the honorable but penniless miller she was in love with. Although the community wasn't exactly wealthy, people were so touched by the couple's obvious love for each other that they took matters into their own hands. They "showered" the bride with small, useful gifts, adding up to even more than her dowry would have been, so that she and her beloved could marry and set up house.

The bridal shower today has evolved from this endearing anecdote into a dreaded social obligation. For most women I know, shower invitations bring to mind not an exhilarating time of female bonding but a boring afternoon of unmitigated hokum. Your shower doesn't have to be a dud. Assuming that you can be perfectly honest with your maid of honor, you may suggest these alternative showers:

- **It's showtime:** Everyone chips in for a block of theater or concert tickets. After the show, you all descend on your favorite pub or coffee bar for a critique and dessert.

- **Jack & Jill:** Make the shower co-ed and center it around a group activity such as beach volleyball, softball, or touch football, followed by a cookout.

- **Movable feast:** The host rents a minivan to take everyone to a different restaurant for each course of a progressive dinner. People send presents ahead of time to your last stop, where the opening of the gifts is the finale.

According to tradition, the maid of honor throws the bride a shower. (The other attendants can chip in, but the bride should keep her nose out of such matters.) For a relative to host this party is way uncool; it looks as if your family is conspiring with you to amass booty. Consequently, if a relative such as your sister or mother is your maid of honor, someone else needs to throw the shower. (Your family may have other opportunities to host events closer to the wedding.)

The "ufruf" for Jewish couples

On the Saturday before the wedding, some Jewish communities have an *ufruf* or *aufruf* — a "calling up" for the groom. In synagogue, the groom is given the honor of being called up to read the blessings before and after the Torah (Hebrew Bible) readings. Many congregations have modernized their services to call up both the bride and groom. Afterward, the congregation sings a congratulatory song as they shower the couple with small packages of candy, nuts, and raisins.

Unless a surprise shower appeals to you, make it clear from the outset that you're not being coy — you really prefer not to be surprised. After the hostess tells you of her plans, be as helpful as possible, supplying a typed guest list with correct names, addresses, phone numbers, and e-mail addresses. If you're going to be "showered" more than once, cross-check the lists so you don't invite the same people — and consequently overburden them with buying too many gifts. You may also want to create a separate registry for your shower, as close friends often like to give brides highly personal gifts such as lingerie, books, music, and so on.

Unlike engagement parties, showers do call for gifts, so invitations should go only to people who are invited to the wedding. The exception is when people from your work, school, club, or some other part of your life throw a shower. In these cases, the groom may also be the guest of honor. In fact, many women who boycott girls-only showers are happy to attend co-ed ones.

Reinventing the bachelor party

Drink, my buddies, drink with discerning
Wedlock's a lane where there is no turning;
Never was owl more blind than lover;
Drink and be merry, lads; and think it over.

— Bachelor party toast

The original bachelor parties were thrown by a group of unmarried friends to give the poor soul about to be incarcerated a stipend of drinking money for the future, when his new wife would make him account for every cent. Before the party ended, they nonetheless offered a toast in honor of the bride, and they smashed their glasses so they'd never be used for a toast of less import.

The best man is now responsible for throwing the bachelor party (usually with the ushers), but the groom dictates the sort of event he feels comfortable attending. Clichés abound that you're supposed to take this one last shot at freedom to the extreme, making crude jokes about the female gender, playing air guitar in your skivvies, mooning passing cars, ogling strippers, swigging beer till you puke, or doing things your buddies may blackmail you with for the rest of your married life. Perhaps because women have made good on their threats to have equally raunchy bachelorette soirees or because many men today have reached a higher state of consciousness, this kind of primal exhibition has become less popular.

Men have other options with which to send off one of their own — options that can actually be more fun. You may even invite your father and future father-in-law to join the fun and chronicle a PG-rated episode of male bonding on video to show the grandchildren — and you don't have to hide any evidence or change any names to protect the innocent. Here are some possibilities:

✔ **Road trip:** Take a train or rent a minivan and drive to a nearby city for a weekend of museums, galleries, movies, rock concerts, and junk food.

✔ **Team trek:** Really take the plunge by jumping out of a plane together (take skydiving lessons the first day and a group dive the second day). Or go on a wilderness trek with an experienced guide over a long weekend. Or learn to cook a seven-course Chinese banquet, and then sit down to an extravagant table.

✔ **Tennis tourney:** Participants are "seeded" and trophies are awarded during dinner at a clubby restaurant.

Waiting until the night before your wedding to have a bachelor party is risky (unless you like the idea of getting married while utterly exhausted), but having your bash any earlier is a problem when ushers and other close friends are coming from out of town. An alternative is to have the bachelor party the day of the wedding — a softball game and barbecue, a golf outing ending with a club lunch, or a treasure hunt of the town, ending at a great brunch spot. These activities are also a terrific antidote to the groom's wedding day anxiety attacks.

Planning the bachelorette bash

In my opinion, bachelorette parties, where the main event is getting as wasted as possible in a stretch limo and stumbling into every joint that features male dancers, is as unattractive as the guy version. If you want to have a more intimate time with your very closest friends, other possibilities may leave you feeling much better:

✔ Take a weekend outing to a spa (even the spiffiest ones, such as Miraval in Catalina, Arizona, offer group rates).

✔ Visit a well-regarded psychic.

✔ Rent a slew of wedding videos such as *Father of the Bride* (both the original and the remake), *My Big Fat Greek Wedding*, *My Best Friend's Wedding*, *Four Weddings and a Funeral*, *The Wedding Singer*, *Bridesmaids*, or *Wedding Crashers* and have a movie marathon. If you and your besties want a little vampire romance before the big day, *The Twilight Saga: Breaking Dawn – Part 1* contains a truly gorgeous wedding scene.

✔ Have a pajama party, one of the most fun bonding experiences known to females.

Doing lunch with the girls

Brides often hold an intimate luncheon or tea to thank their attendants for their services. Inviting both your mother and the groom's, as well as a few close female relatives, is thoughtful. Holding this party the week before the wedding or on the afternoon of the wedding (if the ceremony and reception are in the evening) is usually the most convenient.

Whether you have this event at home or at a restaurant, you can go all-out on the table décor, as you have only one table to worry about. Myriad antique or pottery teapots paired with hand-painted cups and a few tiered cake stands filled with truffles, cookies, petit fours, and tea sandwiches — all served on a quilt or over lace — puts the group in a most divine, ladylike mood. Invitations may even ask the group to "Come to the Mad Hatter's Tea Party."

Revving up: The rehearsal dinner

Held a day or two before the wedding, the rehearsal dinner is more intimate than the actual wedding reception. As everyone is buzzing with anticipation, this meal can be an emotional tour de force, with both teary toasts to the memory of loved ones who are no longer living and slightly ribald anecdotes not suitable for more public consumption.

Take this opportunity to express your deepest gratitude and affection to anyone in the room who helped get you to this point. Thank your parents and family, and toast each *individual* in your wedding party. (See Chapter 5 for a few words about toasts.) Many couples present the attendants' gifts at this time and sometimes also give something to their parents. Sometimes the bride and groom present these gifts in tandem to make clear that the gifts are from both of them.

Showing a this-is-your-life video or slide show (that friends have put together) at the rehearsal dinner can make the whole evening, especially if the video includes secret interviews with your dry cleaner, personal trainer, parking garage attendant, grammar school teachers, and so on. You may also turn the idea around with a slide show of candid photos of family and friends taken over the years.

The guest list for the rehearsal or prenuptial dinner can be as complicated as that for the wedding. This gathering may be limited to just the wedding party and very close family members or it may comprise all the out-of-town guests. (See Chapter 6 for details on hosting out-of-town guests.)

Because the guest list — and the expense — for the rehearsal dinner can balloon out of proportion, and because you don't want this event to compete with the wedding itself, you may want to keep the rehearsal dinner very informal. The neighborhood Mexican, Chinese, or Italian joint can be an economical way to feed a lot of people in a festive atmosphere. The dinner may also be a simple barbecue or picnic.

If you have a number of guests staying in one hotel, you may be able to negotiate a better price there for both your rehearsal dinner and next-day brunch.

Offer such touches as personalized fortune cookies or chopsticks with your names and wedding date (both items made by novelty companies — shop around online). On another theme, napkin rings made of bread and a menu of exotic, colorful pastas can be festive.

In the past, if the bride's family picked up the tab for the wedding, the groom's family did so for the rehearsal dinner. Now the rehearsal dinner cost may be split, depending on the other financial arrangements, who is being invited, and whether you (or a friend) have arranged an alternative event for any out-of-town guests while you're with the wedding party and close family at the rehearsal dinner.

The invitations for this dinner may be straightforward or cute. Because many of the guests may not be rehearsing, you can invite them to a "prenuptial" dinner or ask them to "Celebrate with us the night before Beany and Cecil's wedding . . ." (see Chapter 5 for more info on invitations). Making the rehearsal dinner a bit funky can help loosen you up for the big day — consider sending beach party invitations in the shape of a large shell, tucking invitations to a Chinese dinner in colorful take-out containers, or wrapping an invitation for a barbecue around a can of baked beans and sending it in a padded envelope or box.

Don't think you have to close down the joint at your rehearsal dinner — everyone will understand if you bow out early to get a good night's sleep.

Wrapping up the day after

Often, if you have a large number of out-of-town guests catching planes or driving long distances home, a relative or friend may host a farewell breakfast or brunch the day after the wedding. These events are best planned as light buffets — breads, cheeses, fruits, juices, omelets, individual quiches, and the like. You can include the invitation with your main wedding invitation if the same guests are invited or you can simply call the guests. Because people are on different schedules (and you may drop by for only a short time, if at all), schedule these events over a few hours — "Drop in and have a bite 9:30–1:00," for example. Obviously, seating isn't assigned, and tables should be constantly cleared and reset.

Though feeding your guests before sending them on their way is gracious, a brunch isn't obligatory. After a destination wedding, when just about everyone may be in a hurry to get to the airport, you might offer your guests take-away box lunches in lieu of a sit-down meal. They're convenient and inexpensive. Just talk with your caterer or the hotel staff about providing these lunches for travelers (and see Chapter 6 for more on destination weddings).

Part III
Ceremony Survival Guide

The 5th Wave   By Rich Tennant

"I knew they were writing their own vows, but I expected quotes from Robert Frost poems, not the Geneva Convention."

In this part . . .

I delve into the heart of the wedding: the ceremony.
Besides giving you an overview of traditional rituals,
I provide ideas for personalizing your ceremony through
your selection of attendants, flowers, music, and readings.
This is where you concentrate on the reason you're doing
all this in the first place — to make a public commitment
to someone you love.

Chapter 9

Attending to Your Attendants

*T*he wedding starts in one hour. As the bride struggles into her petticoat, she puts the heel of her shoe through the lace and topples over. Lying there helplessly in a heap, she gazes up to see two sour-faced women with their arms crossed, glaring at each other. "When is someone coming to do my hair?" one of them wails. "Well," the other fumes, "if Muffy would get out of the bathroom I could at least pluck my eyebrows." The bride looks about for her maid of honor to act as referee. She's glued to the mirror in a fit of self-loathing. "I want to burn this dress," she snarls.

Across town in his apartment, the groom and his best man pace, looking at their watches. The doorbell rings; one of the ushers has arrived. "Sorry about the tux, man," he mutters as he sees the groom's eyes cross. "It looked really cool at the prom." As the other gentlemen arrive, one later than the next, a somewhat pathetic display of men's formal fashion parades across the living room. The best man is bewildered — he had, after all, painstakingly briefed the group on the proper uniform. Is this a case of subliminal sabotage or mere apathy?

Don't worry, you won't face this scenario, because in this chapter, I walk you through who to choose as attendants, how to choose them, and how to get the best out of your friends as they help you prepare for your wedding day.

Choosing Your Entourage

Your attendants may be your siblings, cousins, or best friends, but that doesn't automatically qualify them for wedding duty. To prevent major freak-outs, screen your attendants with care and, after you anoint them, brief them clearly but lovingly on your expectations.

When it comes to those who you want to honor in some way, but not as an attendant, be thoughtful. Asking someone to deliver a poem, sing a song, or be one of the chuppah pole bearers is truly an honor. But asking someone to hold the guest book, act as a host or hostess, hand out escort cards, double-check the seating chart, or perform some other "plum" assignment feels like busywork.

Understanding the job requirements

The average wedding in the United States has four bridesmaids and four groomsmen in addition to a maid of honor and best man. Unless you're choreographing your wedding to look like a halftime show, you don't need a cast of thousands fanning out from the altar. Many people have trouble narrowing down the field, feeling that if they ask one friend, they must ask another, and so on. Don't feel that because you were an usher or a bridesmaid at someone's wedding ten years ago, you need to reciprocate the honor. People understand that relationships change. In a seemingly impossible dilemma, here are some possible solutions: Ask your mother or father to be your best person, have your wedding party comprise only children (as done in England and France), or appoint only siblings.

As you decide how many and what kind of attendants to have in your wedding party, think through what you expect them to do. (To figure out where they all go in the processional, see Chapter 10.) Ideally, attendants perform duties to get the wedding off the ground and to keep *you* grounded.

- **Maid (or matron, if married) of honor:** Head cheerleader, sounding board, therapist, saint, gofer (on occasion), and actress, pretending to care about the marital minutiae as much as the bride does. May serve as a fashion consultant for the bride's and attendants' garb and as the schoolmarm, keeping other attendants in line. Responsible for subtly and gracefully getting the word out as to where the couple is registered. Sees to it that the bride is properly corseted, zipped, buttoned, powdered, and primped on her wedding day. May throw a wedding shower and/or dream up a special group gift for the bride (in addition to her own gift to the couple). May also spearhead the bachelorette party.

- **Best man:** A master at strong yet subtle emotional support because most men aren't skilled at asking for it. Telepathy is a good quality. So is punctuality: If the groom arrives late with a crooked tie, the best man takes the heat. Arranges the bachelor party. Selects a gift for the groom from all the ushers. (Also buys his own gift for the couple.) Oversees the ushers if there's no head usher, making sure they're appropriately dressed as well as gentlemanly. Holds the bride's ring at the ceremony. Quietly slips the fee into the clergyperson's hand after the ceremony. Signs the marriage license as a witness. Makes a stirring toast at the reception.

Maid to order

It used to be that if you had both a maid and a matron of honor, the maid took precedence, standing closer to you at the altar and handling more responsibilities. Now, however, if you have both, they may split up the job. For example, one may hold your bouquet, the other the ring.

Remember that not every married woman loves the connotations of the word *matron*. Many brides have dubbed their honor attendants "best woman" or "best person." Which brings me to another point: The person who stands up for you doesn't have to be the same sex as you. If you're a bride whose best friend is a guy, make him your best person. Likewise, if you're a groom whose best pal is a woman, appoint her to the job.

- **Bridesmaid:** Is the epitome of charm at wedding and prewedding events. May collaborate with the maid of honor and other bridesmaids in planning a shower and/or bachelorette party. Should make all complaints about the dress and its cost before purchase. May not apply lipstick at the altar. In theory, is on call for anything the bride needs, particularly in the realm of emotional support. In reality, may be too far out of the loop to be effective.

- **Groomsman or usher:** In most parts of the United States, the terms are interchangeable. Acts jovial and comedic but not raunchy at the bachelor party. Takes ushering duties seriously enough to refrain from downing scotches until after the wedding pictures are taken. Possesses a photographic memory, able to match names, or at least ceremony seat assignments, with faces he's met only once before. A human compass, escorting guests to their seats and directing them to parking lots, bathrooms, dining rooms, and so on. A good ratio is one usher per 50 guests. Two ushers unfurl the runner down the aisle right before the ceremony begins.

  In many areas, ushers and groomsmen have distinctly different roles. Ushers arrive 45 minutes before the ceremony, assist in seating guests, and then sit down before the ceremony begins. Groomsmen stay with the groom, much as the bridesmaids traditionally stay with the bride, and make their entrance as they walk down the aisle and take their places at the front of the ceremony.

- **Flower girl:** Looks adorable. Old enough to make it to the end of the aisle without Mommy or Daddy on their knees, pleading in a stage whisper for her to keep moving. Chosen because the couple is inordinately fond of her and/or her parents, not because she looks like a Ralph Lauren ad. Scatters petals or carries a basket, tussy mussy, or wreath (see Chapter 11 for floral details). Smiles sweetly all the way.

- ✔ **Ring bearer:** This role traditionally goes to an adorable young boy. Like the flower girl, must look precious but be mature enough to complete his journey down the aisle without bursting into tears or taking a detour in midprocession. Carries a pillow with rings (usually fake) tied on. Looks adorable in short pants with white socks and shoes, but can also wear long pants that coordinate with (but don't look like a doll-sized version of) the groomsmen's attire.

- ✔ **Junior bridesmaids and ushers:** The default category for youngsters (meaning anywhere between 7 and 15) who are no longer cute enough to serve as flower girls and ring bearers but not yet grown-up enough to be full-fledged attendants. Like their adult counterparts, they walk down the aisle and act charming. However, girls wear dresses that are similar to but less sophisticated than those of older bridesmaids, and boys wear tuxedos or suits.

Knowing what your friends expect of you

Just as the attendants exist to make your life easier, you must behave with all the grace and magnanimity toward them that you can muster during this anxious time. In the same way that you and your intended wisely chose each other for your wondrous points and in spite of the downsides, don't choose your attendants thinking you can change them. Remember that they're not indentured servants or workers for hire whom you can dismiss because they fail to love (or look stunning in) the mauve taffeta frock or lemon-yellow Nehru dinner jacket you've picked out for them. Compromising on an attendant's costume is just one example of gracious prewedding manner.

Next Stop: Wardrobe

The wedding clone concept dates back to fifth-century Britain, when bridesmaids and groomsmen, exhibiting amazing loyalty, dressed identically to the bride and groom to fool evil spirits that might harass the happy couple on their way to be joined. (Evil spirits being rather nearsighted, apparently.) Somehow, over 17 centuries, the original concept has become a little mixed up. Female attendants now dress to look like one another (yet not enough like the bride to fool even the dimmest evil spirit), and male attendants dress to approximate the groom.

"I thought you were paying for this"

When you ask people to be in your wedding, they're often flattered and honored — until they find out what it's going to cost. Admittedly, some tours of duty are more expensive than others, so be sensitive about asking those who can't afford to be an attendant or be prepared to defray (or pick up entirely) the cost for them. Whatever you decide, the time to explain the expenses and who's responsible for them is when you do the asking. The items that most often produce misunderstandings are

✔ **Appropriate clothing:** Traditionally, attendants are responsible for buying or renting their clothes, but sometimes you may buy a particular item as a gift, such as designer shoes for the bridesmaids or studs for the ushers. If your taste in attendants' garb runs to the extravagant, you must chip in or rent or purchase the clothes for them outright.

✔ **Bridesmaids' hair and makeup:** Clarify whether attendants are responsible for getting and/or paying for their own hair and makeup. If you do pay for any of it, set parameters so you don't end up paying for falls, false eyelashes, or other extra-charge items.

✔ **Local transportation:** You should provide transportation for attendants to the ceremony (and reception, if it's not in the same venue). If, as is common, bridesmaids get dressed in what will later be the honeymoon suite, they need to take their things with them when they leave for the reception. As for ushers, they don't usually get dressed together in the same place, so they get themselves to the ceremony site. If you want them to be at a certain place at a certain time — for photographs, for example, either before or after the ceremony — consider transporting them en masse. After the reception, transporting attendants to where they're staying isn't necessarily your responsibility, as often they neither leave at the same time nor are bound for the same destination.

✔ **Long-distance transportation:** Out-of-town weddings may require a serious financial investment by guests, but at least guests have the option of simply not attending. If your wedding party, however, is expected to pay for plane fare on top of all their other expenses, make sure that your relationship and their wallets can take it.

Bridesmaids' dresses: The honest truth

The budget approach to bridesmaids' dresses is to choose something that has little style, less workmanship, and is very cheap. At least no tears are shed when it disintegrates by the end of the reception. Your second choice — one that's increasingly easy to do — is to outfit your bridesmaids in something they'll feel good in at the wedding *and* may actually wear again afterward. A number of designers — such as Amsale (www.amsale.com), Monique Lhuillier (http://moniquelhuillier.com), and Jenny Yoo (www.jennyyoo.com) — create bridesmaids' dresses in elegant fabrics, trendy colors, and flattering styles. Famed bridal designer Vera Wang offers her White collection, including bridesmaids' styles, at David's Bridal (www.davidsbridal.com), and J. Crew (www.jcrew.com) features a wide selection of chic bridesmaids' dresses in cocktail length, as well as a few full-length styles. If you're feeling indie, the small New York line Sir, by Joanna Baum (www.sirbyjoannabaum.com), makes lovely deconstructed silk dresses to order in a wide range of colors. And if you or your attendants have a luxurious budget for your gowns, New York designer Morgane Le Fay (www.morganelefay.com) is a never-fail source of exquisite and unusual bridal party wear.

A vast array of smart suits, flirty dresses, and stylish gowns is available to choose from; the only excuse for choosing monstrosities in colors cooked up by the mad bridal scientists is pure mean-spiritedness. As a deterrent (or just for a hilarious planning break), take a look at www.uglydress.com, a deliciously hideous archive of the world's ugliest bridesmaid dresses.

Of course, finding a dress that looks good on several different women is another issue. Even if you manage to pull this one off, you can be sure that not all the women will be convinced that they look terrific. The effort you devote to this search depends on how desperately you want your attendants to look like a bridal *party*. Consider, more importantly, who these women are. If your friends are your friends because they're individualists, don't try to turn them into a matched set of septuplets. They'll feel uncomfortable and look it. Many bridesmaids' dresses now come in various styles of the same color and fabric so that your attendants can choose from among a few of these styles and still look like a bridal party. (J. Crew is particularly good for this.)

Another emerging trend that creates a unified look while letting bridesmaids be themselves is for the bride to choose a degree of formality (maybe cocktail, or evening gown) and a color palette (perhaps pale pastels, peacock colors, jewel tones, or shades of gray) and let attendants choose their own dresses. Brides can create a palette to guide their bridesmaids' choices the old-fashioned way, with a little collage of paper and fabric scraps, or they can use a smartphone application like the myPantone Wedding Styleboard, an iPhone app created in collaboration with bridesmaids' dress manufacturer Dessy.

Separates for bridesmaids have become popular in the same way they have for brides, and they're great for accommodating different body types. Bridesmaids may have matching skirts with different tops in the same color, for instance, giving the illusion of unique but coordinated dresses. Or the bride may choose a fresh and forgiving option such as a crisp, tailored white blouse paired with a ball gown skirt for her bridesmaids. (Check out French designer Anne Fontaine, at www.annefontaine.com, for an array of stunning blouses perfect for pairing with formal skirts.)

If you simply must have all your attendants in the same dress, keep it simple and choose a style that flatters the largest size among them. (See Figure 9-1 for silhouette ideas.)

If one of your dear friends is expecting, there's no reason she can't be a bridesmaid. Just take her dress-hunting first, as she'll be the hardest to fit. Go for softer, flowing materials that glide over — and can be let out to accommodate — an expanding tummy. And skip the stiletto sandals. Opt instead for a thick heel with plenty of support.

Figure 9-1:
Tweak a simple silhouette to suit the various shapes of your bridesmaids.

V-NECK   HIGH NECK   STRAPLESS   FULL-LENGTH BALLGOWN   ONE-SHOULDER

Illustration by Elizabeth Kurtzman

Outfitting the guys

The groom and his attendants are as much a part of this set piece as the bride and hers. Ushers should look and feel the epitome of debonair. A heavy wool tuxedo at a midafternoon garden wedding in August doesn't make you feel as crisp and confident as a navy jacket with off-white trousers may. This insight is common sense, but it's easy to get flummoxed in figuring out what *is* appropriate. However, rather than monopolizing valuable brain cells with decoding the difference between, say, informal daytime and semiformal afternoon, I suggest you choose something that makes you and your ushers feel comfortable, dashing, sexy, and in command — not like a band of woeful penguins stranded on an iceberg.

Nonetheless, ushers should be either nattily dressed to match one another or purposely diverse. You especially don't want three ushers who have, say, winged collars and plaid bow ties and one who has a lay-down collar and a black bow tie. The poor guy will look like central casting made a dreadful mistake. Asking groomsmen to wear their best dark suit will produce more cohesive results than a lineup of tuxedos from different eras.

Whether you go for a traditional or trendy look, you need to understand the elements of style at your disposal, as shown in Figure 9-2, and how to carry them off.

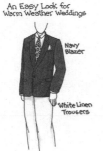

Figure 9-2:
Subtle differences in style convey vastly different moods and messages.

Illustration by Elizabeth Kurtzman

Suits and tuxedos

When it comes to suits and tuxedos, the fit is key. Place your arms at your sides, fingers extended. The hem of the jacket should be no longer than your middle finger. The sleeve should grace the top of your hand, and your shirt cuff should peek out from the jacket sleeve no more than half an inch. Your trousers, neither too narrow nor too full, should skim the heel of your shoes in back and break slightly over the tops of your shoes in front. Because the extra buttons on a double-breasted jacket draw the eye toward your midsection, that style looks best on someone who's tall and slender. To create a more debonair silhouette, consider having some extra padding put in the shoulders and the waist taken in a bit.

The options include

- **Cutaway or morning coat:** In its traditional design, this coat is for the most formal morning weddings. It's a novel experience in dressing up for men used to wearing jeans and T-shirts. Coats are black or gray, with a single button at the waist and one broad tail at back. These coats are worn with a winged-collared dress shirt, striped trousers, and ascot (or a patterned tie for a less formal look). If you're going all-out and — this is important — you can carry it off without looking like you're playing dress-up, add gloves, spats, and a top hat, and perhaps even a walking stick.

- **Dinner jacket:** These typically come in classic white or ivory or a subtle pattern of the same, with peaked lapels or a shawl collar. They work well in summer months, warm climates, afternoons, and evenings, and they're considered an appropriate substitute for a standard tuxedo. They're great for a casual wedding or a rehearsal dinner and look particularly swell with formal black trousers with a side satin stripe — think Humphrey Bogart in *Casablanca.* They're available for purchase or rent at a formalwear shop. (With some vigilance, you may unearth one in a vintage clothing boutique, but examine it carefully for stains, rips, missing buttons, and so on.) You may wear a white dinner jacket even if your ushers are in black tuxedo jackets. Some designers are showing white-on-white suits replete with vests.

- **The gorgeous dark suit:** This is for a dressy but not formal wedding or for the groom who absolutely won't wear a tuxedo. Choose charcoal, black, or navy and a solid-color or subtly patterned tie to dress it up.

- **Stroller coat:** This is a variation of the morning coat, usually hip length. It looks good with fancy waistcoats. Designers such as Kenzo and Christian Dior Paris have in recent years shown versions with a touch of whimsy.

- **Tails:** This jacket is short in front with two longer tails hanging in back. It's worn with braces and a white pique shirt, vest, and bow tie (as in "white tie and tails"). Very formal.

- **Traditional tuxedo or black tie:** The tux is usually worn after 6 p.m., but it can appear at a formal daytime wedding anytime after noon. A black or gray jacket with a single button is the most classic. It has shawl, peak, or notched lapels (see Figure 9-3 and the "Check the lapel" sidebar nearby). The jacket is worn with matching flat-front (or one-pleat) trousers, a bow tie (no clip-ons or glitzy colors), and suspenders, or vest. (A cummerbund is a traditional alternative to a vest here, but it has slipped out of fashion. If you decide to defy the trend, cover your waistband and remember that the pleats always face up.) For some of the elegance of tails without the full grandeur, you can wear a tux with a white vest and white tie.

✔ **Updated black tie:** The evening suit is a newer variation on the classic tux with the satin or grosgrain trim on the lapel and pants legs, albeit subtly. These tuxes are worn with a black shirt and a regular tie in lieu of a bow tie, and often with a belt rather than suspenders.

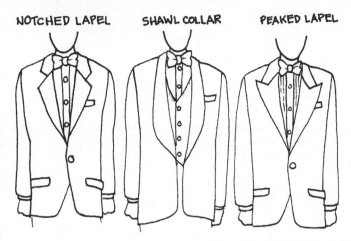

Figure 9-3:
Tuxedos come in several styles and are easily updated with different accessories.

Illustration by Elizabeth Kurtzman

Shirts

You probably haven't gotten this far in life without figuring out what kind of shirts you prefer. But if formalwear is an alien concept to you, you may find that one style of collar (or cuff) doesn't fit all. (See Figure 9-4 for examples of some of these styles.)

✔ **French cuffs:** Roll-back shirt cuffs fastened with cuff links. Spend some time shopping for interesting cuff links for both you and your ushers. Attention to this detail attests to your impeccable taste.

✔ **Mandarin collar:** Flashback to the Nehru jacket of the 1960s. High-necked band collar that has become fashionable for both shirts and jackets and looks good with high-neck vests.

✔ **Spread collar:** Dressy shirt collar with a high band that sits slightly up on the neck. Also called the English spread, as it was invented by the Duke of Kent and is still favored by Prince Charles.

✔ **Turndown collar:** This collar literally turns down, as on a regular business shirt, making it slightly less dressy but more comfortable than the winged collar (see the next bullet). These shirts often feature soft-pleated fronts and French cuffs.

✔ **Winged collar:** Very dressy. The collar band stands up, but the tips fold down. The front panels of a shirt with a winged collar may be pleated. Looks best on men with long, slender necks.

Check the lapel

One of the most important aspects of a jacket's cut is the lapel, especially with a boutonniere pinned to it. Here are the main choices:

✔ **Notch lapel:** This jacket lapel boasts V-shaped cuts pointing inward, where the collar and lapel meet the jacket. It accentuates the horizontal, so it's not a good choice if you're on the heavy side. Though traditionally considered to lend a "businesslike" effect to tuxedos, and thus seen as somewhat less classic, notch lapels are nonetheless having a trendy fashion-statement moment as of this writing.

✔ **Peaked lapel:** A jacket lapel that includes two points of fabric on either side that project upward, with narrow spacing between the lapel and collar. This is considered the most classic lapel choice.

✔ **Shawl collar:** A rounded jacket lapel (as in Figure 9-3) that rolls back in a continuous tapering line. Double-shawl collars roll to reveal satin lining. This looks very elegant trimmed with satin stripe or contrasting piping. It's a great choice whether you're tall and husky, short and stocky, or generally super buff and want to create a more vertical line.

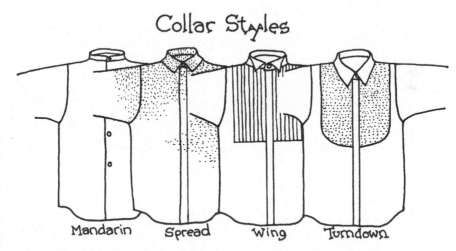

Collar Styles

Mandarin Spread Wing Turndown

Figure 9-4: Choose a collar that flatters your jacket and you.

Illustration by Elizabeth Kurtzman

Neckwear

What you wear around your neck to accessorize a suit or tuxedo can let your personality shine:

✔ **Ascot:** A neck scarf, usually secured with a stickpin. Looks pretentious in almost any other situation except at a formal morning wedding, where it's quite glamorous. Usually complements the gray-and-white stripe of the pants with a cutaway jacket, but may be of another pattern.

✔ **Bow tie:** Worn with tuxedos and dinner jackets. May be the ubiquitous black, but consider silver or an elegant, black-on-black damask. Should match the lapels on a tuxedo (satin with satin, grosgrain with grosgrain) and coordinate with, but not necessarily be identical to, the cummerbund or waistcoat. Hand-tied looks spiffiest, either bat-wing or butterfly style (see Figure 9-5 for instructions on tying the bat-wing). Leave shiny materials and garish colors for magicians. If you want to make a statement, though, larger bow ties are having a trendy moment thanks to the popularity of the talented designer Tom Ford and the very large bow ties in his collection.

✔ **Four-in-hand tie:** A clever term meant to confuse you. Very similar to an ordinary tie, just in a more-formal fabric. To ensure its characteristic fullness, tie it so you create a dimple or crease in the center, below the knot (see Figure 9-6). Silver dresses up a navy suit; a whimsical pattern makes it more casual.

TIP

I know that the thought of tying a bow tie can strike terror in the bravest of male hearts, but it really doesn't have to be so intimidating. Figure 9-5 illustrates the process, but for a live demonstration, just search for "bow tie tutorial" on YouTube.

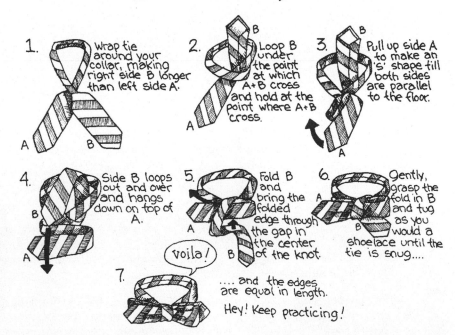

Figure 9-5:
After you learn to tie a bow tie, throw out all your clip-ons.

Illustration by Elizabeth Kurtzman

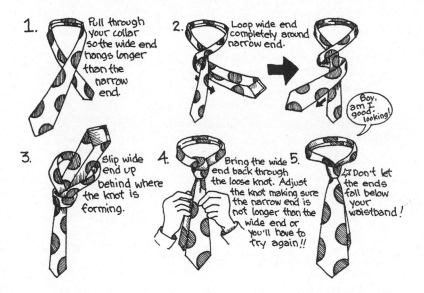

Illustration by Elizabeth Kurtzman

Figure 9-6:
Tying a
four-in-hand
knot comes
naturally
after a little
practice.

Accessories

Even if the groomsmen all wear different styles of tuxedos, they can create a coordinated, unified look through a single accessory in matching or similar fabrications:

- ✔ **Cummerbund:** A satin sash with pleats that face up. Worn in lieu of suspenders or a vest. Should coordinate with the bow tie.

- ✔ **Suspenders or braces:** Wear to avoid the homeboy groom look. Wearing a belt *and* suspenders together, however, makes you look insecure.

- ✔ **Waistcoat or vest:** A vest that covers the trouser waistband, which means that you don't need a cummerbund. May match or contrast with the jacket's fabric. Has become a fashion statement for men's formal-wear and is less constricting than a cummerbund. Designers such as Terence Teng are turning out custom and off-the-rack vests that are as beautiful as tapestries. In rich, colorful satin, white pique, luxurious brocade, or woven grosgrain ribbon, these creations are perfect gifts for ushers.

Make sure to get a vest with a back. Otherwise, if your jacket flaps open or the unheard-of happens (you actually remove it to dance), it won't be a pretty sight.

Footwear

No matter what kind of shoes you choose, they must be in excellent condition — no scuffs, worn heels, or mismatched laces. If you buy new shoes for the occasion, break them in by wearing them around the house a few times. Consider slipping on a pair of the following:

- **Hosiery:** No tube socks! If you buy only one pair of fine-gauge socks in your life, do it for your wedding day. However, do bring a slightly heavier pair as a backup if you plan to do a lot of dancing. And make sure that they're black if your suit or tuxedo is.

- **Patent pumps:** Low-cut slip-on shoes with a ribbed ribbon bow in front have traditionally gone with very formal attire. Many grooms are choosing to wear the more-comfortable plain-toe patent oxfords.

- **White bucks:** Also known as saddle shoes, these beautifully offset a navy or seersucker blazer with white pants. Shoes must be in excellent condition.

Making Mom look good

Traditionally, the bride's mother (hopefully in tandem with the bride) chooses the style and color of her outfit first and lets the groom's mother know what she's picked. The idea is that the groom's mother will then purchase something similar (not identical) in both color and degree of formality. Neither mother needs to match your attendants — they'll just look like ancient bridesmaids.

Although your mom may look a little over the hill to you, trust me, she feels young and wants to look pretty. Don't ruin her fun by dictating exactly what she has to wear or, worse, by forcing her into one of those age-making M.O.B. (mother-of-the-bride) dresses. Arguing because you have some strict vision of your day that allows for no variations is more trouble than it's worth. Remember, your mother may very well have been obsessing about this day far longer than you have.

Dapper dads

As with moms, I don't recommend costuming either the bride's or the groom's father in the exact same way as the ushers. They should wear something that reflects the same degree of formality as the other men in the wedding party, but otherwise let them choose what makes them feel comfortable.

Renting versus buying a tux

Buying a tuxedo or a good suit is always a better investment than renting a cheap tuxedo. Rented tuxedos unfortunately often look like rented tuxedos, as ill-fitting and uncomfortable as bad toupees. They're also not cheap, running between 25 and 50 percent of the purchase price of an average tuxedo. You'll get more wear out of a tuxedo that you own than you may think. Remember, also, that you'll be looking at these photos for the rest of your life.

If you're renting, don't spend the extra dough for the shoe option. Rental shoes by definition fit poorly and look worse. Shining up a pair of your own makes infinitely more sense. You're getting married, not going bowling.

Finding the right suit, tuxedo, and accessories can take as much time as locating the perfect wedding gown. If you're getting married in a popular wedding month and are planning on renting for yourself and/or the ushers, reserve the tuxedos as soon as possible so that you don't wind up with the dregs. Because you'll be on your honeymoon, have the best man return rented outfits the first working day after the wedding.

If you do rent, you can usually pick up the tux two or three days in advance. Check to make sure that all the buttons are on and secure and that the tux has no stains, cigarette burns, or other unattractive extras.

Showing Your Appreciation

So, enough about you. What are you going to do for all those selfless souls who've stood by you during the creation of your masterpiece and are now prepared to deliver a flawless performance at the wedding? You need to give them something that's both a memento of the wedding and personally meaningful to them.

The rehearsal dinner is an ideal time to present these gifts (although some people choose to do it at the bridal tea or luncheon or the bachelor's dinner). As you give each token of your appreciation, make a toast to the recipient.

Just because you're on a budget doesn't mean that you're stuck giving tie clips and fake pearls. Nor do you have to give each person the same thing. Here are some creative ways to say thank-you to your female attendants:

✔ Jeweled hair clips to wear at the wedding and to future festive occasions

✔ A charm bracelet with a starter charm chosen for each bridesmaid

✔ A lovely pashmina and/or a handbag to match their wedding attire

✔ Perhaps most appreciated, a gift of your attendants' dress or shoes

For the male attendants, some tried-and-true gifts include

✔ A set of monogrammed barware, such as tumblers or beer steins

- ✔ A leather dopp kit for traveling
- ✔ Monogrammed cuff links for their wedding tuxedos

You may also consider tokens of appreciation that aren't gender-specific:

- ✔ A silver picture frame inscribed with your names and wedding date. After the wedding, send a photo that fits the frame of the person walking down the aisle at your ceremony or otherwise enjoying herself at the reception.
- ✔ Antique glass, watches, or silver serving pieces wrapped with a hand-written card describing the item's provenance and vintage
- ✔ Monogrammed garment bags
- ✔ Monogrammed terry cloth robes

Search eBay for fun, meaningful, and often inexpensive mementos, such as souvenir postcards (and frames) of your hometown or wedding location, monogrammed jewelry or utensils, or goofy vintage books that fit each attendant's personality. Such gifts can include pulp fiction novels, arcane etiquette books, sports biographies, cookbooks, and so on.

Thank the little ones in your wedding party with gifts that are appropriate for their ages. Some possibilities are birthstone necklaces, initial key rings, binoculars, faux jeweled hair clips, or a portable MP3 player. A lovely gesture is to send their parents a framed photo of them during their grand entrance.

Show your parents how much you appreciate their support during the wedding-planning process by presenting them with something they'll enjoy. Theater tickets, a commissioned sketch of their home, or even arranging to have a bouquet of flowers with a note delivered while you're on your honeymoon are ways to show how grateful you are.

For your beloved

Among ancient Danish and Germanic tribes, husbands traditionally presented their new wives with a special piece of jewelry the morning after the wedding night as a symbol of their love. Today, many couples send something to each other just before the wedding or set aside time soon after the ceremony to give each other an especially meaningful and personal token of their affection. These gifts need not be extravagant; in fact, they may be as simple as a handsomely bound edition of love sonnets inscribed with a heartfelt message, a small keepsake box, or a watch, perhaps engraved with your wedding date. Perhaps the most moving gift is the least expensive: a letter for your beloved expressing your gratitude and your wishes for your married life.

Chapter 10

Sensational Ceremonies

· ·

· ·

*A*lthough the ceremony — the exchange of vows — is the most important part of your wedding, as you bury yourself in prenuptial minutiae, the ceremony could just slip through the cracks. If you and your intended are of the same faith and you belong to a house of worship, the tendency is to assume that everything will fall into place without much thought from you. True, religious ceremonies have a specific structure, but you still need to do your homework. That means investing a good deal of time in thought — deep thought — and soul-searching.

Understanding how you feel about Life's Big Questions prepares you for planning a ceremony that's meaningful to you and those around you. Even if your faith has a fairly set script, you may still need to consider the music, prewedding counseling with your officiant, and the personalization of your vows. If you're of different faiths, you may want an interfaith ceremony. If neither of you subscribes to any religion in particular, you may create a nonsectarian ceremony.

Selecting Your Officiant

Nonreligious ceremonies — called *civil ceremonies* — must be performed by a judge, justice of the peace, notary public, or court clerk who has legal authority to perform marriages. In certain circumstances, a judge or court clerk may give a person temporary authority to conduct a marriage ceremony. As of 1999, ship captains on Princess Cruises can marry couples at sea; Bermuda issues the marriage license and the United States recognizes it. To find out the specific requirements for officiants where you're getting married, check with the county clerk. Don't assume that someone who can legally officiate in one state is automatically able to officiate in another — that isn't the case.

In order for ceremonies to be recognized by a religion, a clergy member (priest, minister, or rabbi) must conduct them. In Native-American weddings, a tribal chief or another official, designated by the tribe, must do the honor. For marriages abroad, local (foreign) civil or religious officials almost always perform the ceremony, not American diplomatic and consular officers.

Evaluating prospective officiants

One of the best ways to see whether an officiant suits you is to see the person in action. If feasible, attend a wedding ceremony, mass, or other service presided over by this person.

Of course, if you want to have your ceremony in a specific house of worship, you may have very little choice as to who your officiant is and how he conducts the ceremony. As a matter of fact, asking too many questions at the beginning of your premarital meetings may be considered disrespectful, so do tread carefully.

If, however, you're interviewing officiants, the following is a list of possible questions:

- ✔ Would the officiant perform the ceremony in a venue other than a house of worship, if that is your preference?

- ✔ What is his fee, and when do you pay it?

- ✔ Does the officiant adhere to a particular ceremony script, and at what points may you include your own vows (if doing so is even allowed)?

- ✔ May you sign the marriage license *before* the ceremony for convenience?

- ✔ Does the officiant impose any restrictions on video cameras and/or flash photography?

- ✔ Will or can the officiant be present at the rehearsal?

You may be getting married by your family clergyperson. If, however, you hire a religious officiant not connected to a house of worship, make sure that you understand exactly what type of official backing your marriage will have. Ask to see the officiant's credentials for performing ceremonies of particular faiths, and call the organization with which he's affiliated to ask for references. Just because someone is licensed by the state to perform a ceremony doesn't mean that he's ordained by a religious body.

If you're having a secular, interfaith, or nondenominational ceremony, you may feel strongly about how the officiant alludes to God, spirituality, or specific religions. Be respectful, but go over these points very carefully to make sure you're comfortable with all religious aspects of the ceremony.

In any ceremony where two people officiate, only one may be the official signatory on the legal documents. Be clear about which one that is.

Choosing an officiant for a same-sex ceremony

In states that recognize marriage or civil unions for same-sex couples, any person who can legally perform a marriage ceremony can do so for a same-sex couple. States that don't permit legal homosexual unions usually have a network of celebrants who'll perform ceremonial marriages or commitment ceremonies. You can access them via word of mouth or through an online search (be sure to include your state in your search terms).

Having a *religious* same-sex ceremony is, of course, a bit more complicated. Many churches are unapologetically intolerant of same-sex marriage. The Southern Baptist, United Methodist, and Mormon churches, for example, forbid same-sex marriages to be conducted by their ministers or in their churches.

A handful of progressive Christian denominations, such as the Universal Fellowship of Metropolitan Community Churches (which was formed more than 40 years ago to address the needs of Christian gays and lesbians) and the United Church of Christ, officially support same-sex marriage. Other tolerant religious groups include Buddhists, pagans, Quakers, and the Reform and Reconstructionist movements within Judaism.

The Unitarian Universalist Church is also known for its inclusive policies. For more information, visit www.uua.org and access the Social Justice dropdown menu.

Still other religious groups are more variable in their support for same-sex unions. The Evangelical Lutheran Church in America leaves it to each congregation to determine whether it will permit same-sex ceremonies, and the Episcopal Church leaves the decision to each individual bishop. And some religious leaders perform same-sex weddings outside of church, even if their faith doesn't allow such ceremonies in their churches. Again, word of mouth and online searches are good sources for info.

Getting Married in a House of Worship

Having a ceremony in a church, temple, or synagogue entails adhering to the house rules. Make sure that you're clear on the following points. Usually the best (and most diplomatic) way to get answers to these questions is to ask a person at the church or synagogue office who's in charge of wedding ceremonies rather than asking your clergyperson.

- Do you have to use the house organist or other musicians, and if so, what are the fees? If not, must you pay a fee not to use them?
- What are the rules and recommendations for ceremony music?
- How long is the ceremony? What are the last words in it (to cue the musicians)?
- What are the rules regarding photography and videography?
- Are premarital programs mandatory? Must you attend weekly services in the months before your wedding?
- How many hours are scheduled between ceremonies?

Special situations call for special officiants

Perhaps trying to resolve religious differences between the two of you has become too complicated, or perhaps neither of you is religious. In either case, a civil ceremony may be appropriate. Check with your town clerk to find out who in your area is licensed by the state to perform civil ceremonies — judges, mayors, registered clergy, and so on. Although these ceremonies are essentially secular, some officiants allow you to incorporate some religious symbols.

You may want to have someone perform the ceremony who isn't officially licensed. States recognize the marriage only if someone else who's licensed by the state fills out the legal documents.

If you want an interfaith ceremony or simply a ceremony that's secular yet spiritual, try contacting the following organizations:

- **The Humanist Society** (www.humanist society.org): A subsidary of the American Humanist Association (www. americanhumanist.org), which promotes Humanism, an offshoot of Quakerism described as "a progressive life stance that, without supernaturalism, affirms our ability and responsibility to lead ethical lives of personal fulfillment that aspire to the greater good of humanity." A Humanist celebrant is analogous to a minister, clergyperson, pastor, priest, or rabbi. Counseling of a pastoral kind is often necessary for preparing a wedding.

- **The American Ethical Union** (www.aeu. org): Ethical Culture is a humanistic religious and educational movement inspired by the ideal that the supreme aim of human life is working to create a more humane society. This organization strives to make weddings "creative, respecting the individuality of each member of a couple as well as the ethical commitment of marriage."

✔ **Universal Life Church** (www.ulchq.org): Founded by Kirby B. Hensley in 1959, this church will ordain anyone, without question of faith, for free. Getting ordained requires only filling out a brief online application.

If you want a good friend or relative to perform your wedding, the more complicated part may involve getting this newly minted ULC minister registered as an officiant at your local marriage bureau. Rose Ministries (www.roseministries.org) and Spiritual Humanism (www.spiritualhumanism.org) also offer similar online ordination.

Deciding on the Order of Events

After you decide the tone or religious nature of your ceremony, you need to think about the sequence of the service. The *order of worship,* as it's also known, determines the spirit and flow. At different points you may have music for drama or scriptural readings for contemplation. You want to keep things moving apace without rushing, and you want each moment to reflect both the seriousness and joy of the occasion.

You may opt to follow the ceremony verbatim as prescribed by your house of worship. However, if you're crafting your own script or having an interfaith wedding, you may want to ad lib or edit the steps.

Most ceremonies incorporate some or all of the following elements:

✔ **Opening words:** Or what David Glusker and Peter Misner call "gathering words" in their excellent book, *Words for Your Wedding* (HarperCollins). The officiant usually speaks these words to welcome the participants, introduce the couple, and state the purpose of the gathering. Opening words set the tone of the ceremony and are formal yet cordial.

✔ **Opening prayers:** Also known as the *invocation,* these words further establish the tone and religious nature of the rites to follow.

✔ **Charge to the couple:** A reminder to the couple that they're taking a solemn vow before God and all witnesses gathered together.

✔ **Declaration of consent:** Words the bride and groom speak before taking their vows, ensuring that they're entering freely into the marriage contract.

✔ **Presentation of the bride:** The ritual of the father giving the bride to her betrothed. Because many people now object to the image of the bride being treated as property, this rite is sometimes modified to express support and affirmation of the union by family and friends.

- **Bible readings:** Scripture lessons are a significant part of the Judeo-Christian tradition. Christian ceremonies typically have three readings — one from the Old Testament, an epistle from the New Testament, and one from the Gospel.

- **Exchange of vows:** The most crucial part of the ceremony, these words express the covenant between two people.

- **Blessing and presentation of rings:** The ring is a physical reminder of the commitment between the bride and groom; they usually choose special words to express this sentiment.

- **Pronouncement or declaration:** The ceremony's climax — the moment when the officiant announces that the couple is officially married.

- **Wedding prayers:** After the bride and groom exchange vows, they ask for God's blessing in celebrating their marriage.

- **Affirmation of the community:** In Christian ceremonies, this part of the script affords the guests a chance to affirm that they'll help the couple uphold their vows. In a Jewish ceremony, this takes the form of the guests shouting "Mazel tov!" after the couple stomps on the wine glass.

Reviewing Religious Rites and Rules

Even devout members of their faith may not be familiar with the faith's specific wedding rituals, which in some cases can be quite involved. Delineating all the particulars of every religious and ethnic wedding tradition is beyond the scope of this book, but I do offer a cursory look at the major religious wedding customs.

Buddhist

Founded in southern Nepal in the sixth and fifth centuries BC, Buddhism is the predominant religion of Eastern and Central Asia, with more than 350 million followers. Buddhists study the teachings of Buddhism's founder, Siddhartha Gautama — known as Buddha, or Enlightened One — who achieved enlightenment *(nirvana)* through meditation and by practicing good and moral behavior. To reach nirvana, however, you must go through repeated lifetimes that are good or bad depending on your actions *(karma).*

Separate but equal

Sometimes, as a compromise or out of respect to the parents or grandparents, couples of different faiths have two separate services (as opposed to having two different clergy members at the same service). A two-ceremony wedding may be a small religious ceremony one day and a larger civil one the next, or perhaps two religious ceremonies within moments of each other at the same venue. For an excellent overview of various religions, from Asatru to Zoroastrianism, including insightful facts about interfaith marriages, check out the website of the Ontario Consultants on Religious Tolerance: www.religioustolerance.org.

Because Buddhism says that humans are flawed, individuals don't marry other individuals but rather make a pledge to the greater Truth, which is perfect and eternal. Ceremonies are simple, usually designed by the couple and based on Buddhist scriptures. Typically, the couple walks down the aisle carrying a string of 21 beads called *o juju.* The beads, which are like a rosary but shorter, represent the couple, their families, and Buddha. The couple uses *o juju* to offer prayers and incense to Buddha. A Buddhist monk blesses the nuptial union, and the couple says their vows. The couple then may share sake (considered by many to be a secular tradition) and, after a few more words from the monk, turn to thank their parents, offering hugs and flowers, thus completing the circle.

Buddhism has no official website, but www.buddhanet.net is a good place for more background, as is *Buddhism For Dummies,* by Jonathan Landaw, Stephan Bodian, and Gudrun Bühnemann (published by Wiley).

Eastern Orthodox

Eastern Orthodox Christians are allowed but not encouraged to marry non-Orthodox baptized Christians. The best man must be of Orthodox faith. Because the Church considers marriage a sacrament, the service must take place inside a church, preferably following the morning liturgy. No one may schedule a wedding during the Lenten season, the Advent and Epiphany seasons (November 28 through January 6), the fasting season that precedes both the Feast of Saints Peter and Paul (June) and the Feast of Dormition (August), and special one-day fast periods.

On the wedding day, the bride and groom approach the confessional and partake of the Sacrament of Penance and then Holy Communion to cleanse themselves of all sin. Orthodox Church members must receive communion on the Sunday before the marriage ceremony.

The bride and groom fast prior to the ceremony, which begins with the betrothal outside the church doors, where the priest blesses the rings before the bride and groom exchange them. (The rings go on the right hand, not the left.) The priest leads the couple into the church and onto a white cloth in front of the wedding platform. Someone in the processional carries a wedding icon, and the couple holds lighted candles throughout the service. The bride wears a veil during the ceremony and reception.

Whereas rings symbolize betrothal, crowns — made of metal or floral wreaths — symbolize the actual marriage. The crowning is the central moment of the service, signifying the formation of a new family unit and recalling the sacrifice of the martyrs. In lieu of Holy Communion, the couple drinks from the *common cup of joys and sorrows*. The bride and groom don't say their vows aloud. While wearing the crowns, they walk around a table or platform containing such holy things as the gospel book. As with other rituals, they perform this act three times to signify the Holy Trinity of the Father, Son, and Holy Spirit. When the couple completes their walk around the circle, the priest removes the crowns and gives the final blessing: "Be thou magnified, O bridegroom."

Hindu

All Hindu weddings are performed by a priest and considered a sacred trust, yet they vary greatly from region to region. Depending on geographic location, family customs, social class, and personal taste, weddings may last a few hours (often the case in North America) or several days. Hindus believe that many paths lead to the same summit, so intermarriage is less of a threat on religious grounds than a potential loss of cultural identity. The wedding rites are prescribed in the holy scripture known as the *Veda,* but ceremonies don't have to take place in a holy temple. The family and priest usually consult astrological charts for an auspicious date.

After invoking all the elements of nature and divine energies to witness and aid the proceedings, the priest sprinkles holy water and chants Sanskrit mantras to purify the bride and groom. The bride wears a traditional red and gold sari and lots of jewelry. The bride's parents may wash the groom's feet while he sits in a chair behind a cloth curtain, offering him gifts of bananas, coconuts, and so on — all the while earnestly asking him to accept their daughter in marriage. The auspicious moment occurs when the bride and groom affix a paste of cumin seeds and *jaggery* (an unrefined brown sugar made from palm sap) with their right palms to each other's head to symbolize their inseparableness. The groom accepts the bride as his wife by tying strings, a pendant, or a gold necklace around her neck. The couple places garlands on each other to show their adoration and showers rice on each other's head to symbolize prosperity.

The bride and groom then take seven steps (called *Saptapadi*) around a sacrificial fire to signify their vows. With each step they pray for different blessings such as wealth, happiness, devotion, and so on. At some point during the ceremony, the bride may stand on a stone to symbolize loyalty and faithfulness.

Hinduism doesn't have an official website, but try the Hindu Universe, `www.hindunet.org`, for more information.

Jewish

Four main divisions of Judaism exist: Orthodox and Conservative, which are very religious, and Reform and Reconstructionist, which can be far less stringent. An excellent resource for Jewish rites and culture is `www.myjewishlearning.com`, which has a brief but informative overview of marriage in the Judaic life cycle.

Who, when, and where

The officiant at a Jewish wedding is the one who *orders* the wedding because Jews believe they aren't married by someone but rather marry each other. The person who presides over the wedding may be a cantor, rabbi, community leader, or scholar. Consequently, a ceremony may be recognized by the state but not the religion or vice versa.

If both the bride and groom are Jewish and affiliated with a synagogue, getting married in that synagogue is no problem. Most rabbis are amenable to co-officiating with another rabbi — the other family's rabbi, for example. If, however, you aren't connected to any synagogue or religious organization, start your search for a rabbi by asking people you know for recommendations.

For Reform rabbis, you can also try the local office of the Union for Reform Judaism (`www.urj.org`). For Conservative rabbis, try the United Synagogue of Conservative Judaism (`www.uscj.org`). For rabbis and cantors who perform interfaith ceremonies, look in the back of local wedding magazines or in the Yellow Pages under *Religion,* or plug the keywords into your favorite search engine.

Finding a practicing rabbi to officiate at the marriage of a Jew and a non-Jew can be difficult. Orthodox and Conservative rabbis won't; Reform and Reconstructionist rabbis often will, depending on the individual circumstances. However, rabbis and cantors who are unaffiliated may preside for a large fee — perhaps even without meeting the couple beforehand.

Weddings may not take place on the Sabbath — from Friday sundown to Saturday sundown. On the Sabbath, work and travel are forbidden, and you may not have two celebrations (the Sabbath being one) at once. If you're planning a religious ceremony, check the dates carefully with your rabbi. Jewish weddings are forbidden on major holidays such as Rosh Hashanah, Yom Kippur, Passover, Shavuot, and Sukkot. Three weeks in July and August and the seven weeks between Passover and Shavuot (usually April and May) are also off-limits. When you set your date, check an almanac to find out the exact time the sun sets. Then find out whether your officiant will travel only after that time and at what time she'll perform a ceremony. Some rabbis insist on an hour and a half after sundown to be absolutely sure not to violate a tenet.

A Jewish ceremony may take place anywhere — and outdoor spots are very popular — but it must take place under a *chuppah* (huppah), or Jewish wedding canopy. The chuppah carries many symbols of ancestral Judaism. Because the Jews were nomads, their weddings historically took place outside under the stars to make the point that the couple should bear as many children as there are stars in the sky. Eventually, ceremonies took place under a tent to protect the couple's spirituality, and today the chuppah is imbued with a variety of meanings: the groom's home into which he brings the bride, a home filled with hospitality (open on all sides), and a metaphor for the groom covering or taking the bride. (See Chapter 11 for tips on constructing a chuppah.)

Before the wedding

In a traditional, religious Jewish ceremony, the groom entertains friends and relatives in a private room before the wedding. In days past, two Jewish adult males, unrelated to each other or to the bride and groom, witnessed and signed a plain document that served as the marital contract — the *ketubah*. Modern ketubahs are ornate and, depending on the rabbi, may be witnessed by both men and women friends. The groom later presents the ketubah to the bride under the chuppah, followed by the ceremony.

Often, the groom and his companions then go to the bride's room for the *bedeken* (the tradition of the groom veiling the bride). Even some very religious women, however, have rejected this ritual because they find it reminiscent of the Middle Eastern *purdah,* or heavy veiling of women.

During the wedding

Although the Jewish wedding processional has no official rules, it usually follows a traditional format, as shown in Figure 10-1. The rabbi and cantor (if you have one) lead the processional, followed by the bride's grandparents and the groom's grandparents, who take their seats in the first row. The right side is the bride's; the left is the groom's.

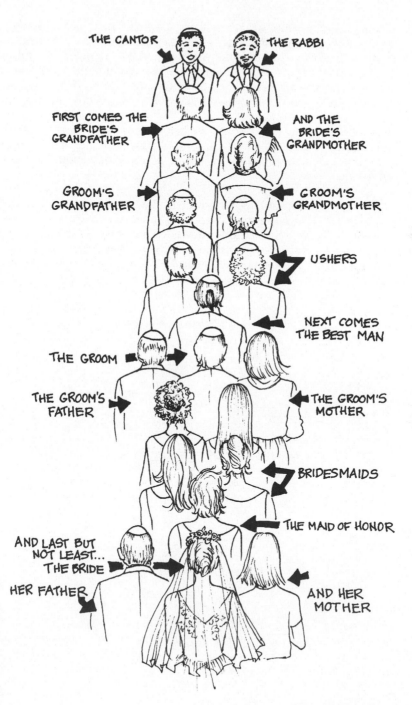

THE CANTOR

THE RABBI

FIRST COMES THE BRIDE'S GRANDFATHER

AND THE BRIDE'S GRANDMOTHER

GROOM'S GRANDFATHER

GROOM'S GRANDMOTHER

USHERS

NEXT COMES THE BEST MAN

THE GROOM

THE GROOM'S FATHER

THE GROOM'S MOTHER

BRIDESMAIDS

THE MAID OF HONOR

AND LAST BUT NOT LEAST... THE BRIDE

HER FATHER

AND HER MOTHER

Figure 10-1: The traditional Jewish wedding processional.

Illustration by Elizabeth Kurtzman

The cantor sings, and guests may sing as well. The music should be upbeat but stately. The wedding party follows in this order: ushers; best man; groom with his parents, who take their places on the left side of the chuppah; bridesmaids, either coupled or single file; maid of honor; and finally the bride and her parents, who take their places on the right. (For tips on pacing the group, see "Places, Everyone — Time to Rehearse," later in this chapter.)

The groom usually approaches the bride before she reaches the chuppah and escorts her to the chuppah, symbolizing his bringing her into his house. Figure 10-2 depicts the basic formation of a Jewish wedding under the chuppah.

Depending on your adherence to Jewish law, you may decide to incorporate some or all of the ceremony's religious aspects. One ritual that's enacted almost exclusively by Orthodox Jews, for example, may seem intrinsically mystical or unbearably sexist, depending on your beliefs: The bride circles around the groom seven times, as if she's enveloping him in the train of her gown. Then she takes her place at his right.

Figure 10-2:
The formation of a Jewish wedding under the chuppah.

Illustration by Elizabeth Kurtzman

More than a piece of paper

The *ketubah,* the Jewish marital contract, may be a plain scroll but more often is a richly painted ("illuminated") Hebrew and English manuscript that an officiant reads during the ceremony and that's kept on display during the reception. Many couples hang their framed ketubah in their home. Some Judaica stores sell premade ketubahs on which you fill in your names. Most synagogues keep a list of ketubah makers who can customize one for you.

After everyone is under the chuppah, the rabbi welcomes the guests, including the bride and groom, and asks for God's blessings. The ceremony begins with the blessing over the wine, of which the bride and groom take sips. Either the bride's mother or a friend has the honor of taking up the bride's veil. The centerpiece of the ceremony is the giving of the ring. The groom places the ring — which should be solid, with no stones, so the bride isn't deceived about its value — on the bride's right index finger. (She later moves it to whichever finger she wants.) The rabbi reads the ketubah aloud, and the groom presents it to the bride (as it is her property), who hands it to an attendant or her parents for safekeeping. The rabbi makes a short speech about the couple, who then may add poems, prayers, or personal words.

The next part begins with another wine blessing. The couple drinks either from a second cup or from the first. (Some couples now bring two kiddush cups, one to symbolize the past and relatives who've died and the other to symbolize the future.) The *sheva b'rachot,* or seven blessings, comes next. The officiant then pronounces the bride and groom legally married and may add a benediction to conclude the service.

The most familiar part of the Jewish ceremony, the breaking of the glass, is next. The groom historically stomps on the glass, but some couples now break it together. This ritual has been interpreted many ways — a reminder of the destruction of the temple, the fragility of marriage, and the intensity of the sexual union.

At a religious wedding, the couple then goes to *yichud,* a private room to convene in for 15 or 20 minutes after the emotion of the ceremony. The caterer often places champagne and hors d'oeuvres in this room for the bride and groom to enjoy before they go out and face their guests. The concept of *yichud* is so appealing that couples of many faiths have adopted it.

If you were married in a religious ceremony, to remarry in a Jewish ceremony you must have a *get,* or religious divorce.

Mormon

Mormons — members of the Church of Jesus Christ of Latter-Day Saints (www.lds.org) — have two kinds of ceremonies. The *temple ceremony,* which takes place in one of 44 Mormon temples around the world, is reserved for active, worthy Church members. The couple, dressed in white, kneels before the altar and is "sealed" together for eternity. The ceremony is considered so sacred that members aren't allowed to divulge many details about it to outsiders. If you aren't a Mormon in the highest standing, you won't be invited to the temple ceremony — guests are usually invited only to the reception.

The other ceremony, the *chapel ceremony,* is far less restricted, but couples are considered married only until death, as opposed to eternity. Many couples have this ceremony first and then eternally seal the marriage in the temple version later — but only if they're both Mormon. A Mormon may marry a non-Mormon only in a civil ceremony. The chapel ceremony is also considered sacred and isn't discussed with outsiders.

Muslim

In Islam, the woman makes the offer of marriage, usually through her father or another male relative. This arrangement is supposed to guarantee that both partners come to the marriage of their own free will. After accepting the proposal, the groom gives the bride a *mahr,* or gift, such as property, jewelry, or even education. (Muslim women must marry Muslim men; however, Muslim men may marry non-Muslim women as long as they raise their children Muslim.)

Although marriage is one of the most desirable states for Muslims, the ceremony is simple and takes only about five minutes. The bride and groom are typically in separate rooms, usually in an office as opposed to a mosque, while the *wali,* the bride's representative, answers questions posed by a religious sheik (an Islamic magistrate). The groom answers for himself as three male witnesses stand by. When the sheik is satisfied that the groom has provided a suitable mahr, they sign the papers, and the couple is pronounced man and wife. A week or two later, the couple has a public celebration with a series of parties and rituals, which the groom and his family pay for.

As with many religions, Islam has no official website. However, at Al-Islam (www.al-islam.org) you can read up on Islamic marriage, among other topics, and the website www.islamicity.com has a mosque locator that helps you find a mosque near you.

Lighting a few candles

Mystical and awe-inspiring, candlelight ceremonies can take place in late afternoon or early evening.

Unity candles usually consist of three candles at the altar. The bride and groom take the outer two, which are lit, and together light the center one to symbolize the joining of two hearts and their shared commitment to the marriage. Other guests may also be given candles, and the couple walks down the aisle, stopping at each row to light the nearest candle, which in turn is used to light the next and so on. In other cases, only parents or other family members join in the candle lighting. The unity candles may also symbolize the joining of the couple in Jesus Christ. The two take the outside lit candles, symbolizing their uniqueness and being single, and light the middle candle to form a union with each other and with Christ.

African-American couples who marry between December 26 and January 1 are lucky to have the drama of the seven candles of Kwanzaa as an option for their ceremony. The candles comprise three red, one black, and three green. The bride and groom start at opposite ends, working their way toward the middle, noting the principle that each candle represents: *umoja* (unity), *ujamaa* (cooperative economics), *ujima* (collective work and responsibility), *kujichagulia* (self-determination), *nia* (purpose), *kuumba* (creativity), and *imani* (faith).

Protestant

The Episcopal Church is the most successful U.S. offshoot of the Church of England, or Anglican Church, with 2.7 million members. Protestantism also has several other major denominations, as well as hundreds of small, independent denominations in local communities.

 Just about every Protestant denomination has an official Church news and doctrine, including the Presbyterian Church (USA) (www.pcusa.org); the United Pentecostal Church International (www.upci.org); the United Methodist Church (www.umc.org); the African Methodist Episcopal Church (www.ame-church.com); the Lutheran Church — Missouri Synod (www.lcms.org); the Evangelical Lutheran Church in America (www.elca.org); and the progressive United Church of Christ (www.ucc.org).

Episcopal denomination

The Episcopal Church views marriage as a sacrament (check out *Christianity For Dummies,* by Richard Wagner, published by Wiley, for the lowdown on sacraments) and says it must take place in a chapel unless the local bishop grants a special exception. *The Book of Common Prayer* (first ratified in 1789) prescribes the marriage ceremony, which may or may not include Holy Communion.

The ceremony is fairly traditional. The bride's father walks her down the aisle. As the procession enters, a hymn, psalm, or anthem is sung or played. The celebrant (who may be a priest, bishop, or, in some communities, a deacon) makes some introductory remarks, beginning with the familiar, "Dearly beloved: We have come together. . . ." A *declaration of consent* follows, which means that the celebrant asks the bride and groom whether they'll have each other in marriage. They reply "I will," and the celebrant asks the congregation whether they'll "uphold these two persons in their marriage." Assuming they all say "We will," a song follows. Next is the *ministry of the word* — a reading from the Holy Scripture. If the wedding includes Holy Communion, a passage from the Gospel concludes the readings. A homily or other response to the readings may follow.

The couple exchanges vows, and the celebrant blesses the rings. After one or more prayers, the celebrant blesses the marriage as the husband and wife kneel.

The peace follows, with the celebrant saying, "The peace of the Lord be always with you." The congregation says, "And also with you," the cue for the newlyweds to greet each other and for greetings to be exchanged throughout the congregation. If Holy Communion follows, the couple may present the offerings of bread and wine and receive the elements first, after the ministers. When both a bishop and a priest are present and officiating, the bishop pronounces the blessing and presides during communion.

Other mainstream denominations

Baptist, Lutheran, Methodist, and Presbyterian denominations consider marriage a holy and desirable union but not a sacrament. Congregations vary in the degree to which they allow you to personalize the ceremony, although almost all allow you to get married outside of a house of worship. Their ceremonies all use biblical passages, involve an exchange of vows and rings, and include a blessing by the celebrant.

Thanks to TV and the movies, most people are familiar with the Protestant ceremony. Indeed, all Protestant weddings include a traditional processional, as depicted in Figure 10-3, and a recessional.

Although Figures 10-1 and 10-3 show ushers paired with ushers and bridesmaids paired with bridesmaids, you may want to pair them as male-female couples for the processional or have them walk to the altar individually and recess in pairs.

Before the processional begins, the bride's mother is the last person to be seated. She usually takes the first seat nearest the aisle, in the first row, leaving an empty seat next to her for the bride's father. If the parents are divorced, the father (and his new significant other, if he has one) sits in the row behind the bride's mother, who sits with her new significant other, if she has one.

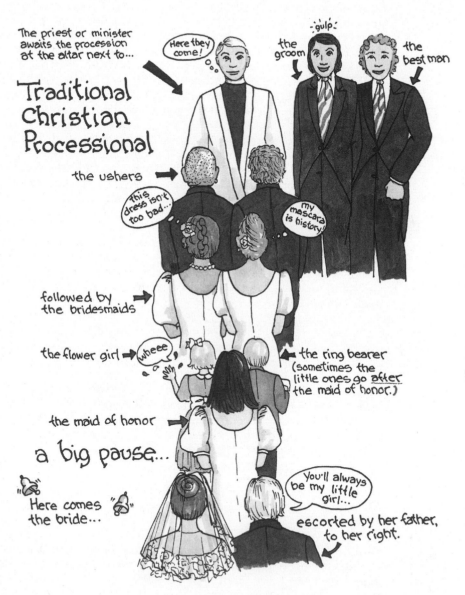

Figure 10-3:
The classic Christian processional.

After the rest of the wedding party is standing in place at the altar, they all turn to face the bride, who starts her walk after a sufficiently dramatic pause.

Before walking down the aisle, the bride should transfer her engagement ring to her right hand, because most people find wearing a wedding ring outside of an engagement ring awkward.

As the bride nears the altar, her father lifts the veil, kisses her, and puts the veil back down. The celebrant asks something like, "Who gives this woman to be married?" to which the father (or whoever is giving away the bride) replies, "I do." (Sometimes both the mother and father say, "We do.") The father may hug or shake hands with the groom before sitting down. The groom offers his left arm, and the bride adjusts her bouquet to accept his arm.

Many couples who believe that the presentation of the bride is patronizing are omitting it from their ceremonies. The celebrant, in that case, never asks, "Who gives this woman to be married?" Therefore, the father sits down after replacing the bride's veil (and greeting the groom). Another variation is to have the bride walk alone or to borrow from the Jewish tradition of both parents escorting her down the aisle.

The bridesmaids and ushers, who fan out from the altar at an angle (see Figure 10-4), should pivot slightly, so they face the bride but don't turn their backs completely to the audience. If you choose to have a flower girl and ring bearer and they're bound to squirm through the ceremony, you may have them sit in the front row.

Mainstream Protestant ceremonies may last only a few minutes, depending on the number of readings and songs. In many ways they're similar to Episcopal ceremonies, with prayers, hymns, and readings.

As soon as the ceremony ends, the recessional music starts. The bride and groom are the first to go down the aisle, followed by the maid of honor and best man. (In some cases, the flower girl and ring bearer follow the bride and groom, but it depends on whether they're old enough to recognize their cue to get back in formation.) The bridesmaids and ushers follow. Next come the bride's parents, and then the groom's.

Quaker

Given their disdain for sacraments and rituals, *Quakers* — members of the Religious Society of Friends (www.quaker.org) — marry in perhaps the simplest fashion. To be married in a meetinghouse, the couple must apply to the Committee for Ministry and Counsel, which generally meets once a month and in turn appoints a *clearance committee* that interviews the couple to determine the clarity of their intention. This process can take a couple of months. The church has no clergy per se; after the committee approves the intended union and appoints overseers to make the wedding arrangements, for the most part, the bride and groom act as their own ministers.

Figure 10-4:
Typical
wedding
party
position
during the
ceremony.

Illustration by Elizabeth Kurtzman

As with a typical Friends meeting, a wedding is characterized by quiet meditation. At some point, when the bride and groom are ready, they stand and make their vows to each other. They then exchange rings and sign a Quaker wedding license. A close friend or relative may read the certificate aloud before the group settles back into silent worship. During this time, guests may rise and speak if moved to do so. Inevitably, many warm and heartfelt messages come pouring forth.

Many non-Quaker couples choose to get a Quaker wedding license, which states in effect that the two people are marrying themselves. You can get the license regardless of whether you have an actual Quaker wedding. You need only to have two witnesses sign the document to make your marriage legal.

Roman Catholic

Marriage is one of the seven sacraments, so if two Catholics are getting married, the wedding must take place in a Catholic church for the marriage to be sanctified. Only the vicar general's office, in any diocese, can grant permission to wed outside of a chapel.

You must provide several documents to prove that you're free to marry in the Catholic Church:

- ✔ **Baptismal certificate**
- ✔ **Letter of freedom** stating that you've never contracted marriage, either civilly or in a church service
- ✔ **Letter of permission** from your parents if you're under 21
- ✔ **Premarital investigation** — actually, just a data sheet, which you fill out during an informal interview with your priest
- ✔ **Publication of *banns*** (the publication or public announcement of the engaged couple's intention to marry), usually read at Mass on three consecutive Sundays before the wedding

Ordinarily, the marriage takes place in the bride's parish, so the groom must get a letter of notification from his parish that his banns will be announced three times. If you aren't a member of a particular parish, speak to the pastor regarding the canonical rule and a dispensation.

You must set the marriage date at least six months, and in some parishes as much as a year, in advance. In the intervening months, you must undergo *pre-Cana* (a Catholic course in marriage). Many parishes offer pre-Cana programs through intensive weekend workshops, which cover such topics as self-awareness, human sexuality, communicating, decision making, natural family planning, sacraments, and so on.

The liturgical celebration is fairly set, although you may — with the priest's approval — amend the vows set forth by the Church, choose to light a wedding candle (see the sidebar "Lighting a few candles," earlier in this chapter), and offer your own prayer or petition of thanks. Before the recessional, the bride may also place a bouquet on the Blessed Virgin Mary's shrine or statue.

Couples may have a ceremony without a Mass or a ceremony incorporated into a Mass (called a *Nuptial Mass*). They may enter the ceremony with a traditional processional (refer to Figure 10-3) or the priest and his assistants may welcome the bride and groom and their families at the door of the church, before they all proceed to the sanctuary. During the ceremony, the bride and groom remain in front of the altar. Throughout the ceremony, they may have to kneel, stand, or sit.

The priest recites an opening prayer (usually of the couple's choosing), followed by readings, including a Gospel passage. The couple exchanges vows and rings, which the priest blesses. If the ceremony takes place outside a Mass, the ceremony concludes with the priest saying another prayer and the Nuptial blessing.

In the case of a Nuptial Mass, the service continues with the priest calling for the sign of peace, in which people turn and shake hands with their neighbors, saying, "Peace be with you," or something similar. A member of the couple's family may then present a gift of bread and wine for Holy Communion to commemorate Christ's Last Supper. The priest consecrates the bread and wine, and the couple takes them as the body and blood of Christ. After Communion, the priest says the concluding prayer and nuptial blessing.

If you plan to have a Catholic ceremony abroad, you may need a letter from your parish priest confirming that you've been through pre-Cana counseling and requesting that the wedding be performed in another church. If you want the wedding outdoors or in a secular setting, you need a special dispensation.

When it comes to interfaith marriages, a Catholic can get a dispensation to marry a baptized non-Catholic or an unbaptized partner, with very specific guidelines. A Catholic can also get a *dispensation from* form to marry in a non-Catholic ceremony. Your partner's minister or rabbi may assist at the wedding by reading a Scripture passage, saying a prayer or a few words, or giving a blessing. Only a priest or deacon, however, may perform the actual ceremony if you're getting married in a Catholic church. Most parishes don't publish the banns for an interfaith marriage unless you request it.

You can find more information about Catholicism at www.catholic.net. This site provides access to leading Catholic magazines and newspapers, papal encyclicals, Church documents, and devotional services in a streamlined format. All content is in accord with the teachings of the Pope and the living magisterium of the Church. You can also check out *Catholicism For Dummies,* by Rev. John Trigilio, Jr., and Rev. Kenneth Brighenti (Wiley).

Shinto

A traditional Shinto-style ceremony is small and rather private, comprising the immediate families, the *nakoudo* (the matchmakers who arranged for the couple to meet), and the priest. The bride wears a white kimono with a fancy headpiece, and the groom wears a black kimono with a striped *hakama* (shirt-like pants) and a black jacket. Before the couple enters, the priest cleanses and blesses the four corners of the room. The couple sits or kneels on rice paper, which covers the floor, as the priest recites Shinto prayers. If the ceremony takes place in a Shinto shrine, imperial Japanese music may play.

Many wedding ceremonies incorporate traditions from both Shintoism and Buddhism. For example, the *sansankudo,* where the bride and groom share sips of *sake* (rice wine), is a Shinto rite that's a part of many Japanese-American Buddhist ceremonies.

See the "Buddhist" section earlier in this chapter and, for information about Shinto practices, check out the Shinto Online Network Association at `http://jinja.jp/english/`.

Sikh

The day before a Sikh wedding, the bride's legs and hands are painted with henna designs. The next morning, her female relatives adorn her with jewels and makeup, and she dons an elaborate traditional sari in red, pink, or white. Whether or not the ceremony is held in a Sikh temple, called a *guardwara,* it takes place in the morning, which is considered the happy time of day.

Before the ceremony begins, the bride's parents welcome the groom and his parents, garlanding them with flowers. The bride enters and garlands the groom with more flowers, and he returns the gesture by garlanding her. Professional singers called *raagis* perform as guests enter and sit around a central platform, upon which the holy book, *Guru Granth Sahib Ji,* is displayed.

The couple sits before the man (a *granthi* or *pathi*) who reads the holy book. Depending on the family's tradition, either the mother or father hands one end of a pink sash to the groom (sometimes placing it on his shoulder) and the other end to the bride. Verses recited from the *Granth* explain the couple's duties in married life. One of the parents, the priest, or the groom may tie the sash to the bride's headpiece — literally tying the knot and symbolizing the bond that joins the couple.

The couple exchanges vows and then walks around the holy book four times *(lavaans),* the husband leading, to signify their journey together. After each circle, the bride and groom kneel and bow toward the *Granth.* The pathi may address the parents and grandparents regarding their roles in supporting the couple. The *raagis* usually sing a concluding song as the bride and groom exchange a sweet food called a *karah parshad.*

This whole ceremony takes about an hour and a half. When it's over, guests greet the couple, placing a hand on their heads, garlanding them with flowers, throwing petals, and often putting a token amount of money into the pink cloth, which the bride and groom still hold.

Two websites offer significant information on the world's fifth largest religion: The Sikhism home page (`www.sikhs.org`) provides an introduction to philosophy and scriptures, and the Sikh Network (`www.sikhnet.com`) offers extensive information for the Sikh community.

Unitarian Universalist Society

By definition, Unitarian Universalists are *noncreedal,* meaning each congregation determines its own affairs and operates within local custom. Though its roots are Judeo-Christian, the religion isn't Christian but rather pluralistic. Believers view marriage as a holy union but not a sacrament. Couples create their own ceremony out of religious and humanistic traditions that are meaningful to them. Consequently, the society has been a haven for interfaith marriages since its founding in 1961. To find out more, visit the Unitarian Universalist Association of Congregations online at www.uua.org.

All Together, Vow!

Besides having an officiant declare you legally married, the other key moment of your ceremony is the taking of vows. There's a lot to be said for the power of history. Many religious services are thousands of years old. Reciting the words that have bound together countless generations before you can give you a feeling of strength and connectivity. You may feel that altering those words diminishes their meaning or insults your forebears. If so, stick with your religious protocol and you'll be happy.

However, couples are increasingly personalizing standard ceremony rituals by cobbling together elements from various religious, ethnic, and cultural traditions and by not only writing their vows but also scripting the entire ceremony.

You may feel that conventional vows fall short in expressing what's truly in your heart. And yet, when you try to articulate the numbing joy you feel about your beloved and the great unknowable before you, the words seem banal, lifeless, trite. What can you say that hasn't been said before? After all, haven't poets been writing about love for eons? Yes, but that doesn't mean you can't give it a whirl. Even if the words are already out there, they haven't been said by *you.*

Creating the script

Whether you create your own vows or simply look for ways to personalize your ceremony, consider these ideas:

- ✔ Start by making a list of all the words that describe your spouse to be, reasons you fell in love with this person, and your hopes for the future.

- ✔ Keep a notebook or journal for jotting down bits of poetry, song lyrics, or movie scenes that strike a chord in you or that have been floating around in your subconscious for ages.

- As obvious as it may seem, look up topics such as love, passion, and marriage in encyclopedias, books of quotations, dictionaries, and on the Internet. Seeing these ideas distilled to their basic concepts may spark your creativity.

- Dig for unusual sonnets, poems, songs, and the like. Really listen to the words. Might a particular piece or a few lines work in your ceremony?

- You may want to briefly acknowledge family and friends, thanking God (or whomever) for the dearly departed who were important to you or saying prayers for the good health of elderly relatives.

- Include your children if you have any, or nieces and nephews. This may be the grandest day of their lives, too (at least for a while). And they'll be around longer than anyone else to keep your wedding-day memories alive.

- Incorporate a ritual or poem from your ethnic heritage or from one you admire.

- As you start putting together your thoughts, keep your vows upbeat and positive. Avoid anything maudlin.

- Remember that you want to create a dialogue, not two monologues.

- Pay quiet tribute to deceased family members through certain flowers, musical selections, or a few simple words of acknowledgment.

Remember, if you're getting married in a church or synagogue, you probably won't have much leeway as to the creation of your own vows. If, however, you're allowed some creativity, make sure that your officiant approves whatever you're planning to avoid inadvertently including anything disrespectful or offensive.

Before you get too creative, keep in mind that although acknowledging the folly of life or the human comedy is fine, this moment is still solemn. In years to come, you want to remember fondly what you said to each other at the altar, not cringe in embarrassment. When in doubt, crib from the standard vows uttered by countless couples through the ages:

- ***The Book of Common Prayer:*** I, [name], take thee, [name], to be my wedded [husband/wife], to have and to hold from this day forward, for better, for worse, for richer, for poorer, in sickness and in health, to love and to cherish, till death do us part, according to God's holy ordinance; and thereto I plight thee my faith.

- **Roman Catholic:** I, [name], take you, [name], to be my [husband/wife]. I promise to be true to you in good times and in bad, in sickness and in health. I will love you and honor you all the days of my life.

✔ **Civil:** I, [name], take you, [name], to be my lawfully wedded [husband/wife]. Before these witnesses, I promise to love you and care for you as long as we both shall live. I accept you with your faults and strengths, even as I offer myself to you with my faults and strengths. I will support you when you need support and turn to you when I need support. I choose you as the person with whom I will spend my life.

✔ **Muslim:** I pledge, in honesty and sincerity, to be for you an obedient and faithful [husband/wife].

Technically, Jewish wedding liturgy doesn't include vows. However, in deference to the American tradition of saying "I do," many rabbis have added commitment vows after the ring ceremony.

Contemporary vows have as many variations on the theme as there are married couples. The language ranges from the prosaic to the mystical. You can find many sources for vows in a number of books and Internet sites devoted to the subject. Here are a few examples to get your inspirational juices flowing:

✔ Our miracle lies in the path we have chosen together. I, [name], enter into this marriage with our knowing that the true magic of love is not to avoid changes but to navigate them successfully. Let us commit to the miracle of making each day work, together.

✔ Respecting each other, we commit to live our lives together for all the days to come. I, [name], ask you to share this world with me, for good and ill. Be my partner, and I will be yours.

✔ Today we move from "I" to "we." [Name], take this ring as a symbol of my decision to join my life with yours until death should part us. I walked to this place to meet you today; we shall walk from it together.

✔ Today, I, [name], join my life to yours, not merely as your [husband/wife], but as your friend, your lover, and your confidant. Let me be the shoulder you lean on, the rock on which you rest, the companion of your life. With you I will walk my path from this day forward.

For more inspiration, search for wedding vows on the web. You'll find sites that provide examples of standard vows for free. Others offer to personalize a ceremony script for a fee.

Reading something meaningful

As you script your ceremony, you may want to incorporate poems, scriptures, lyrics, quotations, or other readings that are personally meaningful. I could fill hundreds of tomes if I were to reprint actual possibilities here. Instead, I give you some general directions to explore:

- ✔ **Scripture:** Genesis, Song of Solomon, the Talmud, 1 Corinthians, Romans, John, Matthew, Ephesians, Psalms, Confucius, I Ching

- ✔ **Literature:** *The Little Prince,* by Antoine de Saint-Exupéry; *The Velveteen Rabbit,* by Margery Williams; *Soul Mates,* by Thomas Moore; *The Art of Loving,* by Erich Fromm; *Letters to a Young Poet,* by Rainer Maria Rilke; *A Natural History of Love,* by Diane Ackerman

- ✔ **Poetry:** Elizabeth Barrett Browning, Shakespeare, Percy Bysshe Shelley, Marge Piercy, Walt Whitman, Carl Sandburg, e. e. cummings, T. S. Eliot, John Donne, Pablo Neruda

Of course, many readings about love will work for any couple, but same-sex couples may want readings that honor their love a bit more explicitly. The site www.gayweddingvalues.com has comprehensive suggestions for religious and nonreligious readings suitable for same-sex couples generally, as well as gay men and lesbians specifically.

If you intend to honor friends or relatives by asking them to do a reading at your wedding, give them ample time to choose it (if applicable), learn it, and practice it. In fact, have them do a run-through at your rehearsal.

If you've written your own vows, and especially if they include a long poem or passage, write them on 3 x 5 cards. Ask someone who will be at the altar or bimah with you, and who has a pocket, to hang on to them until you need them during the ceremony.

Places, Everyone — Time to Rehearse

Rehearsals not only make the wedding run smoothly but also tremendously reduce the angst level. If you have children in the ceremony, the rehearsal helps them get a sensory hold on what they'll be doing. (Come to think of it, that's why adults need rehearsals, too.)

Attendants may be quite blasé when handed a wedding-day schedule (see Chapter 7) at the rehearsal and may even make hilarious jokes about the "mindless minutiae" and the "control freak" who penned it. These are usually the same folks who ask for a new copy an hour before the ceremony and clutch it as if it were a life-support system.

Seating your guests

You can hold the marriage ceremony in a variety of configurations if you aren't in a religious setting (and therefore aren't bound by house rules). For example, you may face the guests as you take your vows. Another option is seating in the round or in a semicircle. In such cases, break up the rows with extra aisles that are smaller than the main one. Allow a center aisle wide enough for double the number of people walking down it. (Make sure that the aisle is of equal width from front to back.)

For a ceremony with chairs arranged in rows chapel-style, allow 3 feet from the edge of one chair to the back of the next. Make each row short enough to provide easy access and egress. Long rows inevitably mean that half the guests have to get up so one person can take a seat in the middle. ("Excuse me. Excuse me. Excuse me. Uh, were those your toes?") If you must have long rows, create a couple of extra aisles so people can get in and out. Also, have an even number of seats in each row because most people come in couples.

Without the formality of pew or within-the-ribbon cards, ushers are usually in charge of seating relatives and others the couple want to have in the first few rows. The rehearsal dinner is often an opportunity to familiarize ushers with the VIPs. At the ceremony, guests often feel that letting ushers know they deserve front-row seats looks presumptuous. If you don't apprise ushers ahead of time, you may find yourselves looking at rows of empty chairs during your ceremony. You may also mark reserved seats with small informal cards.

Doing a quick run-through

You usually hold the rehearsal the night before the wedding, ideally where the ceremony is to be. For an Orthodox or Conservative Jewish wedding, you may hold the rehearsal earlier in the week or slightly before the ceremony so as not to conflict with the Sabbath. The time should be late enough in the afternoon to accommodate those coming from work but early enough so you can greet other guests arriving for the rehearsal dinner. Now isn't the time to start choreographing your rehearsal. With a delineated schedule, a rehearsal shouldn't take more than 45 minutes, even for an elaborate ceremony. If you have people coming to the rehearsal who haven't seen one another in a long time, allot extra time to get hugs, kisses, and gossip out of the way.

Rehearsals in a church or synagogue usually involve the officiant as well as the person responsible for the chapel who puts everyone through the paces. If your officiant participates in your rehearsal, invite him (and spouse) to the rehearsal dinner. You should also invite an officiant who's your family clergyperson or a friend to the reception (with spouse). You may ask the clergyperson to say grace or the rabbi to offer the traditional prayer over the challah bread. However, note that Orthodox and Conservative rabbis most likely won't attend a nonkosher reception, even if you provide a special meal for them. To avoid any embarrassment, clarify this point before inviting them.

If your ceremony is in a space that's always booked for other events, request as early as possible in your planning to reserve the space for your rehearsal. The manager, if given enough time, may hold the space for you or schedule other events around you to accommodate a short rehearsal.

If you're getting married at a hotel or banquet hall that does numerous weddings, the captain or maitre d' will most likely coordinate the rehearsal for you. Your wedding coordinator may also be in charge of the lineup. If you can't rehearse where your ceremony is going to be, improvise in another space, perhaps where the dinner is being held, timing it so you finish before the other guests get there. Set up the first row of chairs with an aisle in the middle; the point is to give participants an idea of where to stand as well as whom they're walking with and in what order.

When setting up chairs for a ceremony in an off-premise location, be sure that you overestimate the aisle's width. Test it and retest it and insist that the caterer go over it with you. Your ceremony will be completely thrown off if you appear in a wide dress with both parents on either side and you can't negotiate the space between the chairs without resorting to single file.

Unless you've hired the church organist to play for your ceremony, getting the musicians you've hired to play at the rehearsal as well is usually cost-prohibitive. Fortunately, music isn't really necessary for a walk-through. If, however, you'll sleep better having the total experience, bring a tape of your music and a portable cassette recorder and have someone cue it at the right moments for the processional and recessional.

You need to give the participants a visual cue so they know when to go next down the aisle. You may tell them to wait until the person(s) ahead of them has reached a certain row. If you don't have a wedding consultant, you need to appoint someone director who can cue the musicians and the wedding party.

Going over the rules and expectations

One round of both the processional and the recessional should be sufficient as a run-through. Just make sure that whoever is running the nonreligious part of the rehearsal goes over these details as well:

✔ Schedule the prelude music to begin when guests start arriving, 15 minutes to a half hour before the ceremony. After the ceremony, the music should continue until the last person leaves the ceremony area or as soon as the reception music starts, if the reception is adjacent.

✔ Ushers should be welcoming and friendly to the guests, not stand in a clump. They should know where the nearest restrooms are and how to get to the reception.

✔ During the rehearsal, go over seating with the ushers, telling them to escort guests to rows directly behind the reserved ones because deserted front rows can be disconcerting to a bride and groom gazing out at the guests.

✔ If children are in the ceremony, escort them to the bathroom before the processional.

✔ Reserved seating, aside from the first two or three rows for close friends or relatives, is rare these days. Because most couples are joining their family and friends together, having the ushers ask, "Bride's side or groom's side?" isn't necessary.

✔ When the bride arrives at the altar or bimah, she should hand her bouquet to her maid of honor so that her hands are free. If she's wearing gloves, she should remove these before the ring portion of the ceremony and hand them to an attendant. The attendant should remember to give these items back to the bride before the recessional.

✔ All who are standing should keep their knees relaxed. If your knees lock at the altar for a prolonged period, the blood flow is constricted and you may faint.

✔ For a Christian ceremony, the bride's mother is the last to be seated. Designate at the rehearsal who will escort her.

✔ If you have an aisle runner, two ushers have the job of unfurling it after the bride's mother is seated and before the ceremony begins.

✔ Ushers and bridesmaids should attempt to look happy and relaxed when walking down the aisle.

✔ Many churches and synagogues have heavy doors at the entranceway. Make sure that someone (usually a sexton or person in charge of the facility) is posted to open the doors and prop them open when the recessional music begins. I hate to see a just-married couple have to stop and wrench the doors open, and then wait for someone to hold them.

✔ If you're getting married in a private home or other space that has a phone, silence the ringer or disconnect the line for the ceremony's duration.

✔ If you don't have a wedding coordinator and you have several cars or limos going to the reception, appoint an usher-and-bridesmaid-traffic-team to serve as ground control.

Getting with the Program

A wedding program serves many purposes — as a lovely memento of the day, a way to honor the participants, and a playbook that guides everyone through the steps of the ceremony.

Some houses of worship create programs for couples getting married, or you can design your own. In either case, make sure your officiant or the person in charge goes over it before the final printing. Programs can be simple or elaborate, photocopied on plain paper or engraved on card stock, written in calligraphy or typeset, unadorned or embellished with artwork, ribbons, and color. A typical layout for a four-page program (front, back, and two inside covers) includes

- ✔ **Front cover:** The couple's name — "The Marriage Ceremony of Charlotte and Charles," for example — goes here, along with the wedding date and place. You may also embellish with a graphic element such as a family crest, personal logo, hand-painted flower, pen-and-ink sketch of the locale, or some other meaningful image.

- ✔ **Inside front cover:** Here you list everyone involved in the ceremony — the officiant(s), the bride and groom, their parents, and the wedding party. Along with names of the attendants, sometimes couples include their relationships to the bride and groom.

- ✔ **Inside back cover:** This page details the ceremony, step by step, complete with music and readings.

- ✔ **Back cover:** Depending on how much room you have, you may put a personally meaningful poem, bit of prose, or blessing. This spot is also a good place to thank family and friends; acknowledge deceased parents, relatives, or friends; provide reception site information; or gently explain that the use of flash or video cameras is prohibited or goes against your wishes.

For a more elaborate program with multiple pages, the inside cover is often where you thank family and friends for their support. On subsequent pages, you may have a more-detailed program, especially if you have many guests unfamiliar with the ceremony traditions — for example, when to respond at particular points during Nuptial Mass. You may also want to include foreign-language translations; words to the readings, songs, prayers, or blessings; or explanations of religious or ethnic rituals or military traditions. Apart from repeating reception site details, don't tell guests more than they need to know about your wedding-day schedule (see Chapter 7).

When listing the music, include the prelude, the processional, music or songs during the ceremony (including hymn numbers), and the recessional. Also list names of soloists and musicians, indicating who's performing what.

Figure 10-5 shows a typical program for a Christian ceremony. Figure 10-6 gives you a structure for planning a program for a Reform Jewish wedding ceremony.

The Marriage

of

Harriet Henshow and Randolph Roosterhaus

Sacred Sea Foam Chapel

Crashing Rocks Bay

August 10, 2013

~ Officiating ~

The Rev. Philip Phetherfrend

The Wedding Party

Matron of Honor	Claudia Cuckold
Bridesmaids	Phyllis Flatface
	Jessica Jacquelope
	Val Liam
Best Man	Peter Porcini
Groomsmen	Stanley Snout
	August Antspantz
	Kevin Kibbutz
Readings	Charlotte Webb
	Ima Biggsow
Organist	Wallace Tuttle

Order of Service

Prelude		
	Canon in D	Johann Pachelbel
	Air (Orchestral Suite No. III in D Major, S. 1068)	Johann Sebastian Bach
Processional		
	Trumpet Voluntary	Jeremiah Clarke
	Grand Triumphal Chorus	Alexandre Guilmant
Call to Worship		
Prayer		
Presentation of the Bride		
Parzival		Wolfram Von Eschenbach
Scripture Reading		Romans 12:1–2, 9–18
Meditation		
The Marriage Vows		
Exchange of the Rings		
Sonnet 116		William Shakespeare
Pastoral Prayer & The Lord's Prayer		
Declaration of Marriage		
Apache Wedding Poem		
Benediction		
Recessional		
	Wedding March	Felix Mendelssohn
	(From A Midsummer Night's Dream)	

Figure 10-5:
An example of a simple program for a Christian wedding.

Illustration by Wiley, Composition Services Graphics

Figure 10-6: A sample program for a Reform Jewish wedding.

Illustration by Wiley, Composition Services Graphics

Within the figure:

Wedding of
Bebe Rebecca Kerfuffleberg
and
Isaac Ezra Blandstein

Saturday
August 10, 2013

Temple Israel
Sea Mist, Florida

Both of us are very happy we are able to spend this special day surrounded by so many of our family and friends. We have decided to include many beautiful traditions in our wedding ceremony. It is our hope that this brief explanation, which we incorporated partly from a booklet written by Rabbi Katzenberg, will help all of our guests to fully understand and participate in our celebration.

~ Bebe and Isaac

The Wedding Processional

Rabbi Philip Katzenberg	
Cantor Mark Tonalman	
Sally Kerfuffleberg	Bebe's grandmother
Adam Kerfuffleberg	Bebe's cousin
Betty Greenberg	Isaac's grandmother
Samuel Greenberg	Isaac's grandfather

Bridesmaids and Ushers

Elaine Kerfuffleberg	Bebe's cousin
Jonathan Schwartz	Isaac's high school friend
Sarah Levine	Bebe's friend from college
Andrew Silverstein	Isaac's friend from college
Tess Hyams	Bebe's cousin
Abraham Silk	Isaac's cousin

Best Man

Michael Blandstein	Isaac's brother

Isaac will walk to the Chupa with his parents, Mark and Tammy.

Matron of Honor

Mimi Kerfuffleberg	Bebe's sister

Bebe will walk to the Chupa with her parents, Theodore and Roberta.

Wedding Ceremony

A Jewish wedding is not merely between two individuals, or their family and circle of friends; it is a cause of celebration for the entire Jewish people. A wedding is not just about two people finding happiness; it's more about the potential of this couple to make the world a better place by the virtue of being together as one.

The upcoming marriage of Bebe and Isaac was announced at an Aufruf at a Shabbat service at Temple Israel on June 22, 2013. Bebe and Isaac were called to the bimah and given honors before the Torah.

Prior to the ceremony, the civil marriage license was witnessed and signed by James Kerfuffleberg (Bebe's brother) and Harry Blandstein (Isaac's uncle). The Ketubah (Jewish marriage document) was witnessed and signed by Fred Solomon (Bebe's uncle) and Kirk Blandstein (Isaac's cousin). The Ketubah was a revolutionary concept, protecting the bride's right and obligating the husband to look out for her welfare.

The wedding takes place under the Chupa, symbolic of the home Bebe and Isaac will build together. The Chupa has no walls; the marriage begins with just a roof, and Bebe and Isaac will build the walls with love and friendship. The Chupa is open on all sides so that family and friends will always feel welcome.

A blessing of birkat erusin, or betrothal, is recited over the wine, followed by another in praise of God, who brought Bebe and Isaac together. Bebe and Isaac drink from the same cup of wine to represent the life that they will share from this day forth.

Next comes the giving and accepting of rings. Jewish custom requires that wedding bands be made of a single piece of metal with no adornments breaking the circle, representing the wholeness achieved through marriage and the hope for an unbroken union. Bebe is using the wedding band of her great-great grandmother when she was married 96 years ago. Isaac will place the ring on Bebe's right index finger and recite the formula of betrothal: "Behold you are betrothed to me with this ring according to the laws of Moses and Israel." Bebe will then present Isaac with a ring and recite, "I am my beloved's, and my beloved is mine."

The Ketubah is then read and presented to Bebe. After the chanting of the seven marriage blessings — sheva b'rachot — the couple drinks from a second cup of wine.

At the conclusion of the ceremony, Isaac will step on and break a glass. This ancient practice has many interpretations. One of the most traditional is that it reminds us of the destruction of the holy temple in Jerusalem and the many losses that have been suffered by the Jewish people. Another explanation is that love, like glass, is very fragile and must be protected because, once broken, it is hard to put back together again. (A special thanks to artist Linda Fishbein for the beautiful colored glass used in the ceremony, which will be made into a mezuzah.)

Yichud (seclusion): Immediately following the ceremony, Bebe and Isaac will leave the Chupa and spend their first few minutes as husband and wife alone together in a private place.

Dear Family and Friends,

We are thrilled and thankful that all of you are able to be here with us today. We are lucky to have such wonderful family and friends. Thank you for being such a special part of our lives.

Dear Parents,

Thank you for your love and never-ending support throughout our lives. We love and appreciate all of you very much.

Dear Siblings,

Thank you for all of your love and guidance through the years. We realize that we are fortunate to have all of you not only as family but also as our best friends.

Dear Bridal Party,

You represent a very special part of our lives. Thank you all for being such good friends through the years and for being a part of this special day.

At this time, we lovingly remember our grandparents, Jerome Kerfuffleberg and Babe Blandstein.

Things to throw

Releasing a tide of helium-filled balloons and watching them drift up and out of sight seems romantic but is in fact environmentally unfriendly. The balloons eventually deflate and become random litter, get hung up in trees, or wind up in lakes and oceans, where animals such as whales, birds, and dolphins ingest them and die. Rice has also fallen out of favor because it expands in the stomachs of birds and other creatures and can be fatal. If you feel you must have guests throw something, try birdseed or flower petals, or have bubbles blown at you instead. Inexpensive but pretty noisemakers, like kazoos or maracas, also let your guests give you a big send-off with little environmental impact.

Chapter 11

Selecting the Perfect Florist and Arrangements

In This Chapter

▶ Choosing a florist

▶ Decorating a house of worship

▶ Adorning your reception with floral arrangements

▶ Selecting personal flowers

▶ Preserving your bridal bouquet

*F*lowers are, with rare exception, the dominant decorative element for a wedding. Even the horticulturally illiterate appreciate the symbolism and elegance that flowers impart. And although "that which we call a rose by any other name would smell as sweet," a loosely tied bouquet of long stems conveys a strikingly different mood from a composite of petals painstakingly wired to resemble one enormous blossom.

Different kinds of wedding professionals handle flowers. A wedding florist creates arrangements for your ceremony and reception as well as all personal arrangements for the wedding party, while an event designer uses flowers as part of creating a complete atmosphere for your wedding, including background, props, lighting, fabrics, and entertainment. (See Chapter 1 for more on different kinds of wedding professionals.) Regardless of the professional you choose, the tips I provide here apply to any floral design.

Before you start interviewing floral artists, get an idea of the kinds of flowers you like. Peruse magazines (not just wedding ones), wedding websites, wedding blogs, and interior design blogs, and keep track of photographs of rooms, arrangements, and bouquets that convey the feeling you want for your wedding. If a floral designer is credited in a photo you like, jot down the name; your florist may know the designer's work and draw inspiration from it. You don't need to be president of the garden club to think about colors, mood, or style, such as romantic, modern, or rococo. Focus on the broad concept first and then find the flowers that go with the image you want.

Finding a Fab Floral Artiste

When choosing the right florist or event designer for your wedding, get recommendations from friends, editors of local bridal or home magazines, and other wedding vendors. But before you even think of scheduling an interview, explore the florist's website to see whether the florist's style resonates with yours. If you want a lush, romantic style, working with someone who specializes in more structured, formal arrangements doesn't make sense, no matter how highly recommended the person is. You'll just frustrate each other.

After you identify one or two floral artists whose work you love, schedule an interview. At the interview, you'll look at more photographs of weddings, individual bouquets, and events for which the floral artist has supplied flowers and/or décor. Here are some questions to consider:

- Has the florist worked at your venue before? If not, will he make a site visit before writing a proposal?

- What props, tablecloths, floral containers, and other extras does the floral designer own? What would need to be rented and by whom?

- Do you like the environment of the florist's space or shop?

- Are his concepts original? How does he respond to your ideas? If you've brought clippings, is he interested in them?

- How does he handle substituting flowers if the ones you've decided on aren't unavailable because of unexpected circumstances?

- Will he make a sample centerpiece or table setup for you? (Note that this is usually done only *after* you sign a contract and put down a deposit.)

- What are the setup and breakdown fees?

- How soon can you expect a proposal?

- What are his payment terms?

- Does he think the budget you're estimating is realistic? If not, how much does he think your ceremony and reception flowers will really cost?

As you chat, carefully note the florist's answers. If you're on completely different wavelengths, move on to the next prospect — no point wasting each other's time.

Expressing Yourself: Decorating the Ceremony Site

Whether your nuptial site is an old church with Roman arches, a yarrow-dotted bluff overlooking the sea, or a whitewashed photography studio, you'll want to add some floral décor for the occasion. That may mean letting a grand site speak for itself with little or no embellishment, enhancing the most eloquent aspects of the space through equally elegant arrangements, or undertaking a major overhaul to turn a secular site into one you deem appropriate for your vows.

Gathering floral ideas and images

Hopefully you've picked a floral artist who "gets" you, but you still need to be able to express your ideas, even if you don't know much about flowers. Fortunately, you have lots of new ways to share images and ideas, even if you have a hard time describing them. If a picture is worth a thousand words, a collection of them should tell your florist or event designer exactly what you have in mind.

✔ Start by exploring wedding magazines (in print or online), wedding blogs, and floral websites. Then use Pinterest (www.pinterest.com) or a smartphone application like Wedding Row (www.weddingrowapp.com) or the Desire Wedding Inspiration Board Creator for iPad (available through the iTunes app store) to capture online images and arrange them, along with your own photos, in a digital inspiration board.

Great sources for flower images include www.prestonbailey.com, www.designsponge.com, www.ritzybee.typepad.com, www.decor8blog.com, and www.thebridescafe.com.

✔ Even easier, the Wedding Flowers Moodboard app for iPhone (available through the iTunes app store) provides a library of wedding flower images that you can select and add to your inspiration board with your own notes.

✔ The Loupe application (www.loupeapp.com) lets you turn any color you encounter into a swatch for your inspiration board.

✔ Of course, if you're feeling nostalgic or just don't have room on your phone for one more app, you can put together an inspiration file by clipping and printing photos as well.

Visualizing your floral design

Visit your ceremony site with your floral designer (or wedding planner) and think about the chronology of your ceremony in relation to what needs decorating. What do guests see as they arrive? What's the view from where they sit? Where are the musicians positioned? Where does the bridal party enter? Where does everyone exit? By understanding how the space works, you can target areas where arrangements add a great deal and where they'd be wasted.

Remember, outdoor ceremonies should be about the outdoors. Wrapping gardens in tulle and fabric is usually gratuitous and incongruous. Let nature speak for itself.

Some people recommend having the chuppah or altar flowers do double duty by whisking them from the ceremony to the reception. Separate venues, however, can make this practice unwieldy. Compare the cost of additional flowers with the moving expense and hassle. If the savings are truly significant, determine with your florist where to place these pieces so that their reappearance isn't obvious.

If you're marrying in a house of worship, churches and synagogues typically have someone on staff who's responsible for specifying and enforcing the rules as to how you may or may not decorate, what time you can begin decorating, and when you have to remove all your décor. Houses of worship can be particularly strict about décor, so heed their rules carefully. For example, churches sometimes have set floral containers and/or candelabras for the altar and aisles. And before you lug your altarpieces to your reception to do double duty, check the rules. Some churches insist that the flowers are a donation to be left behind for the congregation to enjoy.

If your house of worship has booked another ceremony before or after yours, consider splitting the cost of decorating with the other couple. The wedding coordinators at churches and synagogues are usually happy to put you in touch with them.

Rolling out the nuptial carpet

Some limousine services and florists throw in complimentary paper aisle runners. Even if these withstand the ushers' unfurling them before the ceremony, they'll most certainly be in shreds by the time the bride makes her way down the aisle. Canvas or fabric runners are a more durable option, and you can enhance them easily and inexpensively by creating a stenciled border. When in doubt, skip the runner altogether.

Row or pew markers

You can put decorative elements as simple as ribbons tied into beautiful bows or as lavish as elaborate rose topiaries on the ends of rows along the aisle — typically every two or three rows. They can be free-standing or attached to benches with floral holders.

Altar or bimah flowers

Usually an altar is flanked by arrangements. Delicate blossoms disappear at a distance, so these arrangements should be composed of large flower heads. You can use greenery and filler flowers in these pieces advantageously because the arrangements can be quite airy. Because churches and synagogues tend to be dimly lit, light or vibrant hues are preferable, but keep the flowers in one palette. The flowers should enhance you and your surroundings, not call attention to themselves.

Keep the size of the space in mind when choosing these arrangements. You don't want to overpower an exquisite country church that has a diminutive altar with flowers appropriate for St. Patrick's Cathedral. A house of worship's ambiance should remain intact after your design wizards alight.

Other places for flowers

In churches, the baptismal font may seem the perfect piece of architecture for the wedding touch, but check first to make sure you can decorate it. Filling the font with multicolored rose petals or garlanding around the base adds a charming note to the surroundings. Garlands or small pots set on windowsills complete the vision.

A floral and ribbon marker or wreath, attached to the door frame or entrance banister or threaded through a trellised gate, guides guests who are driving, welcoming them to the celebration.

Chuppahs

Although religious law requires Jewish weddings to take place under a chuppah (see Chapter 10), it cites no specifics regarding size or decoration. Generally, a _chuppah_ is a canopy open on four sides and constructed just for the wedding. Some chuppahs are designed to be free-standing, and others are carried and held up by four people whom the couple wishes to honor.

Chuppahs can be beautifully simple covered with a fabric that's meaningful to you, such as a _tallit,_ or prayer shawl, given to the groom by the bride and her family, or a material richly embroidered with symbols of married life or other personal notes.

Chuppahs can also be quite elaborate. These have come into vogue as Jewish or interfaith ceremonies often take place in off-premise sites or hotel ballrooms. Some appear to float above the congregation amid billows of tulle, ivy, and flowers suspended by invisible wires. Others are topped with baskets of leaves and set within garlanded columns of wisteria and branches to evoke the feel of a country garden.

If you make the canopy for your chuppah by hand or have an elaborate one made for your wedding, you may suspend it over your bed (to symbolize the chuppah's original meaning), frame it, or use it as a wall hanging after your wedding.

Take into consideration the size of the table and cloth you're using under the chuppah. When this small table, on which the officiant places the wine goblet and wine and rests the prayer book, is covered with something in hot pink thrown on by a busboy at the last moment, your beautiful setting turns into an eyesore.

Decorating Your Reception Space with Redolent Arrangements

As the most important aspect of your reception's design, flowers are likely to eat up the bulk of your décor budget. (For a larger discussion on decorating your reception space, see Chapter 17.) Flowers themselves are generally expensive; in addition, someone has to select, prepare, transport, and arrange these precious blooms, and that can add up to significant money. If you want them to last through your reception with heads up and color intact, you can't just plop flowers in a vase. They must be conditioned — stems denuded of thorns, anthers, stigmas, and extra leaves (which may decay in water, producing a foul odor); ends snipped or crushed; and stems wired. If you desire a certain look such as fully opened roses, these must be blown open just enough but not one iota too much. Even the seemingly homespun wild-flowers-in-a-pitcher look isn't as simple as it appears. Studied casualness takes *work*.

Making centerpieces measure up

Many hosts are obsessed with table centerpieces being no higher than eye level. Although this design raises manic arguments between designer and client, keep in mind that people tend to converse with those seated next to them rather than those across from them. People like to be able to at least nod at the smiling faces across the way, but in my opinion, as long as center-pieces are airy, you don't have to worry about partially obscuring the cross-table view. You just don't want a mini privet hedge bisecting the table. With the various table sizes and shapes now being used together at one reception, designers must make different sizes and shapes of their floral pieces as well.

If you're fixated on giving guests a clear view across the table, use the elbow test. Rest your elbow on the table and raise your forearm perpendicular to the table, fingers extended. Centerpieces on the table should end below your fingertips (about 14 inches), and elevated centerpieces, where the flowers are above eye level, should start above your fingertips.

For the most part, use filler such as trite flowers and greenery sparingly. Ideally, greenery consists of leaves removed from the flowers themselves and used only to balance an arrangement or hide the mechanics — floral foam, chicken-wire cages, tape, wire, and wired tubes — built in to add height and breadth. In any centerpiece, no matter how elaborate or simple, these materials should never show.

Centerpieces for wedding receptions no longer look as if they came off of a floral assembly line (see Figure 11-1). Designers create rooms as a whole, using a variety of colors, flowers, and approaches for each table. Some tables may have low arrangements with tapered candles, while others feature an elevated centerpiece and votive candles. You frequently find several variations in both color and fabric of the table linens as well.

Styling your centerpieces

You have various styles and configurations of centerpieces to choose from:

- **Branches:** Just one or two flowering branches such as cherry or quince in a tall glass vase. Recently popular. Because of the arrangement's simplicity, the height of the stems, the water level, and the cleanliness of the water are critical.

- **Breakaway:** Several dainty posies in individual glass containers arranged to look like one big bouquet. At the end of the party, each person at the table takes home one of the pieces. (When you make your rounds to all the tables between courses, you can inform guests that they're welcome to take part of the centerpiece.)

- **Candelabra:** A tall candelabra that has four to six arms that hold tall, tapered candles. Flowers start at eye level, stemming from an elevated bowl in the candelabra's center.

Illustration by Elizabeth Kurtzman

Figure 11-1:
Gone are
the days
when cen-
terpieces
came in
one-style-
fits-all.

- **Fish bowl or globe:** Round glass bowls stuffed with mounded flowers, such as roses, for a fairly low centerpiece.

- **Garden:** An abundance of flowers and foliage, such as cabbage roses and ivy tendrils, that look as if a small garden is growing in the middle of the table. The greens either completely obscure the container (which is therefore nothing fancy) or allow at most a peek of the container, which can be a pretty basket or patterned pitcher.

- **Ikebana:** A Japanese style in which each element is meticulously and artfully placed with a strong sense of space, proportion, and scale.

- **Pavé style:** A European-style arrangement composed of flowers whose stems have been cut almost down to the head and arranged in low, mounded patterns. Well suited for side tables as well as centerpieces.

- **Still life:** Arrangements that have not only flowers but also colorful fruits and vegetables, such as artichokes, asparagus, china berries, crab apples, grapes, green apples, kale, kumquats, nuts, vanilla beans, or whatever's in season.

- **Topiaries:** Either natural ivy grown around a metal frame and trimmed to resemble something as simple as spheres or as complex as cupids, or topiary trees made of Styrofoam balls covered with moss and finished with flower heads, fruits, ribbons, and so on.

Flanking the band or bordering the dance floor with floral pieces is generally a waste of money, as you usually have to remove these when the music starts.

At some point, your designer should communicate with your cake maker. If your cake is to have sugar or icing flowers, you may want it to coordinate with the centerpieces or the bridal bouquet. If the cake is to have fresh flowers, the florist needs to know the cake's colors and shape so she can provide them and also so she can make sure that no chemicals have been used in conditioning the flowers.

Cutting costs: Making alternative reception arrangements

One of the biggest costs in the flower universe is labor. If you have the time and the inclination (or a posse of doting aunts dying for a wedding assignment), you might go into do-it-yourself mode. Or, to cut your floral expenditure, ask your florist to come up with some simpler ideas that require less labor and/or fewer stems.

An oft-heard bridal refrain is, "Can't we just use some heavenly wildflowers that we pick ourselves?" Sure you can — if you want to spend your wedding in jail. Federal law prohibits the picking of wildflowers, so if you want them, grow your own or find a supplier who does.

The following strategies help create an eye-catching look with fewer flowers:

- ✔ Use elements other than flowers to create centerpieces: glass bowls of green apples with ivy; tiered plates laden with varieties of grapes, miniature pumpkins, and acorns; or highly stylized, minimalist arrangements such as ikebana. The look of the room comprises all the tables as a whole, so alternating tables that have ornate arrangements with those that have smaller ones doesn't diminish the beauty of your reception.

- ✔ Float apples, limes, or lemons in glass cylinders and finish the arrangement with cut flowers.

- ✔ Use the available banquet cloths for the underlay or bottom cloth and top them with a smaller square of contrasting color or more lavish fabric.

- ✔ Instead of mixed cut flowers, use a moss-covered terra cotta pie dish (used under large flower pots) as a base and fill it with small pots of flowering plants, such as primroses, pansies, African violets, and one orchid for height.

✔ Use petals and greens in lieu of flowers to decorate the cake table.

✔ To accent an escort card table, use small pots of herbs, flowering plants, or a bed of petals rather than an oversized floral piece.

✔ Scoop out apples or pears to make a small well in the top, drop in a disc candle (sold as "floating candles") or votive, and use them to add polish to tables that have small arrangements. Rub lemon juice on the cut parts of the fruit to prevent browning.

✔ Create faux potted plants by pressing soaked floral foam in the bottoms of long or round terra cotta planters, fill with moss or dirt, and stick in flowers that have sturdy stems (wire them if necessary), such as gerbera daisies, sunflowers, and calla lilies.

✔ Tie napkins with ribbons, lace remnants, or raffia and tuck in a sprig of ivy, rosemary, or an inexpensive flower. Creating more visual interest around the entire table makes an imposing centerpiece less necessary.

✔ Surround a candle-filled hurricane lamp with scattered flowers, petals, or, for a beach wedding, sea shells. These are also lovely surrounded by small bowls, each containing a single bloom.

✔ A small cluster of Mason jars with loosely arranged blossoms and/or floating candles, tied with lace or ribbon, creates visual interest with fewer flowers and has a charming rustic look.

✔ Paper and ribbon are low-cost and offer many possibilities. Try stacked Chinese lanterns, deconstructed and grouped paper wedding bells, origami cranes hung from tall branches in a vase, or ribbon flowers.

✔ Grouped julep cups look fantastic filled with simple lemon or galax leaves.

✔ Instead of flowers, put scented candles with a few sprigs of ivy or rosemary in the restrooms.

Putting the Bloom on You: Up Close and Personal Flowers

The term *personal flowers* refers not only to the bride's bouquet and groom's boutonniere but also to all the flowers worn or carried by attendants, family members, or others you want to honor. Men often have preferences, some quite specific, for the boutonniere they sport on their wedding day. For brides, though, the flowers they carry as they walk toward married life are the ultimate — and very visible — accompaniment to their wedding dress.

Specify exactly where you want the florist to deliver your personal flowers and that you want them all labeled to avoid even the slightest chance that an usher may try to pin the flower girl's tussy mussy to his lapel.

Bride and attendants

At the beginning of the 20th century, brides and bridesmaids carried such elaborate bouquets that the women practically needed a wheelbarrow to transport them down the aisle. Bouquets can be striking but should never be distracting; you want all eyes on the carrier, not on her bouquet. As an accessory, the bouquet should complement the dress as well as the size and shape of the wearer. Bridesmaids' bouquets need not be dwarf versions of the bride's; they can be mini works of art in themselves.

Antique lace, organza, or wired ribbon wrapped around the stems finish a bouquet beautifully, although not inexpensively. One of my favorite looks is having each bridesmaid carry a different, vibrantly colored bouquet finished with matching ribbon streamers.

I've also noticed a trend for younger, budget-conscious brides to choose a floral wristlet rather than a bouquet for their attendants. Fresher and hipper than dowdy, old-fashioned wrist corsages, these may take the form of a floral garland, incorporate feathers or crystals, or even feature just one big flower attached to a beaded band.

For years, people considered only one style of bouquet to be appropriate for formal weddings: all roses, stephanotis, and lily of the valley. This idea is no longer the case. At even extremely formal ceremonies, brides now carry a variety of flowers, colors, and shapes.

Flowers, however dazzling and pure, can cause you grief if they aren't prepared with meticulous care. Before handing them to attendants, ask someone to check them to make sure they're dry and that any stamens that may stain dresses have been removed.

Hold your bouquet by placing your elbows at your hipbones and grasping the stems or handle with both hands in front of your bellybutton (see Figure 11-2). (This position shows your waist; any higher and you start to look thick around the middle.) You should be able to carry a bouquet in this position while linking your arm with one person, unless you choose a pageant or presentation bouquet, which you must cradle in both arms. In other words, who's walking you down the aisle and how you walk together affects the kind of bouquet you can comfortably carry.

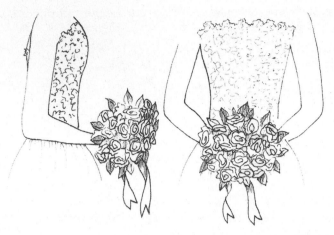

Illustration by Elizabeth Kurtzman

Figure 11-2: How to hold your bouquet.

Some of the following examples of bouquet types are illustrated in Figure 11-3:

- **Ballerina:** A posy-sized bouquet with flowers filled in by tulle or netting. Demanding fewer flowers, it's a pretty budget option that was popular with brides in World War II.

- **Biedermeier:** Tightly composed concentric circles of individual colors, wired into a lace collar or other holder.

- **Cascade or shower:** Classic, elaborate shape with flowers that are wired or pulled out to droop gracefully in a waterfall effect. Can be made with long-stemmed blooms or shorter wired flowers.

- **Composite or glamelia:** A flower constructed of dozens to hundreds of real petals wired together to look like one enormous flower.

- **Crescent:** Composed of one full flower and a flowering stem, often orchids, wired together to form a slender handle that you can hold in one hand. Designed as either a *full crescent,* a half circle with a central flower and blossoms emanating from two sides, or as a *semicrescent,* which has only one trailing stem.

- **Loose-tied:** Flowers loosely bound together with ribbon, with stems left exposed. Unconstructed and looks as if the blooms are freshly-picked, often incorporating flowers and greenery of varying shapes and lengths. Lovely for a more casual or garden wedding.

- **Nosegays:** Round bouquets (16 or 18 inches in diameter) composed of flowers, greenery, and occasionally sprigs of herbs, all wired or tied together. Can be similar in size and general form to loose-tied bouquets but are more tightly arranged and have a more structured round shape, with flowers and greenery arranged at the same length.

✔ **Posies:** Smaller versions of nosegays. Ribbons and silk flowers are often integrated into them.

✔ **Presentation:** The pageant bouquet — long-stemmed flowers cradled in your arms. Has a front "good" and back side.

✔ **Tossing:** A bouquet used for tossing so you can save the actual wedding bouquet for posterity. No need to duplicate the original.

✔ **Tussy mussy:** From the Victorian era, a posy in a small, metal, hand-held vase. Some have attached ring chains for easy carrying.

Instead of a bouquet, consider using fewer flowers in these innovative ways:

✔ A border of flowers on your veil or the hem of your dress

✔ A comb, barrette, or headband covered in lace, ribbon, and flowers

✔ A hat adorned with fresh flowers

✔ An heirloom prayer book accessorized with flowers

✔ A single long-stemmed flower such as a calla lily, rose, or Casablanca lily

✔ A wreath of flowers worn in the hair

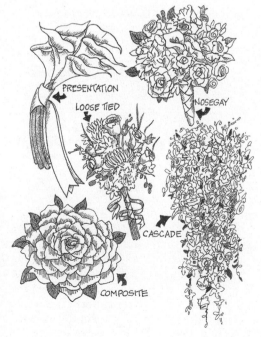

Figure 11-3: A bouquet's shape and style are as important as the kind of flowers it contains.

Illustration by Elizabeth Kurtzman

Bouquet-building basics

A bunch of flowers can almost never be left to its own devices. Creating floral sculptures and even simple arrangements requires the skills of a few magicians. Here's how various arrangements are created and why the prices may vary wildly:

✔ **Arranged in holders:** Floral foam soaked in water is placed in a bouquet holder — a plastic cone with a handle. Flowers are then stuck into the foam.

✔ **Individually wired:** Stems are cut down and taped to wire so the flowers are more malleable. For greens such as ivy, the leaves first have to be stitched with a fine silver wire. This technique is complicated, time-consuming, and, consequently, expensive.

✔ **Tied in bunches:** A natural bunch of flowers tied together with ribbons, which are prettiest when French braided or finished with love knots. For a more natural look, leave the stems showing.

Mothers, stepmothers, fathers' girlfriends, and others

Say "corsage" and many women think "blue hair," not to mention pinholes in their fancy silk frock. Alternatives exist, including *tussy mussies* (ornate Victorian bouquet holders), flowers pinned to a handbag, or the kind of floral wristlet mentioned earlier. Some florists now use magnets to hold corsages in place on a dress. Ask your florist for this option if a pinned-on corsage is a must-have.

Grooms, ushers, stepfathers, mothers' boyfriends, and others

No longer the standard-issue, white, senior-prom carnation, the groom's boutonniere may be the same as one of the flowers in the bride's bouquet — as if plucked from there. The ones he chooses for his ushers and other gentlemen he wants to honor should reflect his personal style and be appropriate for their outfits. These flowers should neither brown around the edges nor wilt in the heat and should be hardy enough to withstand hours of hugs.

A few replacements for trite lapel pins:

- ✔ Acorns
- ✔ Berries backed by a galax leaf
- ✔ Cornflowers
- ✔ A stem of hydrangea
- ✔ Variegated ivy, fern, and pine
- ✔ Vibrant-colored roses set with a sprig of herbs

Also, having the stems wrapped with spiffy ribbon in an unexpected color or design can turn a mundane boutonniere into something dapper.

Men should wear boutonnieres on their left side and pin them on the underside of the lapel so that no part of the pin shows.

Order extra boutonnieres because they're relatively inexpensive, and one or two may not survive ham-fisted attempts at pinning or may get crushed by well-wishers. Besides, it's good to have extras for any forgotten menfolk.

Little touches for little people

When dealing with flower children (or any children, for that matter), keep accessories in proportion to the child's size. You don't want your flower girl to look like an ungainly flowering plant moving down the aisle. Some simple floral alternatives to the traditional flower basket include

- ✔ **Circlet:** A ribbon or twig band accented with blossoms and worn on girls' heads.
- ✔ **Garland:** Birch vines covered with smilax and flowers and carried in tandem by two or three very young children. This arrangement looks adorable and also keeps the kids together.
- ✔ **Hoop:** Made of vine strung with flowers and carried like a tambourine.
- ✔ **Pomander:** A Styrofoam ball, covered in lace and tulle and trimmed with floral heads, which hangs on the wrist.

Fresh petals can be slippery. If you want to follow children strewing petals from baskets, show them how to sprinkle them, alternating sides of the path rather than going straight down the danger zone. Or use silk petals, which are far less dangerous.

The ring bearer's main accessory is the ring pillow, which may be sewn of luxurious fabrics such as satin, silk, velvet, or organza. These pillows are sometimes embroidered or trimmed with silk, natural flowers, or ornate tassels. The rings are tied on with attached ribbons. As special as the pillow is, the ring bearer may be more interested in wearing a boutonniere identical to that of the ushers.

I suggest that the ring pillow never have the real rings on it. To protect the child's ego, attach fake rings and have the best man make a display of untying them. The real rings are, of course, safe with the best man and maid of honor.

Keeping the Bloom On

If you choose not to toss your real bridal bouquet, you may want to preserve it, which you can do in one of several ways:

- ✔ **Air dry:** Hang the bouquet (and the boutonniere, if you'd like) upside down in a dark, ventilated space, separating the flowers by type for best results.

- ✔ **Freeze dry:** Professionally done, this keeps the colors more vibrant than air drying does. You can then display the flowers in a glass dome or shadow box.

- ✔ **Potpourri:** Dry the flowers and remove the petals, which you mix with fragrant oils, herbs, and spices. Put in an airtight jar and shake once a day for six weeks.

- ✔ **Preserving with desiccants:** Simple but time-consuming, this arts-and-crafts project requires you to bury the bouquet in silica gel, available at hobby shops.

In a spirit of generosity, many couples consider donating their leftover flowers to a local hospital. It's a nice thought, but, frankly, most hospitals don't want them. If, however, you want to do something truly charitable, make arrangements with a nursing home, assisted living center, or homeless shelter *before* your wedding as to when and where to drop off small, tidy bouquets after your reception. Negotiate the price for this delivery with your florist. Even better, a few cities around the country have local charities that collect, repurpose, and deliver your flowers to hospitals, nursing homes, or shelters for a small monetary donation on your part. Try the Flower Shuttle in Raleigh, North Carolina; Floranthropy in Seattle; or Blooms from the Heart in San Diego. Your wedding planner or floral designer may be able to recommend local resources. And remember to ask for a receipt for tax purposes.

Another possibility, if the timing is feasible, is to ask your florist to provide floral paper and an assistant to create bouquets from the centerpieces and other arrangements at the end of the reception for your guests to take home.

Chapter 12

Music to Get Married By

The music at a wedding sets the tone for the entire ceremony. The pieces you choose and the way they're played are decisions that you should consider carefully in tandem with the other elements of your ceremony. In this chapter, I provide suggestions for various types of ceremonies and guidelines for creating your own musical menu.

They're Playing Our Song

Dozens of classical music pieces, although beautiful, are used so often in wedding ceremonies that they've lost the ability to inspire. That doesn't necessarily mean that you should be afraid to use such standards. The key is to find musicians who know how to make the music sound as if the pieces are perfect for *your* wedding. Or, if you're using recorded music, choose exemplary versions of the classics or new pieces that are fun and impactful.

If those commonly used pieces aren't your cup of tea, begin your search by listening to CDs or MP3 files of classical wedding music collections (you can preview these on iTunes or Amazon.com before purchase — just enter "wedding music" into the search box). If you don't have any luck with that, expand your musical horizons and listen to other classical selections. Consider, for example, such baroque composers as Handel, Marcello, and Quantz.

Before you get your heart set on a particular piece of music, check to see whether a solo organist can play it or whether it works for the number of musicians in the group you've contracted. Some of the musical pieces that you consider may only work for entire orchestras or may call for specific instruments that aren't in your ensemble.

Generally, I recommend getting a list of approved or suggested musical selections if you're marrying in a religious venue. Don't assume that your selections, even if they're standard, will coincide with the church's guidelines. For many Christians, having the "Bridal Chorus" (commonly known as "Here Comes the Bride") from Richard Wagner's opera *Lohengrin* as the processional and Felix Mendelssohn's "Wedding March" from *A Midsummer Night's Dream* as the recessional are as integral to their ceremony as the vows. Conversely, many churches don't allow those pieces, as they're secular rather than religious. Most synagogues don't allow those selections either, because Mendelssohn converted to Christianity and Wagner was a notorious anti-Semite.

Music in five parts

In general, a wedding ceremony has five facets of music:

- **Prelude:** Played for 15 minutes to a half hour before the ceremony, this music welcomes the guests and plays in the background while they're seated. Keep that in mind when you make your selections — whether you prefer a festive, elegant, or religious spirit.

  The prelude music, if you have no restrictions, can comprise any number of untraditional possibilities — an a cappella trio, an operatic soloist, or a quartet that specializes in classical renditions of Beatles songs. Some couples, tired of the usual variety of classical wedding music, opt for recorded music. Jazz favorites from Duke Ellington to Ella Fitzgerald to Nat King Cole put guests in a romantic mood as soon as they arrive, keeping them amused while they wait for the ceremony to begin.

- **Procession:** This music sets the pace for attendants walking down the aisle. The music should be rhythmic enough for them to keep time to (in a natural fashion). Often, a pause signifies the bride's arrival, followed by a fanfare as she enters.

  Really ambitious couples plan music that changes for each portion of the procession — one piece for the ushers, another for the bridesmaids and maid of honor, followed by a pause before a flourish for the bride's entrance. You must have very adept musicians or a talented DJ to make this work without gaffes.

- **Ceremony:** Couples might designate music to be played or a choir or soloist to sing at some points in the ceremony, perhaps before a reading or during the lighting of a unity candle. (For a religious ceremony, the officiant designates at what points a song or musical piece is appropriate and what the choices are.)

Guests need to be able to hear both the music and the words at a ceremony. Make sure that you, your officiant, anyone who's delivering a reading, and the musicians are loud enough. Depending on the location of your ceremony, you must either use a stand-up microphone or mike the site or the participants.

✔ **Recession:** This music, at the end of the ceremony, should be powerful and joyous. It's usually louder and quicker than the processional music. You might feature a rousing live chorus of gospel singers belting out "When the Saints Go Marching In"; a favorite, applicable rock song on CD; or even bagpipers. Anything may work as long as it's joyous and celebratory and sends people out the door uplifted.

✔ **Postlude:** This is a continuation of music, upbeat and celebratory, that keeps the guests feeling like they're a part of the wedding until they've all filed out of the ceremony space.

A soloist, a choir, or something in between

Planning the music for your ceremony is a mix-and-match process. You choose the musical pieces, the times they're played, and the artist(s) to perform them. Although some scenarios won't work (a solo guitarist performing Jeremiah Clarke's "Trumpet Voluntary" just doesn't cut it), many musical works can be scored for a variety of ensembles.

When selecting which pieces to play, think about the number of musicians you can afford to hire and the equipment they'll need. The following are possible musical configurations:

✔ **A capella group:** Generally three or four vocalists who sing without instrumental accompaniment. Can be very upbeat and fun.

✔ **Choir:** At least six singers with instrumental accompaniment.

✔ **Classical ensemble:** An almost infinite range of possibilities using various instruments (see Table 12-1 for some examples).

✔ **Jazz ensemble:** A trio or quartet consisting of guitar(s), bass, and drums.

✔ **Organ:** This instrument is an integral part of the ceremony at many churches and temples. Some very grand ones sound like a full orchestra.

✔ **Piano:** Either solo or as part of an ensemble, this instrument can be an electric keyboard, a baby grand, or an upright.

✔ **Recorded music:** A CD or MP3 files played on a sound system. Music technology has changed a lot in recent years, so check with your ceremony venue about appropriate media. Your local church may be a bit behind the curve.

> ✔ **Small orchestra:** Six or more pieces, such as a double string quartet or a string quartet, organ, and flute.
>
> ✔ **Soloist:** One singer with either instrumental accompaniment or a capella.

Classical ensembles are the most popular for weddings. If you want to save money, ask whether some members of the band that you hire for the reception can play for the ceremony at an additional hourly fee.

Table 12-1	Classical Ensemble Configurations
Type	*Instruments*
Duets	Flute and violin; violin and cello; two violins; harp and flute; flute and guitar
Trios	Harp, flute, and cello; violin, flute, and keyboard; two violins and a flute
String quartets	Four violins; two violins and two violas; two violins, one viola, and one cello
Woodwind quartet	Flute, clarinet, oboe, and bassoon
Brass quartet	Two trumpets, trombone, and French horn or tuba
Quintets	String quartet and piano; string quartet and harp

If you're planning an outdoor ceremony, classical musicians — particularly harpists — will insist on some covering from the sun and potential rain. Because these instruments are so expensive, even the threat of a drizzle three states away may keep the harpist from performing unless she's in a building or a tent.

Composing musical menus a la carte

Depending on your type of ceremony, different kinds of music may be suitable at various times. In this section, I provide you with some sample musical menus for different types of religious ceremonies.

Protestant

Table 12-2 shows a possible classic lineup of music with the church organ and a string quartet for a ceremony in a Protestant church. Although I don't show it here, a Protestant service may include a vocal of "The Lord's Prayer," as well as a vocal arrangement or instrumental music during a unity candle lighting.

Table 12-2	Examples of Musical Selections for a Protestant Ceremony
Action	*Music*
Prelude	Quartet: *Concerto for Violin in G Minor,* OP. 8 (Vivaldi); "Water Music" (Handel); *Concerto for Violin in E Major,* OP. 8, No. 1 "Primavera" (Vivaldi); *Brandenburg Concerto* (Bach); "Rondeau" (Mouret)
Mothers are seated	Quartet: "Jesu, Joy of Man's Desiring" (Bach)
Groom, best man, and officiant take their places	Quartet continues with "Jesu, Joy of Man's Desiring"
Music stops after groom, best man, and officiant are situated, and then begins again	Organ and quartet: "Trumpet Voluntary" (Clarke)
Ushers, bridesmaids, flower girl, ring bearer, and maid of honor process	Continue with "Trumpet Voluntary"
Doors open	Organ fanfare
Bride and her father process	Organ: "Bridal Chorus, Lohengrin" (Wagner)
Ceremony	No music
Recessional	Quartet and organ: "Wedding March" (Mendelssohn)
Postlude until guests have left church	Quartet: "New World Symphony" (Dvorak); "Canon in D" (Pachelbel); "La Rejouissance," from *Music for the Royal Fireworks* (Handel)
Outside church as bridal party exits and guests exit	Two bagpipers: Scottish folk music (approximately 20 minutes)

Catholic

Table 12-3 shows a program planned for a church organ and a soloist in a Catholic church.

Table 12-3	Examples of Musical Selections for a Catholic Ceremony
Action	**Music**
Prelude	Organ: "Jesu, Joy of Man's Desiring" (Bach); "Ode to Joy" (Beethoven)
Groom's parents are seated; bride's mother is seated; groom, best man, and priest take their places at the altar	Organ: *Preludes and Fugues for Organ* (Bach)
Processional begins; ushers process; bridesmaids process, then maid of honor	Organ: "The Prince of Denmark's March" (Clarke)
Bride and her father process	Continue with "The Prince"; music gets louder
Communion	Congregation with organist: "The Lord's Prayer" Organist: "Lord of All Hopefulness" (Struther); "Panis Angelicus" (Franck)
Lighting of the unity candle	Organist: "When Thou Art Near (Bist Du Bei Mir)" (Bach)
Visit to Mary Shrine	Soloist: "Ave Maria" (Schubert)
Recession	Organ: "Trumpet Tune" (Purcell)
Postlude	Organ: "La Rejouissance" (Handel); "Rondeau" (Mouret); "Aria" (Peeters)

Jewish

In Table 12-4, I show musical selections for all the components that you might include in a Jewish wedding ceremony. Many ceremonies don't have all these components, and others have less-traditional selections.

Table 12-4	Examples of Musical Selections for a Jewish Ceremony
Action	**Music**
Prelude	Organ or piano: "Yedid Nefesh" ("The Love of My Soul")
Cantor	Cantor: "Dodi Li" ("I Am My Beloved's")
Procession	Organ or piano: "Hanava Babanot" ("Beautiful One")

Action	Music
Under the chuppah	Cantor: "Eshet Chayil" ("Woman of Valor") Congregation: "Niggun" (wordless melody)
Recession	Organ or piano: "Siman Tov u'Mazel Tov" ("A Good Sign and Good Luck")
Postlude (and then for cocktail reception)	Klezmer selections

Nondenominational

A ceremony in a nonreligious venue, with officiants who are open to your designing all your wedding's musical elements, may take on a completely different flavor. I show you how you can do this in Table 12-5, where the ensemble comprises a keyboard, guitar, and violin.

Table 12-5	Examples of Musical Selections for a Nondenominational Ceremony
Action	**Music**
Prelude (mother of bride and parents of groom are seated as last piece of music ends)	"Camelot," "Night and Day" (Porter); "Smoke Gets in Your Eyes" (Kern); "Here, There, and Everywhere" (Lennon/McCartney); "Theme from *Chariots of Fire*" (Vangelis)
Groom, best man, and officiant take their places; best man and maid of honor walk down aisle	Soloist accompanied by keyboard and guitar: "In My Life" (Lennon/McCartney)
Rest of wedding party, consisting entirely of children — two sets of ring bearers and flower girls — processes	Trio: "Waltz of the Snowflakes," "Nutcracker Suite" (Tchaikovsky)
Bride and her father process	Trio: Fanfare — "Romeo and Juliet Love Theme" (Tchaikovsky)
After introduction and readings	Soloist accompanied by keyboard and guitar: "Wedding Song" (Dylan)
Recession	CD recording: "Brown-Eyed Girl" (Morrison)
Postlude	Trio: "Embraceable You," "S'Wonderful" (Gershwin); "I've Got My Love to Keep Me Warm" (Berlin)

Choosing Ceremony Musicians

If your house of worship provides the musicians for your ceremony, you don't need a contract — just a confirmation of timing and fees. If you hire an independent soloist, quartet, or other musical entity for your ceremony, you want to get all the particulars in writing.

The music directors in churches and temples are well versed in both the possibilities of ensembles for your ceremony and choices the officiant deems appropriate. If your ceremony is at a site other than a house of worship, you'll likely have far more freedom in creating your musical program. Either way, when interviewing musicians for your ceremony, be sure to cover the following questions, and take notes:

- Do they have a sample CD, MP3 files, or links to streaming media they can send you?
- Will the musicians on the sample be the ones playing at the ceremony?
- Have they worked at this venue before? If not, will the leader have a short meeting with the person in charge?
- Can they give you some direction on musical choices for various parts of the ceremony?
- If you want a particular piece of music, can they configure it for your ensemble? How long will that take, and for what fee?
- If you hire a soloist or other group for the ceremony, will the musicians rehearse with them?
- How many hours are included in the quoted price? If the ceremony goes over the expected time, is overtime available?
- What will the musicians wear?
- Do they have any special requests — armless chairs, music lights, tenting for outdoor ceremonies?
- Are they available for your rehearsal? Do they charge an additional fee? *Note:* If you're having an elaborate ceremony and feel that the cues are complicated, you may want to negotiate a price to have the group (or at least the leader) be present at the rehearsal.

Part IV

A Rousing Reception

The 5th Wave By Rich Tennant

"It's nice that you picked a professional radio DJ for the reception music, but I wish he'd quit announcing the weather and sports scores between every third song."

In this part . . .

1 guide you through the intricate process of planning a memorable party in celebration of your marriage. Whether it's cocktails and cake, tea for 200, or a formal seated dinner, a wedding reception is among the most festive of occasions. I show you how to spend your money wisely when it comes to food, drink, and décor — and how to whip these key ingredients into an event that will make lasting memories for both you and your guests.

Chapter 13

Get Up and Dance

You both are giddy with emotion as you glide arm in arm to the dance floor for your first dance together as husband and wife. For a moment you could swear the bandleader, sounding rather like a cartoon mouse, just mispronounced your names in his introduction, but you're too busy readying yourselves for the foxtrot you've spent weeks perfecting to worry about it. With a flourish, the band begins to play your favorite song. And it sounds, well, like the worst lounge-act cover version you've ever heard. You focus on breathing deeply and start praying that you'll wake up from this nightmare in a cold sweat, just as you have several times in the past month.

The point is that music is an extremely important aspect of your ceremony and undoubtedly the element that sets the tone and pace of your reception. People may not remember exactly what they ate, but they'll remember whether they danced all night or stuffed the dinner rolls in their ears. This chapter helps you keep their feet on the dance floor.

Setting the Tone

To help keep your guests lively and your reception flowing nicely, plan for different types of music during each phase of the party.

Cocktail reception

As guests arrive for cocktails, music should greet them. People tend to drift in, and particularly for the first few guests who enter the space, background music serves as an audible welcome mat. Decide with the maitre d' where to place the cocktail musicians so they don't interfere with the entrance or exits, hors d'oeuvre stations, or bars.

Depending on the number of guests, you should have a minimum of two musicians. No one will hear a solo flute or guitar over the clanking of ice in drink glasses, let alone the din of excited, postceremony chatter. If you have more than 125 guests, seriously consider having three musicians.

Typically, you can strike a deal with the band for a few of them to play for the ceremony and/or the cocktails at a per-musician price. Although this may be a good deal financially, it can be awkward musically and logistically. First of all, unless these musicians are able to play different instruments than they'll be playing during the meal, your whole reception will sound the same. Second, whether your ceremony is in a different location than your reception or in an adjoining room, the musicians have to scurry out ahead of the guests leaving the ceremony or breathlessly set up as guests arrive for cocktails. Later, when you want the full band set up at least 20 minutes before the guests enter the dining room, the same musicians have to thread through the crowd carrying their instruments unless they have a second set. Even though guests may not notice that the music has stopped, they may find the musicians packing up and leaving odd.

If your ceremony features classical music, consider having something different played at the cocktail reception if your budget permits. Even if it's recorded jazz, changing the mood from serious to festive works well. Consider one of the following options:

- **Two or three pieces from the band:** This setup is usually composed of one or two guitars, an electric keyboard, and a trumpet or sax. (These instruments are the easiest to move to the room where the main reception is.) Think in terms of a jazz lounge — Miles Davis, Herb Alpert, Frank Sinatra, Tony Bennett, George Gershwin, Fats Waller, and so on.

- **Piano and singer:** This combination works best with a baby grand piano. It's also a good icebreaker. Think cabaret, a la Billie Holiday or Sarah Vaughn. Be conscious of acoustics; this duo still shouldn't be loud enough to take over the cocktail reception.

- **Something unusual:** Cocktail receptions can be great fun with zydeco, klezmer, doo-wop, or an a capella group placed at the entranceway.

As guests enter the main reception space

After the cocktail reception, guests are escorted to the main reception area. If you want dancing both before and after dinner, the DJ or the full band should be playing as guests come into the room. Choose upbeat and recognizable music; many guests may want to dance before the first dance of the bride and groom, and these first songs should encourage them to boogie.

Here are a few tunes that may fit the bill:

- ✔ *Frank Sinatra:* "I Get a Kick Out of You"
- ✔ **Peggy Lee or Count Basie and Joe Williams:** "Alright, Okay, You Win"
- ✔ **Nina Simone:** "My Baby Just Cares for Me"
- ✔ **Original cast recording or Tony Bennett:** "Anything Goes"
- ✔ **Nat King Cole:** "Just One of Those Things" or "Our Love Is Here to Stay"
- ✔ **Diana Krall:** "Let's Fall in Love" or "I've Got the World on a String"

If you plan to save the dancing until after dinner, consider having only a portion of the band (just keyboard and guitar, for instance) play as your guests enter. If you have a DJ, request that he play softer, less bass-heavy songs before the meal.

First dance

The timing of the first dance varies greatly. Some people prefer that only background music be played until after the main course is served; others like to get their first dance out of the way and continue to have dance sets in between each course.

Some couples prefer to dance their first dance to recorded music even if they've hired a band. They may feel that only the original artist can do their song justice or perhaps they've rehearsed to this specific version and feel edgy about any possible changes. If you decide to use a recording for your first dance, make sure that the timing is down to the minute so the music blends seamlessly with the band starting the second number. Of course, that means having someone there to operate the sound system and pay attention.

Although you have zillions of possible numbers to choose from for a first dance, your two main considerations should be the following: The song should carry special meaning for both of you, and you should feel comfortable dancing to it. Some first-dance classics include

- ✔ **Beach Boys:** "God Only Knows"
- ✔ **Harry Connick, Jr.:** "Love Is Here to Stay"
- ✔ **Bruce Springsteen:** "If I Should Fall Behind"

If your idea of a slow dance consists of hanging on to each other for dear life, start taking dance lessons sooner rather than later.

Although some songs seem romantic enough for your first dance as husband and wife, listen carefully to the lyrics — not just the chorus — beforehand for their true meaning, which may be inappropriate for the moment. For example, Olivia Newton John's "I Honestly Love You" is about the ending of an extra-marital affair. And Whitney Houston's "I Will Always Love You" is a breakup song, as is Garth Brooks' "The Dance." I always find it particularly hilarious when couples choose "Every Breath You Take" by the Police, which is a song about stalking. Ballads are particularly tricky.

Second tune

The second number, played after the first dance, is usually for a series of dances with the parents (see the next section), after which the guests are invited to join in. If you find this awkward because of divorced or widowed parents or for other reasons, instruct the wedding party to join you on the dance floor as the second piece of music starts. Other guests will inevitably join in. If not, the bandleader can invite them.

Dances with parents

On occasion, whether as the second dance or later in the reception, the father of the bride and/or the mother of the groom may want to dance to a particular song with their daughter or son. Although the usual suspects over the years have included such ditties as "Sonny Boy" (Al Jolson), "Sunrise, Sunset" (from the original cast recording of *Fiddler on the Roof*), and "Daddy's Little Girl" (Al Martino), you should choose something meaningful (and, I hope, not foolishly sentimental) to you. One bride and her father spent weeks choreographing a tango and then performed it with great flair, much to the surprise and delight of all the wedding guests. Here are some ideas, including some less well-known options:

- **Bette Midler:** "Wind Beneath My Wings"
- **Bob Carlisle:** "Butterfly Kisses"
- **Catie Curtis:** "Dad's Yard"
- **James Taylor:** "You've Got a Friend"
- **Temptations:** "My Girl"
- **Warren Zevon (or Shawn Colvin):** "Tenderness on the Block"

Ethnic dances

Don't assume that the band or DJ has a full repertoire of traditional or ethnic selections. Most likely, they can play a hora or a tarantella or "Danny Boy," but if you want a full set of ethnic dancing such as Indian music, you need to arrange this with the musicians or DJ far enough in advance for them to find or learn the music.

Special requests

Perhaps some of your friends are talented singers or musicians who would add to the festivities by performing a number with the band. The band needs to know about this in advance and to have the music. Having the friend rehearse the special performance with the band, perhaps while guests are in another room having cocktails, is also a good idea.

Some couples stipulate in the contract that the bandleader or DJ not play any special requests without clearing them with the bride or groom. If you're truly concerned that guests will make ridiculous requests that disrupt the mood, you may want to take this route. However, you'll lose some spontaneity — letting human nature take its course is often more fun. A talented musician or spin doctor should be able to gauge the crowd and create an artful segue. Who knows — doing the Macarena could end up being one of your fondest wedding memories.

Which reminds me, your "don't play" list is far more important than your playlist. Seemingly benign songs that remind you of a past love, your high school chemistry teacher who hated you, or a band you despise on principle may mar your wedding if you don't apprise your bandleader of such. Check the band's own playlist as well.

As a surprise for your new spouse, your guests, or your parents, consider having someone perform a song written expressly for your wedding. To find a songwriter who specializes in customized lyrics, search the web for "custom songs."

Background music

Even if you have dancing between courses, when food is served, you want something soothing and not distracting. Show tunes or instrumentals work well, as does recorded music by a mellow artist.

Cake cutting

When the time comes to cut the cake, a reprise of the first dance song notifies the guests that something is about to happen. If you really want to make an event of this ritual, an energetic, rock-and-roll version of "The Bride Cuts the Cake" (played to the tune of "The Farmer in the Dell") brings down the house.

Late night

If you hire both a band and a DJ or if you decide to keep whomever you hire playing for late-night dancing (after many guests have left), the later hours are when you may want to make the music louder and more contemporary.

Booking the Band

Talented musicians, like prime locations, go fast. No matter how much time you allot for planning your wedding, finding and booking the band should be one of the first things you do.

Before you begin band shopping, put your thoughts in order. Who are your guests? Are they all about the same age or do they cover several generations? Do either of you have strong musical preferences? What do you like to listen to? What can't you bear? Get opinions about music from your parents and friends and find out what keeps them on the dance floor. Bear in mind, however, that in the end you can't please everybody. As with other aspects of your wedding, you must determine whose enjoyment is most important and plan accordingly.

When hiring a band, you can opt for eclecticism or virtuosity. A band that offers a full repertoire, from swing to funk to ethnic favorites, is probably not expert at all of it. If you, like many couples these days, are averse to traditional wedding bands, fearing a parody a la *Saturday Night Live,* you may wish to hire a band that isn't primarily a wedding band. Doing so can be a great idea; just be very specific about any traditions you want to keep.

Music-union rules sometimes specify the minimum number of musicians that are allowed to play in certain on-premise spaces. For most dancing crowds of 100 or more, you probably want to hire six pieces minimum. If you want certain tunes or genres that require specific instruments, discuss with the bands you interview what makes sense and what's overkill. Ask the catering or banquet director's opinion as well. More isn't always better.

Breakfast and lunch receptions are generally lower key and often without dancing. Consequently, you may not require a full band, although background music is always festive whether you use recordings or hire a few classical musicians.

Finding a band

To find the perfect band for your wedding, consider the following:

- **Blogs:** Check wedding blogs for weddings in your area and explore the pictures and the musical credits. If you like the wedding's style, chances are you'll like the musicians too.

- **Concert promoters:** Call the office and endear yourself to someone upfront. Fabulous bands that open for bigger acts are often available for hire.

- **Friends:** Have any friends been to weddings or other parties lately where the band kept the crowd on its feet all night? What kind of music was it? What sort of reception? Can you trust your friends' musical taste?

- **Hotels:** Call the banquet manager of the nearest large hotel. Better yet, ask the maitre d' because he doesn't usually have a vested interest in promoting a particular band but does care a great deal about one that ruins a good party.

- **The Internet:** Do a search for "wedding musicians" ("wedding bands" turns up mostly websites selling rings) to find groups, agencies, and individual players. You can make your search more effective by searching for the specific musical style you want, like swing, cabaret, Brazilian, reggae, doo-wop, and so on.

- **Music agencies/band representatives:** This route is the most common way to find a band of whatever size and style you're interested in.

- **Music colleges:** Call or e-mail the job placement office with your wedding details. Many music schools maintain a list of hiring opportunities for musicians and will post your event on their message boards.

- **Nightclubs:** Call the booker for recommendations and for ways to get in touch with a favorite band's agent.

- **Vendors:** Photographers, caterers, and other vendors who work on-site with bands usually know who's hot.

Looking for the perfect band can bring on audio overload. From time to time you may need a little band-aid in the form of a few days off to keep you from hiring the next group you see because you can no longer distinguish one from another.

Auditioning the band

Wedding books delight in advising you to get dolled up and go hear a band in person before signing the band. I really have a problem with this because a bandleader who invites you to witness his band's talents at another wedding would have no qualms about using your reception as a marketing tool as well. The only time you should audition a band at someone else's wedding is if the bandleader assures you that the bride and groom have magnanimously agreed (out of sympathy, no doubt) to have you drop by. When you do, remain inconspicuous.

Recordings are often your only way to check out a band. Bands often post links to streaming music on their website and may share additional MP3s or a CD on request. Find out when the recording was made and under what conditions. If recorded at an event, the quality may be uneven.

Studio recordings may be technically flawless but bear no semblance to what the band really sounds like. Video can also be technically enhanced, and unscrupulous music agents aren't above showing photogenic band members dubbed with different, more-talented musicians. Unless you work as a sound technician, this fraud is often hard to spot. You must rely on the group's reputation and your own instincts.

If you're interested in a band named for a famous bandleader, find out whether the leader is still with the band or if the musicians have bought the name. Many bands may be named after this person. After you determine that the bandleader is indeed the original and the one you want, schedule a meeting with the leader.

In evaluating a band, ask these questions:

- ✔ Does the contract stipulate that the musicians who appear on the video or play on the audio are the ones who perform at your wedding? Always insist on seeing a photograph with audio.

- ✔ Is the audio or video recorded live or studio-produced? Is the sound technically enhanced?

- ✔ How many musicians are playing on the recording? How many vocalists? How many instruments?

- ✔ When was the recording made? (The band's style or its players may have changed dramatically.)

- ✔ Does the band bring its own sound system? How large a room can it accommodate?

- ✔ Who sets up the instruments, and when do they arrive?

✔ Is continuous music in your agreement? Depending on the band's size, a minimum of one or two musicians should always be on stage while the others are on break.

✔ What do the band members wear? Does formal dress cost extra?

✔ Do you need to rent a piano or does the band use an electric keyboard?

✔ Does the bandleader or another band member act as master of ceremonies?

✔ Does the band have another gig before or after yours? Are band members prepared to play overtime? How much is the overtime rate? Is overtime based on the hour or half hour? What leeway do you have?

✔ No matter what the band's repertoire is, can it play other songs important to you such as a hora or other ethnic classics and favorite pop hits?

✔ If you have an original or esoteric piece you want played, will the band learn it, and how much lead time do you need to provide? What would the band charge to arrange it?

✔ Does the band have a rider attached to its contract? (A *rider* is a contract addendum that contains additional terms and specifications. The more successful the band is, the more likely it has an extensive rider.) If so, read it very carefully to see whether you're willing to honor it, or ask whether the band will alter its rider for a private event.

If you hear a band that you feel certain you're going to book but you need a few days to mull it over, make sure to ask for the *right of first refusal.* In other words, the band will call you if someone else is waving a check for the same date. If the band doesn't agree to a right of first refusal, get out your checkbook.

Getting in tune

After you've written your wedding-day schedule (see Chapter 7), go over it with the bandleader either by phone or in person. Specifically, you want to clarify

✔ **Breaks:** Specify when and where the band will eat, based on a consultation with the maitre d'. If you want continuous live music, the band must eat in shifts.

✔ **Etiquette:** Stipulate no eating, drinking, or smoking on stage (unless you don't mind, of course).

✔ **First dance:** Tell the bandleader the name of the song, when the band should play it, at what tempo, and how to introduce you.

✔ **Gag orders:** Be extremely specific about how and when the bandleader makes announcements. At the same time, be reasonable: Even if you don't want to risk the bandleader running off at the mouth, *somebody* has to tell people when the next course is being served.

✔ **Introductions:** If the bandleader is acting as master of ceremonies and you want to have family and wedding-party members introduced, write down their names phonetically and their relationship to you. Make a special note of people who are divorced, deceased, or not attending to save the bandleader from making a big "whoops."

✔ **Stage set:** Ask what the band's music stands look like and whether they go with your décor or have the band's name emblazoned on them. The stage should also not look like a dressing room. Provide a secure place for the band to store personal effects.

✔ **Who's running the show:** Be certain that the maitre d' and the bandleader work together in deciding when guests are dancing and when they're eating.

Personally, I could do without *medleys,* short renditions of a slew of songs of a similar type. If you want to hear *full* versions of the Rolling Stones catalog or your favorite Motown hits, be sure to mention that to the bandleader.

Although this may be your first wedding, it may be the hundredth that the band has played this year. A good friend of ours, a talented musician who's graduated from playing weddings, has said that the groups he played with were often so bored that they'd fight over the selection of magazines they read surreptitiously on their music stands as they were performing. You can, however, get even jaded musicians to rise to the occasion:

✔ **Be flexible.** Ask the band members what they like to play and include it if possible. Don't dictate the playlist down to the millisecond. Trust the pros to get the party moving.

✔ **Feed the band.** Musicians work weird hours and have erratic habits. Although you don't have to serve the band what you feed the guests, a leftover sandwich from the cafeteria doesn't cut it. A full meal served in a decent place plus a drink or a beer may in fact make them play better.

✔ **Introduce yourselves.** Early in the reception, you and your betrothed should approach the bandstand and tell the band members how happy you are to have them playing at your wedding. This gesture alone may shock them into consciousness.

✔ **Provide special equipment.** If the bandleader or manager specifies certain arrangements, such as a baby grand piano, a two-level platform, extra mikes, or special lighting, make sure these details are attended to. If you can't supply it, tell the bandleader well in advance. Arriving at a gig to find specified items missing unnerves musicians.

Setting up

At sites with an inlaid dance floor, the band's spot is usually obvious. If your reception is at an off-premise site (where everything's catered) such as a tent, you must decide where to place the dance floor. I suggest positioning the band and dance floor so that all the tables are equidistant from the band rather than putting the band at the front of the room so that guests seated at the back must pack a canteen before setting out in search of the dance floor. In principle, having tables between the dance floor and the bandstand cuts off the dynamic between the band and the dancers and can burst the eardrums of guests who happen to be seated in the crossfire. Although you may be tempted to place tables in the round with the dance floor in the middle, you don't want guests gazing at the backs of musicians and their equipment.

Some considerations for setting up the band:

- ✔ Where's the electrical source? Will you require a generator in an outdoor space?
- ✔ Does the band need risers?
- ✔ What type of chairs does the band need?
- ✔ Is special lighting required so musicians can read their music in a darkened room?

You don't want the band rolling its instruments through the cocktail reception on its way to set up. So if you can afford it, pay for early setup. If you're hiring more than one band or a DJ and a band who will be performing at different times, you should still have *all* the equipment set up on stage before the guests arrive. (Picture a double-header concert.)

Checking the sound

Volume perception is very subjective. Generally, the younger the crowd, the greater the decibels. Pumping up the jam is fine when guests are revved up on the dance floor. But when people are being served or eating, the music (if any at all) should be low enough so people can speak in conversational tones. Any group always has someone who'd find a harp deafening. All you can do is seat those folks as far away from the speakers as possible.

You must decide before the reception who's in charge of the sound level. Nothing annoys a bandleader more than getting mixed orders from you and your parents — "Turn it up!" "Turn it down!" "I thought I told you to turn it up!" "Did you see whose signature is on the check? I said turn it down!"

Keeping time

You typically hire a band for four hours, not including ceremony, cocktails, or overtime. A common mistake is to cut the band's starting time extremely close to avoid overtime at the end. Bands, however, are notorious for arriving one minute before showtime. If you don't allow a 15-minute cushion in the beginning, you may find yourself hyperventilating as band members do their sound check while your guests' stomachs growl.

Bands sent out by an agency sometimes refuse to play until paid in full, so I advise you to pay your balance the day before. As for overtime, the band usually bills you later. Clarify with the bandleader who's in charge of deciding whether the band will play overtime. If you and your spouse are paying for the band, you don't want one of your parents blithely telling the band, "Oh, please just keep playing. We're having such a *fabulous* time!"

Spinning with a DJ

A DJ at a wedding used to be as low-budget a choice as macaroni and cheese for the main course. Today, that's not the case but rather a matter of the kind of music you want at your wedding. If your preference in music is mostly current top-40, '70s rock, or a combination of very different styles, a DJ is your best bet.

Although for $25 you may be able to hire your multipierced neighbor and his iPod, don't risk it. Hire a professional DJ — one adept at weddings rather than one who specializes in bar/bat mitzvahs, confirmations, or sweet sixteens. You may not be pleased to have Day-Glo yo-yos and balloon guitars catapulted at your guests as the DJ urges them to do the "Hokey Pokey."

A DJ is only as good as the songs she brings. Even though pros have an inventory of zillions, make a list of specific songs you want the DJ to bring with her or offer to furnish the recording yourself. If you want your DJ to also act as master of ceremonies, be prepared to pay for two people — a front person and the person in charge of the music.

DJs come in a few varieties nowadays. Many select and mix their song set from a laptop computer, and you can also get a DJ who works with old-school vinyl and turntables. (A few also still use CDs.) Scratch Events has a network of trained DJs nationwide that you can access through its website: www. scratchevents.com.

If you can squeeze it into your budget, have a DJ alternate with a live band. That way, the band can play what it's good at, the DJ can offer versatility, and you still get that special energy between live musicians and an audience that you sometimes don't have with a DJ alone.

Aside from the obvious musical questions, interview DJs the same way you would other vendors. As with a band, you may have to go through an agency, which may resist your meeting with a specific one to interview. Your goal is to get past these salespeople and check out the talent. If the company has a reputation for sending out pros, ask to see reference letters for the DJ the agency plans to send to your reception. Also insist that you get to speak to the DJ by phone before the wedding. Among the things to verify:

- What the DJ will wear

- That the DJ or the agency will check out the electrical requirements and acoustics at your venue, especially if the DJ hasn't worked there before

- What the equipment looks like and whether the DJ needs a draped table for the turntables or computer

- The size of the speakers and whether they can be camouflaged (doubtful, as I discuss in Chapter 17)

- Whether the DJ plans on using any effects such as theatrical lighting, bubbles, or smoke

We could have danced all night

When creating a playlist for the band or DJ, keep in mind that you need about 50 or 60 songs for a four-hour reception. Start putting together your playlist by listing a few songs you love to dance to. You can type these songs into Pandora Internet Radio (www.pandora.com or the Pandora smart phone application, available through the website) to get suggestions for related songs. Listen and add the ones you like to your list. If you hear a great tune while you're out and about, you can use the Shazam app (www.shazam.com) or the SoundHound app (www.soundhound.com), both for iPhones and Android phones, to identify it and put it on the list as well. And the Fun Wedding app for iPhone gives you lots of music charts, updated regularly, like the top 200 songs at wedding receptions, the top songs for the first dance, and the most overplayed songs. You can select from these charts to generate your wedding playlist.

If you want some suggestions to get started, the following is a highly subjective list of wedding tunes to get your party moving, particularly into the wee hours. You have umpteen thousands of great tunes to choose from, of course, but in the interest of ecology, I've limited this list — organized by decade — to these favorites that have stood the test of (at least some) time:

1950s

- **Bill Haley & His Comets:** "Rock Around the Clock"

- **Shirley & Lee:** "Let the Good Times Roll"

- **Bobby Darin:** "Mack the Knife"

- **Hank Williams:** "Jambalaya (On the Bayou)"

- **Buddy Holly:** "It's So Easy"; "Rave On"

(continued)

(continued)

1960s

- **Chubby Checker:** "The Twist"
- **Martha and the Vandellas:** "Heatwave"
- **Rolling Stones:** "Honky Tonk Woman"; "Jumpin' Jack Flash"
- **Marvin Gaye & Tammi Terrell:** "Ain't No Mountain High Enough"
- **Beatles:** "She Loves You"; "Got to Get You into My Life"; "Twist and Shout"

1970s

- **Al Green:** "Livin' for You"; "I'm Still in Love with You"; "How Can You Mend a Broken Heart"
- **Bob Marley:** "Jamming"; "One Love/People Get Ready"
- **Chic:** "Le Freak"; "Dance Dance Dance"
- **The Knack:** "My Sharona"
- **The Bee Gees:** "Stayin' Alive"; "Night Fever"; "You Should Be Dancing"

1980s

- **B52s:** "Whammy Kiss"; "Love Shack"
- **Buster Poindexter:** "Hot, Hot, Hot"
- **Culture Club:** "Do You Really Want to Hurt Me?"; "Karma Chameleon"
- **Cyndi Lauper:** "True Colors"; "She Bop"; "Girls Just Want to Have Fun"
- **David Bowie:** "Let's Dance"; "Fame"

1990s

- **C+C Music Factory:** "Gonna Make You Sweat"
- **DJ Jazzy Jeff & the Fresh Prince:** "Boom! Shake the Room!"; "Summertime"
- **Lauryn Hill:** "Doo Wop (That Thing)"
- **Snap:** "Rhythm Is a Dancer"
- **Deee-Lite:** "Groove Is in the Heart"

2000s

- **Gnarls Barkley:** "Crazy"
- **Justin Timberlake:** "SexyBack"
- **Beyoncé:** "Single Ladies (Put a Ring on It)"
- **Kylie Minogue:** "Can't Get You Out of My Head"
- **U2:** "Beautiful Day"

Chapter 14

What's on the Menu?

The ceremony was splendid. You both composed exquisite vows and delivered them beautifully, leaving not a dry eye in the house. Your guests oohed and aahed at the beautiful flowers and creative flourishes you spent months obsessing over. Somehow, though, something was missing in this amazing production; could it be that the food was lackluster?

Don't imagine that just because you're not a "foodie," the food is a part of your wedding reception you can default on. Serving an imaginative, tasty, and enjoyable meal to your guests requires as much thought and time as the other aspects of your wedding day.

Working with the Perfect Caterer

When it comes to the food for your wedding, your first task — if you're renting an off-premise space (see Chapter 4) — is to hire a caterer. The following sections tell you how to find and hire a caterer and what to do at your initial tasting.

Finding a caterer who shares your tastes

Although asking friends for catering recommendations may seem natural, taste in food is really, really subjective. Consider these other sources for recommendations:

- ✔ **Culinary schools:** Ask whether they have an alumni list, association, or job bank. Check out the bulletin boards and post a want ad. Be sure to ask for references and arrange a tasting if you're going to work with students.

- ✔ **Professional associations:** If you're planning a long-distance wedding and have absolutely no clue where to begin, consult a professional association such as the International Special Events Society (`www.ises.com`).

- ✔ **Restaurant chefs:** Ask the chef at your favorite restaurant whether the restaurant caters outside of its premises or if the chef is particularly impressed with any caterer in the area.

- ✔ **Vendors:** The best recommendations often come from other suppliers — bands, florists, party coordinators, and so on — who've worked with caterers and know what really goes on behind the kitchen doors.

Call and ask caterers and banquet managers for an informational package that includes sample menus. If the packet is stuffed with recommendation letters, as is often the case, the majority should be current. Don't be shy about calling references. Write down your questions before you pick up the phone. Be as specific as possible regarding the style you have in mind for your reception and how much help you can expect with the ceremony and other aspects not directly related to food and service.

Questions to ask people about their experience with specific caterers include

- ✔ Did the caterer deliver what it promised?

- ✔ Were expensive items, such as shrimp, plentiful?

- ✔ Was the staff neat and prompt?

- ✔ Were there enough bartenders and service people? Did guests ever have to wait for anything?

- ✔ Was the food tasty and attractive?

- ✔ What were the downsides, if any? (To get an honest answer, qualify this question by saying, "Not that your answer would necessarily keep me from hiring this caterer. . . .")

Asking the right questions

Before making any decisions, meet with caterers in person, preferably at their kitchen/offices. This meeting should give you a fair idea of their manner and workmanship. Are they brusque? Disorganized? Clean? Does their workspace smell yummy? Are they legally licensed? Have they posted a certificate of inspection in the kitchen? Do you relate well to the person you'd be working with? Figure 14-1 lists some key questions to ask.

Caterer Interview Checklist

❏ What ideas, if any, does the caterer have regarding appropriate spaces for your wedding?

❏ If you have found your space already, has the caterer worked there before? If not, will the caterer make a site visit before writing a proposal?

❏ What specific menus can the caterer recommend that will work in that facility's kitchen?

❏ Does the caterer have sample menus? Are there photographs of the work?

❏ What references can the caterer provide?

❏ What are the caterer's specialties?

❏ How flexible is the caterer in planning a menu?

❏ Can you have a tasting? At what cost?

❏ How does the caterer price the menus?

❏ Is a wedding cake included? If not, what are the charges? Can you supply one? Is there a cake-cutting fee?

❏ What are the specific hourly charges for all staff such as waiters, captains, and kitchen staff? What additional gratuities are suggested? What are the overtime charges?

❏ How many staff people would they suggest for your event, and how many hours would each staff member work?

❏ How do they handle the rentals? Must you use a specific company? What choices do you have for rentals, such as glass, silver, china, and linens?

❏ What does the caterer own that will be included, such as props, platters, or kitchen equipment?

❏ Will you receive separate food, service, and rental bills?

❏ How do they handle the liquor?

❏ Assuming that you are allowed to supply your own liquor, what suppliers does the caterer suggest? Ordering suggestions?

❏ What do they charge for setups (soda, ice, fruit)?

❏ How involved will the caterer be in your wedding — just supplying food or helping with the ceremony and other facets?

❏ What is the caterer's educated estimate on *total* costs for food, liquor, rentals, and staff for your party?

Figure 14-1:
Ask the right questions when interviewing prospective caterers.

Illustration by Wiley, Composition Services Graphics

Comparing pricing between off-premise sites and on-premise sites, such as hotels or banquet halls, is slightly tricky. For an on-premise site, tally the cost of the food, beverage, tax, and gratuities. For an off-premise site, combine the site fee with the caterer's estimates on food, liquor, rentals, and service. If you interview several caterers for one site, use an average of their estimated costs as the catering charge for that site. (For an explanation of on- and off-premise sites, see Chapter 4.)

Building rapport with the chef

Find out who's really in charge of cooking your meal — the banquet chef, sous-chef, or someone farther down the totem pole. Having a lovely meeting or tasting with a well-known executive chef or the chef for the restaurant kitchen does no good unless one of them is actually involved in the preparation of the meal at your event.

If at all possible, meet with the chef to determine what the kitchen staff can produce well for a group of your size. Although chefs have a reputation for being intimidating, in my experience they're flattered when someone cares what they think, and that can have a decided impact on what comes out of the kitchen. If the catering manager and chef, as well as the references you've called, all recommend a very basic menu, listen to them and keep it simple.

A matter of tasting

After you book a space or caterer, I feel that you're entitled to a tasting, so make sure that point is spelled out in the contract or in an oral agreement. Schedule the tasting far enough before your wedding date that you have time for a second one if needed, though not so far ahead that key ingredients are out of season.

With increasing competition for jobs, you now sometimes have the opportunity for a tasting *before* you hire a caterer. Some caterers stage tasting events or offer group tastings for prospective clients. Check with the caterer directly about the possibility or ask your wedding planner if she can coordinate a group tasting with other couples.

If your wedding is in a restaurant's banquet space, the meal for your reception may be prepared in a banquet kitchen completely separate from the main restaurant kitchen. Therefore, a meal in the restaurant may bear no resemblance to the food you have at your wedding.

Your caterer will tell you how many people you can bring to the tasting. Besides you and your fiancé(e), the banquet manager should be there to offer professional comments and suggestions. You may also want to include your parents or in-laws.

Because of the cost of labor and ingredients, places often don't let you taste the hors d'oeuvres unless they book huge numbers consistently. In such cases, ask whether they have an event coming up and can make up a take-out tray for you to sample at home. (You will, of course, offer to pay for this.) If they can't accommodate you, can they at least show you photographs and describe ingredients in detail?

At this stage of the game, you want to keep a few things in mind:

- ✔ **Take photographs.** Before you consume anything, snap a photograph. Having pictures later helps you remember what you chose, and they're lovely for your digital photo album or your scrapbook.

- ✔ **Ask to taste two or three options for each course.** You may think you're set on filet mignon, but after tasting the chef's specialty lamb, you may change your mind completely. In principle, a kitchen should shine at a meal for four or six. If it doesn't, the meal served to your guests could be even worse.

  Taste with your eyes as well as your mouth — be very specific about how you'd like the food to look.

- ✔ **Remember the vegetarian option.** Even if you're not a vegetarian yourself, chances are increasing that some of your guests will be. So be sure that you sample the vegetarian offerings for the main course. Spaces and caterers may create an explicit vegetarian option (for which they charge you based on the number of orders) or a "silent" vegetarian option provided at no additional charge to anyone who indicates that the steak or the chicken won't work. Don't forget to include meals for any of your kosher guests, as well as vegans.

- ✔ **Request that the food's presentation be exactly as it would be at your wedding.** If at your tasting you decide on poached salmon that's beautifully plated, rimmed by a painstakingly drizzled nouvelle sauce, and garnished with flowers, then it should look the same on your wedding day, not dumped from a tray by a waiter.

- ✔ **Taste food and wine together.** Either bring the wine you'd consider serving or ask the caterer to supply some selections in your price range.

- ✔ **Go about the tasting professionally.** Don't stuff yourself with every last hors d'oeuvre and lick your plate clean; save room for dessert. Enjoy yourself.

> ✔ **Ask questions and take notes.** Is it possible to have this sauce on that dish? What if we serve this with coffee ice cream instead of vanilla? Take notes, draw pictures, and be ridiculously detailed. Yours is probably not the only event that the chef is working on at the moment, and details that are important to you may fall through the cracks unless you furnish notes or a follow-up letter summarizing your desires.

Ask your caterer to pack a few portions of each course (including the wedding cake) for you to take when you leave your reception to assuage the inevitable 3 a.m. munchies. Now is also the time to arrange for leftovers to go to a local soup kitchen or "harvesting" charity. Food rescue charities gather food from restaurants, caterers, and other sources and distribute it to soup kitchens, shelters, and other care providers. Ask whether your caterer is affiliated with a food rescue charity or search online for *food rescue* plus your city to locate one.

The Beauty of the Feast

As with other things in life, the greater the interest you take in your wedding meal, the better the results will be and the more you'll enjoy it. The best way to start designing your meal is to have some idea of what you want to serve.

Whether you're dealing with an in-house catering operation (such as at a banquet facility, restaurant, club, or hotel) or hiring a caterer for a site you're renting, before you concoct elaborate haute cuisine wish lists, start with the place's sample menus, which constitute its greatest hits. Request to meet with the banquet manager and/or catering director and ask about the kitchen's strengths and weaknesses. To focus your search for the perfect meal, take a few preliminary steps:

> ✔ **Adapt a recipe.** Go through cookbooks and food magazines for ideas. Keep in mind, however, that unless you're holding a wedding for ten people, something like hand-rolled pasta carbonara won't translate. Chefs are usually open to using your favorite recipes, as long as they come from reliable sources such as professional cookbooks.
>
> ✔ **Take a palate poll.** What are your and your intended's favorite restaurants and meals? What do family and friends like to eat? What's considered too exotic? Do most of the guests eat meat?
>
> ✔ **Tap your know-it-all pals.** If you have friends who always know the hot new restaurants or actually work in the food business, ask them for their opinions.

The meal format you opt for has a great effect on your entire wedding. A lunch can be as formal as a dinner, provided both are seated and served, but something about an evening event (perhaps the increased alcohol consumption?) encourages guests to really party. A full meal served from food stations rather than at tables can be as formal or low-key as you want. Ditto for a cocktail reception where you have only partial seating. The number of courses depends both on your budget and how you want to time your wedding. Obviously, the more courses, the longer the party. A buffet meal, as I discuss in the later section "Variety shows: Buffet stations," takes the least amount of time.

Postnuptial nibbles

A cocktail reception usually follows most wedding ceremonies and is then followed by a complete meal. A cocktail time after the ceremony is a good idea, as wedding ceremonies tend to produce great emotional upwellings, and guests need a release before being herded into the dining room. One way of determining the length of the cocktail reception is whether you're taking pictures together at that time.

Choose the hors d'oeuvres after you choose what you're serving for the rest of the meal so you don't duplicate foods, such as following up salmon rolls at cocktails with grilled salmon at dinner. Also take into consideration the rehearsal-dinner menu. When in doubt, the wedding meal takes precedence.

Passed hors d'oeuvres

Passed hors d'oeuvres should be bite-size. That's *one* bite. No knives, forks, or spoons. A toothpick or skewer may be okay. Portions of food served at cocktail stations should be small as well. If necessary, a small plate with a small fork is permissible.

Caterers usually price passed hors d'oeuvres per piece or include them in the meal package with a choice of hot and cold. You're not out of line to ask how many pieces of each hors d'oeuvre they serve within your price level. Caterers I queried agree that between eight and ten hors d'oeuvres per person is ample for a one-hour cocktail reception.

Hors d'oeuvre stations

In addition to passed hors d'oeuvres, having one or two stations with, say, carved smoked salmon and baked brie helps dissuade people from jumping the waiters as they come out the kitchen door and also provides a natural gathering spot.

For hors d'oeuvre stations such as a raw bar, carving station, or pasta assortment, caterers generally charge per head.

The trick is not to show that you can afford umpteen hors d'oeuvre stations followed by a huge hunk of meat but to design a menu that has broad appeal, is appetizing, and leaves guests with energy to party.

When it comes to shrimp, although you can almost never have enough, figure on about three per person; I've never been to a wedding where a single piece was left on a waiter's tray. You're typically charged per piece, even if other hors d'oeuvres are priced as a package. Peeled, tail-on shrimp are graded according to the number per pound by using the following shorthand terms: 26–30, 21–25, 16–20, U–15, and U–10. A pound of 16–20, for example, contains between 16 and 20 shrimp, while a pound of U–15 contains fewer than, or "under," 15. U–10, therefore, are comparatively huge (and rare).

If you like shrimp but whole cocktail shrimp are beyond your budget, ask your caterer about more economical alternatives such as minishrimp toasts or shrimp salad on rye rounds.

Variety shows: Buffet stations

The old-fashioned buffet comprising an endlessly long table with a salad, a main course, a vegetable, and a starch — for which you stand in an endlessly long line — has been (thankfully) relegated to school cafeterias. Food stations that enable you to serve eclectic and creative meals without traffic jams are very much in vogue. Various types of food can be had at stations around the room. One station may offer carved meats; another, fruits and cheeses; another, stuffed vegetables; and still another, seasonal salad combinations.

Your reception will be much shorter with a buffet than with a served meal because downtime between courses disappears. You can add time by serving a seated first course and then inviting a few tables at a time to go to the food stations.

Buffet stations aren't a bargain option. They're at least as expensive as seated dinners, and depending on what assortment of dishes you choose, they can in fact cost more. Having several stations requires extra plates so that guests can take a fresh one at each station — something to keep in mind if you're renting china. Figure on an average of three plates per person. You also need plenty of staff to bus this many plates and man the stations.

The food can and should be a large part of the décor. When choosing your menu, pick a variety of colors, textures, and temperatures. A lineup of even the spiffiest silver chafing dishes looks fairly institutional, so ask to have items served at different temperatures and thus in a variety of bowls and platters in addition to chafing dishes. Ask the caterer: Who decorates the stations? Do you have interesting vessels to serve the food from? Do you have specific props for certain dishes, such as netting for a seafood station?

Playing with your food

Whether for cocktails or the main meal, food stations provide both décor and entertainment opportunities, so have fun.

The food itself on stations serves as a decorative element. Food is more appetizing when everything is laid out at different heights or in different vessels. Some ideas to try:

- ✔ Use painted backdrops, hanging banners, creative signage, and simple props.
- ✔ Display foods at various heights by using tiered candy trays or specially constructed props.
- ✔ Create peaks and valleys by using linen-covered dish racks, milk crates, and bus boxes.
- ✔ Tilt platters by propping them up with upside-down plates underneath.
- ✔ Garnish tables with bunches of beautiful fruits and vegetables, such as grapes, artichokes, and crab apples.
- ✔ Utilize *topiaries* (mini trees) out of foods such as lemons, figs, or nuts.
- ✔ Pile round tables high with dried fruits, nuts, olives, or marinated vegetables — anything that guests can help themselves to without creating a mess — to make interesting walk-around stations. Ask to have a waiter attend to keeping them looking fresh and appetizing.
- ✔ Add a touch of showmanship with food cooked or finished in front of the guests. Pasta, carved meats, shucked oysters and clams, fajitas, and other foods are all the more tantalizing when prepared on the spot by a chef.
- ✔ Create mini vignettes such as a sushi station designed as a Zen rock garden, with a tiny fountain and bonsai trees.

Serving with style

Be clear with the banquet manager or caterer about how and when to serve food and how to set the tables. You've spent a great deal of time (and money) on how these tables will look when you come into the dining room. One of my personal dislikes: tables that are preset with the first course and/or the accoutrements for coffee service. Although sometimes necessary, preset food makes people question how long it's been there, and coffee service on the table looks like the party has to catch a bus.

Food is usually served in one of three ways:

- ✔ **French service:** Waiters heat plates and garnish food at a side table or cart called a *guéridon.* If done properly, this technique is very impressive. Although considered for eons the height of elegance, it's rather slow and requires a great deal of space.

- ✔ **Russian service:** Waiters serve you from a silver platter. This technique is often erroneously called French service.

- ✔ **Plated or a la carte:** Waiters carry the food out on plates. By far the most elegant way to serve plated food is to have waiters carry two plates at a time and, choreographed by the captains, blanket the room, completing one table at a time. The main advantage is that the food arrives at each place the way it was meant to look rather than improvised by the waiters. The downside is that service takes longer than French or Russian service.

People who request alternative meals (kosher, vegetarian, and so on) shouldn't be punished by being served their main course when everyone else has gone on to the wedding cake. The best way to keep this from happening is to give the maitre d' a list of guests, along with their alternative orders and table numbers, as early as possible. (To do this, you need a seating chart; you find help in Chapter 17.)

For food to be certified *kosher,* it must meet the requirements of strict Jewish law. Ingredients and the equipment used to produce the food must not contain or come into contact with foodstuffs or materials that are restricted, such as pork and shellfish. Contrary to a common misconception, a rabbi's blessing isn't part of the koshering process. Kosher rules require, among other things, that animals be slaughtered in a certain way and that meat and dairy products not mix. As inhospitable as it may seem, kosher meals aren't to be unwrapped before they're brought to the table — that's the only way the guest knows that the food has remained untouched.

Figuring the number of waiters per guests is usually based on ten guests per table. Depending on regional standards, the ratio of waiters to guests varies, ranging from two waiters per 10 guests (or one table) for an extremely formal meal to one waiter per 25 guests (or two-and-a-half tables) for a simple meal.

Skimping on the number of servers can be a penny-wise but pound-foolish decision. If you're trying to save money, this isn't the place to cut corners; getting a waiter's attention shouldn't feel like hailing a cab in a typhoon.

If you're hosting a catered reception in your home, the person working with you from the catering company will visit the location and figure out the best traffic flow. He'll also advise you as to what furniture you need to move and what items you need to rent. (See Chapter 17 for information on tented receptions.)

Making Menus Memorable

No matter what kind of wedding feast you have, don't underestimate its powerful symbolism as a grand communion. That doesn't mean you have to pay a grand tab, but do invest time and creativity in its planning. For inspiration, check out the next few sections, which have sample menus that I created by using bits and pieces from several of my favorites.

A seated wedding dinner

If you're serving a seated lunch or dinner, the first course should be light and simple — cold soup in the spring or summer, a composed salad plate, or vegetables vinaigrette — so the guests aren't stuffed to the gills by the time the main course arrives. Also note that if you decide to offer guests a choice of entrees, you may incur a surcharge. Another approach for those who really enjoy eating and want a long and leisurely meal is to offer a tasting menu. This sort of meal is composed of several courses of small servings.

See Figure 14-2 for a very popular Tuscan tasting menu that I've re-created often.

A Tuscan-Style Tasting Menu

ANTIPASTI
Platters of raw seasonal vegetables, cured olives, small pieces of melon wrapped with prosciutto

FIRST COURSE
Eggplant and tomato panzanella

PASTA COURSE
Ravioli stuffed with mozzarella and parmesan cheeses

FISH COURSE
Turbot with artichokes and potatoes

MEAT COURSE
Grilled florentine steak with herbs and olive oil

WINES
Prosecco
Pinot Grigio Di Anterra
Brunello Di Montalcino

Wedding cake and dessert buffet

Figure 14-2:
A sample tasting menu.

Illustration by Wiley, Composition Services Graphics

A family-style wedding supper

Another innovative alternative to a traditional three-course meal is a family-style wedding menu. This can be anything that's suited to being served that way — stews and tajines, for example, work well.

Although tajine (a traditional hearty Moroccan stew) is usually made with mutton, vegetarian versions are equally tasty, making this a good option for a group that includes people who eat meat and those who don't.

Start with a huge salad bowl filled with a variety of lettuces and vegetables passed family-style, serve the stew as a main course, and end with platters of pastries.

Relatively inexpensive to make, stews are a mainstay of frugal gourmets. If done well, they can be a delicious main course of a memorable wedding feast without breaking the bank — even if, to your amazement, one table happens to polish off eight platters of tajine.

For authentic ethnic pastries or other specialty side dishes that are time-consuming to make or require hard-to-get ingredients, consider ordering them separately from an ethnic bakery, deli, or restaurant and having them delivered to your reception site.

When Dinner Is Not Served

Although seated dinners and lunches are the most popular types of receptions, they're not for everyone. The other options include three-hour cocktail parties, afternoon teas, and wedding breakfasts or brunches. Although these affairs are usually less costly and less fussy, they still require thought and ingenuity.

The cocktail reception

Serving solely cocktails and hors d'oeuvres — rather than a meal — for the reception is a fine choice for a variety of circumstances:

- The space you've fallen in love with can seat only a third or fewer of the guests.
- Your reception is a celebratory party that has been postponed for several days or weeks after the ceremony.
- You're an older or previously married couple and don't feel comfortable having a traditional wedding reception.

✔ You have vast numbers of guests you *must* invite but you can't afford a seated meal for all of them.

✔ You simply want an untraditional affair.

I asked top caterers and banquet managers around the country for their most popular hors d'oeuvres, and here are the warm treats they recommend:

✔ Chicken sausage with grainy mustard

✔ Crab cakes with rémoulade sauce

✔ Crispy shrimp spring rolls

✔ Grilled foie gras on brioche with fig butter

✔ Miniature beef Wellingtons

✔ Miniature cones of beer-battered fish and chips

✔ Miniature grilled cheddar sandwiches served with a taste of tomato soup

✔ Peking duck rolls

✔ Portobello mushroom fries

✔ Roasted or deep-fried calamari with cocktail sauce

✔ Spinach-and-cheese-filled phyllo triangles

✔ Steamed vegetable or shrimp dumplings with hoisin sauce

✔ Sweet potato pancakes with frizzled leeks and crème fraîche

✔ Teeny burger sliders

✔ Tiny chicken potpies

✔ Tiny wild mushroom tarts

✔ Vegetable samosas

In addition, you want to serve some hors d'oeuvres that are cold or room temperature:

✔ Caponata (eggplant relish) on toast rounds

✔ Cheddar cheese straws

✔ Endive leaves with red pepper and cream cheese purée

✔ New potatoes stuffed with sour cream and caviar

✔ Oysters topped with wasabi, served on porcelain spoons

✔ Roasted vegetable and goat cheese tartlet

✔ Salmon caviar pizzetta

✔ Salmon tartare on black bread rounds

- Shot glasses of chilled pea soup
- Shrimp salad on corn muffins
- Smoked salmon napoleons
- Tiny biscuits with Smithfield ham and honey mustard
- Tuna tartare
- Vegetable and California sushi rolls

Two-and-a-half to three hours is the optimum length of a cocktail reception. Anything shorter is too rushed; anything longer feels dragged out. If you go an extra hour, make sure that you have ample food, drink, and cake. In fact, you may consider having a dessert table, which can also function as a mouth-watering décor element.

For a cocktail hour, you might serve four hot and four cold hors d'oeuvres. For a two- or three-hour cocktail reception, serve perhaps ten hot and ten cold, in addition to a food station or two. (See "Variety shows: Buffet stations," earlier in this chapter.)

The food should include both passed (or butlered) hors d'oeuvres and food stations that are as simple as crudités with dip or as elaborate as carved Peking duck. In any case, nothing should require more than a fork (if that) because seating is limited and you don't want guests wearing the food. Stagger the selection of passed hors d'oeuvres so guests don't get bored. Although you're not serving dinner, you want to provide enough food so that guests aren't racing to leave for a real meal. The entire room setup should be clearly that of a cocktail reception rather than a dinner gone awry. Tables should be no larger than 32 inches in diameter, and you should only have enough seating for a third of the guests, maximum.

Remember, you must specify on the invitation the fact that the reception isn't dinner, as in, "Please join us for cocktails and hors d'oeuvres to celebrate our marriage." This particular wording also makes it clear that guests aren't invited to the ceremony. Refer to Chapter 5 for more on invitation wording.

Although a corporate cocktail reception may specify both the beginning and ending times (7 to 10 p.m., for example), doing so for a wedding isn't gracious. Serving a wedding cake, dessert, and coffee at the beginning of the last hour and toning down the music is usually enough of a hint for guests to wind down the festivities.

Tea for two (hundred)

Having a tea in lieu of a full meal is popular for many of the same reasons that having a cocktail party reception is, particularly if you want to have a day-time wedding or include children. The menu may feature many of the classic tea foods — cucumber sandwiches, petits fours, English biscuits, and so on — but if you have a sizable crowd, you may consider having the same kind of menu as you would for a cocktail party reception. In fact, you may even include a Champagne toast. Another variation, open-house cake and punch parties, are popular in the South, a holdover perhaps from the days before air-conditioning, when weddings were held almost universally at night and included a large number of guests.

A tea may seem like one of the simplest receptions imaginable, but you can spiff it up by offering several unusual flavored teas, available at gourmet shops and specialty stores, and by using a variety of interesting teapots.

Other ways to munch: Breakfast, brunch, or lunch

The wedding breakfast, a mainstay in England, follows a morning ceremony and is actually lunch. To make matters more confusing, a lunch reception is usually more of a light dinner served in midafternoon. For both brunch and lunch, the cocktail reception (if you have one) is often shorter and less elaborate.

Finesse and impress

Some flourishes to further jazz up your meal:

- A variety of good breads to complement each course (for example, cheesy puff pastry sticks with soup, a crusty sourdough roll with a beef course, and a whole-grain walnut toast with cheese and salad)
- Waiters offering freshly grated cheese and ground pepper at the table
- A small dish of herb-infused olive oil in lieu of butter with bread
- Butter molded into florets or other shapes
- Lemon slices served in the ice water
- A choice of sparkling or still water
- Sprigs of fresh herbs, such as rosemary and tarragon, as garnishes

- Multicolored sugar crystals or chocolate spoons for coffee
- Cappuccino/espresso bar
- Hors d'oeuvres served in baskets, colorful glass bowls, or chintz hatboxes, or on trays lined with various fabrics
- A lush presentation (at each table) of rich chocolates, fresh fruit, and cookies with dessert and coffee
- Finishing touches on hors d'oeuvre trays such as tiny bouquets or offbeat elements such as miniature brides and grooms, balls and chains, or tennis racquets

Brunch is a thoroughly American compromise and can be one of the least costly meals to produce. Following a late morning or midday ceremony, a typical buffet may consist of bagels, cream cheese spreads, smoked salmon, Danish pastries, mini quiches, fruit salad, juices, mimosas, and coffee. Stations can offer omelets, waffles, blinis, and fruit pancakes.

Figure 14-3 shows a delicious brunch menu that caters to many tastes.

A Fabulous Wedding Brunch Buffet

The bride's favorite German apple pancakes
(Grandma Betty's recipe)

Applewood smoked bacon, turkey bacon, and veggie bacon

Sautéed red potatoes with onions and peppers

Spinach asparagus frittata

Corned beef hash with poached eggs

An assortment of smoked salmons:
pastrami salmon, pepper cured, gravlax

American caviar omelets

Tiny muffins, scones, and popovers with homemade jams

Bloody Mary bar — traditional and 'white' with
an assortment of sexy garnishes

Mimosas

Figure 14-3: A brunch reception can be as elegant or casual as you want.

Illustration by Wiley, Composition Services Graphics

Chapter 15

Let's Drink to That

According to the Bible, Jesus performed his first miracle at a wedding in Cana, an ancient town in Galilee, by turning water into wine. Although miracles are wonderful, I believe in using them sparingly. Fortunately, you can also provide drinks with a combination of common-sense planning and good taste.

This chapter is about alcohol and how to serve it at your wedding. My place isn't to moralize about *whether* to serve wine, beer, and spirits but simply to show you *how* to do so intelligently and graciously. And, of course, I firmly believe that when serving any alcohol, you must do so legally and responsibly. If alcohol is an issue because of religion, recovery, or expense, consider having a morning wedding with a breakfast reception, where alcohol is neither necessary nor expected.

Tending Bar

Much to my amazement, I've read in several wedding books that a good way to cut costs is to have a cash bar. Well, so is BYOF (Bring Your Own Food). Remember the purpose of this day: You, your parents, and your future spouse have sent out invitations to have friends and family join you in celebration. I think that this invitation clearly includes food *and* drink. Period. So, the following sections present info to help you decide what sort of beverage service you want to provide.

Speaking in bar code

Before I get too far along, make sure you're conversant in bar-speak— and I don't mean pickup lines. A few terms worth knowing are

- **A.P. glasses:** Caterers usually use "all-purpose" stemmed goblets for mixed drinks and wine served at the bar. These one-size-fits-all glasses make for shorter lines at the bar and are less expensive to rent. (Champagne and sparkling wine, however, are always served in flutes.) If glassware is particularly important to you and your budget can handle it, you might request an assortment of the proper glasses. These include highball, rocks, cordial, and red and white wine glasses, not to mention Champagne flutes.

- **Call liquor:** A specific brand you ask for, or call, as in, "I'll have an Absolut screwdriver."

- **Champagne:** With a capital *C*, Champagne is the sparkling wine produced in France's Champagne region. Using the second fermentation in the individual bottle, winemakers have produced Champagne the same way for approximately 300 years. Although you may enjoy sparkling wines, only Champagne deserves to be called Champagne.

- **Corkage fee:** The amount the site charges to remove the corks from bottles you supply and to serve the wine.

- **House wine(s):** What the establishment serves without an additional charge. Depending on the house, the wine can range from perfectly palatable table wine to rotgut.

- **Pouring** or **well brands:** Generic liquor, as in, "I'll have a screwdriver."

- **Sparkling wine:** Produced by using either the Champagne method or a less-expensive method. To further confuse the two, makers sometimes call these *champagnes* (small *c*). Also includes delicious options such as prosecco, cava, and sekt.

- **Top shelf, premium,** or **super premium:** Call brands that are higher priced, including single-malt scotches, aged cognacs, and rare liqueurs.

When you have your wine and food tasting (see Chapter 14 for details), try the house wine (both white and red). Far from being a minor detail, a glass of house wine is the first thing many people put to their lips at your reception. If you find it undrinkable, request an upgrade.

On-premise pricing

Restaurants, banquet facilities, private clubs, and other spaces where the catering is on-site usually hold a liquor license, allowing them to sell alcoholic beverages with food. (See Chapter 4 for more about on- and off-premise sites.) Their offering full bar service isn't a humanitarian gesture to make your life easier but rather a large profit center for the facility. Consider the tastes and habits of your guests when planning the bar. If you have only a pouring bar — in other words, no specific brands — and your favorite uncle's sole joy in life is a particular single-malt scotch, he won't be happy. Should you opt not to provide cognac or liqueurs and someone orders one after dinner, the waiters will say, as they've been trained, "I'm sorry, but the host hasn't provided for that."

On-premise places typically price wine and spirits in one of four ways:

- ✔ **Per consumption:** They charge you specifically either per bottle or by drink and only for what your guests consume. Some places charge per *opened* bottle of liquor, although the fairest way to be billed is by tenths of bottles consumed. This pricing doesn't apply to wine and Champagne, however, which are charged by bottle opened. Sodas, juices, and bottled water may be served at no additional charge or priced per consumption as well.

  This arrangement is a smart choice if you think your guests won't be drinking much. Advise the maitre d' that waiters aren't to clear half-empty glasses (and thus send guests back to the bar for a new drink). Also have the maitre d' apprise you (or the wedding consultant) of the consumption level halfway through the party. Doing so accomplishes two things: You have an opportunity to moderate the amount of alcohol being poured, and the house knows that someone else is keeping track.

- ✔ **Cocktail reception included, then per consumption:** This pricing scheme means that whatever guests consume during the cocktail hour is included in the agreed-upon per-person price (even if your guests drink like fish) and that whatever they drink *after* that period is charged per drink to your bill. This option is a good one if you're not sure how much people will drink, as booze consumption is heaviest at the beginning of the reception and slows down considerably after the first hour. What's more, if you pour wine with the meal, chances are guests won't request additional cocktails, which keeps the tab for additional beverages down.

- ✔ **All-inclusive:** The total price includes food and beverage. Although the liquor portion may appear hefty, this structure is cost-effective if your guests are heavy drinkers. It also means not having to keep track of what they consume. Wine is included in the bar for cocktails as well as wine service during dinner. You usually choose from a set wine list. If you want to upgrade your selection, you should receive a rebate on the list price per bottle. A Champagne toast may be included, but pouring Champagne from the bar as well is most likely an additional cost.

- ✔ **Corkage fee only:** You pay a fee for wine and Champagne that you bring in yourself. Calculate this fee carefully because you can wind up paying a huge premium per bottle when the fee is tacked on. If you have your heart set on a wine that the establishment doesn't carry, find out what it would charge you to special order it. Believe it or not, even after the place tacks on its markup, this route may cost you less.

Liquor legalities

Laws that relate to liquor licenses for caterers at off-premise sites vary from state to state, so your caterer *may* be able to supply your liquor for you, or at least advise you on quantities to buy as well as types of liquor that are popular in your area or with your guests. Rum and tequila, for example, are more popular with younger crowds. Some local governments prohibit the shipping of wine directly to consumers, so ask your supplier about the law in your area. If shipping wine is legal where you live, the law may dictate that an adult receive the shipment. In some states, you can't buy beer where you buy liquor, so make separate arrangements with your caterer. In any case, it's always a good idea to contact your insurance carrier to get suggestions.

A growing number of states and counties are passing *social host* laws, meaning everyone from the vendor to the host may be held responsible if an intoxicated person injures himself or others — whether the alcohol is served in a public venue or a private home. Specify that the bartenders may not serve minors, obviously intoxicated guests, or known alcoholics. To see what your area's laws are, search the web for "social host liability" and your state and/or county.

Go through your guest list and note how many invitees are under drinking age. Have your contract specify a lower price for them.

Off-premise options

One of the main advantages of holding your wedding at an off-premise site where you bring in a caterer — such as your home or a rental space — is that you can also buy and bring in your own liquor. In some instances, the site may have an in-house caterer you must use, but you're still allowed to bring in your own liquor. In either case, this way you're not locked into an establishment's rigid pricing structure, and you can serve what you want, a plus for specialty bars (covered later in this chapter) or if you have specific tastes in wine and liquor.

Some places where you can shop for liquor and perhaps find deals include

- **Discount warehouses or superstores,** which sell wine at or near wholesale prices, usually only by the case.

- **Liquor stores,** which sometimes have special sales (scan local newspapers for ads). Quantity price savings can be particularly juicy when buying wine and Champagne. Just follow the guidelines for proper storage so you don't wind up with several cases of salad dressing.

✔ **Local wineries,** where you can visit and taste the wine before having it shipped to you.

✔ **Wine shop catalogs,** which often offer lower prices and a larger selection of hard-to-find wines than local markets.

Figure 15-1 covers what you need to take into account whenever you host a party that includes a bar.

Bar Setup Checklist

❑ Does the caterer charge a service or corkage fee on top of the bar "setup" fee that includes ice and fruit?

❑ Is it possible for the hosts to personally supply any wines or Champagne at an in-house venue? If so, what is the corkage fee?

❑ Will the liquor supplier take back unopened bottles of liquor and unchilled bottles of wine?

❑ Do you want to have blended drinks, specialty drinks, or drinks that require special preparation? (For example: drinks such as cosmopolitans, martinis and margaritas that require shaking and particular glasses.) What ingredients and equipment do you need to arrange in advance? Are any of those included in the regular bar setup?

❑ What nonalcoholic beverages will be available? (These might include fruited iced teas, fresh squeezed juices, nonalcoholic beer, or sangria without alcohol filled with slices of fresh lemons, limes, and oranges and served in glass pitchers.)

❑ If you're using a full-service facility, what brands will the banquet manager provide? What is the price difference between inexpensive "well" brands and "premium" or "top shelf," the most expensive?

❑ Are liquor stores allowed to deliver in your state? What arrangements can you make with the caterer to pick up the liquor?

❑ Will your site accept liquor deliveries in advance of your reception? Does it have a secure place to keep it?

❑ If you're supplying the liquor, where should leftover open bottles of liquor be left? Who will pick them up for you after the wedding?

❑ Do you feel comfortable serving liquor to vendors such as musicians and photographers? How do you want to instruct the caterer regarding this matter?

Figure 15-1:
When it comes to the bar, work out a beverage strategy with the caterer.

Illustration by Wiley, Composition Services Graphics

When stocking a bar, bear several points in mind:

- Buy about 10 percent more liquor than you think you need.

- Buy from a liquor store that allows you to return unopened bottles. Just be sure to instruct the caterer not to *crack*, or open, the seal on every bottle. Neither should the caterer ice all the white wine and Champagne, which causes the labels to soak off, unless you're sure they'll be drunk. Bottles without labels look unappealing and are impossible to return. For a catered meal, however, go ahead and open almost all the bottles at once; otherwise, service will be slowed considerably.

- Whether or not you're paying a per-person setup fee (usually $3 to $5 for ice, fruit, juices, mixers, and sodas), go over the particulars with the caterer or banquet manager. Don't assume that the bar will be stocked with ingredients and garnishes for Bloody Marys, piña coladas, margaritas, sours, and other special drinks that you may want to serve.

- Double-check the amount of ice ordered (see the following section for more information).

- Offer nonalcoholic drinks that are appetizing, varied, and festive so nondrinkers don't feel like poor relations. Some possibilities: iced tea with mint sprigs, fresh apple cider, and pink lemonade. People who don't drink usually aren't that interested in pretend cocktails such as virgin daiquiris.

- Make sure that white wine and Champagne are delivered chilled, because most off-premise sites don't have enough space — and you won't have enough time — to chill it adequately.

- To prevent any disappearing surplus, assign a responsible friend to confer with the caterer about leftover liquor and to pick up the unopened bottles within a few days after the wedding (when, presumably, you're on your honeymoon).

Chilling out

Keep these facts in mind when dealing with ice:

- Figure on 1½ pounds of ice per person and 2½ pounds per person if you're also chilling bottles.

- Although you can ice bottles in about 20 minutes by pouring water and salt in with the ice, doing so makes the labels come off. Otherwise, pack bottles in ice for two hours to properly chill them.

- Crushed ice chills bottles faster than cubes do.

Liquid logistics

If you're at the point where you aren't sleeping at all and are obsessing over every detail, here's a little 2 a.m. project to keep you busy: Make a quick reference for stocking the bar.

Calculating how much alcohol to have on hand isn't an absolute science. Several factors come into play — the social habits of your guests, your budget, the time of year, and the time of day. A summer wedding, for example, may require more beer, vodka, and gin than a winter wedding, where people are likely to drink more red wine and whiskey.

You may notice that bar arithmetic is akin to doubling recipes — the number of liters you need doesn't necessarily increase in direct proportion to the number of guests and/or bar stations added. When ordering liquor, take into account the number of bar stations the caterer plans. If you have 250 guests and five bar stations, for example, you need five bottles of bourbon rather than four so that each bar is stocked with the same selection.

As you estimate how much liquor you need, keep in mind the following guidelines on average guest consumption:

- ✔ For a liter bottle of alcohol, estimate 20 to 22 drinks.
- ✔ For a one-hour cocktail reception before dinner, estimate two drinks per person for cocktails and then two to two and a half glasses of wine per person during dinner.
- ✔ For a two-hour cocktail party, estimate three drinks per person.
- ✔ For a four-hour dinner party, estimate three to four drinks per person.
- ✔ A bottle of wine yields approximately five glasses.
- ✔ A liter of soda has five to seven glasses, depending on glass size and ice.
- ✔ Allow six generous glasses per standard 750ml bottle of Champagne. For a Champagne toast, figure on 75 glasses per case.

In Figure 15-2, I show you what you'd typically need for 100 guests with a four-hour open bar, including a cocktail hour. Note that these amounts are only estimates. You're always better off having returns than being caught short with no liquor store open within 100 miles.

If your reception is an extended cocktail party rather than a seated meal, you need to modify the formulas for calculating amounts. For a three-hour affair with 100 guests, plan one drink per person per hour, or approximately one and a half cases of liquor altogether, comprising, in descending order, vodka, scotch, gin, and rum. One liter of liquor yields approximately 20 to 22 drinks.

Bar Checklist

❏	Scotch	4 liters
❏	Vodka	6 liters
❏	Gin	5 liters
❏	Rum	2 liters
❏	Bourbon	1–2 liters
❏	Blended whisky	1–2 liters
❏	Tequila	1 liter
❏	Campari	1 liter
❏	Dry vermouth	2 750-ml bottles
❏	Sweet vermouth	2 750-ml bottles
❏	Assorted beers	2 or 3 cases
❏	Light beer	2 cases
❏	White wine during cocktails	1½ cases
❏	Red wine during cocktails	6 bottles
❏	Champagne during cocktails	1½ cases
❏	Cola	14 liters
❏	Diet cola	12 liters
❏	Lemon lime soda	7 liters
❏	Diet lemon lime	7 liters
❏	Ginger ale	7 liters
❏	Club soda	9 liters
❏	Tonic	1 case
❏	Juices (cranberry, orange, grapefruit)	8 quarts each

Figure 15-2:
A typical order for 100 guests for a four-hour open bar, including a cocktail hour.

Illustration by Wiley, Composition Services Graphics

Hard to believe, but true: Professional waiters do and will arrive at your site without corkscrews. Whether your family is tending bar or you've hired bartenders, it pays to have a half-dozen screwpull corkscrews or waiter's corkscrews — not the wing-type corkscrew. To open special bottles such as Impérials of red wine, you need a bar-mounted corkscrew.

Equipping the complete do-it-yourself bar

If you're setting up your own bar from scratch or insist on driving your caterer crazy by checking over the minutest of details, here's a rundown of nonliquid supplies that you need:

- Bar pitchers (four per 75 guests)
- Bottle openers
- Champagne pliers
- Coasters
- Corkscrews
- Funnels
- Garnish bowls (6-inch)
- Glassware (at least two per person, preferably three):

    12-ounce all-purpose goblets

    8-ounce highball glasses (optional)

    Champagne flutes (optional)
- Ice buckets (one to display Champagne; the others for ice)
- Ice tongs

- Ice tubs (to chill wine and Champagne)
- Knife and cutting board
- Large mixing pitchers
- Lemon/lime squeezers
- Long-handled spoons
- Measuring cups
- Mixing glasses
- Napkins
- Plastic runner (to protect floor behind bar)
- Serving trays
- Shakers/strainers
- Sponges
- Trash bags
- Trash cans

Avoiding Traffic Jams

I can't stress enough how important traffic flow is to the success of your day. One way to make guests miserable is to have long lines at the bar, making it impossible for them to get that first drink they've been salivating for. An easy and festive solution is to have waiters parked at the entrance of your reception area holding gleaming trays of wine, sparkling water, and, if it's in your budget, Champagne. Most people are perfectly happy to drink what's offered and consequently avoid stampeding the bars.

Some couples opt to have the full bar open as guests arrive at the ceremony. Arbiters of taste split hairs on the subject, suggesting that to open a full bar is tacky, but to serve Champagne and/or wine is fine. Somehow, the nuance is lost on us; if you decide to serve alcohol before the ceremony, how much and what kind is a matter of personal style. Just make sure that the guests are ushered to their seats in plenty of time for the ceremony so you don't have an impromptu extended-cocktail reception before your planned cocktail reception. Also be sure to have enough waiters to whisk away glasses from guests as they take their seats so that the dulcet tones of shattering Champagne flutes don't interrupt the ceremony.

Some people consider serving any alcohol before the ceremony an outrage. In fact, some banquet facilities are adamant in their refusal to open the bar before the couple is firmly locked in matrimony. I feel, however, that you (and perhaps your officiant) should decide when to serve the first drink. (Obviously, this point is moot when the ceremony takes place in a house of worship or is an Orthodox or Conservative Jewish wedding on the Sabbath.)

For a cocktail reception that precedes a dinner, the standard ratio of bartenders to guests is 1 per 50 or 75. Unfortunately, however, you can't count on this. If you're paying per consumption (rather than all-inclusive), some banquet managers load up on the bartenders — the better to sell you liquor with, my dears. Conversely, if you're paying an all-inclusive price, guests may feel that getting a drink is like searching for an oasis in the Sahara.

Even if waiters are passing drinks to stave off a crush at the bar as guests are first arriving, contract for extra bar staff during this crucial period. If hiring additional bartenders costs extra, request that some of the waiters (provided it's not a union issue) fill in behind the bar until all the guests have had at least their first drink.

Bar Aesthetics: Set Up and Take Notice

Specify what the bars are going to look like. Determine who's supplying the bar linens — the establishment or your décor person. If linens are an afterthought, you'll probably wind up with institutional white ones that are a blight on your painstakingly designed reception. At the very least, the back bar — the table behind the main — should have linens that match the front bar. Glasses, ice bins, and extra setups should be kept neatly. Sometimes, bartenders forget that their workspace is in your reception space.

A few questions worth asking:

- Will the bartenders *free pour* liquor (estimate the amount in a shot) or use *pourers* (bottle spouts that measure per shot)?

- Are pourers silver-tone or plastic? (Silver looks more elegant.)

- What will the bartenders use as ice bins? If the answer is huge garbage pails (which is often the case), request that they wrap the pails in tablecloths. Champagne should be kept in ice buckets.

- What do they scoop ice with? I hope with an ice scoop. Harried bartenders may resort to scooping ice with a glass, sometimes resulting in tasty shards of glass garnish. I won't even discuss bartenders scooping with their hands, and I hope you won't have to, either.

Other bar aesthetics to keep in mind include

✔ Having bubba-sized half-gallon bottles sitting out on a bar looks like you're expecting an invasion of Huns. A more aesthetic approach: 750ml bottles. If you're serving a variety of beers, a few different wines, or margaritas, display the bottles prominently on the bar so that guests know to request them and the selection isn't just a secret between you and the bartenders.

✔ Stock the bar with clear carafes containing juices for mixing cocktails, and keep them visible. They let guests know what's on offer, and they look truly gorgeous.

✔ Write a few sentences describing the wines you've chosen and give them to the bartenders so they can speak intelligently about what they're pouring. After you and your fiancé(e) have excitedly chosen the perfect cocktail wines, nothing can make you choke on your 1988 Gevrey-Chambertin like overhearing a bartender reply to a guest's query, "Let's see, we got red and we got white."

✔ Another charming touch to highlight your selections is tented menu cards or a hand-lettered chalkboard describing your wines and your specialty cocktail, if you have one. Your guests will feel fully educated when asking for their beverage of choice.

✔ Don't forget the bar snacks; they're gracious and they moderate the effects of a little too much celebration by your guests. Talk with your caterer about providing nibbles guests can pick up along with their drink.

✔ Grand floral creations on the bar inevitably become a target for the bartenders or guests to knock over. A small, tasteful arrangement of flowers in keeping with the overall theme is plenty. The same goes for candelabras and votive candles — an unnerving scenario when dolman sleeves are in the vicinity.

One point, though perhaps obvious, bears repeating: Omit the tip cup from your bar. I believe that tip cups belong only on cash bars, and neither has any place at a wedding.

Specialty Bars: Blithe Spirits

Although they require additional, well-trained staff, specialty bars can be a treat for guests, even at large weddings.

Some festive ideas for specialty bars include

✔ **Cappuccino and espresso bar:** Doesn't it seem as though coffee bars have taken over the world? Well, weddings aren't immune. Some caterers now specialize in supplying coffee bars that offer everything from cappuccino to half-caff double-skim mocha lattes. Hot rum toddies, Irish coffee, and hot chocolate spiced with chocolate liqueur also fit in nicely.

✔ **Dessert bar:** After-dinner drinks are enjoying the same renewed popularity as cigars and martinis. Cordials range from a selection of liqueurs to an assortment of aged cognacs, as well as armagnacs and digestifs. (For ideas of what to serve, see the "Luxurious liqueurs" sidebar in this chapter.) Waiters sometimes take orders for these at the table, but if you decide to go all out, carts wheeled to the table with a selection of cordials and dessert wines — and their proper glasses — are an excellent finale to a sumptuous meal.

One catch: Although immensely gracious, the liqueur cart can be a costly proposition, as people who would never think of having an after-dinner drink will make an exception when offered one in this situation.

✔ **Vodka bar:** With the advent of a multitude of unusual vodkas, from flavored to triple distilled, vodka bars are another possibility. Deeply chilled in iced glasses is the only way to serve this spirit. Vodka drinks work well by themselves or as an accompaniment to a food station serving blini and caviar or smoked fish. Large canisters holding fruit or herb-infused vodkas behind the bar make the station very enticing.

✔ **Wine bar:** Serving an array of interesting and delicious wines works especially well for cocktails-only receptions. You can have some fun here based on your tasting experiences of the past couple of months. The wines don't have to be expensive or rare as long as they make a statement. Display each wine with a card or offer a special wine menu explaining the fine points of each selection. Six wines — some whites, some reds — are enough as long as they include a range of grape varieties, perhaps a cabernet sauvignon, a pinot noir, a chardonnay, a sauvignon blanc, a merlot, and a sauterne. Consider selections from Australia, Chile, and South Africa as well as the better-known wine regions. For a grand touch, have a couple of Impérials (which aren't necessarily more expensive) standing sentry on the bar. To complete the effect, serve each wine in the proper glass.

If you decide to offer a specialty bar, be sure to make any special arrangements required for the full dramatic effect. For example:

✔ Serve these drinks at a separate station rather than at the bars, or have waiters pass them around.

✔ Stock each station with the accessories needed for the particular drink. For example, a martini station should have martini glasses, matching shakers, and a variety of garnishes, including pickled pearl onions for Gibsons.

✔ Plan drinks that both look pretty and taste good. Try having glasses rimmed with colored sugars or using unusual garnishes like a peppermint stick or a long-stemmed strawberry.

Luxurious liqueurs

Serving a liqueur/cognac selection at the end of your reception is a spiffy coda to the festivities. If possible, serve these drinks in brandy snifters or delicate cordial glasses rather than cocktail glasses. A primer of possibilities:

✔ **B&B:** Benedictine and brandy

✔ **Cognac:** From the Cognac region in France; brands include Hennessy and Courvoisier

✔ **Cointreau or Grand Marnier:** Orange-flavored liqueur

✔ **Cordials:** May include either inexpensive or name brands with flavors such as crème

de cacao (chocolate), crème de menthe (mint), peach, apricot, pear, peppermint, and banana

✔ **Kahlúa:** Mexican coffee liqueur; Tia Maria, a Jamaican coffee liqueur, is another option

✔ **Sambuca:** Licorice-flavored liqueur, often served with coffee beans in the bottom of the glass

✔ **Specialty drinks:** Chocolate martinis, mudslides, and Irish coffees are possibilities

A cost-saving option for bar service is to serve just beer, wine, and one specialty drink. There's a trend for couples to have their own specialty cocktail for their wedding, named after the couple or something of significance to them. Some of these concoctions lend themselves to premixing all the ingredients, including alcohol, rather than being made as ordered, while others require skilled bartenders. A few possibilities:

✔ **Coladas** accented with a skewer of mango, kiwi, and pineapple

✔ **Cosmopolitans** made with vodka, triple sec, lime, and cranberry juice — or the white dress–friendly *white cosmo,* made with colorless cranberry juice and usually served in a martini glass

✔ **Margaritas** poured into V-shaped glasses with salted rims and a wedge of fresh lime

✔ **Mojitos** combining rum, sugar, lots of fresh mint, and lime juice

✔ **Sangria** made with red wine and a dash of brandy and then garnished with fruit slices and poured from a lovely pitcher

✔ **Sidecars,** a concoction of brandy, Cointreau, fresh lemon juice, and a flamed orange peel

Selecting Wine, Beer, and Champagne

Many people mistakenly think that serving only wine and beer is less expensive and a way to keep guests from getting drunk. Both are fallacies. First, not every catering establishment charges substantially less for house wine and beer. A better-quality wine served in lieu of hard liquor can, in fact, cost you more money. Second, the idea that wine and beer aren't as potent as hard liquor is preposterous. Trust me, enough of either can get you good and drunk. Should anyone overindulge, remember the immortal words of Dean Martin: "If you drink, don't drive. Don't even putt."

Earlier in this chapter I discuss beer, wine, and Champagne in terms of pricing and amounts. Now I get into the delicate and rather subjective art of choosing appropriate and delicious bottles to complement your party.

Wining when dining

For many people, a good meal by definition is accompanied by wine. The amount of money and time you spend on selecting your wine depends on how important you rate a taste of the grape. Markups on wine and Champagne are typically exorbitant in banquet facilities and hotels, so this area is one where going for an off-premise site can really make a difference in the cost of your wedding.

One of the most fun aspects of wedding planning is choosing your wine. If you're purchasing the wine yourself, buy several selections in your price range to try at home with dinner. If you're choosing from the in-house banquet wine list, get a copy early in your planning and purchase your top picks at a liquor store to try them out. Some establishments include wine tastings with menu tastings. Remember, this is a tasting, not a bacchanal. In fact, a wine tasting is probably the only time in your life when you're allowed to sip *and spit* in public. (See Chapter 14 for info about arranging menu tastings.)

Although American wines have come into their own, they don't necessarily cost less than imported ones. Fortunately, a good wine need not be expensive.

Until recently, when planning a bar, you automatically ordered copious quantities of white wine and a bare minimum of red just to satisfy some pretentious eccentric. As good red wines have become more reasonably priced, they've gone mainstream. Order sufficient red wine for everybody to drink it with the main course if

- You're serving meat or a fish in a red wine sauce
- The wine is particularly delicious
- The wedding occurs in the middle of winter

If you serve white wine (and no red) throughout the meal, half a bottle per person is usually ample. If you serve white wine for only the first course, followed by red or a choice of white or red with dinner, count on a third of a bottle of white per person.

Should you serve the best wine first or save it for last? Some people believe in the power of first impressions and think that guests, after they're somewhat sated, won't notice that at some point during the party the wine ceased to impress their taste buds as much. Others believe that guests only begin to notice what they're drinking after their taste buds have warmed up, so you should serve the good stuff later. One way to circumvent this tangle if you serve more than one wine is to make sure the wines are comparable and complementary.

Don't worry, beer hoppy

Beer and weddings date back to ancient times. In fact, the word *bride* is derived from the Germanic *bruths* and the Old English *bryd,* which in turn come from the root word *bru,* meaning to cook or brew. In the 15th century, wedding feasts were called *bride-ales* (an ale being a party), and the drinking of copious amounts of beer — the stronger the better for a robust marriage — was, naturally, a prime activity at these rather rowdy functions. The bride's mother parked herself in front of the church and sold her specially made brew, known as *bridal,* to anyone who passed by. The proceeds benefited the bride's dowry.

Today, beer at weddings isn't requisite, but with the rising popularity of microbreweries and a growing interest in the complexities and nuances of "the liquid bread," beer is no longer considered too roughneck for weddings. Just be sure to serve it in a glass and from a bottle as opposed to a can or a keg, unless your reception is doubling as a frat party. If you're offering beer, include a light beer and stock up if it's a hot summer day.

For a special beer bar, you might feature recipes from several microbreweries, a selection of exotic imports, beers from countries representing your families' ethnic heritage, or a world tour of beers from every continent (except Antarctica, of course). One way to impress beer aficionados is to get a local microbrewery to make a special batch of its brew for your big day or a prewedding party. Print labels with your names and wedding date.

Bring on the bubbly

Champagne or good sparkling wine is expected at a wedding celebration, whether you serve it throughout the reception or just with cocktails, by request, at dinner, or with the cake for a toast.

Champagnes can be vintage or nonvintage. Any Champagne without a vintage year on the label, which accounts for 85 percent of all Champagne produced, is *NV,* or *nonvintage.* Three or more different harvests are blended for NV. A vintage Champagne consists of 100 percent of grapes from a single year rather than blended with reserves from previous years. Plan on coming into a lot of money if you want to serve vintage Champagne.

Whether vintage or non, Champagne is categorized by sweetness, and the terms aren't self-explanatory, to say the least:

- *Extra Brut* or *Brut Nature* means totally dry (under 0.06 percent sugar).

- *Brut* is still very dry (under 1.5 percent sugar) and in general is your best bet for a wedding. Most of the Champagnes sold in the United States are brut nonvintage.

- *Extra Dry* is sweeter than brut and considered medium-dry.

- *Sec* is slightly sweet. (In French, however, *sec* means dry. Go figure.)

- *Demi-sec* is considered sweet but not as sweet as . . . (see the next bullet).

- *Doux* is *really* sweet. This style of Champagne is the sweetest and should only be served with dessert. However, doux Champagne is hard to find in the States.

A fun personal touch is a cocktail created just for your wedding. For their rose garden reception, one couple I know served rosé Champagne with a rose petal garnish and a strawberry in every glass. As guests entered, waiters offered the drinks from trays adorned with forest-green leaves and roses and announced, "The 'Rose Cocktail' in honor of Loretta and George."

Rosé Champagne has an undeservedly bad reputation among those who think bartenders make it by mixing carbonated something and red wine. Actually, makers do their thing by either adding pinot noir in the beginning of the process to a blend of white wines or leaving the skins on the grapes during vinification to impart a pink color. Rosés are particularly sensuous and romantic for weddings. Unlike many blush wines, rosé Champagnes are brut rather than semisweet.

If you want to serve Champagne but are concerned about the cost, consider serving a good prosecco from Italy, a cava (white or rosé) from Spain, or a domestic sparkling dessert wine with the wedding cake.

One case of Champagne contains approximately 70 to 75 glasses, so for a Champagne toast you need one case per 75 guests. For the cocktail hour, figure on one and a half cases per 100 guests. Some flutes or tulip glasses can be deceptive in that they hold less than they appear to, in which case you may get closer to 80 glasses per case.

After your Champagne has made its bumpy journey from store to wedding, let it rest for several hours before opening, as you would any other carbonated drink. Never remove the wire cages before you're ready to open the bottle unless you want spontaneous cork popping. For the same reason, never use a corkscrew, which releases the carbonation suddenly and much too forcefully. Although the correct procedure for opening Champagne is to gently ease out the cork so it emits a teeny sigh, if you don't mind losing a portion of the contents and are hooked on the Hollywood image of Champagne corks going "Pow!" give the cork a good, hard pull. In any case, point the bottle away from decorations, yourself, and any other living creatures to avoid implanting the cork in someone's forehead.

A Few Words about Toasts

Wedding toasts have adhered in the past to a more or less strict protocol. The best man went first, followed by the groom, who responded with a toast of thanks to his parents and in-laws and perhaps to his bride. Then the bride made a toast, followed by the bride's parents (mother first), the groom's parents, and the rest of the guests. These days, however, the groom and the best man frequently give the honor of the first toast to the father and/or mother of the bride if they're hosting the reception. Often, the bride's parents offer a short welcome toast and save their extended sentiments for later in the reception.

When to propose the first toast depends on what kind of reception you have. If you serve a meal, wait until everyone has been seated and served wine. In the past, people have often served Champagne for the first toast. I feel, however, that Champagne is best saved for a toast with the cake, with which it goes so well. At a standing reception, you can begin toasting when everyone has a drink in hand. (For specific options on when to toast, refer to the wedding-day schedule in Chapter 7.)

To make the toasts go trippingly, be sure to

- ✔ **Nominate a master of ceremonies.** You want someone who is witty, wise, and capable of gently giving long-winded toast makers the hook. Having a stentorian voice doesn't hurt either, as it eliminates the need for a drum roll, strobe light, or puff of smoke to command people's attention. If you don't assign this honor role, the job falls to the bandleader, who may not strike the tone you want. I've known some couples who acted as their own emcee, introducing each speaker with an apropos comment to create a personalized, intimate mood.

- ✓ **Choose toast makers carefully.** I even encourage you to cheat a little. In other words, someone may be a fabulous speaker but not very close to you. Honoring a new stepchild or sister- or brother-in-law by asking the person to speak may make all the difference in your relationship going forward.

- ✓ **Give toast makers a heads-up.** Apprise the people who will make toasts several weeks in advance. Doing so gives them time to come up with a way to be amusing and articulate.

- ✓ **Specify short and sweet.** Any toast that goes on longer than three to four minutes belongs at a coronation, not a wedding reception.

- ✓ **Stipulate the tone.** Inside jokes or private anecdotes may be lost on many of the guests.

- ✓ **Put someone else's words in your mouth.** The web has lots of free resources and quotes to use in wedding toasts, and a few sites also sell toasts for around $10. Just enter "wedding toasts" into your favorite search engine for options. Shop around for a wordsmith whose style is simpatico with the way you think and speak. Rehearse well beforehand so that you feel comfortable. You don't need to be nervous about one more thing on your wedding day.

- ✓ **Give toasts up front, facing the crowd.** The emcee introduces the speaker and demonstrates how to use the microphone. Few situations are more embarrassing than watching the bride's father deliver an obviously heartfelt toast, blotting his copious tears with his handkerchief, as all the guests mouth to one another, "What did he say?"

- ✓ **Set a quota.** Even if you have an entire family of elocutionists, sign up no more than eight for toasting duty. More than that and you may begin to hear the distinct sound of snoring coming from some tables.

A wireless hand-held microphone is a wonderful invention. Most people are more relaxed holding something, and the toasts come off less stilted if the emcee hands the mike to the toaster, who can then stand naturally while speaking. If possible, have a *small* table or a podium that can be wheeled on and off the dance floor so that toasters can lay down their notes. A waiter should always deliver a glass to the toaster.

According to the rules of polite society, during toasts at formal gatherings, everyone should rise but the recipients. Due to the plethora of toasts at a wedding, however, making guests jump to their feet every time someone raises a glass is ludicrous. Tradition also holds that drinking to yourself is gauche, akin to applauding yourself. If you want to follow the well-mannered path, refrain from taking a sip when toasts are made to you. The exception to this rule is often the Champagne toast that accompanies the cake-cutting. Nobody seems to mind the bride and groom sipping along in the moment.

Chapter 16

A Piece of Cake

Since ancient times, cakes have been associated with rites of passage, the wedding cake being a particularly powerful symbol. Embodying the themes of marriage, fertility, communion, and hopes for a sweet life, this cake remains an important aspect of most couples' first meal as husband and wife, and the cake-cutting ceremony is a ritual that guests look forward to witnessing.

Still, until recently, the cake was a white cement afterthought, wheeled out to strains of "The Farmer in the Dell" reworked as "The Bride Cuts the Cake," and guests who actually ate a piece risked going into sugar shock. No longer.

The contemporary wedding cake has evolved into a beautiful centerpiece for the reception, as exquisite to look at as it is delicious. Couples spend as much time choosing the look and flavor of their wedding cake as they do on other significant elements of their nuptials.

A plethora of designs are available today, as many artists who originally worked in other materials have turned their talents to creating edible art. Cakes no longer have to be round, stacked, or white. In fact, they no longer have to look like cakes at all. Many bakers specialize in creating grand trompe l'oeil masterpieces that look like precious jewelry boxes, balls and chains, mosaic tile birdbaths, architectural landmarks, oval Shaker boxes, patchwork quilts, wedding-dress lace — just about anything meaningful to the couple.

Baking Away

The good news is that, although these lavish baked sculptures *can* be prohibitively expensive, you have less-expensive yet still delectable alternatives to choose from. In any case, the cake is usually the last thing that your guests eat at the reception, so send them off with something delicious.

Finding a baker

Unless your Aunt Myrtle is a world-class pastry chef and has offered to bake her award-winning *gâteau de mariage* for your wedding, you need to rev up your taste buds and go cake shopping. Or, more precisely, bakery shopping. To find a baker who can do the job, you can use the same methods you use to find a reputable caterer (see Chapter 14).

Bridal website The Knot (www.theknot.com) has a guide to wedding bakers by state; find it by clicking Wedding Cakes on the home page. And to get some inspiration before you start shopping, check out the book *Sensational Cakes* (Stewart, Tabori & Chang) by sensational wedding-cake maker Sylvia Weinstock.

Don't assume that you have to purchase your cake from your caterer. Most caterers allow you to supply your own cake, particularly if they don't specialize in the splendiferous structure you have in mind. Do, however, double-check your banquet facility's policies regarding wedding cakes. Even if your facility allows you to bring in your own cake, it may have to approve the source for insurance purposes or it may charge a cake-cutting fee, which I discuss later in this chapter. Also, if the cake is included as part of your meal price, you probably won't get a rebate if you bring in your own.

As when dealing with the caterer, assess the bakery's potential and limitations. If you choose the bakery because you've seen and/or tasted its cakes and love them, go through its photo portfolio. Remember that bakeries that don't market themselves as wedding-cake specialists may in fact be capable of producing beautiful creations for your special day, so don't rule them out. Also, don't overlook pastry chefs at restaurants. They're often trained in the sugared arts and may jump at the chance to strut their stuff.

Focus on the cake early in your planning because popular bakers book up quickly. If your area is truly lacking in baking talent, don't despair: Consider having your cake shipped from out of town. Many bakers and pastry chefs you read about in magazines send cakes across the country with meticulous instructions for keeping and setup. Some even have websites displaying their creations; search for *wedding cake, wedding cake bakery,* or *wedding cake baker.* Try to arrange a by-mail taste test as well.

An option that's less costly than having your entire cake shipped is to order a simple tiered cake or even a sheet cake from a local baker and transform it with custom-made cake tops, sugar flowers, dragées, and other decorative elements that you can mail-order. Even upscale grocery and deep-discount warehouse stores with in-house baking facilities turn out remarkably decent wedding cakes these days. This can be an economical way to go, particularly for an informal wedding or if having a confectionary masterpiece isn't a high priority. Also consider spiffing up the cake table rather than the cake itself, which is a less-expensive proposition. Drape the table with an ornate cloth, pile petals or fresh flower heads on the table, or set the cake on an heirloom platter or cake plate (see the section "Cake on Display: No Drooling, Please," later in this chapter).

Before meeting with a baker, amass clippings and photos for ideas. Snapshots of your reception venue, dress, and type of flowers are helpful as well. To become knowledgeable about flavors that go well together, make a point of tasting cakes for dessert when you go out to eat. (I realize that doing so may be a hardship, but try to tough it out.)

Tiers of joy

Tiered cakes are either stacked or separated. The layers of *stacked* cakes are placed one on top of another, whereas *separated* cakes (also called *pillared* cakes) use decorative elements (traditionally, miniature Grecian columns) to physically elevate tiers so they're not touching. Consequently, separated cakes are taller than stacked ones that have the same number of tiers.

The ethereal look of some wedding cakes belies the nuts and bolts needed to make them last through a reception. Constructing a separated tiered cake is an engineering feat that requires reinforcing the layers, which can be quite heavy, so they don't collapse into one another. Wooden dowels or plastic classical columns were once the only structures used to separate tiers, but now you can achieve the same effect with sugar topiaries, cupids, or garlanded Lucite columns — just about anything that can hold the weight of the top tiers. Each layer is then separated by corrugated cardboard. Unless your baker specializes in tiered cakes, ordering a multitiered confection can get you a wobbly tower in which the top layer falls through and becomes the bottom layer.

Topping the cake is another occasion for you to brainstorm. As the formerly universal grimacing plaster bride and groom have gone out of style, cake tops are appearing in myriad ingenious forms. Working from photographs, artisans whose sole business is sculpting edible figurines can accurately replicate the couple in a favorite pose, such as teeing off, skiing, or driving their convertible. Companies that produce the typical cake ornaments have become somewhat enlightened, producing brides and grooms of all ethnicities and selling them to be easily mixed and matched for either interracial or same-sex couples. Jewelry companies are producing crystal cake toppers as well as metallic monograms to add glitz to simply iced cakes, and several Internet sites offer custom-made, handblown, glass cake toppers. Ebay (www.ebay.com) and Etsy (www.etsy.com) are great sources for vintage cake toppers, and some Etsy vendors also offer handmade and customizable toppers.

Classical bakers insist that everything on a wedding cake be edible or at least made out of edible ingredients. For that reason, many purists shun fresh flowers on wedding cakes. A crown of fresh flowers that rests solely on the top of the cake, however, can be inexpensive, delicate, pretty, and easy to remove — just be sure to use flowers that are pesticide-free. Other options include preserved flowers such as candied violets and rose petals, edible flowers such as nasturtiums, or flowers that are made from icing piped out of a pastry tube, which are less time-consuming for the decorator and hence less expensive than hand-molded designs.

Confection selection

The type of cake and fillings you choose are limited only by your imagination and the baker's prowess. The emphasis today is on flavor, from cream cheese–frosted carrot cake to chocolate cheesecake, from a hazelnut torte enrobed in dark chocolate to classic butter poundcake with a white-chocolate ganache.

If you have a gluten sensitivity or if you prefer not to consume animal products, have no fear. Specialty bakers in many cities across the country offer gluten-free or vegan wedding cakes, and these options have gotten steadily more delicious. If you have guests with nut allergies or are expecting lots of kids at your wedding, talk to your baker about ensuring a nut-free cake.

If you're serving another dessert in addition to the cake, choose complementary flavors. Fresh berries with pastry cream go well if the wedding cake is a light butter cake filled with lemon curd, for example. On the other hand, a chocolate truffle bombe is way too rich if you've opted for a chocolate mousse cake. Take the season into account as well; dense cakes with rich chocolate filling are more suited for cold weather consumption, whereas in spring and summer, people appreciate berry or citrus flavors at the end of a meal.

Icing issues and filling facts

In planning the texture, flavor, and look of your cake, a working knowledge of icing and filling options can make communicating with your baker a breeze.

✔ **Butter cream:** Both an icing and a filling that consists of real butter (not shortening), sugar, and eggs. Ranges from ivory to pale yellow in color depending on the number of eggs, the butter's color, and whether meringue is mixed in for whitening. Also used to pipe out beautiful and realistic-looking flowers. Mixes well with liqueurs and other flavorings.

✔ **Dragées:** Gold or silver decorative balls — like BBs — made of candied sugar.

✔ **Fondant:** An icing that's either poured in liquid form onto small cakes and petits fours or rolled out in a sheet, cut, and wrapped around the cake. Its smooth, velvetlike appearance is a perfect surface on which to apply decoration. Refrigerating fondant is not only unnecessary but also unwise because it tends to *weep*, forming unappetizing beads of moisture.

✔ **Gold and silver leaf:** Used in small amounts as a final touch on iced cakes. Painting with edible real gold and silver is both labor-intensive and expensive but quite beautiful for tinted flowers, leaves, and art deco touches.

✔ **Marzipan:** Ground almond paste that can be rolled like fondant to cover the cake or used as a base for the fillings between the layers. Can also be hand-molded into such realistic-looking decorations as individual fruits, bunches of grapes, or figures.

✔ **Modeling chocolate:** Has a consistency similar to that of gum paste, though it doesn't get rock hard. White or dark, it can be rolled out like fondant and used to enrobe an entire cake or to embellish a frosted cake with bouquets of chocolate flowers or other whimsical touches.

✔ **Pastillage, sugar dough, or gum paste:** Used to make hand-shaped, fantastical, and botanically correct flowers, replete with stamens and pistils, as well as other cake decorations. Incidentally, though pastillage flowers are exquisite and supposedly edible, I wouldn't suggest biting into one unless your teeth are made of diamonds.

✔ **Pulled sugar:** Sugar syrup that's made molten and pulled into such shapes as bows and flowers.

✔ **Royal icing:** Egg whites beaten with confectioners' sugar and lemon juice and then piped with a pastry tube to make intricate decorative elements such as lace, trellises, or miniature buds. Very sweet and hardens quickly.

✔ **Spun sugar:** Strands of caramelized sugar thrown to create a magical golden veil over a cake or dessert. You can't refrigerate spun sugar, and it doesn't hold up for long, making it inappropriate for a cake that you intend to display for several hours.

✔ **Whipped cream:** The purist's favorite, as either a cake filling or icing. Pure whipped cream isn't the same as "dairy product"; the latter is mixed with stabilizers that increase its longevity but change the taste completely. Whipped cream must be refrigerated.

Size matters

For variety, each tier of the wedding cake can be a different flavor and/ or comprise different flavored layers. At the other end of the spectrum are smaller cakes — single-serving-size cakes, to be precise — that can be as cute or as elegant as you desire. Increasingly popular are miniature cakes wrapped in chocolate (white, milk, or dark) and imprinted with a logo, monogram, or other design. Possible mini cake configurations include

- ✔ **Centerpiece cakes:** Each table has a miniature, decorated wedding cake as the centerpiece, which the guests then slice up and serve for dessert. Sometimes, cakes at each table are of different flavors, encouraging guests to share.

- ✔ **Cupcake cake:** Multiple tiers of individual cupcakes, each decorated separately and sometimes lavishly, are arranged on a stack of plates in graduated sizes to give the image of one many-layered cake.

- ✔ **Party favor cakes:** Each guest gets a miniature cake for dessert or boxed to take home after the reception.

Slicing and pricing

Depending on the part of the country, the cost per cake slice can range from $5 to $25, although custom-designed extravaganzas can run higher. When calculating what size to order, don't consider only the number of guests. Take into account the look of the cake in the room, the number of courses in the meal (if you're having one), the heaviness of the menu, and whether the cake is the sole dessert or will accompany another one. If you want to save the cake top for your anniversary, deduct the number of portions in it from your count.

If you're having a large wedding reception and you don't want to spend the money for an ornate cake of gargantuan proportions, you can save by having the displayed cake made for fewer guests than are in attendance. Serve the majority of slices from simply decorated sheet cakes sliced and served from the kitchen. Request that neat slices, rather than chunks, are cut from the backup cake so the ruse isn't obvious.

For a very grand room but a rather small guest list, you might order a "cake and a half," just so the cake doesn't look absurdly small for the space.

Two Hearts, Two Cakes

Sometimes, couples have two cakes — the bride's cake, or wedding cake, and a groom's cake. Having never gone out of style in the American South, the groom's cake is increasingly popular in other parts of the United States. As it frequently is a surprise that the bride plans for the groom, this cake usually reflects a specific theme dear to the groom's heart and may be sculpted into the shape of anything from a football to a doctor's bag to a giant Big Mac.

If you're interested in a particular design, color, or flavor that you think may be too far-out for your wedding cake, consider using the idea for a groom's cake.

The groom's cake may be served in slivers alongside the wedding cake, wrapped in a beribboned box and sent home with guests, or presented as part of a dessert buffet. You can either display it from the beginning of the reception alongside the wedding cake (see the following section) or present it later, when the wedding cake is cut.

In the American South, a baker often hides charms attached to ribbons beneath an icing border around the cake's base. Before the cake cutting, each bridesmaid pulls a ribbon. Voilà! Each comes away with a charm that has a specific meaning: a tiny ring (next to marry), a heart (love will come), an anchor (hope, adventure), a thimble and button (old maid), a horseshoe and four-leaf clover (good luck), or a fleur-de-lis (love will flower). *Note:* Not all bakers make these trinket-laden cakes; some states have laws against baking any foreign object into a cake lest some unwitting guest choke on a good-luck charm. Nonetheless, these cakes are also popular at Southern bridal showers, where the bridesmaids frequently collect the charms for a bracelet to give to the bride.

Cake on Display: No Drooling, Please

The wedding cake is usually displayed from the beginning of the reception, so choose a filling and icing that can hold up for the duration. (See Figure 16-1.) Keep in mind the time of year and the length of time the cake will be out so it doesn't look like a Salvador Dali watch by the time it's cut. If you're pin-spotting the room (see Chapter 17 for lighting tips), add a spot for the cake table. Otherwise, park it somewhere well lit and in full sight of the guests but off the dance floor or it may wind up on the bandleader's head during the first fast dance.

The base of the cake determines the size of the table. A huge, round table makes even the stateliest cake look minuscule. Make sure that the table is sturdy and is either on wheels or light enough with the cake for two waiters to carry it.

Ask the bakery what kind of serving piece it delivers the cake on. Some provide a flat silver tray; others just deliver it on a plain piece of baker's cardboard that you'll need to cover. A sweet touch that also makes use of those expensive bridesmaid bouquets after the ceremony is to have the maitre d' or wedding consultant discreetly relieve the bridesmaids of their bouquets and arrange them around the cake with a studied casualness. The bridesmaids, incidentally, are usually grateful, being at a loss for how to balance the bouquets with drinks, hors d'oeuvres, and the arm of their significant other.

Arrange to have the cake delivered at least two hours before the reception begins. Cakes are rarely transported fully assembled. Make sure that you clarify specifically who from the bakery is delivering the cake and setting it up. Tell your caterer the delivery time so the cake table is ready and the delivery person doesn't just leave the cake in its box and disappear.

Figure 16-1:
Make sure your cake table is steady and in proportion to the cake before you decorate it.

Illustration by Elizabeth Kurtzman

Cutting the Cake

In the past, the cake ceremony was such an anticlimax that brides and grooms used it as an opportunity to act out some thinly disguised aggression by shoving cake in each other's faces. Thankfully, this charming tradition has gone by the wayside, and the cake cutting has become a sentimental and romantic moment.

Traditionally, the first shared piece symbolizes the couple's first meal as husband and wife. The cake cutting also used to signal the end of the wedding, as the bride and groom would then change and be off. More often now, the cutting is a natural segue, after which people who want to leave may do so, but the newlyweds and the majority of their guests stay and take to the dance floor.

You can gracefully signal that the cake cutting is imminent with a reprise of the first-dance music. The bride and groom often make their toast at this time, presenting a perfect photo opportunity. (See Chapter 15 for info about toasts.) After the cutting and toasts are completed, the band plays quietly in the background until the bride and groom finish exchanging the first bites, whereupon the music swells into a full-fledged dance number.

When you schedule your wedding day (see Chapter 7), put in bold type: *Entire band should be ready to play immediately after cake cutting.* Many bands seem to think that this is the perfect time for a break. Just the opposite — if the music ebbs now, your party is over.

The headwaiter should show you where to make the first cut, particularly if the cake has a *dummy layer* (a fake bottom layer that serves as support). To symbolize the couples' shared life together, the groom places his right hand over the bride's, which holds the knife. Together they cut a small piece from the back of the bottom tier. (For cutting procedures at military weddings, see Chapter 8.) Traditionally, the groom feeds the bride first, a small mouthful easily washed down by a sip of champagne. Then the bride feeds the groom. Then, if they're feeling particularly nice, the bride and groom serve a piece to their new in-laws.

We're aware that some couples find this ceremony antiquated and would rather skip it. Although I have no objections if you feel strongly, just realize, as I said earlier, that guests do *expect* to see you cut your cake. They feel cheated if they don't. Some even believe the old superstition that the bride must cut the first piece or risk being childless.

That said, cut the cake, eat your pieces, put the plate down, and move away. After the photos, the banquet directors should have the cake taken into the kitchen to be cut quickly and efficiently without showing the guests the mess this work of art becomes during slicing.

Some places charge a cake-cutting fee — usually $3 a slice — allegedly to cover the cost of the setup (plates and forks). I find this charge inappropriate, and you should attempt to expunge this clause from your contract.

If the idea of saving your top tier for future consumption strikes your fancy, take precautions to make the cake as palatable as possible one year later — no mold, freezer burn, or other delightful taste treats. Bring a properly sized box, lots of wax paper, bubble wrap, and an airtight plastic bag. Leave explicit instructions for airtight wrapping (freeze the cake first for a few hours before wrapping it) and charge someone — a cryogenics specialist perhaps — with taking this precious cargo home and popping it in the freezer posthaste. Make arrangements to have it transported to your freezer upon your return from the honeymoon. In lieu of this rather complicated procedure, when ordering your wedding cake, you might cleverly put in an order for a small cake of the same flavor to be scheduled for baking and pickup on your first anniversary.

Chapter 17

Setting the Stage

. . . .

In This Chapter

▶ Planning your wedding's décor

▶ Hiring a wedding designer

▶ Furnishing and decorating your reception site

▶ Embellishing a tent

▶ Sending your guests home with a small gift

. . . .

*B*arely knowing the difference between a pickle and a pin spot, you and your fiancé(e) have entered the lair of the Flying Whoozamawhatzies, a renowned wedding design team. Hours later, having finally figured out that a pew bow isn't a smelly ribbon, a runner isn't the fastest waiter who dashes for ice, and a bud vase isn't a beer container, you realize you should've learned to speak Decorese before getting engaged.

Relax. This is going to be fun. You just need to educate yourself in the particulars of the space and the elements that need a creative touch. First step: Do your homework. Amass ideas and tips, find out the venue's ground rules for decorating (see Chapter 4 for pointers in evaluating a venue), and refine your own personal vision. At that point, you should be in good shape to meet with a wedding designer or begin constructing your wedding fantasy yourself.

What to Contemplate before You Decorate

No doubt with every passing day the wedding you've concocted in your heads has morphed many times over. Be forewarned: You haven't seen anything yet. As your reconnaissance gathering goes into full-tilt boogie, make sure that you

> ✔ **Get a floor plan** (as in Figure 17-1) of your reception space that shows, based on your estimated number of guests, the location of the tables, dance floor, bars, buffet stations, stationary pillars, furniture, kitchen, and architectural features that may affect the setup of your party.

Venues often have precise, computer-generated design plans available online or to share with you on request.

- **Try out different florists** every time you have an occasion to send flowers. Pay a call on the store or design studio in person or, even better, order flowers for yourself. See Chapter 11 for information on flowers and finding a florist that suits your style.

- **Collect swatches, images,** and anything else that helps you describe what you have in mind. You may want to keep both a virtual inspiration board (using `www.pinterest.com`, a smartphone application like Wedding Row, or the Desire Wedding Inspiration Board Creator app for iPad) and a physical file or scrapbook for all those bits of fabric and magazine pages. Going through bridal magazines and blogs is just the beginning. Peruse bridal magazines and websites from other countries, shelter and food magazines, art books, and classic movies. You may be inspired by something as minute as the way a curtain hangs or the way a vase is set on a table. If a window display at your favorite boutique catches your eye, find out whether the stylist is available to do weddings.

- **Keep a "Not in *My* Wedding" list** that may include odoriferous flowers such as rubrum lilies, narcissus (paperwhites), and some alliums and daisies, or any arrangement styles that you find tacky or just *not* your style.

- **Solicit the input of the banquet manager or the caterer,** but differentiate between that person's opinion and fact. She may know what has worked in the past in that space — and may be right most of the time — but you should feel free to make suggestions and ask questions.

A common pitfall of wedding planning is a lack of communication about your wedding décor with the powers that be at your reception venue. Before things get too far along, meet with the banquet manager and go over the ground rules. Among the details you want to get straight:

- What are the décor givens? For example, is the ceiling so low that high centerpieces don't work? Or are the available chairs a particular color?

- How much time is allotted for setup and breakdown?

- Does the venue have another event immediately before or after yours?

- What can be affixed to what? Some places have strict rules about stringing garlands, hanging things on walls, using nails, and the like.

- What, if any, are the restrictions regarding prop rentals, candles, additional lighting, and fabric draping?

- Does the venue have a list of recommended and/or dictated floral designers who can work there?

- Where do the bars, buffet stations, and dance floor go?

✔ Where's the best spot for the bride-and-groom's table, and what are the best and worst spots for other tables?

✔ Can you remove or cover décor elements that you find objectionable, such as taxidermic animal heads, pieces of furniture, and lighting fixtures?

✔ Do the fountains and fireplaces work? Can they be made to work in time?

✔ When will renovations (painting, cleaning, and so on) promised in the contract be done?

✔ Are any new renovations or décor changes in the works before your wedding?

✔ Are any public or shared spaces off-limits for decorating?

✔ Will the room be *turned* (changed over) between the ceremony and reception? How long does that take? (See Chapter 4 for room-turning concerns.)

✔ Does the venue have air-conditioning, and is it sufficient?

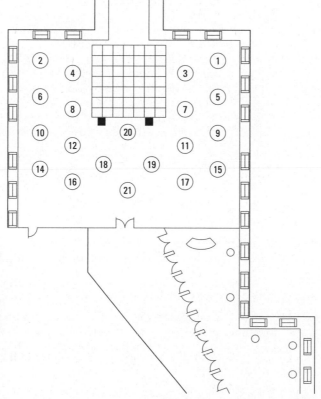

Figure 17-1:
A simple floor plan helps you visualize and design your reception.

Illustration by Wiley, Composition Services Graphics

Choosing a Wedding Designer

For the purposes of this book, I use the term *designer* to refer to any person involved with the décor. You see, once upon a time, only florists were involved. They supplied flowers for parties and weddings, and you may have called them to send a dozen red roses to your sweetheart for Valentine's Day. Now you can find floral designers, party designers, event planners, event producers, happenings specialists, space stylists, and even lifestyle consultants. You can't tell from the title alone whether they design the entire décor (including flowers, linens, lighting, and props), design solely flowers, or even know a poppy from a Popsicle.

The first meeting with a designer you're considering can take place either at your reception venue or at the designer's shop or work space. Set the parameters and be upfront about your budget; no reason to waste your time, and his, by trying to lowball him or by having him suggest outrageous concepts you could never afford. Ask to see photos of possible room treatments. After you choose a designer, take a walk-through *together* as early in your planning as possible, even if he's familiar with your space.

After you hire your designer or company and agree on budget and design details, you should be able to see a sample centerpiece a few weeks before your wedding. If possible, have the designer create a sample table replete with linens, place settings, candles, and table numbers so you have a clear idea of the total effect. Be flexible: When it comes to flowers, what you see isn't always what you get. When possible, get a photo of the centerpiece. Your contract most likely stipulates that, because of unforeseen events such as frost, seasonal changes, and shipping problems, you can make certain substitutions. Find out what those are.

To prevent any misunderstanding, here are some other specifics to include in your agreement:

- Does the designer charge setup and breakdown fees?

- How early will he need to start setting up and how long will he take to break down? (This factor is important for avoiding overtime space-rental fees.)

- Can he arrange to deliver leftover flowers to your home? For what fee?

- At the end of the event, what materials — such as tablecloths, vases, napkins, and table numbers — do you own, and what does the designer own? Can guests leave with the centerpieces intact or do the flowers need to be wrapped or put in other containers?

What's in a Room?

Consider every aspect of your space that could use some decoration. The following overview provides ideas and solutions for design dilemmas, whether your wedding is in a hotel, a banquet hall, or a loft. (For particulars about theme weddings, see Chapter 8.)

When you enter

First impressions count, so as guests enter, give them something to remember:

- ✔ An arched trellis adorned with flowers or a floral monogram

- ✔ A pair of large, fiberglass urns, faux-finished to look like jade, pink marble, or granite and stuffed with flowering branches

- ✔ A welcome sign designed as a whimsical garden plaque, a sports-type pennant, or an illuminated, medieval-looking scroll lettered in gold — especially in lieu of the generic black event board with white plastic letters that many hotels and conference facilities use

- ✔ Waiters bearing trays of drinks just inside the door for an immediate display of hospitality

The driveway

Even before your guests hit the entrance, you can convey a celebratory air without spending a great deal of money. Create a glowing path of footlights by using *luminarias* (votive candles in small paper bags). Either color or plain-brown paper bags will do. Make sure you have a few inches of sand in the bottom of each bag to stabilize it. For an even more-festive touch, cut out patterned windows in the bags symmetrically by folding the bags in half, as if making paper snowflakes.

Tiki torches or lanterns on shepherd's hooks, often found at gardening shops, are dramatic as well as inexpensive. When filled with citronella, these have the added bonus of repelling things that go buzz in the night.

For daytime weddings, use potted plants, staked balloons, or nicely done, billboard-type signs along the drive to guide the way.

The gift table

Except in certain cultures, people seldom bring presents to the wedding anymore, so you may not need to have a fancy table waiting to be piled with packages. (I cover different traditions for displaying gifts in Chapter 18.)

For guests who haven't figured out that gifts brought to the reception are just more stuff for the bride and groom to schlep home, assign a waiter or friend to whisk away the packages and envelopes and check them in the coat room. Do so out of courtesy to those guests who sent their gift directly to your home but may, upon seeing a few ribbon-festooned boxes waiting to be joined by more ribbon-festooned boxes, fear that you expected them to inundate you on the spot.

In cases where guests bring just a card, presumably with a check or money inside, have your gift-keeper put it in a safe place, perhaps even a small lockbox.

Designate someone to gather the gifts at the end of the reception and hold onto them until you and your spouse can arrange to pick them up when you return from your honeymoon. Wait until you get home to open the packages and envelopes — doing so at the reception isn't appropriate.

Up, down, and all around: Ceilings, floors, and walls

Look at the big picture. What parts of the space are crying out for help and need to be disguised? What has potential and should be accentuated? Can you live with the bare acoustic ceiling tiles or should you divert precious centerpiece funds to camouflage them? Does the space contain a singularly exquisite architectural feature — a cathedral ceiling, a sweeping banister, a fountain? You can create an entirely different environment by draping the walls, ceiling, and every possible feature, but if your space requires such a total transformation, why did you book it in the first place?

When it comes to decorating, choose your battles. Neutral walls and even patterned wallpaper may not be noticeable, depending on the time of day. If the walls are decorated in a flamboyant way, go with it rather than trying to do a complete overhaul. Similarly, the flaming-orange carpet may be distracting during a day wedding but inconsequential at night, when the tables are set up and the lights are low. If you have a budget that allows for more than tabletop décor, draping ceilings or walls and hanging floral chandeliers from the ceiling can transform a space completely.

Fabric, table linens, and other decorating materials must adhere to fire ordinances. Fire marshals have been known to spring surprise inspections at even the most glamorous locations and insist that everything be removed. Speaking of fire safety, by law, you can't cover lighted exit signs and fire sprinklers.

Trees or huge plants such as ficus, palm, or philodendron cover a multitude of sins for comparatively little money because you can rent them from nurseries. Some nurseries rent large, hearty, flowering plants also.

Lighting

People often don't realize just how important lighting is for the look and mood of an event. A few shades can make the difference between intimate and institutional. You don't want lights dimmed to such a romantic level that waiters have to set off flares. Nor do you want the room so brilliant that sequin dresses spontaneously combust. However, a pin spot can make even a modest centerpiece pop, and something as simple as dimming the chandeliers for the first dance can conjure an aura of mystery and suspense.

Visit the space at the time of day your wedding will be. Even for afternoon events, where supplemental lighting is often a waste of money, you need to take into consideration the light level. Ask your designer to detail the most appropriate light settings for your reception and mark them for the maitre d'. Some other questions to ask include

- ✔ Is the light blinding so that shades need to be drawn?
- ✔ Do the windows have shades?
- ✔ Should you change the time of your wedding because the light looks best at a certain time of day?
- ✔ If you're having your ceremony at the site, in which direction does the sun set, and can you plan your ceremony around that?
- ✔ Do the lights have dimmers? What are the requirements or restrictions for a lighting designer?

Hiring a professional lighting company may seem extravagant — and it is — but creative lighting can transform a room in ways you never dreamed possible. Properly up-lit, an urn filled with branches not only appears larger but also throws dramatic silhouettes on the wall, turning a single arrangement into a forest. Think about restaurants and homes where you feel extremely comfortable. Chances are, the lighting is very pleasing to both your eye and your psyche.

Some floral designers offer lighting services; others subcontract with companies that supply the equipment. Either way, here are some terms you may hear bandied about:

✓ **Bee, fairy, or twinkle lights:** Strings of tiny lights, like Christmas lights. Used behind diaphanous fabrics, on banisters, or in trees, they add a magical touch. An inexpensive trick is to drop strings of these like vines from the ceiling. In addition, some light strings utilize large-diameter, clear bulbs or globes, with visible filaments, that help create a romantic, European bistro feel. Drape them in organic patterns over your guests' heads or in key areas. You can also substitute colorful bulbs or globes to support the overall color scheme.

✓ **General lighting:** The main light in the room, coming from either natural or artificial sources. This light should soften and flatter; use accent lighting to make specific areas or architectural features stand out.

✓ **Gobos:** Custom-made or rented stencils that go over lights to project patterns such as stars, moons, snowflakes, monograms, or musical notes onto walls, the dance floor, or draped fabric. They create contrast and drama in the room.

✓ **Moving lights:** Also known as *intelligent lighting,* these computerized systems can be programmed to focus the beam remotely, change its size, and project a variety of colors, patterns, and strobe settings that are perfect for energizing the dance floor.

✓ **Perimeter lighting:** Color-washing the walls that surround the room is key to setting the mood. Color-changing LED lights allow any room to be "painted" the color of your choice with a wash of light.

✓ **Pin spots:** Narrow beams that target centerpieces, the cake, or anything demanding special attention. Hung from the ceiling or directed from light poles, they're frequently used in pairs to give cross-directional light. The darker the room, the more dramatic pin spots look.

✓ **Up-lights and down-lights:** These used to be known as *light-cans,* which are usually painted to match the space. Used to project beams of light upward from the base of an urn or tree or down onto a mantle or altar. Although still in use by some lighting designers and venues, these are quickly being replaced by programmable, color-changing LED lights, eliminating the need for a lot of power or lighting filters *(gels)* to create color.

✓ **Washes:** Colors (usually pastels) projected over large spaces such as bars or dance floors that bathe the area in a particular light.

To de-emphasize unattractive areas without spending a penny, simply remove some of the fluorescent tubes in the bathrooms or unscrew light bulbs in wall sconces. If you need *some* light, replace the bulbs with pink or frosted bulbs.

Props and furniture

By *props* I don't mean big, theatrical pieces. You might incorporate unique items that you own — such as delicate chairs, pretty lamps, ceramic pitchers, silver bowls, candelabras, and vases — into your décor scheme. Antique stores often rent items that aren't precious, and many cities have prop shops where you can find all sorts of goodies. Caterers and hotel banquet departments often own props that they wouldn't have thought to use for a wedding but that you may be interested in, such as huge fans, paper lanterns, or even backdrops. (Props are, of course, a critical component of theme weddings, which I cover in Chapter 8.)

The cocktail area

A secret to a lively party is keeping guests constantly amused and entertained with small surprises. To do this, try not to be too predictable with any of the facets of your reception, including the décor. If the dining room is romantic and classical, there's no reason that the cocktail area can't be glitzy or very modern. Whether cocktails are served before dinner or are the main event (see Chapter 14), don't mimic a dining room with large centerpieces and tables for eight. You want guests up and mingling, not planted like carrots.

Here are some other traffic-flow considerations:

- Place bars and food stations around the room, not all together.
- Bars should be visible to guests but not near the entranceway, which can cause bottlenecks.
- Don't set bars or buffets near the dance floor or music.
- In a tight space, don't use one-sided head tables; they take up too much room.

Cocktail tables

Cocktail tables should be small and seat no more than four people. Whether the tables are 28, 32, or 36 inches in diameter, you should provide seating for about a third of the guests — but not more than a third — during cocktails. Having seats for, say, 75 percent of the guests isn't gracious; it's silly and makes people think you forgot to rent chairs for the other 25 percent.

A trend of late is bar-height pedestal tables for guests to lean on (rather than sit at) as they chat. Many rental companies offer bases that turn 30-inch-high tables into high tops.

Escort card table

An escort card isn't the same as a place card. If you're serving a seated meal, an *escort card,* which guests pick up before the meal, tells them at which table they're seated. A *place card* (at the table) informs guests which seat at that table is theirs.

A professional trick: Escort cards work best when they're sets of miniature envelopes with guests' names on the outside and inserts with table numbers — as opposed to having both names and numbers on *table tents* (folded cards) — because the numbered inserts can be done beforehand and changed at the last moment without you having to rewrite the entire name. The envelopes look quite elegant propped up on their little flaps in rows on the escort card table, and they can be calligraphed in bright colors or festooned with teeny silk flowers to add to the table's look.

Because the escort card table stands alone — usually in the cocktail area or in another prominent place (but not where you'll cause a bottleneck!) — and is often the first thing that guests see, make it particularly striking. A large, elaborate centerpiece and an embroidered cloth on the table or a single fabulous prop, such as a portrait of the two of you or an antique lamp, works well. A lovely touch is to put framed photographs — the older the better — of parents and grandparents around the table and arrange the escort cards around them. You have many creative ways to tell guests where they're seated: Some designers hang cards from branches as if they're growing and have them plucked for the guests; others make a bed of orchids or gardenias to rest the cards on, doing away with a centerpiece completely.

Post either a waiter or a friend with an alphabetized list and table numbers to troubleshoot should a card go astray or someone bring an unexpected guest. (Rude, yes, but you still have to find an extra seat.) The list-keeper should also note cards that aren't picked up so that the caterer can remove extra place settings before guests enter the dining room.

Rather than leave your guest book on the escort card table, ask a friend to pass it around at the reception (and be responsible for retrieving it at the end of the party) and encourage people to share their thoughts on the day. Buy a hard-bound album with blank pages (a photo album may work) that matches your wedding's style. A truly meaningful guest book is more than a list of signatures. Besides, you presumably already have your guests' names and addresses from your invitation list, so you don't need them to sign in as if at a hotel. A clever alternative to the traditional guest book is to put a digital camera and a small printer on a table and ask the guests to print photos of themselves at your wedding in addition to their good wishes.

Bars

A banquet table can serve as a bar or the space may have rolling bars. In either case, avoid bottlenecks at the entrance by making sure the bar — and waiters passing drinks — are far enough inside so guests can grab a drink and keep on moving. If your budget allows, either skirt or box bar linens so the table legs don't show; the color of the linens should work with your scheme. (For a full discussion of bars, see Chapter 15.)

For a truly dramatic effect, make a bar out of ice. An ice sculptor carves the entire bar out of ice and then lights it dramatically with colored lights. Another popular but less-extravagant option is large ice sculptures that sit atop the bar and also serve as chillers for flavored vodkas. However, make sure that the ice sculpture (or floral arrangement or candle arrangement) isn't overwhelming. The bar, after all, is a high-traffic spot and work space.

Dining areas

Even if you've had to shoehorn in more than an ideal number of tables, leave adequate room both near the entrance and between tables so guests can make their way gracefully without snagging tablecloths in their wake. Upon entering, guests should feel like they're in a completely different atmosphere than the one they just left.

If you're having a buffet or any kind of food station, you need to place these tables where guests can line up and easily reach them without standing on someone's chair. Because the key decorative element of food stations is the food itself, they're best discussed within the context of planning the menu (see Chapter 14).

Position one or two waiters as traffic cops near the dining room entrance with a floor plan that indicates table numbers and locations. Otherwise, Aunt Myrtle may still be looking for her table when you return from the honeymoon.

Dining tables

One way of making a large room filled with guests look less institutional and more elegant is to vary the sizes and shapes of the tables. A successful floor plan can include squares, rounds, and/or rectangles. The most efficient way of making sure you devise a plan that works is to use a *CAD* (computer-aided design) program, which many hotels and tent companies have. But you can also simply measure the space and map out the floor plan on graph paper.

If you're using round tables, seating eight to ten guests at a 54-, 60-, or 66-inch table works best. Having the same number of guests at every table, however, is virtually impossible.

Seat and you shall find

Although individual place cards are optional (a touch that I believe guests really do appreciate, but it's a lot of work), assigning tables for any seated meal is an absolute necessity. If you don't assign guests to a table, inevitably there will be 30 chairs pulled around one table, and your two camp friends who don't know anyone else will be seated at a table for two in the corner.

When ordering escort cards, you'll most likely need about half of the number of your guests because you place couples' names on one card together. If you've printed a monogram on your seating cards, order extra because they'll come in handy as gift cards later on in life.

The historically grueling seating process has definitely become more fun of late with the advent of online software. The latest technology stores all your data in the cloud so that you can access it from anywhere. A tool I particularly like is Social Tables (www.social tables.com). It has a dynamic drag-and-drop interface and allows you to create your seating charts online and share them with your fiancé(e) and family. The software includes a guest list manager and a floor plan designer as well. A creative and thoughtful seating plan can definitely add a lot to your guests' experience.

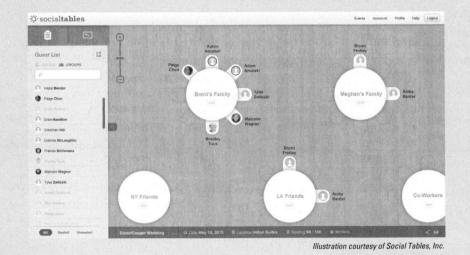

Illustration courtesy of Social Tables, Inc.

Still, you want to keep the number of people at each table and the table sizes in close range. You may have eight tables of ten and two tables of eight, for example, but not two tables of four, two tables of seven, three tables of ten, and so on. This is a party, not a nightclub; people at smaller tables feel like the odd folks out. When you have your final guest count, ask the banquet manager whether you should plan for fewer tables because space is tight or more tables because you have room to spare. If you do use different size tables, inform the tablecloth and centerpiece suppliers as soon as possible so everything is in proportion.

Head table

Wherever the bride and groom sit is called the *head table*. The most important aspect in planning the head table is where you put it because everyone
wants a view of the bride and groom. Two things affect the size of your head
table: the size of your space and the people you want to sit with you. For the
latter, you can do one of two things:

- Seat both sets of parents, the officiant, grandparents, and/or extremely
  close relatives such as aunts and uncles with you. Then you can sprinkle
  the wedding party and their significant others around the room, making
  them mini emissaries for you.

- Give parents their own tables with friends and seat the wedding party
  and their significant others at your table. Traditionally, the bride sits to
  the groom's right, and the best man sits on her other side. Attendants
  are alternately male, female.

Seating significant others at separate tables may result in wistful looks and
goo-goo eyes from across the room, making other guests feel uncomfortable
as well.

Don't assume you're a seating psychic. If your parents are divorced or you
have some other family drama that may erupt, ask before you blithely place
those people where you please. Even if you play the peacemaker at family
events, remember that this isn't the normal family dinner. Your attention will
be elsewhere during the reception. Are you brave enough to leave contentious
relatives to their own devices?

Until recently, seating the entire wedding party on a *dais* (a raised platform)
on one side of a long table so they faced the room was standard operating
procedure. As many couples now find the long head table either unattractive,
silly, or impossible to plan seating for, they're opting to use a round table. If as
a matter of diplomacy or personal taste you use a rectangular head table, you
can make it a focal point by swagging the cloths, planting floral gardens down
the table's length, or situating the table under an airy arbor or gazebo-type
structure.

Some couples, perhaps out of the sheer frustration of determining who should
sit at the head table, have a table for just the two of them, called a *sweetheart
table*. Although it's not my favorite solution, where you sit is likely to be a
moot point because you'll both be working the room for most of the meal.

Cake table

Place this table prominently in the main dining area and decorate accordingly. (See Chapter 16 for a complete cake table report.) If possible, and if the
cake is beautiful, spotlight it.

Dance floor

A built-in dance floor makes life easy, but if you must rent one, interlocking, 3-x-4-foot parquet squares are superior to the flimsy, rolled-up variety.

An extraordinary but expensive proposition is a hand-painted dance floor, a specialty of many designers. One popular design is a couple's monogram in script surrounded by a painted wreath of flowers.

Bandstand

If you're having trouble fitting a large band directly on your dance floor, you simply don't want to give up precious dance floor space, or you just want drama, you can rent platforms to be used as a bandstand. Even though these risers generally run only 8 inches high, your designer should cover the gap between floor and platform with stapled material. Specify who's erecting the bandstand — the house, the rental company, or your designer — and make sure to get the size specifications from the band.

You can't do much about camouflaging speakers because they need to be placed between the musicians and the audience. Mixing boards are big and ugly no matter what, so place them as discreetly as possible on a table with a boxed cloth that matches the dining tables.

Lighted music stands are often emblazoned with the band's name. If having this free billboard for the band doesn't jibe with your décor, specify that you'd prefer the band use generic music stands or none at all. For more band information, see Chapter 13.

Chairs

Hotels and restaurants often spend a great deal of money on their chairs, which are designed to work with the room's décor as well as to seat the optimum number of people around each table. If you need to rent chairs, in most parts of the country wooden and plastic folding chairs are available in various colors. A more elegant option is Chiavari (faux bamboo) chairs, which are smaller — though less comfortable — than most chairs and can seat more people at a table. Although Chiavaris cost more to rent, you may actually break even because you need fewer tables, tablecloths, and centerpieces.

If your venue's chairs are particularly hideous, you may want to rent chair-back covers, full slipcovers, and/or simple sashes. Materials range from polyester-cotton blends in various colors to space age–looking spandex. A ribbon of tulle covered with a floral garland on the backs of the bride's and groom's chairs adds romance. For a funky, chic look, swathe chairs with a few yards of transparent fabric (such as crystal organza or tulle) and tie it into a gigantic bow in the back.

Tabletops

A centerpiece alone does not a table make. You convey an event's flavor and spirit through many details, which, repeated seat after seat, table after table, form a delectable impression as guests enter. After guests are seated, they have time to note and appreciate each and every nuance, from the color of the napkins to the placement of the wine glasses. Consequently, the hours you invest planning these elements are well spent.

Before the guests file into the main dining room, have the headwaiter or your wedding consultant do a table-by-table inspection to make sure that the correct number of chairs and place settings are set at each table, the tables are where you want them, every place is set correctly, the glasses have no spots, the candles are lit, and the chairs are straight — in short, that every decorative detail has been taken care of.

Tablecloths

Anything you can dream up for your wedding is available for rent — for a price, of course — and tablecloths are no different. Many companies rent nationally as well as locally, happily shipping linens anywhere in the country. The typical white restaurant tablecloth, darned and dingy, is best used as an under-pad. You can make just about any tablecloth look more festive, however, with a little creativity and sewing ability. Although some of these ideas are impractical for *all* your tables, they're doable and dramatic for one important table, such as the escort card table or the cake table:

- A thick band of satin edging on a table square
- Block-painted or stenciled designs
- A rolled hem or cording sewn into the hem for a formal, petticoat effect
- Swagged tablecloths
- Fringe and/or tassels sewn on a square top-cloth or used with swagging
- Hand-painted designs, which you can create with inexpensive materials
- A solid-color under-cloth that shows through a lace top-cloth
- A tablecloth of leaves made by gluing green leaves onto the cloth
- Mixed patterns such as floral chintz top-cloths over striped under-cloths
- One-of-a-kind cloths such as patchwork quilts, antique lace, or vintage shawls for a special table
- Overlays made of organza, panne, or cut velvets
- Damask or brocade runners down the center of the table
- Each table a different shade of the same color so the room appears as a sea of blues, for example

✔ Table squares with silk or fresh flowers, tassels, or rings sewn on the corners (to calculate what size square you need, see Table 17-1)

Table 17-1	What Size Square Tablecloth?
Rectangular Table Length	*Square Overlay Length (Point to Point)*
127"	90"
119"	84"
101"	72"
85"	60"
76"	54"
64"	45"

Something about bare table legs draws people's attention away from the rest of the room's splendor. Try to use floor-length cloths at all costs. For rectangular buffet and bar cloths, add 60 inches to both the length and width to get a floor-length cloth. To calculate the size cloth you need for a round table, see Table 17-2.

Table 17-2	What Size Round Tablecloth?
Table Diameter	*Round Floor-Length Cloth*
72"	132"
66"	126"
60"	120"
54"	114"
48"	108"
36"	96"

The clunking of cutlery and china on wood or particleboard can feel and sound harsh, so place a foam pad or another linen between the table and linen.

Napkins

A subtle part of the décor, napkins can go on the service plate or directly on the tablecloth but don't work well fanned out in glasses when a low centerpiece is on the table.

If you're renting napkins, rent plenty of extra for waiter's service and to replace dropped or soiled ones. For cocktail napkins, order at least three per guest.

Tying napkins with wire-edged ribbon or raffia is a lovely finisher and less expensive if you (and your helpers) do the tying. That means picking up the napkins a few days before your wedding if possible.

When it comes to cocktail napkins, starched linen is elegant and formal but not inexpensive to rent. A standard monogram on paper napkins is fine, but creating your own logo by hand or computer and having it printed on paper cocktail napkins and hand towels may be more in keeping with your reception's style.

Candles

Candles have long held a mystical appeal and are currently, if you'll pardon the pun, hot, hot, hot. Where once you may have seen two elegant tapers guarding each centerpiece at a reception, you now find a virtual conflagration composed of hundreds of candles in all shapes and sizes.

Tall tapers can turn into wax-spitting demons in rooms with cross-directional air currents. Even dripless candles can be hazardous. If you're at all unsure, ask the banquet manager what she has seen work the best in the space. Also work out a contingency plan for when the candles burn down: Either have staff replace the candles or adjust the lighting accordingly. And *never* use scented candles around food.

Some places don't allow open-flame candles because of fire codes. Three ways to circumvent this limitation (as well as the air-current problem) are to use hurricane lamps, flame-free battery or LED candles, or "mechanical candles" in which a steel spring pushes up wax through a metal, candle-shaped casing as it burns. From a distance, these look fairly natural, making them suitable for ceremonies and chandeliers.

Developments in battery and LED (light-emitting diode) candles have been truly remarkable. They come in a wide variety of shapes and sizes (from tea lights to pillars to tapers), and they flicker just like real candles. Famed wedding and event designer Preston Bailey is a big fan of these candles. He says that although they may be a bit less romantic than a live flame, they solve all your safety and wax issues while producing an effect that's pretty much the same.

The glass holders for votive candles provide a base for decorating. They're frequently gold- or silver-leafed, covered with galax or lemon leaves, and tied with raffia, beribboned, covered in mesh or fabric, planted in tiny terra-cotta pots, or hung from precisely engineered centerpieces.

Some ways to wax romantic include

- Chunky Roman candles of different heights grouped together
- Hand-dipped spiral candles
- Candles shaped as orbs, squares, and pyramids
- Floral-shaped tea candles floated in rose bowls
- Taper candles, which can be as tall as 3 feet, placed in short, ornate holders or in the tops of tall centerpieces
- Scented candles in the bathrooms (but never around food)
- Candles in votive holders placed on mirrors set in table centers to reflect more light
- Votive candles grouped together and/or set in wreaths of flowers, lemons, or branches
- Table lamps that hold candles, with beaded or silver shades

Dishes, cutlery, stemware, and so on

Frequently, in hotels and restaurants, you don't have a choice in china and silver. Ask to see what the venue uses as a service plate or *charger* (the empty plate that's part of the place setting when you enter the room). If you hate the pattern, skip the service plate and put a napkin in the center of each place setting instead.

For china, silver, and glassware rentals, which you need at some sites, choices abound. At the inexpensive end of the spectrum are heavy, white china, flimsy silverware, and soda-bottle-thick glassware. Attractive options do exist at various price points, and if you and your caterer can agree to use one plate for two courses (in other words, washed in between), renting attractive china may be affordable. Just make sure that every element works with the overall table design. As you can see in Figure 17-2, outfitting a place setting for a five-course meal means a lot of rental charges.

Table accoutrements can be practical as well as enchanting:

- Individual salt and pepper shakers or cellars
- Butter placed on lemon leaves
- Tiny silver tongs for sugar cubes
- Colored stem glasses
- Metallic or faux jewel napkin rings
- Knife, spoon, or chopstick rests

If you're serving meat, be sure to order sharp knives. Regular rental knives usually aren't serrated, forcing guests to engage in Eating Olympics.

Figure 17-2:
Make sure that each place setting includes the specific plates, glasses, and utensils needed for your meal.

Illustration by Elizabeth Kurtzman

Table numbers

Make table numbers easy to read, but refrain from making them big enough for billboards. And put some thought into creative ways to avoid using generic table-number supports. These ways may include

- Rococo frames displaying table numbers
- Leaves painted with numbers, affixed to a long tube, and planted in the centerpieces
- Numbers on table tents that match escort and place cards
- Different flowers or props on each table, with guests assigned to table names — *Gardenia* or *Tango* — rather than by number

Table numbers should be removed at the beginning of the meal — the table is probably too crowded as it is and, after guests are seated, numbers are unnecessary.

When numbering the tables (as in Figure 17-1, earlier in this chapter), do evens on one side of the dance floor and odds on the other, rather than what you think is a consecutive arrangement. The odd-even split makes narrowing down the location of a table that much easier for waiters directing guests. Keep in mind that some people have an aversion to the number 13, so you may want to skip that table number. Use lower numbers at the least desirable tables and high numbers at the best tables. If a guest's table is situated on the third balcony, somehow it feels better if it's numbered Table 6 rather than Table 3,012.

Place cards

Place cards tell guests where at the table they're seated. You can use table tents, centered at 12 o'clock above each plate, or flat cards set on top of each napkin.

In times past, place cards were a must at seated meals. They went out of fashion during the '60s and '70s but made a comeback in the '80s and continue to be popular at weddings today. Fortunately, place cards are increasingly — and sensibly — less formal, using first names and even nicknames so members of the table know how to address one another.

Assigning tables is difficult enough and, admittedly, assigning seats is an even bigger pain. Place cards may also seem a little formal and fussy to you. But trust me, guests really appreciate your having thought about whom they may have to talk to for several courses.

Write or print names on both sides of table-tent place cards so guests across the table from one another can read them.

Designing a menu card

A handsomely printed or calligraphed menu card makes a nice memento. Here are some tips for making yours special:

✔ Put your names or monogram, the wedding date, and the site at the top of the menu.

✔ List the wines to be served to the left of each dish — but only if they're interesting enough (not necessarily expensive) to mention.

✔ Use colorful and descriptive adjectives.

✔ Use the menu cards as place cards, writing each guest's name at the top.

Menu cards

Pretty menu cards don't have to be expensive. You can design them yourself on your computer or download one of the templates available online and then have them offset printed or print them on good card stock from your own computer. (See Chapter 5 for more on DIY printing for your wedding.) If you're having your wedding at a restaurant or hotel that prints its own daily menu, the venue may be happy to do yours in the same fashion. Although you may have one menu per person, two or four per table is sufficient. When you have different food stations, menu cards are a real advantage. Otherwise, after the party you'll hear, "I didn't know there was filet somewhere!"

Restrooms

Women, in particular, get a kick out of bathroom baskets filled with goodies. I suggest throwing in everything from hairspray to breath mints to emergency pairs of stockings in various sizes. In off-premise spaces, the bathrooms can be dreary at best, so bring in your own hand towels, scented candles, soaps, and even toilet paper to replace the particularly torturous variety found in institutional restrooms.

Transitional spaces

You don't have to bedeck vestibules, foyers, and spaces between the cocktail and dining rooms in flowers and finery, but they should at least look like they're a part of the same event. Even if you've already blown your budget on more pressing design details, try to save a few bucks to place some votive candles around on ledges and tables or to cover spare tables and chairs with tulle, the all-purpose wedding material. You can cover potted plants in plastic garden containers with tulle or other fabrics and group them together to soften otherwise neglected spaces.

An In-Tents Experience

I've seen the sad results of people who erected grand tents but ran out of money to decorate them. Although their fantasy may have been to dine in a palace that had somehow magically dropped into their backyard, the reality ran more toward dining inside a great white laundry bag. If the tent itself puts such a gaping hole in your budget that you can't afford to hang a piece of greenery, you really should reconsider your choice of venue.

Some crucial aspects of tent decorating include

- **Banners:** Wide bands of fabric that cover part of the ceiling and are less expensive than a full tent lining but serve the same purpose in drawing the eye away from the ceiling.

- **Fabric linings:** Most tent companies rent pleated fabric linings that cover the ceiling and/or the walls. Linings are rather pricey.

- **Flooring:** If you opt for the floor, carpet is a tony touch that also muffles sound. A less-costly floor covering is black or green AstroTurf. (See Chapter 4 for info on floor issues.)

- **Interior lighting:** If your wedding is in the evening, the tent requires lighting. Options include chandeliers, *starlighting* (bee lights), track systems, inexpensive globes, carriage lights (which look like old-fashioned gas lamps), and oversized Chinese lanterns.

- **Landscape lighting:** Used to emphasize natural features such as ponds or trees, as well as to guide guests to necessities such as restrooms and driveways.

- **Poles:** Many contemporary tent designs avoid poles altogether, creating more open space within the tent. If you do select a pole tent, poles can be up to 42 feet tall for a large tent, depending on its pitch. When planning tent seating, take into account how poles affect sightlines. Metal poles are ugly and need to be covered somehow. Besides painting them, you may wind them in floral garlands or ruche and tie fabric around them. For a touch of organic whimsy, cover the poles in cheap fabric and glue leaves in overlapping rows pointing upward to completely camouflage the metal.

- **Windows:** Tent sides are clear plastic, opaque plastic, or cloth, depending on the season, and often stenciled with windowpanes, arches, and shutters. Some unusual and quite expensive tents also feature glass walls.

Make sure all tents, equipment, and décor comply with local ordinances, including fire codes. The tent company is responsible for getting the proper permits.

Doing Your Guests a Favor

Although sending guests off from your reception with a small gift is very gracious, finding the right item, neither too cheap nor too grand, can be difficult. With wedding memorabilia, the line between cute and kitsch can be mighty thin. I was reminded of this not long ago when I came across an ad for the "perfect wedding favor" in the back of a bridal magazine — a customized air freshener with the couple's invitation reproduced on it. If you can't or don't decide to spend the money to give your guests something they may actually save until they get to their car, you should forgo giving anything at all — it's not necessary. With a little creativity, however, you can probably find or make the perfect party favor. My suggestions:

- The traditional candied almonds, symbolizing the bitter and the sweet of marriage but packaged creatively to evoke your own wedding style (for example, small tins with calligraphed labels that double as place cards)

- Dream pillows, a Native American concept, with a handwritten note explaining their use (to be kept under your pillow to invoke specific dreams) and thanking guests for coming

- If your wedding has a floral theme such as daisies or roses, a full-size plant in a terra-cotta pot with a note on care and treatment

- Herb plants such as basil or sage in a terra-cotta pot, with a printed card of your favorite recipe

- For a desert or urban wedding, small pots with beautiful cactuses or succulents, also with care instructions

- Whole miniature wedding cakes, large enough to be a dessert portion, packaged in white glossy boxes and tied with chiffon ribbons

- Small boxes made of sugar filled with tiny chocolates and packaged in beribboned white boxes

- A tin of assorted homemade cookies in the shapes of tiered wedding cakes, bells, and rings

- Personalized boxes, muslin bags, or glassine envelopes with sticker seals, filled with small treats such as chocolate truffles, heart-shaped Linzer torte, or meringues

- Homemade or purchased hot chocolate on a stick, bundled into cellophane bags and tied with pretty ribbon

- A cellophane envelope or plastic sleeve filled with personalized M & M's in your wedding colors, custom-printed with your first names and wedding date or a small sketch of your faces

- ✔ Attractive glass bottles of high-quality olive oil, flavored with a visible chili pepper or branch of rosemary and tied with raffia

- ✔ A two-, four-, or six-pack of boutique beers with a label dedicating the brew to the bride and groom

- ✔ Homemade preserves or chutneys in Mason jars with handwritten labels

- ✔ Bottles of wine with a custom label from a small vineyard (these should be full-size bottles; what can a couple do with a half bottle or split — rinse their mouths?)

- ✔ A framed portrait of each couple or single guest to take home with them (see Chapter 21)

- ✔ A book of love poems or quotes with a leather bookmark or a metal page-keeper embossed with your wedding date

- ✔ A pair of hand-painted champagne flutes

- ✔ Small topiary trees in faux antiqued pots

Certain party favors must come in pairs. Giving guests (whether couples or single) a lone champagne glass or bottle of beer is beyond useless — it's too sad to contemplate.

If favors aren't part of your tabletop décor, the best way to distribute them to guests is as guests are leaving the reception. Put the favors in small shopping bags with pretty tissue paper and have a waiter hand one to each guest. In cold weather, the coat room attendant may hand them a bag with their coats. Putting the bags on guests' chairs is rarely convenient; the bags end up on the floor, getting trampled every time someone gets up from the table.

For a wedding that ends in the wee hours of the morning, send your guests off with a special favor — a goody bag containing the early edition of the next day's newspaper and some ready-to-eat breakfast fare. Guests will surely appreciate bagels and cream cheese, a mini-loaf of sourdough bread and a wedge of good cheese, or tiny croissants, breakfast pastries, and a small pot of jam.

Part V

Gifts, Garb, Pics, and Trips

The 5th Wave   By Rich Tennant

"I told you we should have registered."

In this part . . .

Don't let the cryptic title fool you — you're about to discover more than you ever wanted to know but were afraid to ask on several key wedding topics. For starters, I tell you how to register for gifts efficiently. As for garb, I thoroughly explore the all-important bridal gown and wedding ring. Pics refers to capturing your big day in photos and on video. Then, it's on to planning a well-deserved honeymoon.

Chapter 18

Greed Expectations and Registry Realities

Christofle claims to have invented the bridal registry in 1856. The French silver manufacturer apparently figured out that wedding guests appreciate some guidance on what to get the happy couple — or else grew tired of couples exchanging their umpteenth set of sterling toast tongs. Many stores recognize that wedding registries aren't only an entree into the profitable bridal market but also a way of winning couples' shopping loyalty for life. Consequently, retailers have gone to great lengths to make the process painless, from dedicating a team of consultants who steer you through the aisles to equipping you with bar-code scanners to zap onto your list any item that your heart desires.

All this consumerist sophistication, and all the glee that comes with choosing gifts, however, doesn't mitigate the emotional trauma of the process. Suddenly, you're shopping for *our* stuff, attempting to meld your personal tastes — and that can be very unnerving. If you doubt this, just go to the housewares floor of any department store on a Saturday afternoon and watch while one couple after another morphs from browsing Jekylls into snarling Hydes as they decide which china pattern to live with *for the rest of their lives.*

In spite of this dilemma, registering remains a brilliant concept — your defense against a deluge of this year's hot gift item as well as grotesqueries from well-intentioned but hopelessly taste-challenged gift givers.

Retail Details

To give yourself enough time to choose your items carefully, begin planning your registry soon after you're engaged. Some people like to consult your list for shower gifts, so you may want to register before those invitations go out.

Even if you're going to manage your registry online, seeing your registry items in person first is a good idea. Make an appointment with a wedding consultant at each store and ask that person to help you with ideas for mixing and matching china patterns or to give you advice on the number of coffee cups you should own — personalized tips can be very helpful. I recommend hitting the stores during the week, as they're likely to be less crowded than on weekends.

Register for a variety of items in different price ranges. Although your eyes may widen at the thought of owning the most elegant designer china and golden flatware, be realistic. Unless your friends and family have collectively won the lottery, you may find yourselves owning no more than a single teaspoon and a gravy boat in those pricey patterns. If your needs are limited to a state-of-the-art sound or video system or something equally unaffordable for one person or a couple to bestow upon you, hint broadly to a close buddy for a group of friends to chip in for a large item.

Don't get carried away by the thought of choosing all sorts of free loot. Whether you're just starting out, are merging two households, or have dreams of trading in the wine crate you've been using for a dining room table, approach registering methodically. Take a careful inventory of what's missing from your lives and use that list to begin selecting items for your registry.

Before you show up at your favorite department store wearing comfortable shoes and clutching a wish list, call the store to find out whether you need to make an appointment. A few other questions worth asking:

- ✔ What's the store's privacy policy? How does the store ensure that only the people you want to see your registry list will see it?

- ✔ Can guests easily access your registry from other branches of the same store or shop from it online?

- ✔ Does the store allow you to opt out of promotional e-mail and other "special offers"?

- ✔ How does the store use your personal information? Does the store promise not to share your info or sell it to marketing partners or anyone else?

- ✔ Are you assigned a customer-service representative who oversees your particular registry?

- ✔ How quickly after you fill out the paperwork is your registry up and running for people to order from?

✔ How quickly does the store update your list when someone buys something, whether in person or online? (Instantaneously is best to avoid duplicate gifts.) How does the store avoid sending duplicates?

✔ How can you add items to your registry?

✔ How long is your registry active after your wedding date? (Up to a year is a good idea, as etiquette dictates that guests have that long to send a gift.)

✔ What are the store's return policies?

Take notes on items and patterns that appeal to you. You may want to scope out the merchandise in person at least once more before signing up for it. Collect lots of brochures and magazine ads to assist in those late-night discussions about nonstick cookware and percale sheets.

If you already own a set of china, crystal, or flatware but it's incomplete, consider registering for the missing pieces rather than a whole new set. Replacements, Ltd. (www.replacements.com) stocks thousands of patterns, some up to a century old. Although eBay doesn't offer wedding registries per se, friends and relatives can send you eBay gift cards (http://giftcard.ebay.com) that you can redeem for merchandise. eBay has numerous listings for all the typical wedding gifts, from flatware to small kitchen appliances.

Try to register at stores that give you a discount on anything left on your registry after it expires.

Beyond Department Stores

Despite the variety and audaciousness of registries these days, finding one store that sells everything you need for your new life together is difficult. Many couples find dividing their registry among two or three retailers useful — for example, a home-furnishings store for decorative items and casual glassware and china; a department store for linens, formal china, stemware, crystal, and kitchen appliances; and a home-improvement center for house and garden supplies. And don't forget boutiques, artisan crafts shops, and galleries, many of which now offer registries as well.

The web also makes it possible to integrate items from different retailers into a single registry. Amazon.com has a registry service that lets couples list items not just from Amazon's huge selection but also from any shopping site on the web. The site www.giftregistry360.com (part of comprehensive wedding website The Knot) integrates lists from all its participating partners and lets you add your own items as well. Newly Wish (www.newlywish.com)

is an online wedding registry service that features offerings from a wide variety of independent shops and service providers that may not otherwise have a national online registry. The service allows couples to register for the usual loot and also for nontraditional gifts like yoga lessons, artwork, dining out, and even dance lessons for that first dance on your big day. And the smartphone application WeddingScan allows couples to scan *any* bar code using their mobile phone and adds scanned items to a centralized online registry at www.weddingscan.com. (GiftRegistry360 also has a scan-and-add feature.)

Asking for nonessentials for wedding gifts seems a trifle self-indulgent but not out of the question. After all, who's to say that an annual membership to the Metropolitan Museum of Art or a new set of golf clubs isn't exactly what you need to get your marriage off on the right foot?

Some nontraditional registry concepts include

- ✔ **Charity:** For nonmaterialist types and previously married couples. Guests are directed to make a tax-deductible contribution in your names to one or more charities of your choice. Just Give (www.justgive.org) and the I Do Foundation (www.idofoundation.org) enable you to create donation registries. Or have it both ways: Register with I Do's partner stores and they'll donate up to 5 percent of gift purchases to the charity of your choice.

- ✔ **Hobby:** For the couple who either has everything or cares more about keeping their inner children happy than having matching sets of towels. Hobby gifts can range from sporting goods to wine to personal electronics. Look for these in specialty stores and websites or travel agencies.

- ✔ **Home improvement:** Not just a guy thing, this category includes tools, lawn mowers, gardening paraphernalia, hot tubs — anything a couple of fledgling homeowners may need. Check out hardware stores, large home-improvement centers, and garden shops.

- ✔ **Services:** These can include spas, massages, steak-of-the-month clubs, housecleaning — use your imagination.

Grandiose gifting

In recent years, there's been a lot of talk about registries for extremely unconventional and high-ticket wedding gifts, such as mortgages, cars, and personal debt relief. However, the idea hasn't really caught on. Few if any companies know how to market the concept without appearing crass, and much of the wedding-going public isn't ready to give up the box tied with a bow. If you can pull it off tastefully, more power to you. Some banks, in their zeal to promote this creative approach to building a house fund, automatically send out letters to your prospective donors. That's a bit much; make it clear that you'll take care of notification.

Is once enough?

If you or your future spouse have already been married (and presumably cleaned up the first time around), you may feel uncomfortable registering again. If so, trust your instincts. But, in my opinion, just as a previously married bride may wear white if she chooses, so may an experienced couple register. You can't stop people from giving you gifts, and they may appreciate your guidance all the more because they don't know whether you or your ex got custody of the lead crystal decanter.

The only exception may be if your last marriage was extremely short-lived. If you go through spouses the way some people go through coffee filters, perhaps you should register for premarital counseling.

✔ **Travel:** Sites such as www.thebigday.com allow your guests to pay for parts of your honeymoon, including airfare, hotel, restaurants, snorkeling, tennis lessons, horseback rides, parasailing, or whatever else you've planned. Companies such as Best Western, American Airlines, and Alaska Airlines also offer travel gift cards that you can use toward your honeymoon.

Not everyone appreciates a nontraditional registry. If you can't manage to integrate your nonstandard requests into your standard registry, then treat them like you would cash gifts — drop the hint (and just a hint) to only your closest friends and relatives, and only if they ask.

Hinting and Hoping

After you sign up for all those goodies, you may have to keep reminding yourself that you only registered for them — they're not yours until people purchase them for you. As tempted as you may be, restrain yourself from shouting the store's toll-free number or web address from the rooftops, renting out a freeway billboard, or ticking off the places you've registered on your answering machine.

If you're wondering whether you can "be helpful" by discreetly printing a store name or two at the bottom of your wedding or shower invitations, the answer is an unequivocal *no*. That's right. Under no circumstances should an invitation mention a gift in *any* way. Nor should you have the store send catalogs, cards, or e-mail notices to guests. Even though some online companies offer to e-mail your registry list to all your guests, refrain from using such services unless someone makes a specific request. And though many wedding website providers will offer to host your registry for you, I prefer that the only mention on your personal wedding website is a *link* to your separate registry — not a listing on the site itself.

Show us the money

In some cultures, giving money for weddings is a revered custom:

- A Nigerian tradition carried on by some African Americans is to shower the bride with money during the reception. The bride carries a specially decorated moneybag into which guests slip envelopes with checks.

- The parents of Japanese grooms present a cash gift (about three months of the groom's salary) to the bride's family in a special envelope. Knotted gold and silver strings, which are supposed to be impossible to undo, adorn the envelope, which is called a *shugi-bukero*. The amount and giver's name is written on the back of the envelope.

- Chinese brides serve a ritual tea to their new in-laws, who then give them money in lucky red envelopes called *hung boas*.

- At a Polish wedding, in order to dance with the bride, guests pin money to her dress.

The only graceful and acceptable way to get the message out is by word of mouth. But never volunteer the information; someone must first inquire, "Where are you registered?" Then you or your mother or your attendants can respond, "My, that is so sweet of you to ask," while whipping out a card with the store's name and phone number. For those who phrase the magic question as "What do you need?" or "What do you want?" don't be coy. Give them some general parameters and then direct them to your registry.

Although your intentions are certainly the best, be aware that to many guests, writing something like "No gifts, please" on an invitation is both presumptuous and offensive. Doing so is actually likely to backfire, as people who feel they must give you something rely on their own devices and taste.

Also, if what you really want rhymes with honey, you may have to have a little bird (of the close-friend species) mention your wishes. The very idea of the gift of a check puts some etiquette mavens beside themselves, but I think money is a very thoughtful gift. But as with gift registries, posting your checking account number in conspicuous places is considered quite rude.

Most money gifts come as personal checks or U.S. Savings Bonds, which some people like to slip to you in envelopes during the reception. Before you leave for your honeymoon, endorse all the checks, fill out a deposit slip if necessary, and have someone you trust deposit them while you're away.

Keeping Track of Your Gifts

The minute you receive a present, write down what it is, who gave it to you, and the date. This information can go on an index card with the guest's other vital information, in a spreadsheet (try Excel or Google Docs), or in the guest-management function of your wedding website (handy because you'll already have entered guest names and addresses). Also record when you send a thank-you note. Many stores will send an e-mail that notifies you of the gift, the giver, and any message but will hold the gifts for you until they're amassed. This enables you to write prompt thank-you notes but not have to contend with receiving one set of silver at a time.

Also save the paperwork (such as a receipt, which probably doesn't list the price). You may need this to prove the item's origin if you return or exchange it. Receipts are also helpful if the store sends duplicates or fails to send out the gift because of some oversight.

Displaying the gifts is an integral part of wedding tradition in some cultures. In 1893, for example, when Princess May and the Duke of York married, their wedding presents were displayed at Marlborough House — all 3,500 of them! In the U.S. South today, friends and relatives may drop by the bride's mother's home a few days before the wedding to see the gifts arranged in all their glory. (Companies there even specialize in creating a tableau of gifts amid damask linens and cut flowers.) Some people like to keep the cards with the gifts; others feel that doing so is indiscreet and clutters up the effect. Checks should stay in their envelopes well out of sight. However, don't display gifts at the wedding or reception. Appoint someone to whisk presents away to a safe spot out of sight.

Giving Thanks

People may give you a gift at any time, from the moment you announce your engagement until one year after your marriage. Even if you're knee-deep in packing peanuts, keeping up with your thank-you notes is imperative.

Although I encourage you to deputize whenever possible, thank-you notes aren't one of those situations. You must write them yourselves. By hand. ASAP.

Although opinions vary, I feel that you have a month to send a thank-you note. (Honeymooners are cut some slack, but only a few weeks' worth.) If you fall behind, prioritize the situation: Send notes first to people such as dear, neurotic Aunt Myrtle, who's probably losing sleep wondering if the vase arrived intact; send the next batch to folks whose checks you've already deposited; and then take care of the rest.

Thank-you notes in general should be short, sweet, and uncomplicated. (See Chapter 5 for details on proper stationery.) A well-written thank-you note mentions the gift, how much you like it, and how you intend to use it. You may also add a few words to the recipients regarding how much you enjoyed (or missed) them at your wedding. For example:

August 11

Dear Aunt Myrtle and Uncle Hal,

Thank you so much for the exquisite hand-painted vase. It looks like it was made for our mantle, and we have already put it to use holding a bouquet of daffodils. We were thrilled that you came all the way from Pucktawket for our wedding – your presence made this an even more memorable family event.

Again, our deepest thanks. We are crazy about the vase.

With love and affection,
Crystal & Howie

Illustration by Wiley, Composition Services Graphics

Both of you may sign the note. A sweet touch is for the other spouse to append a brief postscript: *P.S. I so enjoyed meeting you after hearing Howie say such nice things about you for so long. Thank you again. We hope to see you soon. —C.T.*

If the gift is actually quite hideous and destined to be exchanged or donated to charity, brush up on your euphemisms — *unusual, unique, bold, conversation piece* — and focus on the thought behind the gift.

Thank-you notes for money gifts are exercises in the oblique. Don't mention the words cash or check — refer to it as *your gift* or *your generous gift* — and never mention the exact amount. You may, however, indicate how you intend to use the money: *We have earmarked it for our house fund.*

For people who send you gifts before you've sent them an announcement or invitation, don't stuff everything in one envelope; send the other missives via separate post. You aren't obligated to invite people to your wedding just because they send you an early gift.

Some etiquette gurus advise using printed acknowledgment cards when you don't have time to pen the real McCoy right away. These cards say that you received the gift and that you'll send a personal note of thanks soon. In other words, they're an elaborate form of procrastination. Simply get on with the thanking, and if you have a legitimate delay — the gifts were sent to your parents' home and had to be reshipped long distance, or you're both taking the bar exam — so be it. No need for lengthy explanations or excuses; even the most cryptic scribbled message is better than none or a generic printed one.

Please don't even think of sending those pre-printed thank-you cards that let you escape putting pen to paper. They just tell your guests that, despite their thoughtfulness and trouble in getting you a gift, you can't be bothered to thank them personally.

Send thank-you notes to all those people who got you through your day — the hairdresser, caterer, photographer, florist, and so on. Service professionals rely on letters of reference for their business, and a laudatory letter often means more to them than a monetary tip (although they like a little moola, too).

On the mark

Before the days of wedding registries and Victoria's Secret, women spent years tatting doilies, needlepointing pillows, and embroidering monograms on bedclothes for their daughters' hope chests. The real excitement came when the girl got engaged. Suddenly her *trousseau* (French for the "little trusse" or "bundle" the bride carried to her husband's house) expanded to include frilly lingerie and enough new clothes to get her through the next year. She might even get a few saucepans to boot.

Today the bridal hope chest and trousseau seem quaintly old-fashioned (although who wouldn't like any excuse to go out and buy an entirely new wardrobe?). However, if you've already started stockpiling sheets, tablecloths, and tumblers for your wedded life, you may be wondering whether and how to monogram or mark them. As shown in the upcoming figure, the best spots for your initials are as follows:

- **Crystal:** Can be etched anywhere, though initials are usually centered.

- **Flatware:** Engraved on the front, near the tip of the handle, or on the back to leave the integrity of a sleek, classic pattern intact. Ornate flatware styles may take the monogram on the spine of the handle.

- **Napkins:** Embroidered diagonally in one corner or centered on a rectangular fold. You may use just one initial centered on a cocktail napkin.

- **Pillowcases:** Embroidered centered 2 inches above the hem.

(continued)

(continued)

✔ **Sheets:** Embroidered in the center so the monogram shows when the top of the sheet is folded down.

✔ **Tablecloths:** For rectangular ones, embroidered in the center of a long side, where the cloth hangs down. For square ones, embroidered in one corner so it shows on the top of the table.

✔ **Towels:** Embroidered in the center of one end, so the initials show when the towel is folded in thirds lengthwise and hanging on a towel rack.

Which initials, then, to use for your monogram? Traditionally, brides have used their birth surname monogram on their stationery and a combination of their birth and married surnames on their linens (which they theoretically pass down to their daughters). For example, Lydia Scooter marrying Michael Blip may use *LB* or *LBS* (with the *B* larger) or *S*B*. Other items, such as flatware and crystal, would take the husband's last name initial.

But these traditions are changing. A bride and groom may choose any combination of their initials, perhaps intertwined and on an angle, with the bride's initials overlapping the groom's, or a design that incorporates some symbol of their lives together such as an acorn or leaping salmon.

Same-sex couples may want to monogram too. A standard solution, assuming each partner is keeping his or her own name, is the combination of the two surname initials in a unified monogram, intertwined and ornamented as they see fit.

Note: Hold off on monogramming anything until you decide what name(s) to use after you're married, and request that your registries do the same because engraved items aren't returnable.

Illustration by Elizabeth Kurtzman

Problem Presents

Some gifts never make it to their destination. Weeks after you receive a notice from the store or a friend mentions that a present is on its way, you realize that something has gone awry. First, call the store. Then notify the giver, who's no doubt wondering whether you just hated the gift or are too inconsiderate to write a thank-you note.

If a gift arrives damaged, take or send it back to the store from which it came. (Returns and exchanges shouldn't be a problem with reputable stores, which want to keep you happy.) If the giver personally shipped the present, check the wrapping to see whether the gift was insured so that the person can collect the insurance and send a replacement.

Unhappy returns: The wedding is canceled

The only time you return items to the giver is if the wedding is canceled. No big explanation is necessary, but you can ease any awkwardness with a simple note along the lines of, "Thank you, but under the circumstances, we can't accept your wonderful gift. We greatly appreciate your thoughtfulness. . . ."

If you've already used the gift, you must send the giver an identical replacement. Of course, waiting to use gifts received before the wedding until you're legally a couple seems overly superstitious to me. I say go for it; if you don't make it to the altar, you'll have bigger problems to worry about than whether you already slept on the sheets from Aunt Priscilla.

Consolidation techniques

Michael C. Fina (www.michaelcfina.com), a New York-based purveyor of fine jewelry, tableware, and home décor, has pioneered the concept of the *consolidated registry*. Here's how it works: The company tracks all gifts ordered through the registry and notifies the recipients but doesn't hold or ship the merchandise immediately. The couple has up to 60 days after their wedding to "release" their registry or change their minds about what they requested. They can accept any portion of what their guests have chosen and apply the remaining credit to any other items in the store.

Trading in versus pawning off

Sometimes, in spite of registering and making sure everyone is notified of your registry, you receive perfectly nice gifts for which you have no use, but exchanging them seems like more trouble than it's worth. You put the present in a drawer, with the idea that one day you'll find someone who can truly appreciate it. *Regifting,* as it's known, seems like a harmless way to recycle, but these gifts tend to have a vibe (perhaps it's guilt) that can come back to haunt you. And you have to remember who gave it to you and whether that person would ever come across it in the secondary recipient's home or notice its absence from yours. In a world where everyone nods when you say "six degrees of separation," regift at your own risk.

So even if regifting seems easier, I recommend returning gifts for exchange. This practice carries with it no guilt penalty, and you don't need to inform the sender of the switch, although close friends usually don't mind and even enjoy knowing what you actually got. In any case, thank the giver of the original gift — fib a little if you must — and let the matter rest.

Chapter 19

And the Bride Wore . . .

. . . .

. . . .

*P*rincess, queen, siren, vixen/maiden — fashion designers are immensely creative in imagining what roles women want to play. As frivolous as some designers' visions seem, buying into a fantasy is easy because the garment known simply as a *wedding gown* is so loaded with meaning that it can throw even the most confident women for a loop. Perhaps the costliest item of clothing you'll ever buy, this dress symbolizes the start of a new phase in your life. It must also endure several nerve-wracking hours of being inspected by umpteen pairs of eyes and will be photographed relentlessly. Thinking about it, shopping for it, and purchasing it can induce nothing short of sheer panic. It doesn't have to be that way.

For starters, bear in mind that the dress that ultimately makes you happiest is the one that reflects your inner self — the woman with whom you're most content. If you're not a slave to fashion in everyday life, why start now? Even though most wedding dresses are inevitably long, some shade of white, and possibly ornamented, you don't have to feel like a carbon-copy bride. And although dresses tend to be a major line item in any wedding budget, by shopping smartly, you *can* find a stunning dress without breaking the bank.

Sizing Up Your Style

If you bought this book in the hope that I'd tell you exactly what is appropriate dress for your wedding's precise time and degree of formality, I'm sorry to disappoint you. If nit-pickers want to debate the proper glove length for "formal daytime" as opposed to "semiformal evening," that's their business. If your invitation specifies "black tie" and you're hosting several hundred guests for a six-course, seated meal with a 20-piece orchestra serenading them, somehow I know that you're not going to show up in a pinstriped suit.

Remember that you're the central character in this show, and all the players' costuming revolves around your ensemble. When dress hunting, you need to focus on three aspects of your wedding:

- **When:** As in the season and time of day. Heavy fabrics such as brocades, velvets, and satins are most comfortable in late fall and winter. A spaghetti-strap crepe dress works best in hot weather. A simple suit with a beaded bustier or a lavender sundress is intrinsically more appropriate for a luncheon than for a dinner dance.

- **Where:** Are you getting married in a church or synagogue, where bare shoulders may seem disrespectful (or be prohibited)? Consider both the ceremony and the reception site. If, for example, your ceremony is in a church and your reception is in a garden, keep those locales in mind when determining the length of your train or the height of your shoes.

- **Price:** How much are you willing to spend? And how likely are you to change your mind? Be realistic and upfront with salespeople about your dress budget. You can save a lot of time if everyone isn't playing cat and mouse. Being upfront also saves you from the depressing scenario of falling in love with a dress that you can't possibly afford.

Selecting the right silhouette

Those brave souls who sell bridal apparel for a living all agree that you need to begin your dress quest with the *silhouette,* or overall shape of the dress, in mind. Here are some silhouette options (see Figure 19-1):

- **A-line:** A structured gown in which the skirt gradually flares out from a fitted bodice. Looks like an upright letter A and is also called a *princess line.* An A-line is a flattering silhouette for just about everyone. A *modified A-line* is a contemporary version in which the skirt is cut a bit closer to the body, flaring out somewhat less dramatically.

Figure 19-1:
Wedding
gowns
come in a
range of
silhouettes.

Illustration by Elizabeth Kurtzman

- **Ball gown:** A fitted corset with a very full skirt that brushes the floor. The waist may be nipped in at your natural waist, shaped in an elongated triangle (called a *basque waistline*), or dropped to hug your hips. This is the classic, fairy-tale wedding-gown silhouette, and when the dress is highly embellished with sequins, lace, or crystals, you've got your very own Cinderella fantasy costume. The ball gown silhouette looks particularly good on women with small waists and is most flattering for the less-buxom bride.

- **Empire:** The bodice is cropped and the waist seam ends just below the bust line to create a flattering, elongated effect. May be sleeveless or short-sleeved and may have various necklines. Works particularly well on women with medium to large breasts and less-than-tiny waistlines.

- **Mermaid:** A narrow, body-hugging gown that flares dramatically at or below the knee, like a mermaid's tail. Also known as a *trumpet skirt*. Good for showing off your curves, especially if you're tall. Some women find the cut constricting, but others like the shimmy effect.

- **Sheath:** A narrow, close-fitting gown that goes to the floor in an unbroken line. This shape is more reminiscent of an evening gown than a wedding dress and is currently very popular with buff brides. Particularly revealing when cut *on the bias* (diagonally to the fabric's grain). Not suitable for kneeling. Basically, a sheath is the mermaid style without the flared bottom.

- **Slip:** Like a long tank top, may be backless or bias-cut (see the preceding bullet), but usually without ornamentation. Looks most elegant on someone tall and slender.

- **Two-piece:** Less a silhouette than a method of construction, two-piece gowns involve a separate bodice and skirt. This style is particularly good for those who are a different size on top or on the bottom, allowing a more precise fit. If chosen to match, the two pieces may look like one, but brides may express personal style by choosing different fabrics, colors, or styling for top and bottom.

Figuring out the neckline

The neckline is next in the style triumvirate (along with the waistline and sleeves) that determines the *bodice,* or part of your dress that covers from your waist up. Possibilities, some of which you can see in Figure 19-2, include

- **Bateau neck:** Follows the line of the collarbone straight across, is high in front and back, and usually skims both shoulder blades. Also known as a *boat neck.*

- **Halter:** One or two straps go around the neck or across the back to hold up the bodice. Backless (or keyhole-backed), it's revealing but, when worn with a strapless/backless bra, surprisingly comfortable and sexy on women of all sizes.

- **Jewel:** A simple curve at the base of the neck, like a necklace around the collarbone.

- **Keyhole:** A keyhole- or tear-shaped opening at the neckline or in the back of the dress.

- **Off the shoulder:** The neckline connects to (usually short) sleeves or wider straps on the arm, leaving the shoulders bare.

- **One shoulder:** An asymmetrical dress where one arm is bare and the other may be long-sleeved, short-sleeved, sleeveless, or anywhere in between. Very dramatic.

- **Portrait:** A fold of fabric creates a shawl-like collar, framing the face. Usually worn off the shoulder. Can be flattering on angular bodies but matronly if not cut low enough.

- **Sabrina:** A nearly horizontal line from shoulder blade to shoulder blade. Like a bateau neck, but it starts 2 inches in from each shoulder, so the neck opening is narrower.

- **Scoop:** Rounded but lower than a jewel neck, perhaps even revealing a hint of cleavage. When the dress is sleeveless with deeply cut armholes, this neckline resembles a tank top.

When you shop

For a successful, less-stressful dress-hunting expedition, having a plan helps:

✔ **In preparing to shop, get a handle on wedding-dress lingo.** Knowing that *Juliet* isn't just the girl who fancied Romeo and that *flyaway* doesn't refer to a bad hair day keeps you from feeling intimidated or exasperated when dealing with salespeople.

✔ **Bring along pictures and fabric swatches.** Take a trip to a fabric store and gather some swatches that appeal to you. Clip pictures from both bridal and general-interest magazines and download images from the Internet that convey the style or mood you want for your wedding. Then winnow the looks down to four or five.

✔ **Skip the plastic and entourage.** The first time you venture out to try on dresses, leave the credit cards at home. Even if you love a dress, come back and try it on again to be sure it's The One before making a purchase. Bring only one trusted friend with you; a chorus of different opinions will only confuse you.

✔ **Wear appropriate underwear.** That is, pantyhose, a thong, a strapless bra, or whatever foundation feels comfortable, looks pretty, and is what you might wear under an evening gown. Keep in mind that you'll be in a dressing room with a sales consultant and whomever you've brought with you, and you don't want to have to hide in a corner as you undress.

✔ **Take notes and pay attention to first impressions.** In a perfect world, you could take a snapshot, but most salons prohibit doing so until you make a purchase.

✔ **Spaghetti straps:** The neckline may be cut straight across or in a V to show some cleavage and is finished with slender straps that may or may not be embellished. A good choice for those who want a bare-shouldered look but aren't comfortable with a strapless gown.

✔ **Strapless:** The gown's neck and shoulders are completely bare, usually with a tightly fitted bustier or corset-type bodice. The top line of the bodice may be cut in a shallow curve or in a sweetheart shape. The strapless neckline, if made from stiffer fabric and ornamented with gathers or ruffles that stand out from the body, is called a *crumb catcher* neckline. Strapless gowns are currently very popular. (In fact, they're so popular that I've started to notice something of a backlash as brides seek a greater variety of neckline styles.)

✔ **Sweetheart:** Open, somewhat revealing, sweeping down, dipping to a point in the middle of the bust, and forming a heart shape.

✔ **V-neck:** Forms a point, making the neck look longer and slimmer.

✔ **Wedding-band collar:** A band high on the neck usually in a fabric that contrasts with the rest of the bodice; often made of lace. Emphasizes a long, slender neck. Also called a *high neck* or *mandarin* collar.

BATEAU   HALTER   JEWEL

PORTRAIT   SWEETHEART

Illustration by Elizabeth Kurtzman

Figure 19-2:
Dress neck-
lines come
in a variety
of styles.

Arm negotiations

In bridal and other fashion, you can no longer determine the season by
the length of the sleeves you see people wearing. After countless hours at
the gym, many toned brides are going sleeveless no matter how chilly the
weather, while women who don't love their arms or never feel completely
dressed in anything but full-length sleeves are wearing sheer sleeves to their
wrists, even during the dog days of summer.

One word of warning: A tightly fitted, long-sleeved dress can be very restrict-
ing. Think twice about choosing one if you intend on dancing, hugging anyone
taller than you, or tossing your bouquet with more than a wrist flip.

The most common sleeve styles include the following, some of which you can
see in Figure 19-3:

- **Balloon:** Wide, puffy, wrist-length sleeves. Pouf sleeves are a variation,
  with a short, gathered sleeve sometimes worn off the shoulder.

- **Bell:** Narrow at the top and widely flared at the bottom.

- **Cap:** A short, fitted, set-in sleeve that barely covers the shoulders.

- **Dolman:** Wide armholes extend out from the waist of the dress and tighten at the wrist. Also called *bat wings.* A bit of Morticia from *The Addams Family,* but heavy drama with the right dress — a tight and slinky one.

- **Fitted:** Long and tapered, these sleeves are sometimes designed to come to a V-shaped point at the top of the hand — that type is cleverly called *fitted point* sleeves.

- **Juliet:** A long sleeve with a short pouf at the shoulder and the rest tapered. A period look, à la the Shakespearean heroine.

- **Three-quarters:** Ends just below the elbow and is finished with a small cuff or band. Very '50s.

- **T-shirt:** As the name implies, sleeves are closely fitted to the shoulder, slightly fuller and longer than a cap sleeve.

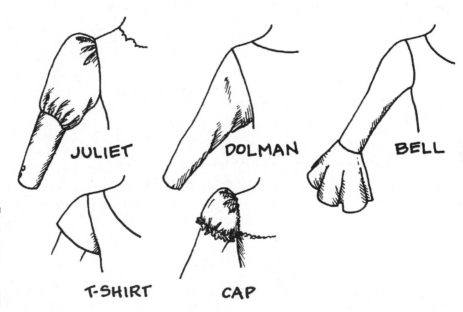

Figure 19-3: Some common sleeve styles.

Illustration by Elizabeth Kurtzman

Looking behind you

Take into account that guests will be gazing at you from behind during the entire ceremony, so the back of your dress should have at least some detailing. With the trend toward sleeker dresses, the lines of the dress, particularly the back, have become more important. In fact, some dresses are virtually plain in the front with all the ornamentation on the rear. (Of course, women who are larger on the bottom than the top may think twice before plastering a dramatic butterfly bow across their tush.)

If you have a lovely back, you may want to consider a dress that shows it off. Among the possibilities:

- A dress that dips *below* the small of the back
- A halter neckline
- A scooped back edged with silk flowers or composed of *illusion* (a fine, almost transparent, meshlike netting usually made of silk)
- A strapless gown that's completely backless

To what lengths will you go?

The length of the wedding dress you choose largely depends on the silhouette, your height, and what height heel you feel comfortable wearing. Typically, wedding dresses come in these lengths:

- **Ballerina:** Usually associated with full skirts; just graces the tops of your ankles.
- **Full length or floor length:** The toes of your shoes should show. The back hem should be short enough to dance in without you or your partner stepping on your dress and tripping you.
- **High-low or intermission:** The skirt is cut shorter in front, usually to midcalf, and goes to floor length in back.
- **Mini:** Ends right above the knee or shorter.
- **Street length:** The hemline covers the knees.
- **Tea length:** Ends at the lower calf or right above the ankle.

Happy trains to you

Perhaps more than any other aspect of your dress, the bridal train has transformative powers. This extended length of fabric forces you to walk a little differently, swishes around luxuriously, and makes you feel positively regal. The longer the train, the more you may want to decorate it with bands, bows, pearls, or sequins. Even an embroidered monogram is exquisite on the right dress.

Possible train lengths include

- **Chapel:** Extends 3½ to 4½ feet from the hemline.
- **Cathedral:** Extends 9 feet from the waist (roughly 5 or 6 feet behind the bride).

- **Royal cathedral or monarch:** Extends longer than 9 feet. From the waist, can actually be upward of 25 feet long.

- **Sweep:** The shortest train, just brushing the floor or the tops of your shoes. Also called *brush*. Looks great as is but isn't a wonderful choice for someone who plans to dance a lot because it doesn't bustle well.

The shape of your train is determined as much by its length as by the way the fabric is attached to your dress. Usually, the train is the same piece of material that makes up the back of your dress, but if it's a separate piece of fabric, you may choose one of these styles:

- **Court:** Attaches at the shoulders and falls to the floor.

- **Detachable:** Attaches with hooks and loops either around the waist, like a long skirt over a short dress, or just to one point at the back of the dress.

- **Watteau:** Attaches at the shoulders, forming box pleats, and falls loosely to the hem and sweeps into a train.

More common than a detachable train is a train that can be gathered up into carefully orchestrated folds and layers to form a *bustle*. Bustles come in several styles:

- **Floor length:** The dress is bustled underneath to create an even hem. The train essentially disappears under the dress.

- **French:** The train is pulled up under the back of the gown and attached with either ribbons or buttons and loops, creating a two-layered, scalloped effect near the hem. This offers a lovely and dramatic look, and, if placed low, doesn't add bulk to the backside (see Figure 19-4).

- **Traditional:** The hem is brought up and attached to loops at the back of the dress, creating symmetric layers (see Figure 19-4).

- **Wristband:** The train is picked up and held by a loop at the bottom that attaches like a bracelet around the wrist. Although this look can be very glamorous and perhaps even impart some drama to the first dance, it's an impractical and uncomfortable choice for an entire reception.

Often overlooked until the last fitting, the way you bustle the dress is extremely important. If, for example, the train is long and the fabric quite heavy, efficient bustling is difficult. And having a yard of heavy material attached to your derriere can seriously cramp your style on the dance floor.

Bring your maid of honor (or whoever will be bustling your dress) to your last fitting for an instructional session and request that the various ribbons are color-coded or numbered to make it easier. You want to avoid being away from the party for hours while someone figures the darn thing out.

Figure 19-4:
Two
common
bustle
styles.

TRADITIONAL
BUSTLE

FRENCH
BUSTLE

Illustration by Elizabeth Kurtzman

She comes in colors

By the late 1800s, when white became the standard in bridal gowns, *Ladies'
Home Journal* advised readers: "Thought must be given to the becomingness
of the shade, for after all, there are as many tints in white as in other colors;
the one that may suit the pale blond is absolutely unbecoming to the rosy
brunette. Dead white, which has the glint of blue about it, is seldom becoming to anyone. It brings out the imperfections of the complexion, tends to
deaden the gloss of the hair, and dulls the brightness of the eyes. The white
that touches on the cream or coffee shade is undoubtedly the most artistic."

Although the terminology has changed, the advice remains important. Lots of
different whites exist, and some look better on you than others:

✔ What the bridal shops call *diamond white, silk white,* or *natural white* is
   soft white, found only in natural (more expensive) fibers like silk, cotton,
   or linen. These tones are usually flattering for fairer brides.

✔ *Blue-white* or *stark white* is generally polyester and, though unflattering
   to most blondes, can be stunning on dark-skinned women.

✔ *Ivory, eggshell,* or *candlelight* is a creamier shade of white with golden or yellow undertones. It generally looks good on fair brides, but don't take it for granted, as a huge disparity lies between what different designers call *ivory.*

✔ *Champagne* or *rum* is off-white with pink undertones. This shade looks particularly nice on olive or darker skin tones.

Ah, but you've probably already realized that things in Bride Land are never that simple. Thanks to designers such as Vera Wang, Monique Lhuillier, Badgley Mischka, and Reem Acra, bridal gowns are taking increasingly more cues from mainstream fashion, which means that white is just the beginning. Badgley Mischka, for instance, has recently shown gowns of pale blush and buttercup, and Vera Wang has designed gowns of pale taupe, spring green, silvery gray, and even sheer black net. I've also seen a recent, surprisingly lovely trend for subtle prints (usually in one color on white). If a certain color looks particularly great on you, consider incorporating it in your dress; you can add it in subtle touches if you love the romance of a white gown. Consider trimming your dress in brilliant yellow satin or opting for the surprise of a dainty row of black velvet ribbons running down the back of a full skirt. A peach or blue sash can add oomph to a traditional dress, and a pale-colored underlayer under white or cream lace or net is a way to have it all. And if you're feeling particularly daring, do away with white completely and walk down the aisle wearing a gold brocade ball gown or even a burgundy sheath.

Fabrics for fantasy

Several fabrics are popular in the design of bridal gowns, and each imparts a different feeling to the wearer. Here, I list the most common. With the exception of silk, these fabrics are available in less-expensive versions, either rayon or synthetic.

✔ **Charmeuse:** A lightweight satin that clings to the wearer and is less shiny than regular satin.

✔ **Chiffon:** Semitransparent fabric with a very soft finish. The fabric moves with the wearer and drapes well. In addition to being used for dresses, this material is used for veils, sleeves, or layers over other fabrics.

✔ **Faille:** A soft fabric with slight horizontal ribbing and a low-key sheen. Despite its softness, it has good body and drapes well.

✔ **Organza:** Flowing but stiffer than chiffon, this fabric is often used for multitiered skirts.

- **Satin:** Heavier fabric that's glossy on the front side and dull on the other side. *Duchesse satin,* a blend of silk and rayon, is lighter and less expensive than silk satin.

- **Shantung:** Has a nubby texture similar to raw silk from a combination of thick and thin yarns.

- **Silk:** This fiber, made from the cocoon of silkworms, is luxurious, resilient, and strong.

- **Taffeta:** Crisp and almost papery feeling, this fabric can be slightly shiny or have a matte finish.

Amazing laces

For some brides, the fabric of their dress is far less interesting than the lace involved. Here I list the most common lace types used in wedding gowns, either as the fabric of the gown itself or in the form of lace trimming.

- **Alençon:** Sometimes called the *queen of lace,* it's a fine lace with patterns of flowers and swags. It's delicate but can look a bit more substantial than chantilly, as the edges of the patterns are re-embroidered with cording. In wedding gowns, it's frequently beaded.

- **Chantilly:** Quite delicate, with a pattern of flowers and ribbons on fine mesh netting or organza. The patterns are detailed and often outlined in fine cording.

- **Duchesse:** Not to be confused with duchesse satin, a lace with larger floral designs, often raised, linked by net rather than fine mesh.

- **Guipure:** A less delicate lace with a more graphic look. Large motifs, such as flowers or geometric patterns, are connected by thin threads.

- **Ribbon:** Ribbon stitched in a random or stylized pattern over net. An old technique, but depending on the pattern, can feel more modern than floral laces.

- **Schiffli:** A light lace with delicate, regular patterns embroidered over fine net.

- **Venetian (or venise):** Heavy, embroidery-like designs of flowers, leaves, or other motifs arranged in a scroll pattern.

The icing on the dress: Finishers

A dress gets much of its sparkle and individuality from *finishers,* which are trims and ornaments that usually work best when applied with masterful restraint as opposed to with a shovel. These elements may include one or more of the following:

- **Appliqués:** Additions either re-embroidered or sewn onto the gown's fabric.

- **Belts and sashes:** Attached to the gown or separate, belts and sashes (best for a gown with a natural waistline) highlight a small waist. Belts are usually a bit stiffer and thinner than sashes, and sashes often tie with a bow in front or back. Both can be made of matched or contrasting fabric and come plain or embellished with silk flowers, crystal buckles, or other ornamentation. (Waist emphasis in wedding dresses is in fashion lately, and I particularly like the selection of belts and sashes at J. Crew.)

- **Border trims:** Braids, ribbon, ruffles, or scalloped edges.

- **Bugle beads:** Small, cylindrical, glass or plastic beads used for ornamentation. Beads are hand-sewn on expensive gowns and hand-glued on less-expensive ones.

- **Edging:** Lace, cord, embroidered band, or silk satin that outlines a section of fabric. For example, a bodice with alternating bands of lace and satin.

- **Embroidery:** Can be sewn over *illusion* (a fine, almost transparent, meshlike netting usually made of silk) or other bridal fabrics in the same or contrasting colors. Some designers use metallic thread in gold or silver.

- **Fringe:** Used as an embellishment or all over for a flapper look. Some designers bead the fringe.

- **Jewels:** Crystals are often used to embellish gowns or veils.

- **Ribbons and bows:** Used in various sizes and lengths, from one giant butterfly bow in back to many tiny bows sprinkled over a tulle skirt, and from silk ribbon closures on a corseted gown to floor-length streamers.

- **Seed pearls:** Very small and often irregular pearls used to adorn garments, headpieces, and shoes.

- **Sequins and paillettes:** Flat, disc-shaped, plastic beads sewn on to give dresses a twinkly, modern look. Unlike sequins, paillettes jiggle.

- **Silk flowers:** Used to highlight a specific area, such as the back or neckline, or as an all-over embellishment, either in the same color as the dress or in contrasting colors.

Getting the Goods

When looking for your "perfect" gown, you should look at lots of options to find out what you really like. If you haven't been poring over bridal magazines and planning your dress since you were 8, or if trying on 50 dresses in a weekend doesn't sound like your idea of a good time, some new smartphone applications can help get you educated before you actually spend time in the dressing room. *Brides* magazine offers the Brides Wedding Genius 2.0 for iPhone. Along with various wedding planning features, the app lets you browse and bookmark hundreds of dresses. The iBridalGown app for iPhone and Android phones helps you compare dresses by storing pictures and information as you shop, letting you share pictures of gowns with friends by e-mail or on Facebook, and providing a glossary of fabric, shape, and other gown-related terms. And The Knot's Wedding Dress Look Book app (for iPhone) provides suggestions based on your body type, your personality, and the style of your wedding and helps you find local salons that carry a dress that interests you.

Even in this age of online shopping, the majority of wedding dress purchases go something like this: You try on samples at a salon. When you find one you like, the salon takes your measurements and any other custom-order information ("substitute jewel neckline for sweetheart," for example) and sends the order to the manufacturer. Depending on the designer and manufacturer, your dress is both custom cut and finished to your specifications or simply ordered in the closest size on the manufacturer's sizing chart and altered by the salon to fit. For the majority of brides, this dress is the only piece of clothing created solely for them that they'll ever own.

The perfect dress for you is out there, even if it has yet to be designed and sewn. Here's where you may find it:

✔ **Bridal salons:** Most brides purchase their gowns at these places, which range from Kleinfeld, the famed wedding-gown emporium (you may know it from the New York edition of reality show *Say Yes to the Dress*), to mom-and-pop stores to salons located in department stores. Many bridal boutiques offer everything for the bridal ensemble, including headpieces, shoes, and accessories. These shops almost always operate by appointment only, and you can save tons of time and undue teeth clenching by scheduling your appointment during off-peak hours. You'll be seated in a private dressing room, and the sales consultant will bring you dresses to try on. The larger the store, generally the better the prices because of the store's buying power. Some couture bridal designers allow you to order your gown with myriad changes, from the neckline to the entire bodice, while others allow only specific changes. In any case, ask whether the salon does alterations in-house.

✔ **Designer or couture:** Some well-known private designers work with brides personally to create one-of-a-kind dresses. Starting with the bride's vision, they work together to choose fabrics, create the style, and decide the detailing. The designer oversees each fitting as well as the hand-sewing and finishing. Many bridal salons may refer you to capable designers willing to create a dress from scratch. These dresses vary greatly in price depending on the designer, the fabrics, and the embellishments. Aside from the obvious advantages, these dresses generally take less time to make than those from manufacturers, which are produced in much greater volume per season. If you love the work of a particular designer, get yourself on the designer's e-mail list as soon as possible. You'll get notification of trunk shows and sample sales, and you may be able to get your dream gown at a lower price.

✔ **Discount bridal shops:** These shops have a large variety of mass-produced gowns in all sizes. Although they're substantially less expensive than a full-service store, their atmosphere is definitely for those on a mission to shop, not to be pampered. One plus: These off-the-rack dresses are usually ready to take home when you buy them.

✔ **Internet:** Many salons and designers have websites where you can browse the collection or order catalogs. Some shops also let you place orders online, but be careful. In many cases, sales are *final*. If they do offer refunds or exchanges, they may charge a restocking fee. Before ordering online, try on dresses at a store to become familiar with the way different styles and sizes fit you and the way various fabrics feel. You may be able to save money (including sales tax, in some cases), but, as with almost any dress, be prepared to have alterations made.

A few particularly good online gown-shopping options have emerged recently. J. Crew (www.jcrew.com; click "Weddings & Parties") offers nice gowns at a range of reasonable prices, and if you check its sale section regularly, you may be able to score an excellent deal. But if you see something you love on the site, don't wait for it to go on sale, as your size may sell out. BHLDN (www.bhldn.com) is a relatively new site, affiliated with the bohemian women's store Anthropologie, that offers pretty and unusual dresses in a range of prices.

If you can get yourself invited, the invitation-only membership site The Aisle (www.theaislenewyork.com) offers curated designer gowns and accessories at significant discounts and donates a portion of all proceeds to a charity of the designer's choice. More democratic is Bride Power (www.bridepower.com), which offers sample and over-stock designer gowns at discounts up to 50 percent and lets you search its stock by designer, silhouette, sleeve/neckline, size, and price. The gowns still aren't cheap, but if your heart is set on a designer gown, this is an economical way to go. Brides Against Breast Cancer (www.brides againstbreastcancer.org) has sales around the country of both gently used and new dresses donated by designers, and all proceeds go to help victims of breast cancer .You may find the dress of your dreams and do some good at the same time.

Thousands of dresses are for sale every day on eBay — some new, some used — and you can find incredible bargains if you shop and bid carefully. To ensure a positive transaction, check the seller's feedback, shipping fees, and return policy. And don't hesitate to e-mail the seller with questions ("What's the fabric? Has the dress been worn or altered? Does it have any stains? Why are you selling it?").

✔ **Rentals:** The idea of renting a dress you wear only once may sound good, but it requires extensive research because rental stores are few and far between. The rental companies claim that bridal magazines discriminate against them, refusing to cover them or let them advertise for fear of alienating the retail trade. The magazines contend that people simply don't want to rent wedding dresses. In any case, consider what a psychic friend of ours says on the subject: "The confluence of vibes from who-knows-how-many previous wearers could send you over the edge on your wedding day."

✔ **Sample sales:** Stores and designers regularly hold sample sales where dresses that have been tried on often as samples or special-ordered and canceled are sold to the general public at huge reductions (usually 20 to 50 percent off the original price). On the downside, sizes are limited (that's what alterations are for), and the gowns may be slightly shopworn. But many brides have hit the jackpot at these sales.

✔ **Sew your own:** Making your own dress is definitely not for novices. The fabrics are delicate (and expensive), so if you aren't a skilled seamstress, consider carefully before undertaking a project that could make you unravel.

✔ **Tailors:** A talented tailor or seamstress may be a frustrated designer or at least skilled enough to create a pattern from a magazine photo. The tailor makes a pattern and then cuts the actual fabric precisely to your measurements. But creating a bridal gown is a specialty, and you don't want to be the bridal guinea pig. Make sure you get references, look at photos of other dresses the person has done, and be very specific about what you want.

✔ **Trunk shows:** Often held at bridal salons and occasionally at hotels, these shows enable you to see a designer's dresses (a larger selection than the store ordinarily carries) on live models. If you purchase a dress at that time, the designers may advise and fit you personally.

✔ **Vintage:** If you can fit into your mother's or grandmother's dress, you may want to accessorize it with vintage jewelry or accessories. If the moths have turned the dress into a large lace hankie, however, you may want to find a designer who can incorporate remnants into a contemporary design. Some antiques dealers specialize in vintage dresses and accessories, but finding an antique dress can be tricky. Depending on the era, you may need a girdle or corset. Alterations are virtually impossible depending on the fabric's fragility.

Some excellent online sources of vintage bridal gowns include www. vintagetextile.com, www.thefrock.com, and www.antique-dress.com. Cities such as San Francisco, Santa Monica (both www. vintageexpo.com), and New York (www.manhattanvintage.com) host vintage clothing expos, usually twice a year, where you can explore many vintage vendors at once.

Pregnant and postpartum brides are hardly novelties these days, but the bridal industry doesn't cater to them. Fortunately, a growing number of maternity stores carry elegant evening wear that you can sometimes adapt for weddings. Custom-made dresses are the other option. Just be sure to put off the final fitting until as close to your wedding as possible (see the upcoming section "Getting the right fit" for the scoop on dress fittings).

Quality control

For most people, deciphering whether a dress is *mass-produced* — cut en masse by laser and sewn with machines — or individually cut and sewn is virtually impossible. But don't get hung up on that point. When shopping, inspect the sample gown carefully, checking the quality of the workmanship. Don't expect the quality of the dress you order to be much better than that of the sample. If the sample doesn't have, say, covered buttons, then neither will the one you order.

When trying on dresses, your inspection checklist should cover

- **Aesthetics:** If a long row of buttons goes down the back, do they have a zipper underneath? Are cloth-covered buttons the same fabric as the dress? Is the interfacing fused to the outer layer? (It shouldn't be!) Check for loose threads on beading — one tug may undo an entire row.

- **Fabrication:** Do naps on separate fabric panels run the same way? (You don't want one shiny panel and another matte panel.) Is the lace free of snags? Is the fabric in good shape (as opposed to being pilled or worn)? Does the dress have a lining? Can you tell exactly what the fabric is? Does the style take advantage of patterns in the lace?

- **Security:** Are beads, loops, and appliqués sewn on well? Does the dress have extra hooks and eyes at such crucial stress points as across the bust? Does the zipper extend to the widest point of your hips to prevent tears? If the gown is strapless, does the bodice have boning for support?

- **Sewing:** Are seams sewn straight and smooth? Is the fabric free of tiny telltale holes from ripped-out stitches? Are lace patterns matched up or laid out evenly? Are the lace seams invisible? Are the hems of heavy fabrics stitched with horsehair to make them stand out? Are seams finished with surge stitching so the inside edges won't fray? Is the seam allowance generous? Do illusion panels lie flat? Are all layers sewn separately rather than stitched together as one piece? (If sewn all together, they may pucker.)

> ✔ **Stains:** If the dress is off the rack, rented, or on consignment, does it have any perspiration, food, or lipstick stains? Can they be removed? Is it free of glue marks?

Getting the right fit

When it comes to sizing, bridal dresses follow a peculiar logic all their own — if you're a size 4, then you may be at least a size 8 in a wedding dress, so don't get obsessed with the size. (It's just a number, after all.) Put your ego aside and order a size larger if necessary. Don't buy a smaller dress thinking you're going to lose weight before the wedding. If you've been known to go up and down when under stress (due to nerves, many brides gain or shed up to 10 or 15 pounds before a wedding), go with a larger size and have your final fitting close to your wedding day. Making the dress smaller with tucks and darts generally works better than letting out seams, especially if the seam allowance is minimal.

Keep in mind, however, that when a gown fits poorly as a sample, it likely can never be made to feel right. When you try on a sample dress, it should curve in where you want it to, the waist should sit where it feels comfortable, and the neckline should be flattering. Often, if the sample size in a bridal salon is way off, the salon uses giant clips to show how the dress may fit you after it's altered.

After you get your dress, plan on two to four fittings. From your second fitting on, bring the right undergarments and shoes (see the upcoming section for more information). Your gown may need minor or major alterations. Minor alterations include tweaking to make the bodice lie flat and adjusting the length of shoulder straps. Major alterations involve such things as shortening sleeves with buttons or detail trim on the wrist from the shoulder (rather than turning them under at the wrist) and shortening a hem with a special finish such as detail scalloping from the waist, not the bottom.

Play Simon Says to find out whether you can move. Sit. Kneel. Do the twist. Can you rotate your arms like a windmill? Does the fabric pull across your hips or bust? Can you reach up to hug a tall guest?

When buying your gown and setting up your fitting schedule, find out about the shop's policies ahead of time. Specifically, you want to check

> ✔ Whether you've incurred any additional charges such as for a plus size, rush order, design change, special color, or custom bustle.

> ✔ Whether design specs, exact color, and wedding date are all on the sales slip. In other words, you want proof that the shop has a tracking system so your order doesn't get lost in the shuffle.

✔ How many fittings you'll need and approximately when the first one will be.

✔ How much the shop charges for alterations.

✔ How much it costs to add extra beading or ornamentation to the headpiece.

✔ The cancellation policy and how much of the deposit is nonrefundable. (Typically, you forfeit the deposit if the dress has been cut.) Oh, and get that policy in writing.

Underneath It All

What you put on before you get into your dress makes a big difference in the overall effect. Many gowns require elaborate foundations to enhance the silhouette. As you search for these underthings, go to lingerie shops where you'll get personal attention.

By the second fitting, you should have all the correct undergarments and your shoes. It also helps to have any other accessories you intend to wear, such as gloves, so you can decide whether to edit your look. At this point, you can bring a camera to the salon and take a picture to help you obsess after the appointment.

A little bra-vado

The most important part of your under-attire is the bra. If your dress doesn't have a custom-made or built-in bra, you need to find an off-the-shelf number that packages your assets in the best possible way.

Different dresses require specific brassieres:

✔ **Low-cut back:** A backless bra that hooks at the waist is a good bet.

✔ **Low-cut front:** Push-up or demi-cup bras are the way to go.

✔ **Strapless or spaghetti straps:** Go for a bustier, preferably a seamless one to keep the look of your torso smooth.

Even totally buff babes may find that their fantasy wedding dress needs some filling out. If you need to give Mother Nature a nonsurgical boost, invest in a pair of silicone bra inserts, available at fine lingerie stores and on the Internet.

To keep your bra from playing peekaboo on a low-cut dress, sew a few snaps on the front and back of the bra to attach it to the dress. On a sleeveless dress, sew little catches with snaps in the straps through which you thread your bra straps. Or have a seamstress tack your bra into your dress. If you want to show some skin and do it with nonchalance (that is, without tugging at your dress all night), buy a roll of Hollywood fashion tape, a special double-sided tape — the "stars' secret" — that holds bra straps in place, strapless dresses up, and revealing necklines in place. This tape is also good for last-minute disasters like a hem that has come down. To order some, go to www.hollywoodfashionsecrets.com.

Perfecting your proportions

With some wedding gowns, you may need specialized undergarments to fill out and tuck in. Here's what else may be going on beneath your dress:

- ✔ **Body shaper:** These used to be called girdles, but today's versions do the job better and don't make you feel like you're wearing a body cast. You can find them in a variety of styles — slimming shorts, bottom boosters, full-body smoothers, thong-cut bodysuits, full-support slips, long-waist panty-girdles, and so on — and in comfy fabrics such as spandex, Lycra, and microfiber.

- ✔ **Garter:** In the form of straps suspended from a wide elastic belt (called a garter belt) or an elastic band wrapped around the thigh, a garter helps hold up your stockings. Although you may feel personally titillated by wearing a garter belt and thigh-high stockings, they don't give you the smoothest line in a sheath dress or even under a ball gown, and they can come unsnapped during a strenuous session of "Hot, Hot, Hot!"

- ✔ **Petticoats:** Many gowns have built-in petticoats, which are underskirts usually made of tulle, lace, or *crinoline* (a stiff, open-weave fabric made of horsehair or cotton) to give fullness to the silhouette, especially on ball gowns. Or you can buy them separately in the same silhouette as your bridal gown. Experiment with the number of crinolines; even if two look perfect, add one more just to be sure. Big gowns need fuller and stiffer petticoats. Wear them for all your fittings.

- ✔ **Slip:** For a long sheath dress, you probably want to wear a slip. New body-hugging slips act as gentle, long-line girdles, extending from waist to midcalf. Just make sure yours doesn't ride up when you walk.

- ✔ **Stockings:** Bare legs don't look finished unless you're wearing strappy sandals. Avoid patterned stockings. Your mother may want you to wear stockings with reinforced toes, but that's a no-no with open-toed shoes. If you plan to wear open-toed shoes but want the smoothing effect of control-top pantyhose, go with a sheer footless style such as Spanx Power Panties. To avoid panty lines, buy butt-friendly undies or stockings with built-in underwear. When in doubt, wear pantyhose without underwear.

No Mean Feet

Don't think that because your dress is long, your shoes are invisible. They aren't. Your feet are actually seen again and again: getting in and out of the car, walking down the aisle, during the first dance. An ill-chosen pair can sabotage your look just as easily as a well-chosen pair can complete it.

You have many options for bridal footwear, as shoe designers have become keenly interested in the bridal market. Designers from mid-price line Stuart Weitzman to the ritzy Christian Louboutin make shoes specifically to be worn with wedding gowns. J. Crew (www.jcrew.com) is a good source for bridal shoes (click "Weddings & Parties" and then "Shoes"), and behemoth shoe website Zappos features an online wedding shop (www.zappos.com/bridal-shoes). Anthropologie-affliated wedding shop BHLDN (www.bhldn.com) also offers a diverse and lovely selection.

When shoe shopping, keep these guidelines in mind:

- ✔ **Plain skirts call for beautifully detailed shoes.** Try some trimmed with bows, beading, lace, or jeweled clip-ons.

- ✔ **Ornate shoes with an ornate dress may be overkill.** A subtle embellishment on the heel, toe, or *throat* (the opening in the vamp of a shoe at the instep) may be enough.

- ✔ **A shoe's fabric doesn't have to match that of the dress.** In fact, mixing textures often looks better. The same goes for color; a pair of hot pink satin heels can look very sexy peeking out from the hem of a white dress.

- ✔ **Comfort is key.** If you plan to dance all night, try buying professional dance shoes, which are extremely light and flexible. With padded, textured insoles, they're built to perform. Another dancing option is ballet slippers dolled up with bows and grosgrain ribbon or covered in lace or eyelet fabric.

For dress shoes, I recommend Foot Petals Tip Toes self-adhesive shoe inserts. They keep the balls of your feet padded and your toes from scrunching forward. The flower-shaped pads are virtually invisible, even on strappy, open-toed styles.

- ✔ **Shoes with back straps must fit perfectly.** Make sure they're neither too tight nor a smidgen too loose. Maneuvering in your dress may be tricky enough without having to mess with slipping heels or painful straps.

- ✔ **Get height while still walking gracefully.** If you want extra height without losing your balance, platforms or wedgies are chic.

An inexpensive pair of shoes in satin or *peau de soie* (a soft, silk fabric of satin weave with a dull finish) can be dyed to match your dress or a subtly colored underlay of silk on your dress. Unfortunately, cheap shoes usually aren't very comfortable. Bring a pair of ballet shoes as a backup for the reception. Just make sure the dress is short enough to accommodate the difference in height between the two.

To avoid a wedding-day spill, gently roughen up your shoes' soles with sandpaper and, if necessary, a sharp kitchen knife. Be sure to remove the size sticker from the soles, especially if you'll be kneeling during the ceremony. Also, practice walking and dancing in your wedding shoes (on a clean floor, of course) until you feel completely comfortable in them.

Heads Up

In ancient Rome, brides appeared enveloped in a saffron-colored haze that symbolized the flame of Vesta, the goddess of home and the provider of life. Today, putting on a headpiece and veil completes the transformation from your daily persona to (hear the cymbals?) your alter ego: THE BRIDE!

Veiled intentions

For most brides today, the veil functions more as a fashion accessory than a religious necessity. Among your options for veils are

- **Angel:** This veil can be any length, but the cut is the distinctive part. It comes to a gentle point in the back from wide sides, giving the look of angels' wings.
- **Ballerina:** Ends at the ankles. Also called *waltz.*
- **Birdcage:** Falls to just above the nose, just below the nose, or below the chin. Often worn attached to a small hat or headband.
- **Blusher:** A short, single-layer veil that covers the bride's face as she enters the ceremony and then is pushed back over her head. Usually worn layered over a longer back veil.
- **Cathedral:** Falls 3½ yards from the headpiece.
- **Chapel:** A yard shorter than a cathedral veil. Often worn with a sweep train to give the illusion of a longer train.
- **Circular:** Can be any length and attaches to the head with a flat comb just to keep it in place. If worn long, it creates a very ethereal look with the bride swathed in a pouf of tulle.
- **Elbow:** A veil that goes to your elbows.

- **Fingertip:** Extends to your knee. Only kidding. The veil touches the tips of your fingers, a length that often works with ball gowns and is therefore one of the most popular.

- **Flyaway:** A multilayered veil that just touches your shoulders. Sometimes called a *Madonna* veil.

- **Mantilla:** A long, Spanish-style, circular piece of lace that frames the face. It usually isn't worn with a headpiece but rather is draped over a comb. The fabric is either lace or lace-edged tulle. Sew clear plastic snaps on both your mantilla and the shoulders of your dress to keep the fabric draped gracefully.

- **Pouf:** A short, gathered piece of veiling that fastens to a headpiece or comb at the top of the head to add height to the veil.

Some etiquette mavens consider veils, particularly blushers, inappropriate for second-time or pregnant brides. Some brides, on the other hand, object to a veil's other connotation: the handing over of the woman to the man. Besides, they want to see where they're going. If you have stage fright, a veil can certainly help to calm your nerves. Either way, unless religious considerations are in order, these days it's your call.

Take a few tips to heart when veil shopping and you'll be sure to find a look you love:

- **If your dress is ornate, wear a plain veil.** A simple dress, however, can take either a plain or ornate veil.

- **Any ornamentation on the veil should start below where your dress ornamentation ends.** Decoration (such as flowers or crystals) on a cathedral veil, for example, should cover only the bottom third.

- **Opt for crystals in lieu of rhinestones.** Crystals reflect light and usually photograph better than rhinestones, which can look like black dots.

- **The adornments on your veil don't need to match those on your dress.** All the elements, such as seed pearls, sequins, or other adornments, should merely complement one another.

- **A ribbon trim may not be your best bet.** Ribbon trim may look better to you than unfinished tulle, but depending on your veil's length, a ribbon can create a horizontal line across your middle, effectively stopping the eye and making you look shorter. I suggest considering trim only for veils that fall above or below your waist.

A poufy veil or headpiece doesn't necessarily make you look taller. In fact, if you're short, a voluminous veil can make you look like a mushroom. Many women opt for narrow-cut veils, which create a vertical line. Remember, your head isn't flat. (At least I hope not.) Examine a veil from all angles and, if possible, try it on with your dress and an approximation of the way you intend to wear your hair. A veil that suits you from the back may not flatter your face, or vice versa. Suzanne, a *couture milliner* (in plain English, a hat designer for rich folks) in New York and Palm Beach, suggests you disregard current trends in headpieces (tiaras, hair sticks, and so on) and concentrate first on the placement of the veil/headpiece on your head. A big hairdo, for example, looks best with a veil that attaches at the back of your scalp. Generally speaking, you should align the headpiece with your ears — as with a headband — for the most flattering look.

If you're lucky enough to have lace from your mother's or grandmother's wedding dress, you can use it to create a veil. Avoid making the mistake of trying to dye an antique veil, however. Its appeal lies in its uniqueness, so it shouldn't match the dress exactly.

Hats, headpieces, crowns, and doodads

Although your fantasy may be to look "bridal" by wearing your veil during the reception, doing so may not be the best idea for photos, particularly profiles where the pouf of the veil obscures your face. Many brides opt for the best of both worlds — detachable veils that they can remove after the ceremony, leaving a headpiece to maintain the bridal aura.

A *headpiece,* another of those great wed-speak terms, is what a bride wears on her head. Worn either alone or as an anchor for the veil(s), it's an integral part of the ensemble.

The key to finding the headgear that works best with your hairdo, veil, and dress is to try on many variations of the basic styles, which include

- ✔ **Cloche:** A small, helmetlike cap, usually with a deep, rounded crown and narrow brim. You can have netting attached to create a pouf, a cloud, or an eye veil.

- ✔ **Fascinator:** A headpiece that's generally larger than a barrette but smaller than a hat, a fascinator is usually ornamented with feathers, flowers, ribbon loops, and/or beads and attaches to the head using a comb, hair band, or a small, flat disk that's secured to the hair with bobby pins. Popular in the 1940s, they're enjoying a resurgence after the royal wedding of William and Kate.

- ✔ **Hair jewelry:** Often used in lieu of a classic headpiece, many types of barrettes, jeweled bobby pins, and wired crystals are available. These look lovely embellishing an updo or keeping hair away from the face, particularly after the ceremony, when the veil has been removed. African-American brides sometimes wear Goddess Queen Nzinga braids wound around the top of the head and forgo a headpiece.

- ✔ **Hat:** Can be in any variety of styles and sizes — large-brimmed hats trimmed with lace, flowers, and/or pearls; pillboxes; or wispy little cocktail concoctions.

- **Headband:** Come in various widths that follow the shape of the skull and are decorated with fabric, seed pearls, and flowers. They can serve as the base for saucer-styled tulle in lieu of a veil.

- **Juliet cap:** Often made of elaborately decorated mesh. A larger version is called a *skullcap*.

- **Nefertiti headdress:** Some African-American brides wear these kinds of headpieces, which are wrapped in ethnic fabric.

- **Profile:** A comb decorated with sprays, pearls, or sequins and worn on one side of the head or at the nape of the neck.

- **Tiara:** The key accessory for playing queen for a day. Extremely popular of late. In Eastern Orthodox and Byzantine Catholic ceremonies, the most solemn moment is the crowning of the bride and groom, when metal crowns or floral wreaths are held over their heads. This part of the ceremony symbolizes that they're king and queen of a heavenly kingdom on earth.

- **Wreaths, garlands, and circlets:** Composed of flowers, twigs, and/or ribbon. The maker needs your exact cranium measurement. A romantic, organic look with a couple of drawbacks: By the end of the day, a flower wreath can feel like the world's heaviest doughnut on your head, and in photographs, twig wreaths can make you look like you've sprouted antennae.

When shopping for a headpiece, imagine a picture frame extending from the neckline of your gown to several inches above your head. A big, elaborate headpiece on top of a big, elaborate hairdo may look like you're modeling the wedding cake.

Resist if a salesperson pushes you to purchase the veil and/or headpiece at the same time you purchase your dress. You should have time to do this after your dress comes in. You'll be much happier choosing the veil and headpiece based on how you want to wear your hair rather than trying to design a hairstyle that accommodates a headpiece you chose in a frenzy.

From Hair to Eternity

Your hairstyle should complete the image of yourself that you've been creating for your wedding. If your gown is very formal and romantic, you'll probably want a fairly ornate do, whereas if you're wearing a sexy sheath, you may opt for something sleeker and edgier.

When deciding on a style, take into consideration how it looks from all sides (particularly how it looks with the back of your dress) because you'll be photographed from many angles, not just head on.

To get a look that's perfectly suited for you, make an appointment with a trusted hair salon and get the hairdresser's opinion on how you should wear your hair and what sort of headpiece would best accommodate that style. Experiment with some possibilities and take a photo to help you when you shop for a headpiece. Perhaps you'll decide on two slightly different hairdos — one for the ceremony and another for the reception. You might take some of your hair down for a modified updo after the ceremony or add hair jewels or fresh flowers after you remove your veil.

If you have fine hair and plan on wearing it in a *chignon* (with a knot at the back of the neck), you may want to wash your hair the day before the wedding, rather than the day of, to give it more oomph. Otherwise, your sleek knot may slip out.

The fact of the matter is that brides wilt, even in subzero weather. Start the day with your hair a little higher, wider, and more done than you're accustomed to. By the time you get to the reception, you'll be lucky if it looks teased at all. But remember that people are less interested in seeing your new cutting-edge hairdo than your face.

Insist on smelling and feeling anything that's put in your hair. You don't want products that clash with your perfume or stick to anyone's face while you're dancing.

Hair today . . .

Your classic pageboy cut is fine for business, but your wedding vision features you with flowing tresses that rival Rapunzel's. If you don't have time (or patience) to grow your locks, fake it. Many salons specialize in temporary, clip-on hair extensions and falls, often made with real hair and dyed to match your hair color, that can give subtle, extra fullness to an updo.

. . . Gone tomorrow

If your dress is sleeveless and you have dark hair on your arms, you may consider waxing, which many women find more satisfactory than depilatories or shaving. Although the process doesn't tickle, it's not torture either. Many salons offer European-style cold waxing, which is less painful than the traditional wax. Other areas that may benefit from a treatment are your underarms, legs, bikini line, upper lip, and eyebrows.

Making Your Face Wedding-Proof

Although you want to look special on your wedding day, deviating too much from your routine is asking for trouble. I'd hate to see your groom shaking his head in panicked confusion as a white-clad someone who looks only vaguely familiar marches toward him down the aisle.

If you want a slightly different look, rehearse your makeup as you would the ceremony, but do so well in advance, not the day before. Your wedding day isn't the time to try out anything new such as contact lenses, acrylic nail tips, or perfumes. Because of the healing time required, schedule acid peels at least two months before your wedding and facials, sunless tanners, and vigorous luffa scrubs at least a week before. Unless you want to look in your photos like you just stepped out of Madame Tussauds wax museum, avoid trendy makeup techniques such as white lipstick or heavy black eyeliner. Stick with timeless, neutral colors, but be careful about using colors that are too subtle because you may look washed out.

I asked several of New York's best makeup artists for their tips in putting your best wedding-day face forward. Their advice:

✔ **Blemishes:** If you get a blemish right before the wedding, try to find an all-night dermatologist. If one isn't available, paint the area with concealer by using a thin eyeliner brush before applying foundation.

I know your mother told you this, but it bears repeating: Attempting to pick or squeeze the problem away only makes it worse!

✔ **Brushes:** A good set of makeup brushes is the number-one tool for achieving wonderful results when applying makeup.

✔ **Cheeks:** For the blushing bride look, use rosy hues and blend well. If the wedding is in the evening, you can use darker shades of contouring blush to get the sculpted cheekbone look.

✔ **Eyes:** To make the whites of your eyes crystal clear, use white or blue pencil on the inner rim of the lower lid. (If your eyes are sensitive, however, they may try to flush out the liner, making for unsightly globs in your tear ducts.) Grays, taupes, and smoky colors, as well as charcoal liners on the eyelids, usually photograph well. Laura Geller, a New York makeup artist who specializes in wedding makeup, advises that before you apply mascara, use a colorless lash thickener as the base (rather than a specialty mascara that says it contains fibers). Modern tube mascaras (such as Blinc, available at www.sephora.com or www. blincinc.com) also provide a natural but long-lashed look with almost no risk of smudging due to bridal tears.

✔ **Face:** Use a primer on your entire face to provide an especially smooth skin surface and stabilize your base foundation. Laura Geller markets a primer appropriately called Spackle (available at www.beauty.com or www.qvc.com). Blend well for a minimum makeup look. Use feather strokes toward the bottom of your face to avoid showing a line along your jaw.

✔ **Lips:** Use a lip liner and lip sealer so color doesn't bleed, cake, or peel. Red lipstick works best for dark skin and olive complexions. Otherwise, unless it's your signature look, use soft pastels. Matte lipsticks last longer than glossy ones. To apply, use a silicone-based lipstick or apply your normal lipstick, blot it thoroughly, and color over your lips with a pencil.

Lip gloss is a magnet for hair, veils, gnats, and other people. Save it for after the ceremony and before photographs.

✔ **Skin tone:** To get an even skin tone all over your body, avoid tanning beds, sunless tanning lotions (which can turn your skin, eyebrows, and hair orange), and body makeup. For problem spots — scars, brown spots, discolorations, and so on — inquire at a good makeup counter about waterproof camouflage creams such as Dermablend (or even better, try airbrushing; see the next paragraph). If you tend to get blotchy or break out in hives, use a Benadryl cream on the affected area.

For the closest thing to permanent perfection, try *airbrushing,* an amazing technique that until recently was used only for theatrical special effects or cover girls. A trained professional sprays the makeup on in a very fine coat, and it dries almost immediately on contact. No brush marks or imperfections to deal with, only excellent color and coverage. Having this done is a bit pricey, but the result is a sheer finish that miraculously minimizes pores and stays on until you wash it off. You can use the technique to cover scars, tattoos, and freckles; apply nail polish; and provide an all-over, even tan. (The latter isn't for the modest, as the technician essentially paints every part of you.) Look for a salon or studio that offers airbrushing near you. If the professional route doesn't appeal, Temptu (www.temptu.com) offers an at-home airbrush system for makeup application.

Finishing Touches

After devoting so much time and energy to getting your dress and headgear under control, accessories may seem like an afterthought, but they shouldn't look like it. Try different combinations of jewelry and gloves until you get the right balance.

Covering up

Getting to and from the ceremony may require protection from the elements. Your wool winter coat simply won't do, nor will your best white sweater. Some options to consider coordinating with your dress:

- ✔ **Bolero:** A cropped jacket, ending at or above the waistline. Can match the dress to give a tailored look or be beaded to enhance the gown. Works well with long, draped skirts.

- ✔ **Capes and cloaks:** A dramatic statement in either a complementary shade of white or, for real flair, an intense shade of red.

- ✔ **Muffs:** The Dr. Zhivago look is perfect for winter weddings, especially a vibrant color in faux fur.

- ✔ **Shawls:** In matching or contrasting fabric or color, something simple to drape over your shoulders. Worn threaded through arms and tied in the back, leaving long streamers to look more glam than granny. Lace, chiffon, raw silk, or appliquéd velvet may be sheer enough to wear over your dress at the ceremony and heavy enough to wear as a coverup in early spring or fall.

- ✔ **Shrug:** Basically, two sleeves that meet in the back and cover the very top of the shoulders.

Hand-some gloves

If you feel perplexed when you look in the mirror, like something is missing, the right pair of gloves may do the trick. Generally, you wear over-the-elbow (called *opera*) gloves with strapless or sleeveless gowns, short gloves (considered less formal) with short-sleeved or long-sleeved gowns, and elbow-length gloves with cap-sleeved gowns. The style, fabric, and texture should complement the dress. Kid leather is considered the dressiest, but satin spandex, crushed velvet, and sheer organza can look ultraelegant. The fabric should be matte; shiny looks chintzy and will bring undue attention to your hands and arms. Gloves can also have jeweled cuffs or iridescent sequins, tiny pearls, or beads down the length of the arm.

Glove lengths are expressed by the number of buttons they have (or would have). A one-button glove is wrist-length. Two-, four-, six-, and eight-button gloves all end between the wrist and elbow. The longest is a sixteen-button glove, which ends above the elbow. In addition to knowing the glove length, you must know your glove size, which generally corresponds to your dress size. Stretchy gloves come in small, medium, and large sizes.

Somehow, your ring finger needs to be exposed during the ceremony. Although you have various ways to maneuver gloves at the altar (a slit at the ring finger or at the wrist), these are usually clumsy and distracting. Your best option is to remove the gloves altogether. This procedure should look like neither a strip tease nor a tug of war. Practice removing your gloves before the ceremony by gently tugging on each left-hand finger and sliding the glove off, right side out. (If you remove only one glove, you'll want to put it back on before the recessional, unless you're Michael Jackson.) Hand the gloves to your maid of honor when you hand her your bouquet; she'll return the gloves to you after the recessional. And when you eat, daintily remove your gloves. You don't want to turn them into five-fingered napkins.

Gloves or no gloves, get your nails in tiptop shape. Get regular manicures (and pedicures) for several weeks before the wedding. On your wedding day, consider springing for a manicurist to make a house call. Painting your nails the night before can result in sheet prints and gives you all the more time to mar the lacquer.

Selecting your jewelry

Opinions about jewelry are as varied as wedding dresses themselves. An off-the-shoulder gown may look best with no embellishment. Pearls are the bridal favorite, and wearing your mother's may be touching, but unless they're the perfect length for the neckline of your dress, they may take away from, not add to, the effect.

Many brides are now choosing to wear funkier jewelry than in the past. Beautiful faux jewel earrings or a chunky necklace may set off a gown beautifully, particularly in white gold or silver. Proportion is the key. Bracelets are overkill with gloves; they may detract from your hands and also catch on a tulle dress or veil, so put them on last and carefully.

Don't feel compelled to wear a suite of jewelry just because it's your big day. Try on necklaces or earrings (maybe not both) to see what looks best with your dress. You may find that large pieces, or too many pieces, compete with an embellished dress.

Notice that if you're perusing dress ads, a vast majority of gown designers show their dresses without any necklaces and with dainty earrings. They do that for a reason; with rare exceptions, brides look most beautiful with a clean line from the bodice up to the headpiece, emphasizing their radiant faces.

Bagging it

When it comes to bags, the best advice is to get a good night's sleep — oops, wrong page! Seriously, even if you normally need a tractor-trailer to transport your daily necessities, the exquisite handbag that accompanies your attire can accommodate only a minimum of survival tools — lipstick, powder, breath mints, mascara, handkerchief. Stow bigger, bulkier items (hairbrushes, hair spray, hair dryers, and so on) in the bathroom or your dressing room.

This miniature purse doesn't make the trip with you down the aisle. In fact, you don't wear it at all. Arrange for someone to hang on to it during the ceremony and leave it on your seat at the reception.

Getting into the Gown

Getting dressed on your wedding day is a two-person job. Check on the cost of hiring an alterations person from your dress shop to assist you in getting dressed. That may sound ridiculous, but believe me, they can be very helpful both in getting the dress ready (if last-minute steaming or minor alterations are necessary) and in cinching up a complicated bustle after the ceremony.

Another life-saving tip (albeit a tad indelicate): Visit the loo before you get into your dress (for reasons that should be obvious).

Now you're ready to get dressed.

1. **Unzip the dress all the way down.**

2. **If you have a separate petticoat, put it into the dress.**

   Make sure the waists match up.

3. **Have your designated lady-in-waiting hold up the dress for you with the bodice falling forward.**

   Put your hands on your waist, arms akimbo, and step into your dress instead of pulling it over your head. If you must do the latter, cover your head with a zippered head netting (available at drugstores) or a scarf so your makeup doesn't ruin your dress or vice versa.

4. **Fasten any buttons, zip any zippers, and so on.**

   To pull the loops over a parade of covered buttons marching from neck to hip, a crochet hook may seem like the eighth wonder of the world as you try to get dressed in less than three hours.

5. **Put on your headpiece.**

6. **Sit on a backless stool to finish your makeup, with the dress fluffed out around, not under, you.**

Caring for Your Gown after the Party

After all you spent in terms of time, money, and emotional reserve, it doesn't seem fair that you get to wear your wedding gown for only one day. Whether you decide to recycle your gown or stow it in your closet, the first step is to have it professionally cleaned.

Preserving for posterity

While you're away on your honeymoon, have someone take your gown to the cleaners and point out all the spots, such as sugar stains, needing special treatment. Some people suggest waiting a week because such stains as Champagne don't show up for a few days. Use a cleaner that specializes in wedding dresses and make sure the place uses clean fluid and does each dress individually.

Specify how you want the dress packed and inspect it when you get it back. The dress should be wrapped in acid-free tissue and stored in an acid-free box that isn't airtight, because natural fibers need to breathe. If the box has a window, it should be acetate (which is acid-free), not plastic. Store the headpiece separately; metal parts can rust or turn a dress brown. You may store both the dress and veil without a box in a clean white or muslin sheet in a dry, dark place. *Warning:* A basement may be too damp and an attic too hot. Wherever you store the dress, check it every year in case stains such as mildew start to develop.

Cleaning and preserving your wedding gown can be very expensive (often several hundred dollars), so get an estimate based on the condition and material of your gown before you leave it with the cleaner.

Recouping your investment

If spending a lot of money on a dress you wear only once makes you crazy, consider getting a bit more mileage out of the gown by recycling it. You can do this in one of several ways:

✔ **Donate:** Find a thrift store in your area that's clean and well run (it's heartbreaking to see wedding gowns dumped in a pile in some smelly shop). Better yet, seek out an organization that caters to brides or other needy formalwear clients. Brides Against Breast Cancer (www. bridesagainstbreastcancer.org) accepts donated gowns and sells them at their nationwide "tour of gowns," with all the proceeds going to support cancer patients. In the New York City area, Bridal Garden (www.bridalgarden.org) is a nonprofit boutique that sells donated designer gowns and donates all profits to local educational charity. (Of course, these sources are also great places to look for a gown.) Another idea: Two organizations that outfit financially strapped teens for the prom are the Glass Slipper Project (www.glassslipperproject.org) in Chicago and Fairy Godmothers, Inc. (www.fairygodmothersinc. com), based in Hatboro, Pennsylvania.

✔ **Restyle:** Take your gown to a good tailor and have it reconfigured into a ball gown for you, a christening gown for a child, or a fairy princess costume for Halloween.

✔ **Sell:** Put the dress up for sale at a consignment shop. You may find one that specializes in wedding attire or, if you have a creation by Vera Wang, for example, designer apparel. Another option is to sell it yourself on eBay, which does a brisk business in bridal paraphernalia (see Chapter 2 for more eBay details).

Transporting the gown

One of the hairiest feats of planning a faraway wedding is getting your wedding dress from A to B with a minimum of wrinkles (to either you or it) or other damage, especially if you have a poufy ball gown the size of Nebraska that can stand up by itself. After the final fitting, have the shop pack it in acid-free tissue paper — lots of it — and a special hanging bag. If you're flying, try to take an off-peak flight, when you have a better chance of getting an empty seat for your companion. Most airlines charge you, but others may give you a break because you're a bride.

Another option is to pack the garment bag in reams of bubble wrap in a large box and ship it overnight or by second-day air. I don't suggest that you check the dress with your baggage. Ditto with your headpiece and veil(s) — despite its airiness, tulle can actually crease, so don't scrunch it into a suitcase. To be totally safe, bring a portable steamer or find out whether the hotel has one. Even better, try to find a professional cleaner or tailor who can steam your dress — as you watch. Never, ever let anyone with an iron near your dress unless you've ordered the special asbestos model. Also, if your dress is heavy, avoid hanging it for more than a day or two; the weight may stretch it out. Pack other clothes in plastic dry-cleaning bags and leave them on hangers.

Chapter 20

Rings That Rock

· ·

In This Chapter

▶ Assessing a diamond using the four Cs

▶ Considering alternatives to diamonds

▶ Choosing a ring's setting and metal

▶ Shopping for rings

· ·

*E*ven if your idea of commitment is matching nose rings, you may want to devote special attention to finding the right engagement and wedding rings. For one thing, they undoubtedly qualify as major purchases for most couples. For another, you'll wear them for the rest of your lives.

Despite the cliché of the man proposing by springing open a jewelry case under his beloved's nose or surreptitiously sinking a ring in her champagne glass, many brides and grooms prefer to shop for the engagement and wedding rings together — or at least preshop together so the groom doesn't buy something that is his taste, not hers. When you do go looking, consider your lifestyle. For a woman who runs stockings by just looking at them, a pointy pear or marquise shape would be a disaster. For a mechanic, a ring of any kind may constantly get in the way or get damaged. I suggest trying on many different rings before you buy anything. Using the guidelines in this chapter, you may develop an eye for quality stones and craftsmanship, but your final choice is extremely personal and should reflect your taste, your feelings for each other, and, as unromantic as it sounds, your budget.

Evaluating a Diamond

A diamond is nothing more than a hunk of carbon, yet in its pure, crystallized form, it's the hardest transparent substance known to man — a hundred times harder than ruby or sapphire. Only another diamond can cut a diamond. This durability, along with the way it reflects light, has made the diamond an enduring marriage symbol.

Today, most engagement rings in the United States feature diamonds, so you probably haven't gotten this far in your engagement without having heard about the *four Cs* — cut, color, clarity, and carat weight — by which all diamonds are judged. Chances are you're even sick to death of the four Cs, but just in case you've been hiding under a rock, read on.

Cut

A diamond's *cut* and proportion determine its brilliance and fire, making the cut perhaps the most important factor in a diamond's beauty. Because each facet acts as a light-dispersing mirror, more facets generally mean greater beauty. To appreciate a stone's cut, you should be familiar with the anatomy of a well-proportioned diamond, as shown in Figure 20-1.

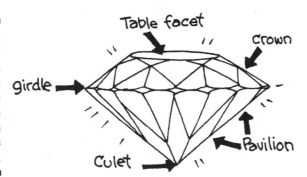

Figure 20-1: The different parts of a stone can vary in proportion and thus affect its brilliance.

Parts of a Diamond

Table facet · Crown · girdle · Pavilion · Culet

Illustration by Elizabeth Kurtzman

A modern, round-brilliant-cut diamond has 58 facets, which makes it more brilliant than other shapes. When light enters an ideally proportioned diamond, it reflects from facet to facet and back up through the top, maximizing its fire and sparkle. In a well-proportioned diamond, the crown appears to be roughly one-third of the pavilion depth. In a diamond that's cut too deep, light is lost through the sides, and the center appears dark. A diamond that's cut too shallow in order to make it look larger appears dull.

Don't confuse *cut* with *shape*. Figure 20-2 shows various shapes: oval, pear, round brilliant, emerald, baguette, and marquise. (However, just to confuse you, a diamond may be emerald cut, and an emerald may be cut like a round brilliant typical of diamond solitaires.) Note that straight and tapered baguettes are often used to surround and complement center stones.

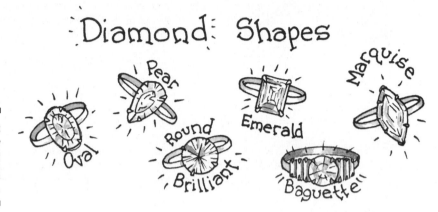

Illustration by Elizabeth Kurtzman

Figure 20-2:
A few
traditional
diamond
shapes.

Color

For some people, a diamond can never be too white. The Gemological Institute of America (GIA) grades color starting with the letter *D* (colorless) through the alphabet to *Z* (progressively more yellow).

Some diamonds possess natural *fluorescence,* which produces a yellowish, bluish, or whitish glow when viewed in daylight or under fluorescent lights. Professional gemologists test for fluorescence to ensure that the diamond color is graded properly; otherwise, a strong fluorescence may throw off the color. A stone that fluoresces blue can mask a yellow tint or make a white diamond look blue-white — a kind of bonus, actually. A white diamond that fluoresces yellow, however, can make the stone look less white, decreasing its value.

In nature, diamonds occur in virtually every color and shade — blue, pink, lavender, yellow, green, red, and even black. Known as *fancies* in the trade, colored diamonds are increasingly popular for engagement rings — Ben Affleck famously sealed his engagement to Jennifer Lopez with a pink diamond — and some rare colors are quite pricey.

Clarity

Internal imperfections — such as small cracks, whitish dots, or dark spots — are called *inclusions.* External flaws — such as *naturals* (unpolished portions), nicks, pits, and scratches — are *blemishes.* Generally speaking, the fewer the inclusions and blemishes, the clearer and more brilliant the diamond, the rarer it is, and, of course, the more it's worth. Note that cutters some-times leave naturals along a diamond's girdle — the area normally grasped by prongs when a stone is mounted into a setting — to produce a larger-cut stone. However, naturals confined to the girdle don't normally affect the diamond's clarity grade.

You can find slightly imperfect stones that actually have better color and more brilliance than some flawless stones. In fact, even an *I3* diamond — the lowest category of the imperfect grade (see the bulleted list that follows) — is 97 percent clean. A perfectly clean stone is less important than a well-cut one. Many jewelers stress that you should *never* sacrifice cut.

Although you may not be able to determine a stone's clarity with the same precision as a professional, you can judge brilliance and light and see certain imperfections by using a ten-power jeweler's *loupe,* a small magnifying glass that covers the eye.

Most jewelers in the United States grade flaws according to the GIA system, which has a large range of classifications:

- **FL:** *Flawless,* meaning without any surface characteristics or internal imperfections. These diamonds are extremely rare.

- **IF:** *Internally flawless* with only minor external blemishes that a jeweler can polish away.

- **VVS1** and **VVS2:** *Very, very small inclusions* that are difficult for a qualified observer to detect.

- **VS1** and **VS2:** *Very small* inclusions visible only under magnification. These are usually a good buy. As a point of reference, Tiffany sells only *VS2* diamonds or better.

- **SI1** and **SI2:** *Small inclusions* that are readily apparent under magnification but not to the naked eye, making them desirable.

- **I1, I2,** and **I3:** *Imperfect* grades in which the flaws may or may not be visible to the naked eye. These are much lower in price and generally don't appreciate in value.

Carat weight

Gemologists measure the size of diamonds in terms of weight, specifically in carats (ct). A carat contains 100 points. Therefore, if a jeweler says, for example, that a stone weighs 25 points, it is ¼ carat. *Note:* Don't confuse carats with *karats* (kt), which in the United States refers to gold quality.

If you ask jewelers how large a stone is and they tell you it has, say, "a 2-carat spread," watch out. Many diamonds are *spread,* or cut with thin proportions, to maximize weight rather than brilliance. Therefore, a diamond that *spreads* 1 carat isn't the same as a stone that *weighs* 1 carat. The correct way to phrase the question is, "What is the stone's exact actual weight?" The jeweler should then give you the number of carats — with no mention of the word *spread.*

A "c" change of sorts

In the past few years, concern has grown over *conflict diamonds* — diamonds used to finance conflict and civil wars, particularly in Africa. The Kimberley Process Certification Scheme, launched in January 2003, is an international agreement to eliminate the trade in what are also known as *blood diamonds*. To ensure legitimacy, industry leaders and about 70 participating countries have instituted self-regulatory measures that include tamper-proof containers for transporting uncut gems, counterfeit-proof warranties, and electronic record-keeping. Although participants aren't allowed to trade in diamonds with nonparticipants, at this writing human rights groups are pushing for more stringent monitoring, without which there's no way of making sure that diamonds aren't sourced from areas held by rebels opposing legitimate governments.

I won't go so far as to say that size doesn't matter, but size is virtually meaningless outside the context of cut, clarity, and color. A large stone that's dull, flawed, or improperly cut is worth less money than a perfect little diamond. The larger a good-quality diamond, however, the more it's worth.

The fifth C — cost

The jewelry industry has very thoughtfully devised a formula to determine how much you should spend on a diamond ring. If you really love her, they say, spending the equivalent of two months' salary is quite reasonable. Although that doesn't seem outrageous to me, it does seem rather arbitrary. You surely have your own priorities and can figure out for yourselves what is appropriate.

If Diamonds Aren't Your Best Friend

Although the majority of American brides wear diamond rings, colored gemstones — such as emerald, garnet, ruby, and sapphire — have become increasingly popular. In fact, since ancient times, people have prized colored gems, believing they endow their owners with power, status, luck, and good health. Various stones were associated with each of the 12 tribes of Israel and the 12 apostles; Hindus and Arabs ascribed stones to the signs of the zodiac. In 1952, the jewelry industry adopted a list of birthstones, which has become the standard in America, although lists of stones for days of the week, hours of the day, states of the union, and each of the seasons actually exist. In short, if you like a stone for its color, you can find many kinds of meanings attributed to it through the ages to further justify your purchase.

Judging gemstones

Although clarity is an important factor in buying a gemstone, flawlessness is a harder characteristic to find than in diamonds. A far more important consideration is color. The closer a stone comes to a pure spectral hue, the higher the quality. In other words, in a red stone, the purer the red, the better.

To accurately assess a stone's true color, look at it in several types of light. After examining many ruby rings, for example, you may notice they range in hue from bluish-red to brownish-red to pink, with several gradations in between. In fact, while a true ruby is corundum, some of those "rubies" may actually be from other gemstone families — beryl, garnet, spinel, tourmaline, or zircon — and should be priced accordingly. Certification for gemstones isn't as institutionalized as with diamonds, but a jeweler should be able to verify the stone's color grade and whether the stone is natural or synthetic.

Scintillating synthetics

If you want more diamond than your budget allows, synthetic diamonds, which are grown in a lab rather than in nature, are a good alternative. Many imitation diamonds have appeared over the years, and some have gained a large following. Known as zircon, GGG, Fabulite, and Wellington diamond, these fakes have proven soft and/or brittle compared to the real thing. Since it was introduced in the 1970s, however, the most popular imitation has been *cubic zirconi* (known as CZ) because it's more durable and less prone to scratches and cracks than other synthetic and imitation stones.

Now, however, CZ has competition from a new substance called *synthetic moissanite,* which is the second hardest gemstone next to — and more brilliant than — diamond. Synthetic moissanite has even fooled thermal testers, the standard way jewelers detect CZ.

Synthetic moissanite costs only 10 to 20 percent less than real diamonds, making it significantly more expensive than CZ. So if wearing several thousand dollars on one little finger makes you nervous, CZ is a good alternative — at least as a backup for day-to-day use. (I actually know many Park Avenue women who wear CZ copies of their most expensive baubles while the real thing sits in a safe, and no one is the wiser.)

The next generation of synthetics has succeeded in growing cultured diamonds that are literally perfect and significantly less expensive than natural ones or moissanite. The high-quality stones have been so impressive that De Beers Diamond Trading Company, the London-based cartel that controls the diamond business, has launched a program to help international gem labs distinguish between man-made and mined stones by using high-tech equipment. It remains to be seen whether consumers care about the difference between a test-tube diamond and a hand-mined one, as long as they get more rock for the buck.

Setting Pretty

A ring's *setting* is like the right picture frame that sets off a masterpiece to its best advantage. The ring must also be in proportion to your hand. An elaborate setting may camouflage flaws in a stone. In fact, an *illusion setting*, which looks like a little box in which the stone sits (see Figure 20-3), is almost certainly a sign that the stone has something to hide. Particularly distinctive settings, however, may bear the designer's insignia inside the ring, whether the design is elaborate or minimalist.

Classic settings include

- **Bezel:** Streamlined setting with no prongs. The stone sits close to the finger. May reduce appearance of brilliance because light can't enter from the sides. Works well with two different metals such as yellow-gold and platinum.

- **Carved scroll:** Victorian setting that became an international trend. Elaborate scrollwork surrounds the stone.

- **Channel:** Used in mounting a number of smaller stones of uniform size in a row. (See Figure 20-3.)

- **Cluster:** A large stone surrounded by smaller stones.

- **Gypsy:** Stone lies flush with the band. Metal around the stone is much heavier than around the shank. (See Figure 20-3.)

- **Invisible:** No visible metal prongs or channels. Stones are cut and fit so precisely that no gaps exist between them. These settings cost more because stones must match very closely.

- **Pavé:** Small stones set together in a cluster with no metal showing through.

- **Prong:** Four or six metal claws grasp onto the gemstone. A six-prong setting is often called a Tiffany setting.

- **Silver cups:** Edges crimped beneath the stones to reflect light. This design originated in the late 1700s.

- **Solitaire:** A single gemstone mounted without ornamental side stones, usually with four or six prongs.

- **Tension:** Diamond appears to be almost floating, barely held in place at the girdle.

- **Tiffany:** Uses six prongs.

Settings

Illusion   Gypsy   Channel

Figure 20-3: A stone can look vastly different depending on what kind of setting it sits in.

Illustration by Elizabeth Kurtzman

Metal Matters

The metal of your ring should flatter both your skin tone and the stone's color. You may need to weigh aesthetics against practicality. For example, 18-karat gold is a brighter yellow than 14-karat, but it's more expensive and not as hard. On the other hand (so to speak), 18-karat white gold is white, less likely to cause allergic reactions, and more affordable than 14-karat white. Platinum is the most expensive metal, but it's beautiful, hard, and resilient. If you want to go the gold route and can't decide whether you like yellow, white, or pink gold the best, tricolor rolling rings feature all three.

Whatever metal you choose, you may have the ring designed with a matte or satin finish, patterns such as delicate flowers or swirling paisleys, or detailed edgings such as *milgrain* (like tiny beads) or a soft bevel known as *comfort fit*.

Orthodox Jews believe that wedding rings should be plain, with no jewels or stones that may impede the eternal, heavenly circle of life and happiness.

Don't Leave Out the Groom

Despite the invention of *gimmal rings,* men rarely wore wedding rings until after World War II. Even the romance-obsessed Victorians preferred a plain gold band for women and no ring for men. Today, 98 percent of all weddings are double-ring ceremonies.

The groom's ring is usually a larger, wider version of the bride's. Although his ring may be a completely different style, like hers, it should slip easily over the knuckle and hug the base of the finger, leaving just enough room to slip a toothpick through to account for fingers swelling when the temperature changes.

Finding the Right Ring

Whether you decide to buy a brand-new, never-worn wedding set or opt for a set with some history, searching for a ring can be an exciting experience. Like the wedding gown and the groom's ensemble, the rings you choose should be distinctly you.

In the loop

Many couples have a special message engraved on the inside of their engagement or wedding rings. This inscription may be their initials or their wedding date. Others are downright tomes requiring a fairly wide and large band. Here are some classics:

- *DODI LI V' ANI LO* (Hebrew for "I am my beloved's and my beloved is mine")

- LOVE ~ HONOR ~ CHERISH

- CONSTANCY AND HEAVEN ARE ROUND AND IN THIS EMBLEM FOUND

- I DOE RECEIVE IN THEE MY CHOYCE (from a 17th-century ring)

- MAY THIS CIRCLE BE UNBROKEN

- WHOM GOD HAS JOINED TOGETHER LET NO MAN PUT ASUNDER

- PUT IT BACK ON

Left hand, fourth finger?

Through the ages, every digit of the hand — including the thumb, in the 17th century — has been used as the wedding-ring finger. The Egyptians used the fourth finger of the left hand, believing that the *vena amoris* ran straight from that finger to the heart. That no such vein exists hasn't deterred people from favoring that finger for wedding rings. In fact, the English Prayer Book of 1549 specifies the left hand. Perhaps that explains why Roman Catholics used the right hand until the 18th century.

Buying new

As with just about everything else these days, you now have the option of shopping for engagement and wedding rings at a local jeweler or online. An in-person purchase lets you see what you're getting and is more likely to come with lifetime cleaning and maintenance of your ring. But shopping online allows for easy comparison, can save you money, and is getting ever-more sophisticated. For example, Blue Nile (www.bluenile.com) allows you to build your own ring and search by stone shape or price. The company can also finance your purchase (not that I recommend buying more ring than you can afford) and help you insure it. Similar sites like Diamond Ideals (www.diamondideals.com) and 25 Karats (www.25karats.com) also get good consumer reviews. And Brilliant Earth (www.brilliantearth.com) allows you to build your own ring while specializing in ethical stones and metals. If you decide you prefer to shop in person for your ring, the Diamond Review (www.diamondreview.com) is a consumer education site (no shopping) that can connect you with prescreened local jewelers and offer you tutorials and forums to answer your questions.

Surprisingly (or not), warehouse store Costco has recently emerged as a place to shop for engagement and wedding rings, either online or in person. (Other warehouse retailers like Sam's Club are doing the same.) Shopping for a ring at Costco is a no-frills experience, and though you get a gem appraisal with your ring, you don't get resizing, customization, or maintenance. But you may be able to score a beautiful ring for significantly less than you'd pay at a local brick-and-mortar store. Costco offers rings in a wide range of styles and price points, but if you decide to shop in person, know that each store carries a different selection, and rings may come in only a limited number of sizes, so checking a few stores in your area may be worthwhile. If you change your mind about your purchase, Costco has a very generous return policy.

When it comes to buying a diamond, beware of deals. If a price sounds too good to be true, it probably is. Although you're usually safe when buying from a reputable retailer, scams do abound. These range from counterfeit or altered certificates to bait-and-switch advertising to deceptive pricing schemes. A legitimate jeweler should have no problem with having a ring checked out by an appraiser of your choosing.

The appraiser should be a Graduate Gemologist (G.G. degree) from the Gemological Institute of America or an F.G.A. (Fellow of the Gemological Association of Great Britain). Certification from the American Gem Society or the American Society of Appraisers is also worthy.

Whether based on an hourly rate or per carat for diamonds, appraisal fees should be posted in your face. The appraisal should be conducted in your presence and provide

- ✔ The millimeter dimensions, quality, weight, and identification of each stone
- ✔ The cut, color, clarity, and carat weight of the diamonds
- ✔ The hue, tone, intensity, transparency, and clarity of colored stones
- ✔ An identification and assessment of metals used in mounting
- ✔ A thorough description or photograph of the item
- ✔ The estimated value of the piece

You need an appraisal for insurance. In addition, take photos of all your precious jewelry and store them in a photo-quality, fireproof box. (Color photocopies of your ring are also a good record, with the added bonus that you can write on them.) Keep these photos with a GIA grading report (often erroneously called a certificate), which is issued when the stone is finished by the diamond polisher. The report doesn't evaluate price but does describe the characteristics of an unmounted diamond.

If you have a diamond, you may go a step further and get a Gemprint, a special laser image that fingerprints your stone. A copy is then registered with the Gemprint Central Registry in Chicago. The process takes only a few minutes and usually costs less than $50, and some insurance companies offer a 10 percent discount on annual premiums for Gemprinted diamonds.

Analyzing antique pieces

If you're interested in finding an antique wedding ring, watch for upcoming jewelry sales at reputable auction houses and antiques shows. Attend previews and inspect the goods. In many cases, the auction house has an expert on hand to answer questions and give you a tutorial in evaluating a ring's attributes. Be sure to also ask about the ring's *provenance* — previous owner(s) — as that may imbue the ring with more meaning for you.

Recognizing the appeal and value of antique jewelry, many jewelers have introduced *estate jewelry* departments. Bear in mind, however, that estate jewelry isn't necessarily the same as *antique* (at least 100 years old); jewelry that once belonged to someone else may actually be only a few years old. The easiest and surest way to know is to check a diamond or colored gemstone certification.

If no certificate is available, the cut may date a stone. Developed in the 16th century, the *rose cut* was characterized by a flat base and facets in multiples of six. In the 18th century, the *old mine cut,* which had unprecedented brilliance and fire, was popular, and by the mid-19th century, the *old European cut* proved even more brilliant. Like today's modern brilliant cut, old mine and old European cuts (see Figure 20-4) have 58 facets. But they aren't as brilliant as stones cut after the 1920s and therefore are typically appraised for less.

Figure 20-4: From the side, old mine and old European cuts have a deep pavilion and high crown.

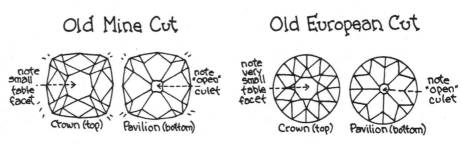

Illustration by Elizabeth Kurtzman

Dirt and grease deposits can collect in and around a diamond setting, making the stone appear more yellow than it is. An old diamond ring may clean up whiter than you expect.

An antique diamond ring may be an antique all right, but not a diamond. It was common in Victorian times to use paste or leaded glass gems in precious metal settings, so you may need an expert to determine a stone's true identity.

Although an heirloom ring may hold great sentimental value, it isn't necessarily a paradigm of great taste. If the style looks dowdy, you may be able to strike a compromise by having the stones reset in a more contemporary or flattering setting. First have the stones appraised; you want to make sure the stones are legitimate and also check for any damage that may affect what you can do with them.

If you opt to have a new setting designed, choose a jeweler who specializes in styles you like. Unless you're absolutely sure of what you want and can provide detailed sketches of the top and side views, try on many rings of various weights and styles and clip magazine photos of rings you like. As you work with the jeweler, request a wax model so that you can make any last-minute changes before your ring is permanently cast.

Chapter 21

For Posterity: Photos and Videos

After you return from your honeymoon, write the last thank-you note, and retrieve your wedding garb from the dry cleaner, you may wonder whether it was all a dream. Until, that is, your photographs or video arrives. These images are the key to keeping each memory as sharp as if you were married this morning. The final products — both your wedding album and your video — should re-create the mood of the day. How effectively that's accomplished depends on who does the shooting, what kind of equipment she uses, and how skilled she is. Figuring out your options is what this chapter is all about.

Getting Focused

Photography and videography are two distinctly different fields, but both require extensive training to produce high-quality results. Depending on your personal taste and budget, you may want to capture your wedding in more than one format.

Your photographer and videographer are two people with whom you must painstakingly go over your wedding-day schedule. Send it to them early and then make a point of addressing any questions or important details to make sure they've read it. (See Chapter 7 for tips on creating your schedule.) If you want either of them to document every millisecond of your day, arrange for them to travel in the car with you if your ceremony and reception are in different venues.

If your photographer and videographer haven't seen your ceremony or reception site before, request that they scout the space and surrounding grounds before the wedding. ***Note:*** Not many photographers make time to do this, but it doesn't hurt to ask.

Photographers and videographers often have smart ideas about selecting the perfect spots for posed and portrait shots, positioning background floral arrangements, arranging chair groupings, and refocusing lighting fixtures. They're also responsible for following the guidelines for photography and videography in the church or synagogue — something that shouldn't be given short shrift.

If your photographer and videographer haven't worked together before, have a meeting with them in person or by conference call. You don't want them falling over each other in their zeal to capture key moments such as the cake cutting. At one wedding I know of, a knock-down, drag-out fight ensued between the two, and the unfortunate groom got injured attempting to break it up. Most professionals, though, are used to choreographing their movements in tandem so they can get the shots they need. Be sure to tell the videographer very clearly that, when in doubt, the photographer's shot comes first.

Take Your Pic

One of the really important choices to make regarding your wedding is who you want to photograph it. The photographer's talent and style are obviously important, but a good photographer is also intimately involved with your wedding — helping you think ahead of time about photo opportunities that may arise during the celebration, gauging the crowd's mood, capturing subtle moments as well as intense emotions, and yet all the while remaining unobtrusive. The photographer is also one of the few vendors you deal with after the wedding as you order prints and put together albums, so pick someone you work well with, and don't pull any bridezilla numbers on him.

If relatives or friends who are photography buffs ask to photograph everything as well, tell them politely that you prefer them to be true guests and enjoy themselves. Flashes from other cameras may set off lights that the photographer has set around the room, ruining the professional shot and producing a continuous disco light show. If you prefer to have no flash photographs during your ceremony, state your wishes in the program.

Finding a photographer you click with

PLAN AHEAD

Good wedding photographers, especially those who specialize in particular styles, book up early, so start your search as soon as you've set the wedding date. To find a good photographer:

✔ Call recently married couples that you know well and ask to see their wedding photos.

✔ Call catering professionals, banquet directors, and wedding consultants (even those you aren't using), as well as editors at local bridal magazines. They're usually willing to recommend someone whose work they respect.

✔ Browse wedding blogs and Facebook pages. Many wedding professionals — such as florists, caterers, and event designers — maintain blogs featuring their work through lots of photographs. Take note of the credits on the photos you like or e-mail the blogger if you can't find a credit. Many wedding photographers also keep their own blogs, a great way to check out the quality and diversity of their work. Search for *wedding blog* and/or *wedding photographer* plus your preferred city.

✔ Check out "real wedding" features in bridal magazines. Often, talented photographers shoot these, which is why they're featured.

✔ Obtain a list of wedding photographers in your area by looking online at a trade organization such as the Professional Photographers of America (www.ppa.com). ***Note:*** These lists are regional referrals, not recommendations.

✔ Surf the web for studios in your area. The Knot's city-by-city guide (www.theknot.com) and the local directory on www.wedding channel.com are good places to find names.

✔ Consider flying in a photographer from another area. Airfare and room rates, depending on the season, may be reasonable. Because many photographers enjoy traveling, their rates may also be negotiable.

Before hiring a photographer, interview as many prospects as time and energy permit. If you're looking for a particular style, ask about their ratio of *candid* shots to *portraits.* (See the section "Choosing a photography style" later in this chapter.) More important, do the photos they show you reflect the style you want? This may seem obvious, but if people tell you they're adept at black and white and you see only color shots, something's amiss. Look at albums that feature an entire wedding. Is the narrative of the day conveyed well? Ask to see shots from weddings in a variety of locations. You also want to see film from weddings in various stages — from proofs or contact sheets to completed wedding albums.

Ask questions that bring out the photographers' feelings about weddings. How do they refer to brides and grooms — warmly or with great eye-rolling? Do they bad-mouth past clients? Do they seem enthusiastic about their work or burned out? Among the questions to ask:

- ✔ What are your favorite moments to photograph? Which weddings have been your favorites, and why?

- ✔ Do you have one or more assistants? Does the assistant take pictures or just carry equipment?

- ✔ What sort of equipment do you use?

- ✔ Do you always come with backup equipment? How many cameras do you bring to a job?

- ✔ How many weddings have you shot? Where did you learn your craft?

- ✔ Will you shoot in color, black and white, or both?

- ✔ How much do you charge, and what does that price include?

- ✔ Do you charge for travel, parking, or other expenses?

- ✔ Who owns the negatives or digital images?

- ✔ Will I get low-resolution images, high-resolution images, or both? At what point in the process?

- ✔ If you use the Internet to transmit or post images for viewing, what's your privacy policy with regard to website passwords and e-mail addresses? (Many photographers have websites where you can view your album and order prints, but you may not want the whole world to have access.)

- ✔ Are you used to working with videographers? Do you have a plan of action for working together?

- ✔ Will you work with me to put together the albums after the photographs are ready?

Ask photographers whether they charge *twilight fees* — extra fees if your event takes time away from another wedding they could book that day or evening.

Even with a highly reputable professional photography studio, you need to focus on the photographer as an individual; the studio itself doesn't shoot your wedding. And those stunning shots in the studio's sample album are the best culled from thousands taken by the studio's stable of pros, who may number in the dozens. Even assuming that everyone is identically trained or that the representative is showing you specific albums shot by each photographer, I strongly suggest that you meet with the photographer assigned to your wedding. Secondly, this person will be with you all day, so you'd better have an excellent rapport with her. When you decide on the specific photographer, make sure that's whose name appears on the contract.

If you like a photographer but feel you need to do more homework, say so. Ask the photographer to hold the date for a short while or at least give you the right of first refusal. Then make your decision as quickly as possible.

Choosing a photography style

Professional photographers understand that their main function is to cover the wedding. They can do the classic shots in their sleep — the first dance, the cake cutting, the bouquet toss, and so on. Deciding the style and format, however, is up to you. Think about how invisible you want the photographer to be, how many formal shots you want, whether you want close-up portraits or candid action shots, and whether to get a photograph of every guest.

Many photographers specialize in one or more styles. The two main styles are

- ✔ **Classic (or traditional):** The best photographers in this genre pose their subjects artfully and use creative setups. Their "candid shots" are obviously more posed than spontaneous, but the subject looks natural and comfortable nonetheless. In other words, you won't get a trite shot of the bride gazing at her train as if looking for moth holes. The photographer takes the couple's portraits with great care and then retouches and custom-crops the photos.

- ✔ **Photojournalistic:** The photographer chronicles the day as it unfolds rather than staging situations. Styles vary — some photographers look for natural situations to occur and then stop the action to get a good shot; others just look for great moments and capture them discreetly. Unfortunately, as this style has become more in demand among couples who have an aversion to classic wedding shots, some photographers who really don't get it are marketing themselves as photojournalists. An attempt to capture the mood of the day by taking a shot of your cat, complete with ragged ribbon around her neck, plopped on a bridesmaid's bouquet, and obviously dying to scram, somehow lacks that sweet, spontaneous feeling that a good candid shot captures.

If photographs are at the top of your priority list (in other words, you've appropriated a large chunk of your budget for them), consider hiring more than one photographer. For example, have one photographer do the formal shots and have another photographer who specializes in candid photos shoot the rest of the wedding.

Shot talk

When discussing the way you want your wedding photographed, knowing the kinds of shots that photographers can take is helpful:

✔ **Candids:** Results appear unposed and natural, as the subject isn't aware of the camera. Positive aspects include the photographer being less intrusive, capturing some unexpected wonderful moments, and everyone looking like their true selves. Downsides include everyone looking like their true selves (if you have a less-than-movie-star profile, you can't hide it), unexpected décor elements showing up (such as balled-up cocktail napkins and cigarettes floating in half-empty drink glasses), and unidentified bits of food captured in people's teeth for posterity. The photographer needs to shoot extra exposures to ensure that enough desirable ones turn out.

✔ **Formals:** These include lineups of family, attendants, and friends, posed individually and in groups. A good classic photographer is very exact, arranging the subjects as a painter does a still life. Photojournalists tend to be more seat-of-the-pants, and the lighting or staging may suffer.

✔ **Portraits:** Close-up photographs of the bride, groom, or both. These are staged, such as the bride posed on a staircase with her train trailing down the steps as she gazes into the camera. Also, this is the term used for head shots submitted to newspapers.

✔ **Setup or stock shots:** Classic photos taken during a wedding, such as the groom and best man toasting each other, the bride and her attendants lifting their legs cancan-style, or the two mothers with their arms around each other.

Deciding on the photography format

Although the shift to digital has pretty much taken over everyday photography, wedding photographers can still present brides and grooms with a choice between digital and film. High-end photographers, in particular, may still shoot on film or offer a mix of digital and film.

So how should you choose? Depending on the camera type, film can offer higher resolution (hence higher-quality images), and those with a very sensitive eye may simply prefer the look of film. On the other hand, finding a lab to process the negatives if you want additional prints is becoming harder and harder, and you don't have the ease of e-mailing digital files to others.

Digital images are good and getting better all the time (particularly with the highest-end cameras). Photographers can manipulate images easily and add effects if desired, and you can share images electronically when you have the files. One additional issue to consider is that a digital photographer may not use a flash, so if your lighting designer uses colored effects at your wedding, you'll get a colored effect in your photographs. If this bothers you, you can always ask for some images to be shot in black and white.

Really, given that image quality is now very good for both film and digital and that you can scan and digitize film images, I recommend choosing based on photographer, not format. If you love the look of his photos — make sure that you see them in print form — the benefits or drawbacks of each format probably won't matter very much.

Don't mistake the use of digital photography as a means to save money. Although digital cameras save time and labor, you're still selecting a craftsperson who's studied the art of photography and is paid appropriately. However, you may be able to save some money by asking your photographer to give you all the digital files on a compact disc, which you can view on your computer, crop, and touch up as you like, and then have the photos developed on a commercial website or at a photo kiosk. Some online companies even offer framing and album-making services. (See "Compiling the wedding album" later in this chapter.)

However, not all photographers are willing to relinquish their digital proofs, as your tinkering may "ruin" their carefully wrought art. Who can blame them? Their reputation is only as good as the printed product. Considering that you presumably hired them for their expertise, you may want to play it safe and have them make an official album or set of prints, and then upload a bunch of images to a password-protected photo website, where you and your guests can order copies.

Just because images are displayed online for everyone to see, don't assume you own them. The issue of who owns the originals — be they negatives, as with traditional photography, or jpeg files with digital photography — is always tricky. Some photographers give you the files but maintain the copyright, others charge you extra to own them, and still others download lower-resolution copies of the images onto a CD for you but keep the original, high-resolution files that would be appropriate for enlargement. Make sure ownership is spelled out in the contract.

The corner photo booth

Renowned New York photographer Terry Gruber is the originator of the wedding photo booth. He sets up a truly candid self-portrait studio with a customized canvas backdrop (which can be anything from an ocean scene to faux marble) and offers props or shoots in sepia tones for a vintage look. He can also add digital titles like "Ida and Wylie's Wedding" and the date. Guests pose and pop the camera themselves by using a cable release. As the party picks up speed, the various formations can be hilarious. The popularity of these photo booths has skyrocketed, and they now come with many different options. Digital photography allows for on-site printing so that guests can take home their photos and place one in an album with a few words of congratulation for the wedding couple. Photos can also be turned into flip-books that are printed and bound almost instantaneously.

Another reason to leave the printmaking to your photographer is human nature — postwedding procrastination is inevitable. You may take months, even years, to get around to ordering hard copies. In the interim, you risk losing all those digital files from a computer crash or simply the march of technology.

 If you do get digital files of your wedding pictures, it's worth investing in good photo software such as Adobe Photoshop. These programs have improved tremendously in recent years, enabling you to organize images, add text, erase unwanted objects, correct color, straighten crooked shots, arrange layouts, create photo videos, print index sheets for easy reference, and even whiten teeth and vaporize tan lines. Just make sure that you save, save, save — archive the images on your hard drive, burn CDs, make prints, and upload them to a commercial photo website that stores them for you as well. Every few years, update the storage medium before the technology or software to view the images becomes obsolete.

Creating special effects

By using special lenses, your photographer can create unusual photos for your album. If any of these techniques interest you, ask your photographer if they're available. Some of the different specialty lenses include

- **Fish-eye lens:** This technique distorts a photo, almost as if shot through a magnified keyhole. These shots are bizarre, but including a few can be fun.

- **Macro lens:** This lens provides extreme close-ups and is great for capturing details such as place cards or wedding rings.

- **Panoramic:** These pictures are shot with a wide-angle or *rotation* lens. Photos are long and horizontal, covering a large expanse.

- **Soft-focus or portrait lens:** Traditional photographers use this technique to make people look younger, "vaporizing" wrinkles. Pictures look slightly out of focus.

You may also want to mix it up by having your photographer alter the images after the fact. Some cool techniques include

- **Colorizing:** Hand-painted detailing of black-and-white film shots, usually with soft colored pencils. This technique works well with infrared shots to beautifully fill in such details as bouquets. The same effect can be achieved with digital black-and-white photography through computer manipulation.

✔ **Cross processing:** By using special software or by manually developing film in noncompatible chemistry, the photographer produces wonderfully intense, over-the-top colors and heightens contrast.

✔ **Infrared:** Outside photos are shot with black-and-white film that reads heat instead of light, giving a dramatic, otherworldly feel. Photos are high contrast — grainy black and white — with no middle tones.

Calling the shots

If you've already chosen a photographer, you probably chose that person because her style matches your style. Still, just to be sure, you should specify types of photos you do and don't want. Although some couples love dressing-room shots, others are deeply offended by the suggestion. Table shots, where half of the guests get up and pose around the other half of the table, are horrendous to some, but they're an integral part of a wedding album to others. Here are a few suggestions:

✔ **Explain dynamics:** Sharing family dirt with the photographer isn't indiscreet. In fact, not doing so may cause you far more embarrassment. If your parents are acrimoniously divorced, one of them is with a second spouse or friend that the other detests, or your sister hates your new spouse's brother — whatever the case may be — full disclosure is the best course of action. Otherwise, the hapless photographer or assistant may naively attempt to take an endearing photo and wind up with an altercation.

✔ **Identify VIPs:** If you don't have a wedding consultant, appoint an attendant or close friend to show the photographer the guests who are important to you so the photographer can make a point of including them in candids. Do so in advance so that your designee can put faces to names of new acquaintances at the prewedding events. Your appointed picture police should also be prepared to gently advise the photographer of who doesn't merit major camera time, such as the new hunk or babe your ex has in tow.

✔ **Shoot the rehearsal dinner:** You may want to hire your photographer to take photographs at the rehearsal dinner, where many poignant moments often transpire. Doing so helps loosen up the subjects for the next day and familiarizes the photographer with the key players. The rehearsal dinner usually requires the photographer to be present for two hours at most.

✔ **Specify groupings:** For formal shots, give your photographer a specific list of the groupings you want, such as the bride and groom and her family, and the order you want them in (and do so under the advisement of the photographer). Include groupings that may not seem obvious, such as the bride and groom with the bride's stepmother and stepbrothers.

Request that the photographers and their assistants and/or video person eat at separate times so someone is always watching for a spontaneous toast or other photo-worthy occurrence.

Figuring out fees and packages

Photographers use so many different pricing structures that comparing them dollar-to-dollar or photo-to-photo is impossible. Although asking how many frames a photographer typically shoots at a wedding can help you gauge the value of his services, knowing what percentage of those photos are keepers is more important. Because candid shots are less controlled than posed ones, the photographer must shoot substantially more frames to get the same number of usable pictures.

You may be surprised to discover that, in most areas, bottom-line price differences for wedding photographers, with the exception of superstars, may be negligible. Photographers generally charge in the following ways:

- **Flat fee, no frills:** You pay a single fee for the photographer's time, film, and expenses. The fee is usually based on an estimate of the amount of film to be shot during the event. The photographer gives you proofs and negatives, but the rest is up to you. So if your photos need retouching or *custom cropping* (trimming the photo to emphasize the main action by removing extraneous people or background), you must find a lab to do it. You also put together your own album, which requires a great deal of time, creativity, and energy. If you aren't up for a big project, be prepared for your wedding photos to remain in their lovely paper film-store envelopes for years to come.

- **Flat fee, including albums:** The albums may include one large and two smaller ones or a combination of albums and enlarged, matted photos. Although the shooting is less expensive upfront, additional prints cost dearly. The album may be of good quality but a standard configuration. If you prefer to supply your own album, the photographer may give you a discount. Some photographers retain ownership of the proofs, meaning that you must return them after choosing the images you want. Some photographers sell you the negatives for a nominal price or release all the digital images to you after your album is complete or on your one-year anniversary.

- **Hourly fee or flat fee, including contact sheets, proofs, and (usually) an album:** Photojournalists often charge this way. The upfront (hourly or flat) price is hefty, because they don't make much money selling you additional prints at a great markup. You typically contract for a specific number of hours and/or rolls of film and pay extra for overtime. Negotiate a generous time frame in advance so you don't feel rushed.

Photographers may take four months or longer to prepare your custom album after you choose the shots you want. Be patient. The photographer has to go through every photograph carefully to ensure the quality of color and cropping.

Ask your photographer to shoot a special roll — perhaps with everyone posed in a special way — and give you the film to develop right away. You can easily have these turned into glossy postcards for thank-you notes, amusing announcements, or holiday cards.

Selecting which shots to enlarge

Because developing every shot from your wedding in full size and on quality paper would cost a fortune, look at all the frames in a less-expensive format and choose only the ones you really want developed. These preliminary formats include

- **Compact disc or flash drive:** Digital images are loaded onto a disc or drive that you can view on a personal computer.

- **Contact sheets:** A compilation of the shots from a roll of film in miniature sizes, which you then examine with a magnifying glass or photographer's loupe. Mark the photos that you want with a grease pencil, perhaps indicating where you want the photo cropped. Some photographers give clients enlarged contact sheets that are easier to see.

- **Internet album:** You view digital images on a password-protected website and make selections. Images are usually organized into categories, such as "ceremony," "guests," and "reception," and they may also be subdivided into "posed" and "candid" shots. You can generally order prints and albums directly through the site and release access to guests who may also want to order.

- **Prints:** Photographs that have been cut and blown up from film negatives but not cropped or retouched.

- **Proofs:** A preliminary set of simply developed photos, all numbered and cataloged, from which you choose your album shots. They may be arranged in proof books or boxes. The ones you choose are then enlarged, custom printed, and cropped to your specifications.

Compiling the wedding album

Wedding albums come in many styles, and new concepts are constantly being created. Classic photographers often include a *flush* album, where the photographs extend to the edges of the page with no borders. These are most often 8 by 10 inches but sometimes 10 by 10 inches. Often, at least one photo spans two full pages. Candid-style photographs are usually compiled in books that have different-size matted photos on each page. Some studios prefer archival boxes, and others turn your images into a coffee-table book. If you're designing your own album, go through your photos with your photographer and specify the size and shape you want each one to be.

A particularly exquisite and memorable album that one bride created included calligraphy surrounding tiny photos, artwork and doodles around larger photos, shots in color as well as black and white, newspaper clippings of amusing events that happened the day of the couple's wedding, and the couple's invitation and announcement.

Assembling a dozen or so highlights from the wedding in individual albums for family and attendants can earn you major points. Matte the photos or mount them with photo corners in petite handmade albums or accordion-fold albums that tie with a ribbon, often available in stationery and art stores.

If you're buying your own album, note that an archival-quality album features

✔ Covers made of quality materials such as leather, fine fabrics, wood, or metal

✔ Acid-free pages, double-sided archival tape, mats, or photo corners as opposed to rubberized pages covered in cellophane

✔ A durable spine with raised ribs

Scheduling picture time

One of the most hotly debated wedding-day details is whether to take photos before the ceremony or after. Wedding photographers almost universally prefer taking formal shots before the wedding because they can take their time to make them perfect. But don't let anyone pressure you one way or another. Here's the true picture, based on the facts, so *you* can decide which time works for you.

If you want to be photographed at a public space such as an atrium, garden, or park, you may need to apply for a special license from a government office such as a parks commission. Also, don't be surprised if a beautiful public site is crowded with other couples taking wedding photos at the same time.

Photos before the ceremony

The main advantage of shooting before the ceremony is that faces aren't streaked with tears yet, your hair is as perfect as it's ever going to look, and nobody is impatient to get to the reception. As I discuss in Chapter 7, pre-ceremony photos are necessary if you have a receiving line at the reception. On the downside, however, these shoots can be fatiguing and can take away the magic of seeing each other dressed as bride and groom for the first time when the bride approaches the altar. The sense of anticipation may in fact be dampened for everyone involved.

Preserving memories

As your wedding planning progresses, you'll probably (I hope) have a great many moments that are touching, humorous, or even weird enough that you want to remember them. Chronicle these by taking snapshots, jotting down conversations, and saving notes, menus, and other similar items. When the hoopla's all over, you can arrange all this stuff in one big, annotated scrapbook — along with your professional pictures. Or you might turn a special box or other container into a wedding time capsule full of mementos from your engagement through the first year of marriage, including letters from friends and loved ones that you leave sealed until you open the capsule a decade or two later.

In general, unless your wedding is very small, prewedding photos take about one-and-a-half to two hours. Parents and close relatives from both families, the two of you, and your wedding party should arrive dressed, coifed, and made up. You distribute bouquets and boutonnieres, and then the participants pose and smile until their faces and feet ache.

If you choose to take your photos before the ceremony, consider these points:

✔ Arrange for the two of you to have some quiet time alone to see each other before the mayhem of the photo session begins.

✔ Remember that shooting too early means you rush to get dressed hours before your ceremony. Cutting it too close, however, means that your guests are left waiting.

✔ Have *stainless* drinks such as ice water and club soda for the group.

✔ Avoid rumpling, crumpling, and smudging by instructing everyone to air kiss until after the ceremony.

Photos after the ceremony

Shooting formals in the short window of time between ceremony and reception precludes having a receiving line, unless you want your guests to wait four hours to eat. The wedding party and families must make a fast getaway after the ceremony to the spot where the formals are to be taken, and unless you spend the money for an assistant photographer, you must wait for the photographer to set up. On top of that, people are usually quite emotional after the ceremony and need a little while to pull themselves together and focus.

But the merits of waiting to shoot formals are many. I believe that no moment in your life compares to that instant when you lay eyes on each other for the first time from opposite ends of the aisle on your wedding day. It's up to you to decide whether the sacrifices are worth this magical experience. Even though taking as many photos before the ceremony as you can manage (you and your attendants, parents, and siblings, for example) expedites things somewhat for after the ceremony, the shots that you'll most likely want to put in your album are those that include both of you.

If you wait to take photos until after your ceremony, keep these points in mind:

- ✔ Plan the session to be short and efficient. The best way to do so is by providing a list of specific shots you want and indicating any groupings that can be taken later during the reception. If people other than your wedding party are to be in group photos, be sure to tell them at the rehearsal dinner or before. Tracking down people so the photographs can be finished is an annoying waste of time.

- ✔ Arrange your photo session from the largest group to the smallest so that people can be dismissed to join the reception as soon as possible.

- ✔ Skip the return shots at the altar or bimah. Coordinating everyone again to reenact your ceremony takes up too much time.

- ✔ Have the photographer's assistant (if you've spent the money for one) set up the lights or other necessary equipment so everything's ready as soon as you are after the ceremony.

- ✔ Have a waiter serve drinks, but unless your wedding party is ravenous, refrain from serving hors d'oeuvres — waiting for people to swallow between shots holds things up.

- ✔ Realize that you (and others in your wedding party) *will* miss part of the cocktail hour — it's inevitable. You shouldn't punish your guests by forcing them to stand around for two hours just so you can do post-ceremony photos *and* get in your full cocktail hour.

Ready for your close-up?

Many people underestimate the degree of stage fright they may suffer at their wedding. If being thrust into the starring role unnerves you, your photos will show it. The most important — and sometimes most difficult — thing is to relax. Continually remember to breathe from your diaphragm, particularly when the camera is on you. Be aware of your shoulders — are they hunched up around your ears? Shake your arms out and loosen your shoulders. Also, watch your posture; you want to neither slump nor stand at formal attention. And whatever you do, don't lock your knees — doing so keeps your blood from circulating properly.

During your formal shots, appoint someone to keep guests away, or even better, choose an area away from the main reception area. You don't want guests distracting you or the photographer. Don't feel you have to converse with the photographer during the shoot — your mouth will look strange in the photos while your eyes are making contact with the camera. Remember that looking up at the camera for affirmation during candids or while being filmed ruins the sense of spontaneity.

If at all possible, have a friend take digital photos of each of you in complete wedding gear (brides should definitely have photos taken when their hair and makeup rehearsal is done) weeks before the wedding. You may very well find things that you want to change — the tiara that looks so good in the mirror may look like a Barbie accessory in a photograph, or the *very*

white sleeves that seemed just a smidgen long peeking out from the tuxedo jacket may look like gauntlets in a portrait shot. If you'll be kneeling at the altar during your ceremony, consider blackening the bottoms of the groom's shoes with an indelible marker so they don't pop out in the photos. You may even want to practice smiling, as silly as that sounds. Although scars, pimples, and wrinkles can be expunged from your photos, a frozen grimace can't.

Videorecording Your Day

If you want your celebration videorecorded but are worried about ruining your professional lighting scheme or hate the idea of having your reception lit up like a basketball court, don't despair. The art of video has evolved greatly in the past few years. Unlike old tape, which required floodlights, new super-light-sensitive equipment means that you need much less light than you needed in the past.

Although the newer equipment requires less light, that doesn't mean ultra-dim lighting achieves the best results. Many reception halls have virtually no lighting; they consider mood lighting a room as making it a place where bats would feel at home. This total lack of lighting assures that both photographs and videos will come out poorly. The videographer may illuminate individual guests, but the room itself may film as a large, black hole. Design your room so that the lighting works to create the mood you want without compromising the video quality.

Casting for a filmmaker

Many of the new-style videographers also specialize in subtlety, sensitively capturing special wedding moments without getting in everyone's way — and with exceptional results.

Use the same criteria in finding a videographer as you would a photographer: state-of-the-art equipment, a good rapport, and an aesthetic style you like (and can agree to in writing). In short, you want a professional videographer who works with professional equipment, not some hack who ran into a deal at a pawnshop and videotapes weddings on weekends when his aluminum lawn-furniture business is slow. Ask photographers who aren't affiliated with a video company to recommend a videographer. Because many photographers have an aversion to working with any video person, any recommendation they make is probably a stellar one. Also ask banquet managers — they know whom their clients (and staff) have loved and loathed.

Find out whether the videographer you're considering uses a tripod, and ask how many people he brings with him. Consider how much this crew will intrude on your day and whether extra people are worth the trade-off for more video material.

Thinking like a movie director

Ask to see complete videos — not composites — that the videographer has recently shot. In evaluating the work, note whether the image is sharp, in focus, and steady. Is the sound clear? Are the shots varied? They should include the following: long shots, which give a sense of setting from afar or by panning horizontally; medium shots, which are a little closer, showing, for example, the entryway to the reception; and close-up shots of the guests. The video should tell a chronological story rather than bombard you with random, disconnected images.

No matter how talented someone is at handling a camera, unless the finished product is edited stylishly and cohesively, the video won't be fun to watch. Pacing is crucial. Does the video open with an *overview* — a sense of the action to come, such as a montage of the city where the wedding was held or a Harry-and-Sally sort of interview with the bride and groom? Do the special effects look like an amateur music video? For that matter, is the music in sync with the action? Does the end of the video consist of a recap of the best parts of both ceremony and reception? Does the editor use *time-shifting* techniques, the method Hollywood uses to put scenes that are shot out of order in the proper sequence? If you want to splurge, you may have computer-generated graphics, animated titles, interspersing of still photos, and quick-cut techniques, making your wedding video look like a major theatrical release.

You can contribute to the unique flavor of your video by choosing meaningful music and having it dubbed in to cover up background noises, adding photos from your honeymoon, or scripting wit-provoking questions for on-camera interviews with guests. You may also want to create a continual reel that includes video footage or stills from your shower, rehearsal dinner, bachelor/bachelorette party, and honeymoon. Most videographers don't allow clients to participate in the editing process, so you need to be very clear about all the elements you want and how you want them used.

Although most videographers (like photographers) do retain the rights to their own material, you may save money if you can get a first-generation DVD that you then have duplicated. Look in the Yellow Pages under audio/visual services for companies that reproduce videos.

Although your family and friends may say they care deeply about reliving every moment of your wedding with you, asking them to wade through four hours of real-time video is pushing it. At most, your video should be an hour and a half. Ask your videographer to create a *highlight disc* or a selected-scenes section on the DVD. If it's affordable, make duplicates for your fans. Also, negotiate to retain your *master disc* (the unedited version). The videographer really has no need for it, and you may find that this uncut version contains parts that you're happy to have in later years.

Getting miked

For a ceremony in a church or temple, the optimum place for the microphone is within 3 to 5 feet of the bride, groom, and officiant. When that isn't feasible, your videographer must get creative. In a church or temple that doesn't permit recording near the altar or bimah, the videographer may be able to put a microphone near the PA system to pick up the ceremony, although doing so can produce inferior results. For an outdoor ceremony, hiding a wireless microphone in the chuppah or in a tree or other stationary element works best.

Because most wedding gowns have no lapel or collar, putting a wireless microphone on the bride is virtually impossible. If your videographer wants to wire the groom or officiant, be aware that in some areas, these microphones may pick up outside radio signals — and you may end up having random cellphone conversations and radio transmissions punctuating your ceremony.

Safekeeping the Past for the Future

Heat, light, and fumes can damage photographs and DVDs. Taking a few precautions can ensure that they're still around for your great-grandchildren to see:

- ✔ Store photos and videos in moderate temperature and humidity, away from any direct light.
- ✔ Protect DVDs from dust and extremes in temperature.
- ✔ Keep a second copy of your DVD (and the negatives of your photos if your photographer used any film) in a separate place, preferably in a fireproof box made especially for photographs and negatives.

Chapter 22

Handling the Honeymoon

. . . .

In This Chapter

▶ Narrowing down your honeymoon options

▶ Searching for honeymoon info online

▶ Going with a travel agent

▶ Stretching your travel budget

▶ Taking care of remaining travel details

▶ Honeymooning overseas

. . . .

*T*he word *honeymoon* comes from the idea that the first month of marriage is the sweetest. More accurately, the honeymoon is a well-deserved break from the stresses of getting married, a delightful interlude during which you decompress after the hubbub of your wedding. For most couples, this entails a vacation or trip that allows them to adjust to being married free from the pressures of everyday living.

Like a wedding, a successful honeymoon owes much to careful planning and budgeting. The good news, though, is unlike a wedding, you only have to please yourselves. In this chapter, I show you how to approach this greatly anticipated sojourn, from figuring out the honeymoon that's right for you to finding the best deal. Although this chapter is devoted to traditional honeymoons, many of the tips also apply to destination weddings. (See Chapter 4 for info on faraway venues and Chapter 6 for the scoop on weekend weddings.)

Determining Your Honeymoon Style

Devising a honeymoon itinerary is much like planning a wedding. You and your spouse-to-be should start by sharing your fantasies of where and how you envision yourself on a honeymoon. Try to recall the last photograph in a travel magazine that knocked you out. Then ask yourselves some questions:

✔ What's the vacation of your dreams?

✔ Do you like active vacations or do you prefer to move as little as possible?

✔ Do you view your honeymoon as a time to relax, take a grand tour, explore an exotic locale, or simply spend time alone together?

✔ What are your priorities in terms of romantic settings, privacy, activities, accommodations, and mode of travel?

✔ Do you have any special needs in terms of cuisine, physical access, or lifestyle?

✔ How much time can you take off from work or other commitments?

✔ What's your budget?

✔ Can you use frequent flier miles, hotel awards points, or another incentive program to defray the cost?

Most American newlyweds flock to spots where the living is easy — places synonymous with sun and surf. On the other hand, couples who find sitting like lumps on a beach as exciting as learning their multiplication tables may choose an adventurous itinerary that gets their adrenaline pumping. If you and your partner have different ideas about what makes a perfect honeymoon, a compromise may be in order — a cruise that makes stops for rock climbing or heli-skiing, or a long weekend in a rustic cabin followed by a few days at a luxury spa.

Whatever your style of getaway, heed this advice:

✔ **Give yourself enough time.** In scheduling, too little realism can spoil the romance. If your idea of fun is to follow the Silk Road from Xi'an to Khunjerab Pass or dine with maharajahs in India, you need more than a week away. And don't compromise quality for quantity: Whizzing through 22 countries in nine days is hardly conducive to focusing on each other, which is one of the main points of taking a honeymoon. If you can't afford the time now, scale back your plans and make the grand tour a goal for later.

✔ **Keep it simple.** Trust me — you've never been as bone-tired as you'll be the day after your wedding. Unless you have a full staff attending to your wedding and your only job is to get dressed and show up, by the next day you may feel like you've just completed eight triathlons. Your jaunt doesn't have to be boring; just don't plan on extremes. Don't try to squeeze in so many excursions or activities that you'll need a vacation after returning from your honeymoon.

✔ **Know your physical limitations.** If you've never climbed a mountain or scuba dived before (and you haven't been training for a recent Ironman competition), now isn't the best time to start. Getting married may make you feel like a new person, but you're not bionic. If your goal is to do something totally new and exhilarating together, take time before the wedding to prepare, whether that means training in a particular sport, getting in shape, or buying the proper gear.

If you're passionate about a particular part of the world, cuisine, or activity, check the blogs or subscribe to the e-mail lists kept by various organizations, companies, and travel experts. Their insider tips can steer you to little-known spots and good deals.

If you've been someplace extraordinary with a former significant other, don't go there on your honeymoon. Three's a crowd, especially with the Ghost of Relationships Past.

If possible, reserve tours or appointments for special services before your arrival. You don't want to be playing tennis at 3 a.m. because the courts are booked for the rest of the day. A travel agent can be very helpful with these reservations.

Medical school, law school, high-pressure jobs — sometimes you just can't fit in a honeymoon right after the wedding. Still, don't deprive yourself entirely. Try taking off just two days. A long weekend in a nice hotel, ordering room service, may do wonders to ease you back into reality.

Bringing the whole family

Planning a honeymoon as a family vacation is increasingly common for remarried couples where one or both spouses have children. These *familymoons* can be a valuable transition time for merging families *Brady Bunch*-style, and they're a powerful way of conveying to all that life is about to become a joint venture.

Large resorts such as Beaches, Westin Resort and Villas (St. John in the U.S. Virgin Islands), and Disneyland cater to newlyweds who want to include their children in the postnuptial vacation by offering packages that feature both romantic and family-oriented activities. Some things to keep in mind:

✔ **Balance your time:** Don't dump the children in a kids' camp all day, but do set aside time for just the two of you. Just as important: Spend time with each child one on one.

✔ **Be democratic:** This may sound obvious, but pick a place with activities everyone enjoys. That's another reason large resorts

are popular — they have something for everyone.

✔ **Don't push it:** Give kids time to get to know one another on their own terms.

✔ **Live large:** Big resorts and cruise ships often work best because they have flexible accommodations (adjoining rooms, living-room suites, activity areas) where family members can congregate and — just as important — get away from one another. Camping may seem like a great bonding experience, but not everyone (especially teenagers) appreciates the lack of privacy.

✔ **Pick a neutral territory:** Choose a destination where neither of you has spent a previous honeymoon or family vacation. Experiencing things together for the first time fosters bonding.

✔ **Take two honeymoons:** If possible, take a conventional, couples-only honeymoon after the familymoon.

Researching Destinations Online

The Internet is the best place to start your honeymoon research. Type possible destinations, activities, or simply the word *honeymoon* into a search engine and see what comes up. You may find that booking everything directly yourself is easy enough or you may discover a company or agent that can handle all the particulars. Some types of sites to scope out include

- **Bridal publications:** All the major bridal websites include links and copious information on honeymoons. For example, Brides features location listings and a "honeymoon finder quiz" (www.brides.com/honeymoons), and The Knot recommends hot spots by region (http://wedding.theknot.com/honeymoons.aspx). The website of Destination Weddings & Honeymoons magazine (www.destination-weddingmag.com) also offers information on all things honeymoon, including destinations and travel packages.

- **Discount airfares:** You can often find good airfares by booking on such sites as www.priceline.com or www.expedia.com. Always double-check these fares with those on the airline's site to get the best price.

- **Travel agencies:** Many companies and agents specialize in honeymoons. MoonRings (www.moonrings.com), for example, is geared toward the adventurous couple — people who might, say, want to blow all their frequent flier miles on an around-the-world trip. Other agencies offer promotions with all-inclusive resorts or specific destinations.

- **Travel clubs:** Credit card companies, zoos, universities, conservation organizations, hostel groups, and luxury tour operators may offer special travel packages through their websites.

Is making reservations a man's job?

Until fairly recently, all honeymoons were pretty much a surprise for the bride. After all, she planned the whole wedding, so it was only fair for the groom to take care of the honeymoon. He agonized, researched, and hypothesized in silence and then prayed that his bride wouldn't find his plan abhorrent. Now, brides and grooms often plan their honeymoons together. Still, a good many grooms feel that planning the honeymoon is *their* primary responsibility.

I recommend that even if the groom does most of the researching and reserving, he include the bride in the big decisions about where to visit, what to see, and what to do. (That trend for surprise honeymoons, requiring the bride to pack everything from a bikini to ski gear, thankfully seems to have declined.) Unless the groom is a mind reader, good communication makes for a much happier honeymoon (and married life!).

As with any Internet shopping site, check the company's track record at watchdog sites such as Consumer Affairs (www.consumeraffairs.com), the Better Business Bureau (www.bbb.org/us/consumers/), or PlanetFeedback (www.planetfeedback.com). You can also contact the local or state department of consumer affairs where the company is based.

Working with a Travel Agent

Most people have become proficient at planning their own travel online, finding the best prices on flights and hotels. But for a trip as important as your honeymoon, working with a travel agent instead of planning the trip yourself may be worth it. Yes, travel agents work on commission, and some may charge a fee or even expenses, depending on the sort of place you're interested in. But the good ones steer you to exactly where you want to be, recommend experiences you may otherwise miss, and can help you get the most for your money.

When interviewing a travel agent, bring a list of your wishes, possible venues, and desired amenities such as a hot tub, an ocean view, or a room with a four-poster bed. Have a good handle on your budget parameters. The more work you do before you start your chat, the more helpful travel agents can be. Questions to ask include

- ✔ Based on what we've told you, what are the options you'd recommend?

- ✔ Have you personally stayed at the site, done the tour, flown the route, or sailed the line that you're suggesting?

- ✔ Do you have guidebooks or videos we can look at?

- ✔ What sort of vacations are your specialty? Do you usually work with individuals rather than businesses or groups?

- ✔ Where are the deals? What kind of discounts can you get? Will you research special honeymoon packages?

- ✔ How do you work in conjunction with tour operators?

- ✔ How quickly can we expect you to return our phone calls when we're working together?

- ✔ Will you supply us with references of other couples whose honeymoons you've planned, preferably those with similar budgets and interests?

- ✔ Will you help us obtain visas, passports, and other documents we'll need?

- ✔ Can we expect you to deliver all tickets, vouchers, and necessary papers to us a few weeks before our wedding?

- ✔ If something goes awry with our trip, what will you do to straighten it out? Do you have a 24-hour help line that we can call?

You can start your search for a travel agent online. The Knot (www.the knot.com) provides lists of travel agents by city (from the home page, click Local Vendors and then U.S. Honeymoons + Travel), and The Honeymoon (www.thehoneymoon.com) lets you search for local agents and provides travel ideas and reviews. Of course, simply searching for "honeymoon travel agent" (include your desired destination if you know it) can give you options to explore.

If you already know where you want to go or what kind of trip you want to take, your task is slightly different: Hire an agent who's a *destination specialist* on that particular location or one who specializes in a specific type of travel, such as adventure trips.

Making Your Money Travel Farther

Your honeymoon need not be a *moneymoon* to be memorable and romantic. Here are some possible ways to save a few bucks and avoid travel fiascoes:

- ✔ **Avoid peak season:** Go in the off-season or *shoulder-season* (in between peak and off-peak). Doing so may mean not taking your honeymoon right after your wedding, but the savings can be substantial.

- ✔ **Book ahead:** Buy cruise tickets far in advance — you may save up to 50 percent off brochure rates and be more likely to get the cabin of your choice.

- ✔ **Buy airline tickets on Tuesday:** Airlines tend to announce sales on Monday nights, and other airlines match those sales Tuesday mornings, so travel experts recommend purchasing domestic tickets online between noon and 3 p.m. on Tuesdays, when the maximum number of sale seats are available.

- ✔ **BYOB:** Stock your minibar with your own snacks, soft drinks, bottled water, and (preferably duty-free) spirits. Ask the hotel room steward for ice and glasses. Limit room service orders — the prices are usually exorbitant.

- ✔ **Check taxes:** As you call around to get price quotes on rates for accommodations, ask whether the price includes tax — all taxes. (In addition to sales tax, some places charge a room tax, which can be more than 20 percent.)

- ✔ **Exchange money carefully:** The first exchange bureau you see in the airport or hotel kiosk usually isn't the best place to exchange money — you'll likely pay a surcharge for the convenience. ATM withdrawals are generally the easiest and cheapest way to get money while traveling. However, carry debit and credit cards in case an ATM isn't available. Check your bank's rules for foreign-currency ATM withdrawals before you leave and perhaps get at least cab fare in the appropriate currency for your destination.

✔ **Fly on off-peak days:** Traveling on a Tuesday, Wednesday, or Saturday gets you lower fares (and less crowding) than other days of the week. Leaving a day or two after your wedding instead of straight from the ceremony may save you some cash.

✔ **Follow the headlines:** A resort recovering from a hurricane or a region rebuilding after a war may offer bargain rates to rebuild tourism. However, avoid areas that have a clear and present danger.

✔ **Guard against scams:** Don't put down any money on a trip until you've pinpointed your hotel's name and location on a map. Some tour operators advertise desirable cities and then stick customers outside of town. And be skeptical of win-a-free-honeymoon contests and come-ons.

✔ **Investigate honeymoon travel insurance:** Depending on your investment in your trip, getting insurance may be worthwhile.

✔ **Pack accordingly:** Bring enough sunscreen and toiletries to last the trip. Hotel and cruise gift shops charge outrageous prices to captive guests.

✔ **Protect the nest egg:** If you go to a casino, set a limit for how much to gamble and stick to it. Better yet, don't gamble. Every game favors the house.

✔ **Register for a honeymoon:** Some travel agencies and such websites as The Honeymoon (www.thehoneymoon.com), Distinctive Honeymoons (www.distinctivehoneymoons.com), and The Knot (www.theknot.com) set up honeymoon registries where guests can contribute to your airfare, hotel, or specific services such as massages or a tour. However, please observe proper registry etiquette, which I discuss in Chapter 18.

✔ **Rent a house:** You may be surprised to know that renting a private home (especially during the off-season), part of a villa in the Caribbean or Mediterranean, a *palazzo* (apartment) in Venice, a motor home in France, or a lighthouse or estate cottage in the United Kingdom can be quite affordable, particularly if you buy alcohol and groceries at a local market and prepare most of your own meals. Of course, if you decide to throw financial caution to the wind, some private villas come complete with a cook and chauffeur. Either way, this option is an exciting way to feel like a native in another place.

✔ **Skip the tour guide:** Limit the number of shore excursions on cruises or plan your own with the help of a good guidebook and travel agent.

✔ **Use miles:** Even if you rarely fly, join the frequent flier club of the airline you take most often. Ask for an application when you reserve your flight; being a member doesn't cost anything, and the miles add up to upgrades and free trips. Also check out charge cards that give you miles for dollars charged.

✔ **Use student discounts:** Some youth hostels have private rooms that may be nice enough for a few honeymoon nights.

✔ **Weigh the benefits of all-inclusives:** Compare package rates with a la carte rates for your particular needs.

When in doubt, bring it

Should you bring stationery on your honeymoon to write thank-you notes? Absolutely not. Sure, you'll have all the more to write when you get home, but nobody expects to hear from you now.

However, you may forget to throw a few items in your suitcase as you're swept into the swirling wedding vortex. Do your essential honeymoon packing far in advance so you make sure you bring all you need. My suggestions:

- Adhesive bandages
- Antacid
- Antibiotic cream
- Aspirin
- Birth control
- A blow dryer
- A bottle opener
- Camera, film, and batteries
- Copies of birth certificates, drivers' licenses, and vaccination records
- Diarrhea medicine
- Earplugs
- An electrical adapter
- A flashlight
- Hats

- Insect repellent
- A journal and pens
- Lingerie and new sexy underwear
- Liquid detergent (small bottle)
- A manicure set and nail polish and remover
- Massage oil, feathers, and special toys
- A mini steamer
- Music (favorite CDs or your MP3 player)
- Scented candles
- Spot remover
- Sunscreen
- Tickets for planes, trains, or boats
- A travel neck pillow
- Vitamins
- Water shoes

One more thing: Resealable plastic bags are handy for stashing snacks and wet bathing suits, organizing travel items, or rescuing leaking bottles of suntan oil.

It pays to advertise. When you make your hotel reservations, and then again when you arrive, make a point of telling the reservationist and/or concierge that you're on your honeymoon. Better hotels do something special for honeymooners to encourage them to come back for anniversaries and vacations. Letting everyone know that you're just married (without being obnoxious about it) *may* result in little perks, ranging from extra solicitous service to discounts at attractions to a bottle of champagne in your room.

Hitting the Road (Or Sky): Tips before You Travel

You may decide to drive to a not-so-faraway destination for your honeymoon. If you're renting a car and your licenses don't have the same address yet, tell the agent that you're just married so you don't have to pay an extra-driver fee. (This announcement seems to melt even the toughest of hearts.) Know ahead of time whether you need to buy extra insurance from the car rental company. Chances are, if you already have comprehensive homeowner or renter, car, and health insurance policies, you're set. Also, some credit card companies extend coverage when you pay with their card.

If your travel plans include driving in the United States, major car rental companies such as Hertz, Avis, Budget, and Enterprise generally impose a surcharge on drivers between the ages of 21 and 24 (usually around $25 per day). So if you're under 25, be sure to budget for the extra cash. (Also check by state — some states have lower age limits and lower fees.)

Whether you travel in the United States or abroad (see the next section), return rental cars with a full tank of gas, which is usually less expensive than the rental company's per-gallon charge.

Whether you're driving or flying to your destination, if possible, have your honeymoon luggage brought to the hotel where you're spending your wedding night so you can leave the next day without returning home. Leave your wedding clothes with the concierge and have someone pick them up and take them to be cleaned (or returned to the rental establishment) so you don't have to drag them along on your honeymoon.

Going Abroad

A trip outside the United States requires some extra planning. For example, asking for a king, queen, or double bed usually gets you just that in the United States or the Caribbean. But in other parts of the world, double beds mean two single beds, so specify a large matrimonial bed. Cruise ships have a limited number of cabins with double beds, so you must reserve them well ahead of time.

Renting a car rather than taking a tour bus is often cheaper in other countries, so compare the two. For the best prices, prepay through a travel agent to avoid fluctuating rates.

For your convenience and safety, don't put off certain administrative and health matters:

- ✔ **AIDS/HIV testing:** An increasing number of countries have established regulations regarding AIDS testing, although mostly for long-term visitors. Check with the embassy or consulate of the country that you plan to visit to verify whether being tested is a requirement for entry.

- ✔ **Passports:** Make sure your passports are current and won't expire during your trip. The U.S. State Department has an excellent website for more information: `http://travel.state.gov/passport/passport_1738.html`. *Note:* Some countries require that your passport be valid at least six months or longer beyond the dates of your trip.

- ✔ **Vaccinations:** Many countries require proof of certain immunizations, which may take several weeks to get. The National Center for Infectious Diseases provides up-to-date information on disease outbreaks, vaccination requirements, and other health-related travel matters on its Travelers' Health website (`wwwnc.cdc.gov/travel`).

- ✔ **Visas:** If a visa is required, obtain it from the appropriate embassy or nearest consulate of the country you're planning to visit before proceeding abroad. Allow sufficient time for processing your visa application, especially if you're applying by mail. You may need to provide passport-size (2-x-2-inch) photos. Most foreign consular representatives are located in principal cities, and in many instances, you may be required to obtain visas from the consular office in the area of your residence. As soon as you receive your visa, check to make sure it doesn't have any mistakes. Processing and visa fees vary, and most aren't refundable.

For a current list of foreign entry requirements, go to the State Department's website at `http://travel.state.gov/travel/travel_1744.html` and choose the relevant country from the drop-down menu.

All international flights are subject to U.S. Immigration and U.S. Customs fees paid in advance as part of your ticket. In addition, many countries have departure fees that are sometimes collected at the time of ticket purchase or upon exiting the foreign country.

For a list of countries for which the State Department has issued warnings noting that you should avoid those places, go to `http://travel.state.gov/travel/cis_pa_tw/tw/tw_1764.html`. At the State Department site, you can also get consular information for any country in the world. Be sure to carry the address and telephone number for the U.S. embassy or consulate for each country you visit. In case of difficulties, contact the U.S. authorities promptly. If you plan to stay in a foreign country for an extended period, register and leave your itinerary with the embassy or consulate.

Part VI
The Part of Tens

The 5th Wave   By Rich Tennant

Okay — let's get one of the parents.

FOTO FUN

"I don't care how kitschy it is, I still would have rather had a professional photographer."

In this part . . .

I understand very clearly the difference between *devising* a realistic budget and *staying on budget.* In this part I offer some tips for adhering to your budget that I've gleaned over the years. I also asked some good friends of mine in the wedding biz to give me one tip that they consider to be invaluable to someone planning a wedding and got some very interesting results.

Chapter 23

Ten Tips for Staying on Budget

This is the part of the book where I give you the straight dope on the big "B" word — budget. I've been producing weddings for a long time, and yes, I know how to spend lots and lots of money to make a wedding very beautiful and exceptionally memorable. I also know that you'll have a life after your wedding, and it's a good idea to keep that in mind. Here are some tried-and-true tips for staying on budget that I've learned over the years; ignore them at your own risk.

Do Away with Magical (Money) Thinking

Perhaps you and your fiancé(e), or your parents, or all of you together, have been smart enough to come up with a budget early on. Just because you throw out a number or put it on paper doesn't mean that everything you have in mind will *actually fit* in that number. Figure out what you really can afford (or what you really *want* to spend, which may be two different numbers) and then painstakingly map out what really works within that budget, not what you imagine should work. Weddings tend to be quite costly, and before you decide to take your 100 nearest and dearest friends to a Caribbean island to celebrate, get the real facts about what it's going to cost.

Don't Play Cat and Mouse with Vendors

Everyone I've ever worked with had some sort of budget in mind, but not all of them wanted to share it upfront. This is risky business. Though letting vendors come up with ideas without any guidelines may seem clever, doing so is just the opposite of smart for lots of reasons. Aside from the fact that it wastes everyone's time, it also puts you in the position of being shown designs (dresses, flowers, food stations) that you can't afford. Unfortunately, everything you see after that will likely pale in comparison. Better to be upfront going in and let the team you hire come up with the best possible ideas for the money. My experience is that they'll appreciate your candor and rise to the occasion.

Track Your Spending

You can get myriad smartphone apps for devising your wedding budget — iWedding, for example, has a good budgeting component. But just like pen and paper, they don't help if you don't use them and *keep* using them. One of the big tricks to staying on budget is to consistently compare what you've budgeted with what you've spent and what you're planning on spending. That way, if you go over budget in one category, you'll immediately realize that you must cut back in another. This helps alleviate those horrendous after-wedding surprises.

Do Sweat the Small Stuff

Stamps, calligraphy, gratuities, vendor meals, and boutonnieres — each and every seemingly small expenditure is still part of the same budget. Keep tabs on these expenses the same way you keep on top of the biggest items. They can add up to a surprisingly large amount if you aren't careful.

Work Together: It Takes Two Baby

Sorry to remind you again, but this is the beginning of your life *as part of a pair*. That means that if you pay for your bridesmaids' dresses, your groom will likely want to pay for what his groomsmen wear as well. It's the same pot of money, my dear — one budget — so this isn't the time or place for unilateral decisions. You both get a vote.

Don't be Trendy

If all the wedding magazines and blogs are featuring brides changing three times during the wedding or showcasing extravagant after-ceremony parties, don't get bullied! Our job as professionals in the wedding industry is to excite, entice, and inspire you with ideas for one of the most important days of your life. That doesn't mean that each concept is right for *you*. Be a ruthless editor when deciding what to include in your big day, and remember that *simple* and *elegant* aren't dirty words.

Be Flexible

If you're absolutely set on a date, a band, or a specific photographer with *no* wiggle room, you have no negotiating power. Certainly keep in mind your first choices, but go into the process willing to consider other possibilities.

Be Careful about Overtime

When you schedule your wedding day, go through each portion and add up the hours. If the venue price includes a one-hour ceremony and a four-hour dinner dance, each minute over that will incur additional charges. Overtime fees can be pretty hefty, so it's far better to figure them into your budget going in and stick to that schedule.

Stop Watching Wedding TV!

There's no such thing as "reality television"; really and truly, it's an oxymoron. If you see me or any of my colleagues putting together a spectacular event on TV for what the host tells you is an absurdly low price, use your common sense. Vendors *donate* their goods or services to be on these shows, and the prices that are quoted don't have anything to do with a wedding in the real world — presumably where yours is taking place.

Control Yourself (No Last-Minute Spending Frenzies)

As the weeks before your wedding dwindle, you'll undoubtedly panic and begin thinking you just haven't included enough stuff. That's no reason, however, to start adding all the items that you originally decided not to spend money on. Realize that you're in the throes of wedding hysteria and stay your course. Resist the temptation to add that extra floral piece, spring for the caviar station (because you were just at a wedding that had one), or schedule an additional limo. If it didn't fit into your budget before, it still doesn't fit. Take a deep breath and walk away from your credit cards.

Chapter 24

Ten Tacky Temptations
I Beg You to Resist

In This Chapter

▶ Avoiding pre-wedding blowouts and gauche gift announcements

▶ Being considerate of your guests

This is the part of the book where I share my pet peeves with you. Don't get me wrong — I like to have fun as much as the next gal. But that doesn't mean anything goes just because it's your wedding. As you exhibit your creativity and personal style, do keep hospitality foremost in mind. When I talk about tackiness, I'm really talking about thoughtlessness. Here is a *very subjective* list of some of the items and behaviors I hope you avoid.

Indulging in Pre-Wedding Debauches

Embarrassing, drunken, macho/macha, G-string-pulling, divorce-inducing bachelor or bachelorette parties are archaic and dumb. Convey to your wedding party that you really don't want to do anything that would endanger your relationship with your future spouse. If your own sense of dignity isn't enough to keep you well behaved, a good gauge of what's okay is to envision your fiancé(e) in the identical scenario. If it makes you blanch then I suggest it's not a good idea for you either. Although these events can be a time to let down your hair, you have lots of ways to hang out with friends and have fun without having to burn the photos afterwards. (For ideas on pre-wedding parties, see Chapter 8.)

Broadcasting Your Registry

I'm all for efficiency, and I do believe in registering, but enclosing your registry information with any kind of invitation is gauche. It conveys that your main agenda appears to be a gift grab, with the invitation itself an afterthought. I can't imagine that, between your parents and close friends, there isn't somebody with a big enough mouth to pass the word of where you're registered. (For more on this subject, see Chapter 18.)

Bankrupting Friends and Relatives

Attending a wedding can be an expensive proposition when you add up gift, clothing, possible travel, and so on. Expecting friends to attend multiple showers and buy gifts for each, as well as an elaborate destination bachelor or bachelorette weekend, may really be the last straw for some with modest finances. Be thoughtful about this and your friends and family will be very thankful.

Playing Musical Chairs

I'm not insisting that you assign each guest a specific seat at each table (although for a formal dinner, it's a lovely thing to do), but leaving guests to fend for themselves inevitably results in a few odd ducks making several embarrassing laps around the room and asking pathetically, "Is this seat taken? How about that one?" Stave off this awkwardness by assigning guests to specific tables. In fact, get creative with the blend of guests at each table — it can give your reception some extra verve.

Bad-Mouthing In-Laws-to-Be

If your prospective spouse is a frustrated stand-up comic who loves to regale the crowd with his or her "hilarious" anecdotes about your parents, nip this sweet habit in the bud now. Such jokes often veil a certain hostility, and you can only wonder what your spouse will be saying about you in years to come.

Procrastinating with Your Invitations

Yes, you have a finite amount of space and a finite amount of money, so it makes sense to get the first round of regrets before you send out the second round of invitations. First off, always be careful not to include an rsvp date on the reply card that may have already gone by before the guest receives the invitation. Secondly, at a certain point, stop sending invitations at all — it's just rude to invite someone to your black-tie, sit-down dinner wedding two weeks before.

Making Yours the Longest Day

Weddings where the ceremony is in the morning or early afternoon and the reception is several hours later are extremely hard on guests, particularly those who have come into town for just the day. What exactly should they do for the four- or six-hour break? Are they expected to change outfits? If so, where? Whenever possible, schedule the reception to immediately follow the ceremony.

Knocking Others' Weddings

Be kind to those who have gone before you: Restrain yourself from criticizing other people's weddings as you plan your own. Catty comments made in passing — "Well, we would never dream of serving *fake* Champagne" — inevitably come back to haunt you. Reserve these observations for private discussions with your fiancé(e), best friend, and tight-lipped parents. Better yet, banish such thoughts completely. (Besides, after you add up everything, you may decide that sparkling wine ain't so bad after all — see Chapters 2 and 15.)

Having an "Adult" Garter Grab

A holdover from the quaint medieval practice known as *stripping the bride,* where guests yanked off the bride's underclothes to hasten the consummation of the marriage, the garter toss hasn't lost any of its charm. I realize you may think this bit of vaudeville, with the band playing the theme from *Gypsy,* is jolly fun, or at the least something you've always thought of as part of your wedding day. If that's the case, try to remember that it's your wedding — not a frat party. Keep the spectacle short, sweet, and playful rather than X-rated. (Ask the bandleader or DJ to help you by cutting it short.)

Forgetting That Those You've Invited Are Guests

Yes, it's *your* day, but that's no reason to torture your friends and relatives. For example, even if you've always dreamed of tying the knot in an outdoor ceremony, move inside if it's cold and damp on your wedding day. The same holds true for not indulging in a three-hour photo shoot between the ceremony and reception as guests wait around, growing increasingly famished, exhausted, and inebriated. It's simple: Think of your guests first, even if it means changing your plans somewhat.

Index

• C •

• E •

• F •

...ple & Mac

...ad 2 For Dummies,
...d Edition
...8-1-118-17679-5

...hone 4S For Dummies,
...h Edition
...8-1-118-03671-6

...od touch For Dummies,
...d Edition
...8-1-118-12960-9

...ac OS X Lion
...r Dummies
...8-1-118-02205-4

...ogging & Social Media

...tyVille For Dummies
...8-1-118-08337-6

...cebook For Dummies,
...h Edition
...8-1-118-09562-1

...m Blogging
...r Dummies
...8-1-118-03843-7

...witter For Dummies,
...d Edition
...8-0-470-76879-2

...ordPress For Dummies,
...h Edition
...8-1-118-07342-1

...siness

...sh Flow For Dummies
...8-1-118-01850-7

...vesting For Dummies,
...h Edition
...8-0-470-90545-6

Job Searching with Social
Media For Dummies
978-0-470-93072-4

QuickBooks 2012
For Dummies
978-1-118-09120-3

Resumes For Dummies,
6th Edition
978-0-470-87361-8

Starting an Etsy Business
For Dummies
978-0-470-93067-0

Cooking & Entertaining

Cooking Basics
For Dummies, 4th Edition
978-0-470-91388-8

Wine For Dummies,
4th Edition
978-0-470-04579-4

Diet & Nutrition

Kettlebells For Dummies
978-0-470-59929-7

Nutrition For Dummies,
5th Edition
978-0-470-93231-5

Restaurant Calorie Counter
For Dummies,
2nd Edition
978-0-470-64405-8

Digital Photography

Digital SLR Cameras &
Photography For Dummies,
4th Edition
978-1-118-14489-3

Digital SLR Settings
& Shortcuts
For Dummies
978-0-470-91763-3

Photoshop Elements 10
For Dummies
978-1-118-10742-3

Gardening

Gardening Basics
For Dummies
978-0-470-03749-2

Vegetable Gardening
For Dummies,
2nd Edition
978-0-470-49870-5

Green/Sustainable

Raising Chickens
For Dummies
978-0-470-46544-8

Green Cleaning
For Dummies
978-0-470-39106-8

Health

Diabetes For Dummies,
3rd Edition
978-0-470-27086-8

Food Allergies
For Dummies
978-0-470-09584-3

Living Gluten-Free
For Dummies,
2nd Edition
978-0-470-58589-4

Hobbies

Beekeeping
For Dummies,
2nd Edition
978-0-470-43065-1

Chess For Dummies,
3rd Edition
978-1-118-01695-4

Drawing For Dummies,
2nd Edition
978-0-470-61842-4

eBay For Dummies,
7th Edition
978-1-118-09806-6

Knitting For Dummies,
2nd Edition
978-0-470-28747-7

Language &
Foreign Language

English Grammar
For Dummies,
2nd Edition
978-0-470-54664-2

French For Dummies,
2nd Edition
978-1-118-00464-7

German For Dummies,
2nd Edition
978-0-470-90101-4

Spanish Essentials
For Dummies
978-0-470-63751-7

Spanish For Dummies,
2nd Edition
978-0-470-87855-2

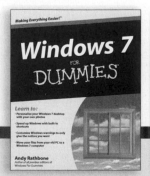

Math & Science

Algebra I For Dummies,
2nd Edition
978-0-470-55964-2

Biology For Dummies,
2nd Edition
978-0-470-59875-7

Chemistry For Dummies,
2nd Edition
978-1-1180-0730-3

Geometry For Dummies,
2nd Edition
978-0-470-08946-0

Pre-Algebra Essentials
For Dummies
978-0-470-61838-7

Microsoft Office

Excel 2010 For Dummies
978-0-470-48953-6

Office 2010 All-in-One
For Dummies
978-0-470-49748-7

Office 2011 for Mac
For Dummies
978-0-470-87869-9

Word 2010
For Dummies
978-0-470-48772-3

Music

Guitar For Dummies,
2nd Edition
978-0-7645-9904-0

Clarinet For Dummies
978-0-470-58477-4

iPod & iTunes
For Dummies,
9th Edition
978-1-118-13060-5

Pets

Cats For Dummies,
2nd Edition
978-0-7645-5275-5

Dogs All-in One
For Dummies
978-0470-52978-2

Saltwater Aquariums
For Dummies
978-0-470-06805-2

Religion & Inspiration

The Bible For Dummies
978-0-7645-5296-0

Catholicism For Dummies,
2nd Edition
978-1-118-07778-8

Spirituality For Dummies,
2nd Edition
978-0-470-19142-2

Self-Help & Relationships

Happiness For Dummies
978-0-470-28171-0

Overcoming Anxiety
For Dummies,
2nd Edition
978-0-470-57441-6

Seniors

Crosswords For Seniors
For Dummies
978-0-470-49157-7

iPad 2 For Seniors
For Dummies, 3rd Edition
978-1-118-17678-8

Laptops & Tablets
For Seniors For Dummies,
2nd Edition
978-1-118-09596-6

Smartphones & Tablets

BlackBerry For Dummies,
5th Edition
978-1-118-10035-6

Droid X2 For Dummies
978-1-118-14864-8

HTC ThunderBolt
For Dummies
978-1-118-07601-9

MOTOROLA XOOM
For Dummies
978-1-118-08835-7

Sports

Basketball For Dummies,
3rd Edition
978-1-118-07374-2

Football For Dummies,
2nd Edition
978-1-118-01261-1

Golf For Dummies,
4th Edition
978-0-470-88279-5

Test Prep

ACT For Dummies,
5th Edition
978-1-118-01259-8

ASVAB For Dummies,
3rd Edition
978-0-470-63760-9

The GRE Test For
Dummies, 7th Edition
978-0-470-00919-2

Police Officer Exam
For Dummies
978-0-470-88724-0

Series 7 Exam
For Dummies
978-0-470-09932-2

Web Development

HTML, CSS, & XHTML
For Dummies, 7th Edition
978-0-470-91659-9

Drupal For Dummies,
2nd Edition
978-1-118-08348-2

Windows 7

Windows 7
For Dummies
978-0-470-49743-2

Windows 7
For Dummies,
Book + DVD Bundle
978-0-470-52398-8

Windows 7 All-in-One
For Dummies
978-0-470-48763-1

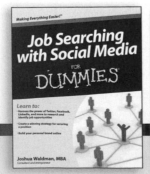